A 'CATCH-22' CASEBOOK

Thomas Y. Crowell Company New York, Established 1834

edited by Frederick Kiley

UNITED STATES AIR FORCE ACADEMY

A 'CATCH-22' CASEBOOK

and Walter McDonald

TEXAS TECH UNIVERSITY

Library of Congress Cataloging in Publication Data

Kiley, Frederick T   comp.
    A Catch-22 casebook.

    Bibliography: p.
    1. Heller, Joseph.   Catch-22.   I. McDonald,
Walter, joint comp.   II. Title.
PS3558.E476C335   813'.5'4   72-10418
ISBN 0-690-18170-1

1 2 3 4 5 6 7 8 9 10

PREFACE

Let it be clear at the outset that the labors involved in making this text were labors of love. The editors feel, without reservation, that *Catch-22* is a masterpiece. Although it is set against the background of a major campaign during World War II, it is not *about* that war, and in that sense not to be pinned wriggling among the great and varied corpus of prose fiction called, unfairly, "war novels." *Catch-22* is about us as a nation and a people, *now* as much as then. It is a grand Rabelaisian, Swiftian, Faulknerian "No! In Thunder" which also suggests yes, perhaps there are ways if only we first cease perverting the uses of reason. As Yossarian gradually perceives and is able to contemplate the horror man creates, we sense the hollow laughter early in the novel turning to chill ripeness in the last chapters. No one else in our time has written such a successfully tragic funny book. *Catch-22* hands us a metaphor. "They have the power to do whatever we cannot stop 'them' from doing." The irony? "They" and "them" are ultimately "we" and "us." Only the sick among us can fight "them." And Yossarian is sick. He has a liver condition. Rarely has anyone hit upon so right a metaphor.

This text is organized into five major sections. First a group of book reviews beginning in October 1961 displays what we feel is a fair representation of the range of early reactions to the novel. Included are reviews from a variety of journals, magazines, and newspapers, large and small, English and American. Second is a gathering of criticism that we have arranged into four subunits according to the principal concern (should we say "thrust"?) of each piece. The first of these subunits centers on *form*, the second on *structure*, the third on *theme*, and the fourth on *the Absurd*. The first deals largely with external patterns, with attempts to place *Catch-22* in a genre. The second goes within, examining internal structure, interior organization. The third focuses upon what several critics think Mr. Heller has *said*. And the fourth subunit deals with *Catch-22* in relationship to that latest literary pose (should we say "posture"?), the Absurd.

If the first two major sections represent opinion and analysis, the next two represent factual background and primary sources. There are interviews with Mr. Heller, one marking the first anniversary of *Catch-22* in 1962, the other marking the ninth in 1970, and a reminiscence by a retired Air Force officer about his days as a bombardier (like Heller) in B-25s on Corsica and what *Catch-22* has grown to signify to him. Then there are two original pieces by Mr. Heller, one a chapter of *Catch-22* cut from the manuscript before publication, the other written upon his return to Corsica more than twenty years after the end of the war.

The final major section is a little unusual for a text of this sort. In 1970, *Catch-22* was made into a stunning and controversial motion picture. The problems of making such a book into a movie are enormous; so we have reprinted two pieces about them—the first, a magazine story about the actual filming itself in Mexico, the second, comments by Mr. Heller (who had almost nothing to do with the movie) about translating *Catch-22* into film. Then follows a selection of reviews and criticism of the film itself.

A detailed Bibliographical Note and suggestions for discussion and writing are included in the closing pages of the book. The questions provide an extensive variety of suggestions for research and writing as well as discussion. The Bibliographic Note mentions in detail the primary and secondary source material the editors feel serious scholars should examine in addition to the core material in the text itself. For convenience, the note is arranged in the same pattern as the text.

There are two basic editions of *Catch-22*. The original, published by Simon and Schuster in 1961, is 443 pages long. (The British and Modern Library editions are the same as this edition.) The second, published as a Dell paperback in 1962, is 463 pages long. Recognizing that the Dell edition is now the one most readily available, we have standardized all page references in the selections to it. Therefore, anyone working with a Simon and Schuster edition will be slightly inconvenienced because our page references to the 400's will occur about twenty pages earlier in his edition, to the 300's about fifteen pages earlier, to the 200's about ten pages earlier, and so forth.

Bracketed figures in the essays indicate the end of the page on which the selections appeared in the original sources; for example [81], marks the end of page 81 in the original. If a page of the original ended with a hyphenated word, our page number follows the entire word.

There are many to whom we are grateful for assistance in preparing this volume but to none more than Joseph Heller, who has been unfailingly gracious and encouraging. It would have been a poorer book without his generous help.

F.K.
W.McD.

CONTENTS

TWO INTERVIEWS AND
A REMINISCENCE   271

TWO OTHER WORKS
BY JOSEPH HELLER   307

CATCH-22: THE FILM   333

NOVEL INTO FILM   335

FILM REVIEWS AND CRITICISM   363

Shall I tell you what I consider to be wrong? What I consider to be wrong is that most of the people in the Western Hemisphere are stark, staring mad and the few people who recognize this are regarded as lunatics by all those stark, staring mad people.

Ashley Montagu, from remarks made at the University of Wisconsin Symposium, "Alternative Futures for America," Spring 1971, which appeared in Cleveland Amory's column "Trade Winds," *Saturday Review*, April 10, 1971.

HUNGRY JOE – DOBBS	ORR	MILO	AARFY CAPTAIN BLACK	CHAPLAIN	DOC DANEEKA DR STUBBS
HUNGRY JOE A PHOTOGRAPHER	POOR AND RUSTIC	MARRIED; A FAITHFUL HUSBAND	AARFY A COLLEGE ALUMNUS	MARRIED; WITH YOUNG CHILDREN	DANEEKA: POOR STAR & PRACTICE BEFORE W. KLEPRACKS DRAFTING
		MILO IS A PILOT			
HUNGRY JOE AND DOBBS ARE BOTH PILOTS	ORR IS A PILOT IN A WING PLANE AND IS ALWAYS BEING SHOT DOWN	VOLUNTEERS FOR MESS OFFICER AS SOON AS HE ARRIVES OVERSEAS	AARFY IS YOSSARIAN'S NAVIGATOR. BLACK IS THE SQUADRON INTELLIGENCE OFFICER	THE CHAPLAIN DOES NOT FIT IN AND HAS NO FRIENDS	
HUNGRY JOE HAS 25 MISSIONS AND IS WAITING TO GO HOME. HE IS PUT BACK ON COMBAT DUTY		HE PRODUCES FRESH EGGS AND BEGINS ORGANIZING HIS BUYING SYNDICATE		HE FEARS BOTH COLONELS AND IS BULLIED BY THEM.	
HUNGRY JOE HAS WRECKED A PLANE NEEDLESSLY. HE WAS GIVEN A MEDAL TO COVER UP HIS MISTAKE			AARFY MISLEADS YOSSARIAN, MAKING IT NECESSARY FOR THEM TO GO AROUND TWICE		
	ORR GOES ALONG ON THE TRIP TO EGYPT TO BUY COTTON.	MILO FLIES TO EGYPT AND BUYS THE WHOLE COTTON CROP	BLACK STARTS HIS LOYALTY OATH CRUSADE AGAINST MAJOR MAJOR	HE LOVES HIS WIFE AND MISSES HER.	
HUNGRY JOE IS AMAZED BY ALL THE NAKED GIRLS IN THE APARTMENT		MILO ARRANGES THE MISSION TO ORVIETO AS A BUSINESS DEAL, WORKING FOR BOTH SIDES	AARFY SPEAKS OF NATELY'S GIRL WITH SMUG CONTEMPT		
HUNGRY JOE HAS NIGHTMARES BECAUSE HE IS NOT SCHEDULED FOR THE MISSION TO BOLOGNA		MILO HAS DISBANDED THE LOYALTY OATH CRUSADE BECAUSE IT DISRUPTED BUSINESS	BLACK REALIZES THAT MEN ARE GOING TO BOLOGNA AND HANDS THE HARDSIGN ON THE CLOSED MEDICAL TENT		STUBBS IS SORRY FOR THE MEN AND FEELS YOSSARIAN MIGHT BE THE ONLY SANE PERSON LEFT
HUNGRY JOE TRIES TO TAKE PICTURES OF YOSSARIAN IN BED WITH LUCIANA	ORR HAS AN ENGINE AND HIS LANDING GEAR SHOT OUT BUT CRASH LANDS SAFELY.		AARFY GETS EVERYTHING ON THE BOLOGNA MISSION & NEARLY SHOOTS		
		MILO BOMBS HIS OWN SQUADRON WHEN PAID TO DO SO BY THE GERMANS		HE WORRIES CONSTANTLY ABOUT THE HEALTH AND SAFETY OF HIS WIFE AND CHILDREN	DANEEKA BEHAVES WITH COURAGE WHEN MILO BOMBS THE SQUADRON
DOBBS PANICS, SEIZES CONTROLS, AND PLUNGES PLANE DOWN INTO FLAK		MILO HAS THE MONEY FROM THE AND IS			DANEEKA TAKES CARE OF YOSSARIAN WHEN HE EMERGES FROM THE PLANE IN A STATE OF SHOCK
		OUT SANDWICHES FOR HELP IN DISPOSAL OF COTTON		CHAPLAIN SPIES YOSSARIAN NAKED IN A TREE AND THINKS IT IS A MYSTICAL VISION	
			AARFY IS		
HUNGRY JOE KEEPS FINISHING MISSIONS AND KEEPS BEING RETURNED TO COMBAT DUTY	ORR IS YOSSARIAN'S ROOMMATE & KEEPS IN MAKING A TENT	MILO TRUSTS YOSSARIAN BECAUSE HE WILL NOT STEAL FROM THE COUNTRY HE LOVES	A YOSSARIAN'S INCOMPETENT LEAD NAVIGATOR	THE CHAPLAIN MEETS YOSSARIAN IN THE HOSPITAL.	DANEEKA IS A SELF-PITYING HYPOCHONDRIAC WITH WHOM YOSSARIAN IS FRIENDLY
	ORR HAS STARTED TO WINTERIZE THE TENT WHILE YOSSARIAN WAS IN THE HOSPITAL	MILO IS AWAY BUYING FIGS			
				NO AUTHORITY TO HELP; BUT THEY	THEY KNOW TO HELP BUT SAY H ADVOCATES

The illustrations on the part titles and on the cover are reproductions of portions of the desk blotter on which Joseph Heller plotted Catch-22.

Nelson Algren
The Catch

There was only one catch and that was Catch-22, which specified that a concern for one's own safety in the face of dangers that were real and immediate was the process of a rational mind. Orr was crazy and could be grounded. All he had to do was ask; and as soon as he did, he would no longer be crazy and would have to fly more missions. Orr would be crazy to fly more missions and sane if he didn't, but if he was sane he had to fly them. Yossarian was moved very deeply by the absolute simplicity of this clause and let out a respectful whistle:

"That's some catch, that Catch-22," he observed.

"It's the best there is," Doc Daneeka agreed.

Yossarian was moved deeply day and night and what moved him more deeply than anything else was the fact that they were trying to murder him.

"Who's 'they?'" Clevinger wanted to know. "Who, specifically, is trying to murder you?"

"Every one of them," Yossarian told him.

"Every one of whom?"

SOURCE: *The Nation*, Vol. 193 (November 4, 1961), p. 358. Reprinted by permission of the publisher.

"Every one of whom do you think?"

"I haven't any idea."

"Then how do you know they aren't?"

Yossarian had proof, because strangers he didn't know shot at him with cannons every time he flew up into the air to drop bombs on them, so it was of no use for Clevinger to say "No one is trying to kill you."

"Then why are they shooting at me?"

"They're shooting at everyone."

"And what difference does that make?"

"I'm not going to argue with you," Clevinger decided, "you don't know who you hate."

"Whoever is trying to poison me."

"Nobody is trying to poison you."

"They poisoned my food twice, didn't they? Didn't they put poison in my food at Ferrara and during the Great Big Siege of Bologna?"

"They put poison in everybody's food," Clevinger explained.

"And what difference does *that* make?"

There was no established procedure for evasive action. All you needed was fear, and Yossarian had plenty of that. He bolted wildly for his life on each mission the instant his bombs were away. When he fulfilled the thirty-five missions required of each man of his group, he asked to be sent home.

Colonel Cathcart had by then raised the missions required to forty. When Yossarian had flown forty he asked to be sent home. Colonel Cathcart had raised the missions required to forty-five. When Yossarian had flown forty-five—there *did* seem to be a catch *somewhere*. Yossarian went into the hospital with a pain in his liver that fell just short of being jaundice. If it became jaundice the doctors could treat it. If it didn't become jaundice and went away they could discharge him. Yossarian decided to spend the rest of the war in bed by running a daily temperature of 101. He had found a catch of his own.

To preserve his sanity against the formalized lunacy of the military mind in action, Yossarian has to turn madman. Yet even Yossarian is more the patriot than Lt. Minderbinder, the business mind in action. Even Yossarian has to protest when Minderbinder arranges with the Germans to let them knock American planes down at a thousand dollars per plane. Minderbinder is horrified—"Have you no respect for the sanctity of a business contract?" he demands of Yossarian, and Yossarian feels ashamed of himself.

Below its hilarity, so wild that it hurts, *Catch-22* is the strongest repudiation of our civilization, in fiction, to come out of World War II. *The Naked and the Dead* and *From Here to Eternity* are lost within it. That the horror and the hypocrisy, the greed and the complacency, the endless cunning and the endless stupidity which now go to constitute what we term

Christianity are dealt with here in absolutes, does not lessen the truth of its repudiation. Those happy few who hit upon Terry Southern's *The Magic Christian* will find that, what Southern said with some self-doubt, Heller says with no doubt whatsoever. To compare *Catch-22* favorably with *The Good Soldier Schweik* would be an injustice, because this novel is not merely the best American novel to come out of World War II; it is the best American novel that has come out of anywhere in years. [358]

John J. Murray

Review of 'Catch-22'

Everything's A-OK and suddenly there you are on your back in the regions of Dryden's thin partition, flying on the edge of madness, maneuvering your mind to the antics of a bedlamite bomber squadron of WW II, performing some of the zaniest stunts of the rationally-illogic since that time the Marx brothers proposed to build a building next door to the one they couldn't escape from. Catch-22 is the escape clause the Air Force uses in its contract with its officers to keep them flying (and dying). If there are 60 missions to fly before rotation, Col. Cathcart raises them to 70. He quotes Catch-22. If a bomber pilot needs grounding because he's near mental collapse, the flight surgeon tells him, "Catch-22 says you've always got to do what your commanding officer tells you to." Since you must obey regulations, and since regulations tell you to obey every order, that's the catch. A neat little syllogism? There are more—bombs more—than that.

This strange novel of the serio-comic is like no other you've ever read. In fact, it's not a novel at all but a series of Overburyean (and overbearing) character sketches connected loosely by the picaresque hero, Captain Yossarian. Yossarian is slightly off his rocker; he has an unnatural fearful fear of death. He watches in horror Snowden's, the young tail gunner's, guts fall out ("Where are the Snowdens of yesterday?") and later appears in the trees, like Mad Sweeney, naked in protest against risking his life on another bomb run. He is also slightly oversexed and almost loses his life being solicitous of his pal's whore's kid sister. Other crackpots in order of rank are the brass who run the war for the greater honor and glory of them-

SOURCE: *Best Sellers*, Vol. 21, No. 16 (November 15, 1961), p. 345. Reprinted by permission of the publisher.

selves—there's Col. Cathcart, an equivocator who will even sacrifice his men in order to make the *Saturday Evening Post*; there are the Generals Dreedle and Peckem, rivals for command, who are superseded by Lieutenant Scheisskopf (he's nuts over parades and lets more than rank go to his head); then come the lesser ranks—there's Chaplain Tappman, so inept and fear-struck that his chaplain's assistant puts the fear of God in him; next there's Major (the IBM machine erred) Major Major, the squadron commander, so anthropophobic he allows no one to see him and so bored with red tape that he amuses himself by signing official documents "Washington Irving," "Irving Washington," or when really bored, "John Milton"; then there's still Milo Minderbinder; there's always one who thrives on war in war novels; it is he who has the best formula for running a war—form a corporation, "everybody has a share," contract with the Germans to bomb your own installations at a profit, or when faced with financial catastrophe by buying unwisely into Egyptian cotton, sell real cotton candy.

All of these characters are drawn in the tradition of good classical farce. I found myself laughing uncontrollably at most of the tipped-mind situations they involve themselves in. But if you list, as the old morality play has it, leave out the serious parts. Regrettably Mr. Heller chooses to give us a message, and it turns out to be the now old existentialist one: in the face of suffering, endure; ripeness is all, and all that. Why a good comic novel suddenly veers from insanity (the stuff of the ridiculous) to sanity (that way madness lies) is beyond me. Maybe figuring out the author's mixed purposes is catch-23. [345]

Robert Brustein
The Logic of Survival
in a Lunatic World

"The man who declares that survival at all costs is the end of existence is morally dead, because he's prepared to sacrifice all other values which give life its meaning."

[*Sidney Hook*]

". . . It's better to die on one's feet than live on one's knees," Nately retorted with triumphant and lofty conviction. "I guess you've heard that saying before."

SOURCE: *The New Republic*, Vol. 145 (November 13, 1961), pp. 11–13. Reprinted by permission of *The New Republic*, © 1961, Harrison-Blaine of New Jersey, Inc.

"Yes, I certainly have," mused the treacherous old man, smiling again. "But I'm afraid you have it backward. It is better to *live* on one's feet than die on one's knees. *That* is the way the saying goes." [*Catch-22*]

Like all superlative works of comedy—and I am ready to argue that this is one of the most bitterly funny works in the language—*Catch-22* is based on an unconventional but utterly convincing internal logic. In the very opening pages, when we come upon a number of Air Force officers malingering in a hospital—one censoring all the modifiers out of enlisted men's letters and signing the censor's name "Washington Irving," another pursuing tedious conversations with boring Texans in order to increase his life span by making time pass slowly, still another storing horse chestnuts in his cheeks to give himself a look of innocence—it seems obvious that an inordinate number of Joseph Heller's characters are, by all conventional standards, mad. It is a triumph of Mr. Heller's skill that he is so quickly able to persuade us 1) that the most lunatic are the most logical, and 2) that it is our conventional standards which lack any logical consistency. The sanest looney of them all is the apparently harebrained central character, an American bombardier of Syrian extraction named Captain John Yossarian, who is based on a mythical Italian island (Pianosa) during World War II. For while many of his fellow officers seem indifferent to their own survival, and most of his superior officers are overtly hostile to his, Yossarian is animated solely by a desperate determination to stay alive:

It was a vile and muddy war, and Yossarian could have lived without it—lived forever, perhaps. Only a fraction of his countrymen would give up their lives to win it, and it was not his ambition to be among them. . . . That men would die was a matter of necessity; *which* men would die, though, was a matter of circumstance, and Yossarian was willing to be the victim of anything but circumstance.

The single narrative thread in this crazy patchwork of anecdotes, episodes, and character portraits traces Yossarian's herculean efforts—through caution, cowardice, defiance, subterfuge, stratagem, and subversion, through feigning illness, goofing off, and poisoning the company's food with laundry soap—to avoid being victimized by circumstance, a force represented in the book as Catch-22. For Catch-22 is the unwritten loophole in every written law which empowers the authorities to revoke your rights whenever it suits their cruel whims; it is, in short, the principle of absolute evil in a malevolent, mechanical, and incompetent world. Because of Catch-22, justice is mocked, the innocent are victimized, and Yossarian's squadron is forced to fly more than double the number of missions prescribed by Air Force code. Dogged by Catch-22, Yossarian becomes the anguished witness to the ghoulish slaughter of his crew members and the destruction of all his closest friends, until finally his fear of death becomes so intense that he refuses to wear a uniform, after his own has been besplattered with the guts of his dying [11] gunner, and receives a medal standing naked in formation. From this point on, Yossarian's logic becomes so pure that everyone thinks him mad, for it is the logic of sheer survival, dedicated to keeping him alive in a world noisily clamoring for his annihilation.

According to this logic, Yossarian is surrounded on all sides by hostile forces: his enemies are distinguished less by their nationality than by their ability to get him killed. Thus, Yossarian feels a blind, electric rage against the Germans whenever they hurl flak at his easily penetrated plane; but he feels an equally profound hatred for those of his own countrymen who exercise an arbitrary power over his life and well-being. Heller's huge cast of characters, therefore, is dominated by a large number of comic maligni-ties, *genus Americanus*, drawn with a grotesqueness so audacious that they somehow transcend caricature entirely and become vividly authentic. These include: Colonel Cathcart, Yossarian's commanding officer, whose con-suming ambition to get his picture in the *Saturday Evening Post* motivates him to volunteer his command for every dangerous mission, and to initiate prayers during briefing sessions ("I don't want any of this Kingdom of God or Valley of Death stuff. That's all too negative. . . . Couldn't we pray for a tighter bomb pattern?"), an idea he abandons only when he learns en-listed men pray to the same God; General Peckem, head of Special Services, whose strategic objective is to replace General Dreedle, the wing com-mander, capturing every bomber group in the US Air Force ("If dropping bombs on the enemy isn't a special service, I wonder what in the world is."); Captain Black, the squadron intelligence officer, who inaugurates the Glorious Loyalty Oath Crusade in order to discomfort a rival, forcing all officers (except the rival, who is thereupon declared a Communist) to sign a new oath whenever they get their flak suits, their pay checks, or their haircuts; Lieutenant Scheisskopf, paragon of the parade ground, whose admiration for efficient formations makes him scheme to screw nickel-alloy swivels into every cadet's back for perfect ninety degree turns; and cadres of sadistic officers, club-happy MPs, and muddleheaded agents of the CID, two of whom, popping in and out of rooms like farcical private eyes, look for Washington Irving throughout the action, finally pinning the rap on the innocent chaplain.

These are Yossarian's antagonists, all of them reduced to a single exag-gerated humor, and all identified by their totally mechanical attitude to-wards human life. Heller has a profound hatred for this kind of military mind, further anatomized in a wacky scene before the Action Board which displays his (and their) animosity in a manner both hilarious and scarifying.

But Heller, at war with much larger forces than the army, has provided his book with much wider implications than a war novel. For the author (apparently sharing the Italian belief that vengeance is a dish which tastes best cold) has been nourishing his grudges for so long that they have expanded to include the post-war American world. Through the agency of grotesque comedy, Heller has found a way to confront the humbug, hypocrisy, cruelty, and sheer stupidity of our mass society—qualities which have made the few other Americans who care almost speechless with baffled rage—and through some miracle of prestidigitation, Pianosa has become a satirical microcosm for many of the macrocosmic idiocies of our time. Thus, the author flourishes his Juvenalian scourge at government-subsidized agriculture (and farmers, one of whom "spent every penny he didn't earn on new land to increase the amount of alfalfa he did not grow"); at the exploitation of American Indians, evicted from their oil-rich land; at smug psychiatrists; at bureaucrats and patriots; at acquisitive war widows; at high-spirited American boys; and especially, and most vindictively, at war profiteers.

This last satirical flourish, aimed at the whole mystique of corporation capitalism, is embodied in the fantastic adventures of Milo Minderbinder, the company mess officer, and a paradigm of good-natured Jonsonian cupidity. Anxious to put the war on a businesslike basis, Milo has formed a syndicate designed to corner the world market on all available foodstuffs, which he then sells to army messhalls at huge profits. Heady with success (his deals have made him Mayor of every town in Sicily, Vice-Shah of Oran, Caliph of Baghdad, Imam of Damascus, and the Sheik of Araby), Milo soon expands his activities, forming a private army which he hires out to the highest bidder. The climax of Milo's career comes when he fulfills a contract with the Germans to bomb and strafe his own outfit, directing his planes from the Pianosa control tower and justifying the action [12] with the stirring war cry: "What's good for the syndicate is good for the country." Milo has almost succeeded in his ambition to pre-empt the field of war for private enterprise when he makes a fatal mistake: he has cornered the entire Egyptian cotton market and is unable to unload it anywhere. Having failed to pass it off to his own messhall in the form of chocolate-covered cotton, Milo is finally persuaded by Yossarian to bribe the American government to take it off his hands: "If you run into trouble, just tell everybody that the security of the country requires a strong domestic Egyptian cotton speculating industry." The Minderbinder sections—in showing the basic incompatibility of idealism and economics by satirizing the patriotic cant which usually accompanies American greed—illustrate the procedure of the entire book: the ruthless ridicule of hypocrisy through a technique of farce-fantasy, beneath which the demon of satire lurks, prodding fat behinds with a red-hot pitchfork.

It should be abundantly clear, then, that Catch-22, despite some of the most outrageous sequences since A Night at the Opera, is an intensely serious work. Heller has certain technical similarities to the Marx Brothers, Max Schulman, Kingsley Amis, Al Capp, and S. J. Perelman, but his mordant intelligence, closer to that of Nathanael West, penetrates the surface of the merely funny to expose a world of ruthless self-advancement, gruesome cruelty, and flagrant disregard for human life—a world, in short, very much like our own as seen through a magnifying glass, distorted for more perfect accuracy. Considering his indifference to surface reality, it is absurd to judge Heller by standards of psychological realism (or, for that matter, by conventional artistic standards at all, since his book is as formless as any picaresque epic). He is concerned entirely with that thin boundary of the surreal, the borderline between hilarity and horror, which, much like the apparent formlessness of the unconscious, has its own special integrity and coherence. Thus, Heller will never use comedy for its own sake; each joke has a wider significance in the intricate pattern, so that laughter becomes a prologue for some grotesque revelation. This gives the reader an effect of surrealistic dislocation, intensified by a weird, rather flat, impersonal style, full of complicated reversals, swift transitions, abrupt shifts in chronological time, and manipulated identities (e.g. if a private named Major Major Major is promoted to Major by a faulty IBM machine, or if a malingerer, sitting out a doomed mission, is declared dead through a bureaucratic error, then this remains their permanent fate), as if all mankind was determined by a mad and merciless mechanism.

Thus, Heller often manages to heighten the macabre obscenity of total war much more effectively through its gruesome comic aspects than if he had written realistic descriptions. And thus, the most delicate pressure is enough to send us over the line from farce into phantasmagoria. In the climactic chapter, in fact, the book leaves comedy altogether and becomes an eerie nightmare of terror. Here, Yossarian, walking through the streets of Rome as though through an Inferno, observes soldiers molesting drunken women, fathers beating ragged children, policemen clubbing innocent bystanders until the whole world seems swallowed up in the maw of evil:

The night was filled with horrors, and he thought he knew how Christ must have felt as he walked through the world, like a psychiatrist through a ward of nuts, like a victim through a prison of thieves. . . . Mobs . . . mobs of policemen. . . . Mobs with clubs were in control everywhere.

Here, as the book leaves the war behind, it is finally apparent that Heller's comedy is his artistic response to his vision of transcendent evil, as if the escape route of laughter were the only recourse from a malignant world.

It is this world, which cannot be divided into boundaries or ideologies, that Yossarian has determined to resist. And so when his fear and disgust have reached the breaking point, he simply refuses to fly another mission. Asked by a superior what would happen if everybody felt the same way, Yossarian exercises his definitive logic, and answers, "Then I'd be a damned fool to feel any other way." Having concluded a separate peace, Yossarian maintains it in the face of derision, ostracism, psychological pressure, and the threat of court martial. When he is finally permitted to go home if he will only agree to a shabby deal whitewashing Colonel Cathcart, however, he finds himself impaled on two impossible alternatives. But his unique logic, helped along by the precedent of an even more logical friend, makes him conclude that desertion is the better part of valor; and so (after an inspirational sequence which is the weakest thing in the book) he takes off for neutral Sweden—the only place left in the world, outside of England, where "mobs with clubs" are not in control.

Yossarian's expedient is not very flattering to our national ideals, being defeatist, selfish, cowardly, and unheroic. On the other hand, it is one of those sublime expressions of anarchic individualism without which all national ideals are pretty hollow anyway. Since the mass State, whether totalitarian or democratic, has grown increasingly hostile to Falstaffian irresponsibility, Yossarian's anti-heroism is, in fact, a kind of inverted heroism which we would do well to ponder. For, contrary to the armchair pronouncements of patriotic ideologues, Yossarian's obsessive concern for survival makes him not only *not* morally dead, but one of the most morally vibrant figures in recent literature—and a giant of the will beside those weary, wise and wistful prodigals in contemporary novels who always accommodate sadly to American life. I believe that Joseph Heller is one of the most extraordinary talents now among us. He has Mailer's combustible radicalism without his passion for violence and self-glorification; he has Bellow's gusto with his compulsion to affirm the unaffirmable; and he has Salinger's wit without his coquettish self-consciousness. Finding his absolutes in the freedom to *be*, in a world dominated by cruelty, carnage, inhumanity, and a rage to destroy itself, Heller has come upon a new morality based on an old ideal, the morality of refusal. Perhaps—now that Catch-22 has found its most deadly nuclear form—we have reached the point where even the logic of survival is unworkable. But at least we can still contemplate the influence of its liberating honesty on a free, rebellious spirit in this explosive, bitter, subversive, brilliant book. [13]

Philip Toynbee
Here's Greatness — in Satire

When I began reading *Catch-22*, I thought it was a farcical satire on life in the United States Army Air Force. Later I believed that Mr. Heller's target was modern war and all those who are responsible for waging it. Still later it seemed that he was attacking social organisation and anyone who derives power from it. But by the end of the book, it had become plain to me that it is—no other phrase will do—the human condition itself which is the object of Mr. Heller's fury and disgust.

A reviewer must always keep an anxious eye on the state of his currency. If he announces too many masterpieces he risks inflation (though it is sometimes forgotten by some of us that the cowardice of perpetual crabbing receives its own kind of punishment). It does not seem many weeks since I was proclaiming that Malcolm Lowry's *Under the Volcano* is one of the great English novels of this century; and not long before that I was urging that attention should be paid to the magnificent and neglected talent of William Gerhardt.

But at the risk of inflation I cannot help writing that *Catch-22* is the greatest satirical work in English since *Erewhon*. For the fact is that all my successive interpretations of this book now seem to me to have been accurate, even if the earlier ones were also incomplete. The book has an immense and devastating theme, but this theme is illustrated, as it should be, by means of an observed reality.

Reality Inflated

I am not suggesting that *Catch-22* is a realistic account of life in the wartime Air Force of America or any other country. The method of satire is to inflate reality so that all its partially concealed blemishes turn into monstrous and apparent deformations. The effect of good satire is to make us laugh with horror. And this means that the social and personal evils which are being satirized must have been *there*, and must be felt by the reader to be there even while he is laughing at the results of the satirist's inflating

SOURCE: *The Observer* (London), June 17, 1962. Reprinted by permission of the publisher.

imagination. Here is an example. Among the vast number of hallucinatory characters in *Catch-22* there is an officer called Milo Minderbinder who devotes all his time to infinitely elaborate commercial enterprises in the Mediterranean field of operations. At one point he bombs his own airfield in exchange for a promise from the Germans of the cost of the operation plus six per cent. Several of his friends are killed, but Milo is much too valuable to be reprimanded, let alone punished, by the American authorities.

Murderous

Utterly impossible? No doubt; yet when I was stationed on the north-east coast in 1941 the new concrete dragon's teeth on the beach began to corrode away after only three months. It was found that the contractor had built brittle shells of concrete and filled them with sand. Yet when I expressed outrage at this murderous piece of cheating it was explained that the man was of too much local importance for any action to be taken against him. His behaviour had, indeed, been less dramatic than Milo's; but was it any less flagrant or appalling?

In the same way the frightful Colonel Cathcart of *Catch-22* cares about nothing but keeping in well with his superiors at any price. To do so he continually increases the quota of missions which his men must fly before being sent home on leave. The original number was 40, but by the end of the book it has reached 80.

We may reasonably guess that higher authorities would have prevented this from happening, even if the flyers themselves had not achieved some sort of resistance. Yet I haven't the least doubt that many a colonel in the armies involved would have behaved like Colonel Cathcart if he had believed that he could get away with it. Was Haig's behaviour very different at the third battle of Ypres?

If *Catch-22* has any continuous theme it lies in the tireless efforts of Yossarian, the Assyrian-American hero, to evade combat duties. The book demands the right, indeed almost the moral obligation, of men to be physical cowards. It is pointed out, for example, that the brave almost always involve others in their senseless and unfeeling co-operation with the forces of war. The man who has the courage of his physical cowardice may be the only kind of man who will eventually make war impossible by refusing to play any part in it at all.

This is, in fact, the position which Yossarian—one of the most sympathetic heroes in modern literature—finally arrives at:

"From now on I'm thinking only of me."

Major Danby replied indulgently with a superior smile, "But, Yossarian, suppose everybody felt that way."

"Then I'd certainly be a damned fool to feel any other way, wouldn't I?"

Exactly; and it is clearly Mr. Heller's fervent hope that everyone will, in the end, feel that way.

Raging Pity

This is an arguable attitude, I suppose, though I have never been able to think of much to be said against it. But though it places Mr. Heller in a very strong satirical position it would not, of itself, have enabled him to write a great book. He has done this because he is a man of deep and urgent compassion whose raging pity is concerned with the nature of human existence itself no less than with specific and curable iniquities.

"And don't tell me God works in a mysterious way," Yossarian continued, hurtling on over her objection. "There's nothing so mysterious about it. He's not working at all. He's playing. Or else He's forgotten all about us. That's the kind of God you people talk about—a country bumpkin, a clumsy, bungling, brainless, conceited, uncouth hayseed. Good God, how much reverence can you have for a Supreme Being who finds it necessary to include such phenomena as phlegm and tooth decay in His divine system of creation? What in the world was running through that warped, evil, scatological mind of His when He robbed old people of the power to control their bowel movements? Why in the world did He ever create pain?"

"Pain?" Lieutenant Scheisskopf's wife pounced upon the word victoriously. "Pain is a useful symptom. Pain is a warning to us of bodily dangers."

"And who created the dangers?" Yossarian demanded.

But it is death itself which is the principal target of this book, the principal object of Mr. Heller's horrified resentment. Unlike that old philistine, Carlyle, he does not find it necessary to accept the universe. This comparatively early passage is confirmed in the magnificent sustained horror of Yossarian's nightmare peregrination of the streets of Rome. And this is placed near enough the end of the book to act as a peroration.

Yet it can hardly be too much insisted that *Catch-22* is a very, very funny book and by no means a depressing one. To counter his horror of death Mr. Heller celebrates sexuality in a richly comic tone which is blessedly un-Lawrentian. What is so remarkable, and perhaps unique, is that Mr. Heller can move us from farce into tragedy within a page or two, and that we accept the transition without demur.

In *Candide* the hero suffers the most drastic physical injuries, yet we are never tempted to take them seriously. Candide's mutilations are a convention of the satirical genre, and nothing more. But when, for example, Kid

Sampson is suddenly cut in two while bathing we share the horror and shock of the onlookers.

Subversive

I suppose the book has faults. It is a little too long and repetitive. Very occasionally the humour turns into a rather brittle and slick form of verbal wit. ("He advocated thrift and hard work and disapproved of loose women who turned him down.") There is rather too much Lewis Carroll nonsense humour, and sometimes the passages of "straight" horror or pity sound a little raucous. If anything Mr. Heller tends to be over-explanatory, and to ram home his messages beyond the point where they have been well taken.

But I mean these complaints to be trivial, for this is a book that I could wish everyone to read. It is a genuinely subversive book in the best sense—written, incidentally, by a . . . New York "promotion executive," whatever that may be—but it sounds deplorable. It is a book which should really help us to feel more clearly.

And Catch-22?

Yossarian looked at him soberly and tried another approach. "Is Orr crazy?"

"He sure is," Doc Daneeka said.

"Can you ground him?"

"I sure can. But first he has to ask me to. That's part of the rule."

"Then why doesn't he ask you to?"

"Because he's crazy," Doc Daneeka said. "He has to be crazy to keep flying combat missions after all the close calls he's had. Sure I can ground Orr. But first he has to ask me."

"And then you can ground him?" Yossarian asked.

"No. Then I can't ground him."

"You mean there's a catch?"

"Sure there's a catch," Doc Daneeka replied. "Catch-22. Anyone who wants to get out of combat duty isn't really crazy. . . ."

"That's some catch, that Catch-22," Yossarian observed.

"It's the best there is," Doc Daneeka agreed.

Shimon Wincelberg
A Deadly Serious Lunacy

As the theater lately has discovered, or rediscovered, when the artist deals with human experience at those levels which are almost literally worse than death, the resources of naturalism prove pitifully inadequate. The alternative, requiring not only a high order of poetic vision but also a willingness to shock, to challenge, to spit in your audience's eye, is what goes currently under the label of the Absurd. This encompasses farce, gibberish, surrealism and even that sub-branch of show-business called "sick humor"—all with good, honorable roots reaching back to Aristophanes, Homer, Cervantes, Swift and just about every other writer, painter or poet who ever had the audacity to attempt works of art out of the meaningless deaths, tortures and degradations some men undergo at the instance of others.

At the moment, of course, Absurdity as a literary or theatrical device is not only respectable but fashionable. And while fashion creates the hazard of attracting opportunists, it also makes it possible for the occasional work of genuine originality and power to find a far wider audience than someone like Nathanael West did in his time.

Joseph Heller's novel, *Catch-22*, lives up almost completely to its ecstatic notices. It is a sprawling, hilarious, irresponsible, compassionate, cynical, surrealistic, farcical, lacerating and enormously readable account of what happened (though it couldn't have, really; not quite *that* way) to some American flyers on a small island in the Mediterranean during the Italian campaign of World War II. Despite its determination to be as unreliable as possible about that particular war and why it might have been fought, it manages to reduce such fine, naturalistic war novels as those of Norman Mailer, James Jones or Irwin Shaw to mere talented journalism, and their portrayal of the bumbling or malevolent high brass into a positive whitewash.

Having served *my* time both on the other side of the globe and as close to the ground as I could get, I don't know whether the term "Catch-22" is an authentic piece of Air Corps folklore or the author's own happy inven-

SOURCE: *The New Leader*, Vol. 65 (May 14, 1962), pp. 26–27. Reprinted by permission of *The New Leader*. Copyright © The American Labor Conference on International Affairs, Inc.

tion. But, as the central symbol of his characters' predicament, it serves his purpose with devastating precision.

Catch-22 is the principle which keeps the half-crazed and exhausted bomber crews of the unspeakable Colonel Cathcart's squadron flying a quota of missions outrageously raised each time they are about to reach it. One of its definitions goes, "they have a right to do anything we can't stop them from doing." "They" are Heller's preposterous (perhaps just a shade too preposterous) colonels and generals, a gallery of childish, senile, vain, malicious, frightened incompetents playing a paper-helmet war for the gratification of their corkscrew egos and titanic insecurities, for some nebulous form of social or commercial [26] advancement, little exercises in one-upmanship between rival brass, or simply to get themselves written up in the *Saturday Evening Post*.

There is almost no plot to speak of, at least until the very end, by which time practically everyone you care about, with the exception of the hero, is dead or missing. There is only a string of sometimes overlapping, sometimes disconnected, events, some as outrageously lunatic as an early Marx Brothers film, some as realistic and sickening as anything ever written about the strange things war can do to the fragile bodies and minds of a lot of once-healthy young animals in uniform.

The book's "hero" is Captain Yossarian, engaging, stubborn, lecherous, saintly, and excruciatingly sane as he flails back at the system symbolized by Catch-22. Sample dialogue between Yossarian and his friend Doc Daneeka, the crabbed, self-pitying, powerless medical officer:

"Is Orr crazy?"

"He sure is." . . .

"Can you ground him?"

"I sure can. But first he has to ask me to. That's part of the rule."

"Then why doesn't he ask you to?"

"Because he's crazy. . . . He has to be crazy to keep flying combat missions after all the close calls he's had. . . . But first he has to ask me to." . . .

"And then you can ground him?" . . .

"No. Then I can't ground him."

"You mean there's a catch?"

"Sure there's a catch. . . . Catch-22. Anyone who wants to get out of combat duty isn't really crazy."

At times, however, Heller's brilliant and original comic vision, as well as his splendid rage at the homicidal and suicidal stupidity with which wars may be fought at the headquarters level, is somewhat weakened by his evident delight in his own cleverness. Not that the jokes, by and large, aren't both fresh and funny—especially the grisly ones. But it soon becomes apparent that most of his characters can be summed up in terms of a joke, which might make them easy for a reviewer to describe, but greatly limits their ability to grow, develop, or expose themselves to revelation.

There is Colonel Cathcart, the one who keeps raising the number of missions, and before a particularly nasty one exhorts his men to be sure and make tight bomb patterns in order to produce "a good clean aerial photograph he won't be ashamed to send through channels." All the disclaimers in the world will not convince me that this man is fictitious.

Another far from atypical character, I suspect, is the sweet and crushingly ineffectual chaplain, who "used to think it was immoral to be unhappy." It is his ambitious but lazy assistant who is responsible for that moving and time-saving form letter to the next-of-kin, which reads:

"Dear Mrs., Mr., Miss, or Mr. and Mrs.————: Words cannot express the deep personal grief I experienced when your husband, son, father or brother was killed, wounded or reported missing in action."

There is also Doc Daneeka, bitterly resentful of the impending collapse of the German armies because it means he will be sent to the Pacific. And the "licensed psychiatrist" who accuses Yossarian of being immature, "with a morbid aversion to dying" and "deep-seated survival anxieties." And the luckless flyers forced to abandon their plane in the waters off Marseilles, who find that their Mae Wests wouldn't inflate because their mess-officer, the remarkable Milo Minderbinder, had stolen the carbon-dioxide capsules to make ice cream sodas for the officers' mess. Nor will I find it easy to forget "ex-Pfc." Wintergreen, the elusive mail clerk, who is "probably the most influential man in the whole theater of operations."

For the last 30–40 pages Heller seems abruptly to have been persuaded that even a novel as original as his would be better for some sort of a plot, preferably in chronological order. So he hastily furnishes one, involving his startled hero in one of those soul-searching conflicts between conscience and self-interest which used to be so popular on live TV. It is very well done and all but, in contrast to the rest of the book's splendid contempt for such niceties, I find it a little on the square side.

That, however, is a minor quibble against a novel which, on almost every page, offers such felicities as: "There are now fifty or sixty countries fighting in this war. Surely so many countries can't *all* be worth dying for." [27]

Julian Mitchell
Under Mad Gods

Joseph Heller's *Catch-22* is an extraordinary book. Its basic assumption is that in war all men are equally mad; bombs fall on insane friend and crazy enemy alike. But wherever bombs fall, men die, and no matter how often the process of bombs falling and men dying is repeated, it is always terrible. Ostensibly a black farce about an American bomber squadron stationed on an island in the Mediterranean towards the end of the Second World War, it is, in fact, a surrealist *Iliad*, with a lunatic High Command instead of gods, and a coward for hero.

Yossarian, the coward, is a rational man trying not to be killed in a wholly irrational world, forced to resort to even more irrational behaviour than that of his superiors in order to survive. He is an expert malingerer; he performs minor acts of sabotage on his own plane; he takes every possible form of evasive action. But he cannot succeed against the appalling Colonel Cathcart, who continually raises the number of missions the men have to fly before they can be sent home, solely to get a reputation as a tough leader of men. Whatever Yossarian does, there is always a catch—Catch-22: 'Catch-22 says they have a right to do anything we can't stop them from doing.' It is an unwritten law which is ruthlessly enforced.

Epic in form, the book is episodic in structure. Each chapter carries a single character a step nearer madness or death or both, and a step, too, into legend. The action takes place well above the level of reality. On leave or in action the characters behave with a fine disregard for the laws of probability. Yet they follow the law of Catch-22 and its logically necessary results. Within its own terms the book is wholly consistent, creating legend out of the wildest farce and the most painful realism, constructing its own system of probability. Its characters are as boldly unlikely as its events, but when they die, they die with as much pain as any 'real' men, and when they are dead, they are wept for with real tears. There is a scene in which Yossarian bandages the wounded leg of one of his crew, only to find that inside the man's flak-suit his vital organs have mortally spilled, a scene which is repeated again and again, each time with more detail and more dread. It acts as a reminder that *Catch-22*, for all its zany appearance, is an extremely serious novel. Against Catch-22 the man who does not wish to die

SOURCE: *The Spectator* (London), Vol. 208 (June 15, 1962), p. 801. Reprinted by permission of the publisher.

has only his wits: war is not civilised, and to be caught up in it is to be reduced to a state of nature far worse than that visualised by Hobbes. *Catch-22* is a book of enormous richness and art, of deep thought and brilliant writing. [801]

Andrew Leslie
A Comedy of
Horrors

It is a long time since the mad futility of war was so cleanly exposed as in Joseph Heller's *Catch-22*. His line of approach to a subject which by now must be faint with exposure is a relatively original one—the detail which is certainly all his own, freshly ground.

Heller's theme is not so much to illustrate the idea that war is squalid, brutal, and life-wasting, though these come as undertones, rather as a sombre cello might sound in the middle of a toy symphony played by eccentrics. It is not the immorality of war which he attacks so much as our ineptness in waging it. Just look—he seems to say, like a *compère* of an army pantomime—at the crazy, vain, and pompous thing a military organisation is, how irrational its confusions about heroism and self-sacrifice. Until the human race is ready to tackle more grandiose concepts—morality and such—this will do as a deterrent.

Heller's exemplary outfit is a section of the United States Air Force in the Italian campaign. His chief protagonist of sanity and virtue—no, his only one—is a certain Captain Yossarian [bombardier of a B-25], whose instinct for personal survival is as robust and remorseless as nature intended in any jungle.

He is an anti-hero of shameless proportions. His dream is to have a seat right over his aircraft's escape hatch. When directing his [B-25's] evasive action over enemy flak the rational objective is not only to escape the enemy but also to zoom away from your friends in case their loads blow up (Heller's depiction of panic, subdued or naked, is shakingly funny). Yossarian is sane because all the seemingly earnest people around him are so clearly mad; or maybe it's the system.

The staff officers are limitless in their courage: they will pick up a phone

SOURCE: *The Guardian* (Manchester), June 15, 1962, p. 5. Reprinted by permission of the author.

and volunteer their boys for any operation, the more hazardous the better. The fliers are afraid of death; the staff colonels terrified of missing promotion. It is a taut network of anxiety from which there is no escape. If you see a chink of light at the end of the tunnel there is always that vague rule in the book, Catch-22, which says you must fly just a few more missions. You can't win. The only temporary escapers are men like Milo, the mess officer, who have something positive and rational to pursue, like money-making. Startling in a small way, his black-market enterprises soon cover all the theatres of the war. [B-25's] arrived painted with the legend "M & M Enterprises, Fine Fruits and Produce" and are redistributed by other sections of the war machine.

At 443 pages, the book is rather long to sustain itself without a firmer story-line than it has. But in about one chapter in three, Mr. Heller soars sweetly up into zones of the quite brilliantly comic. [5]

Milton R. Bass

Review of 'Catch-22'

There is nothing in the world so satisfying as to come unexpectedly upon genius. It stirs the very bowels of your being, gives pleasure and excitement in the present and engenders hope for the future.

These were my reactions upon getting involved with *Catch-22*, a first novel by a 38-year-old writer named Joseph Heller. There is a genius in Mr. Heller. Perhaps minor genius, but pure genius nevertheless. I can't recommend this book to everybody. Children and teenagers are out. The same goes for all women and perhaps men who have not lived through a war as an active combat participant. There are universalities for all (including the children and teenagers) in the book, but they must be interpreted on an individual basis.

Ernest Hemingway once commented that the great war books are not the ones that come out immediately after the fighting ceased. It takes at least five years for the creative mind to assimilate the physical vastness of what has happened and transmute it into literary form." Heller started

SOURCE: *The Berkshire* (Mass.) *Eagle*, October 31, 1961, p. 6. Reprinted by permission of the author.

this book in 1953 and finished it this year. Meanwhile, he attended New York University, Columbia University and Oxford University, the last on a Fulbright Scholarship. He taught in college for a while, and is now working as a promotion executive on a magazine. From 1942 to 1945 he served as a bombardier in the 12th Air Force, stationed on the island of Corsica.

The uniqueness of the novel is that although it is relating events that occurred in World War II, it does so from the viewpoint of all that has taken place since then, including the advent of McCarthyism and the John Birch Society. The people in the novel are always having the impression that what is happening to them has happened before, and since the author does look forward and back, the book is really an exposition of the cyclic theory of history. It's a terribly sensible *Finnegans Wake*.

Our hero of the book is a brave man who is a coward. He is Everyman, trapped in a world he never made. His name is Captain Yossarian, a bombardier who has decided to live forever even if he has to die in the attempt. However, any man in combat has only so much luck and Yossarian's is on the verge of running out. His main trouble is his commanding officer, Colonel Cathcart, who raises the number of required missions in multiples of five any time anybody in the squadron gets near enough to rate rotation home.

The characters in this book are either rogues or nuts, somewhere a combination of both. The most amusing one is Lieutenant Milo Minderbinder, the mess officer who organizes international cartels for black-market activities. His outfit becomes so big that he even bombs his own airfield for the Germans, at cost plus 6 per cent. Then there is a Major Major Major, whose tragedy is a sick resemblance to Henry Fonda; Lieutenant Scheisskopf, who loves nothing more in the world than a parade; Major————de Coverley, whose face is so foreboding no one has ever dared to ask him his first name; and Orr, the pilot who sticks chestnuts in his cheeks and perfects the most brilliant combat dodge in the history of warfare. There are innumerable other characters, all too beautiful to believe.

Catch-22 is one of those books that annoys you for the first 50 pages, mostly because you can't understand what the devil is going on. The sentences are of the nice, simple declarative type, but there is an oddness to the people, a seeming disorganization to the plot and a weirdness to the atmosphere that makes you feel trapped in a mental institution after the caretakers have left for the day. And then all of a sudden the pattern falls into place, and you realize that there is fantastic organization to the spider web of the plot and that the people are everybody you know carried to their logical extremes and the incidents are everything that has happened, is happening or will happen to you. And you rush through to the end just to find out how you will make out, hoping your end will be a happy one, but prepared for the worst.

This is one of the funniest tragedies I have read. Most of the time you can't cry for the laughing and you can't laugh for the crying. I don't know how many people will embrace the book the way I did, but if you think there is the slightest chance it may be for you, don't let this opportunity get away from you. There are so few of us and we have to stick together. [6]

Richard Starnes
Review of
`Catch-22`

Yossarian will, I think, live a very long time.

All the way through *Catch-22* Yossarian knows that thousands of people are trying to kill him. Everybody. His squadron commander, Colonel Cathcart, and his pilot, McWatt, and Milo Minderbinder, the cosmically dishonest black-market entrepreneur, even Doc Daneeka, the whining, self-seeking squadron surgeon, who was declared dead and could never thereafter persuade the ponderous Army bureaucracy to reverse the decision, even though he was as alive as he had ever been—all are part of the huge conspiracy to destroy Yossarian.

Catch-22 is a novel by Joseph Heller. It is very, very good and tremendously exciting. The book, which was published by Simon and Schuster, is already a commercial success. It is, moreover, surely destined to be one of the enduring monuments in our language.

Yossarian is the hero of *Catch-22*. He is gentle, intelligent, sensitive, and quite mad. The whole insane focus of man's most grandiose insanity is aimed at destroying Yossarian. Before one is very far along in the book the question of whether Yossarian (who is humanity) will survive becomes very important—just as it becomes terribly important to learn Snowden's hideous secret.

Catch-22 is variously defined, but perhaps best of all by the abandoned crone in the raided bordello in Rome: "Catch-22 says they have the right to do anything we can't stop them from doing."

SOURCE: *The Washington Daily News*, March 1, 1962, p. 25. Reprinted by permission of the author.

Catch-22 enables Colonel Cathcart to order Yossarian and the rest of the squadron to fly more combat missions than any other bomber group. It is responsible when Snowden yields up his grisly secret, which is everybody's secret, to Yossarian in the tail of a shot-up airplane.

Yossarian, too sane and too decent to endure the mad obscenity of war, cannot live with the terrible burden of Snowden's secret—but Catch-22 makes him live with it, just as it makes him live with the starving children and the brutalized prostitutes of wartime Rome.

Yossarian's despairing walk through the rainy Roman night is a nightmarish, surrealistic evocation that approaches the terrible, tortured insight with which Leopold Bloom was cursed. Indeed, not since I first read *Ulysses* has any novel taken me up as *Catch-22* did. I don't believe it is unreasonable to suggest that someday it may mean as much to us as does the tormented tale of Bloom's quest for his lost son.

By this I don't mean to suggest that *Catch-22* is as troublesome or as unnecessarily arcane as *Ulysses* is. *Catch-22*, for example, is convulsively funny in spots—until the reader's preoccupation with Snowden's unbearable secret and the awful tension of wondering whether Catch-22 ultimately will crush Yossarian becomes too much even for the gifted Mr. Heller's mad dialog to make funny.

The jacket blurb says *Catch-22* presents the world of this century as it might appear to one who was dangerously sane. This it does, but more than that it shows us that we all carry the dreadful burden of Snowden's secret—that when it is revealed with all its painful explicitness we can't avoid sharing it. [25]

Anonymous
The Heller Cult

"It's not a book you like a little," says . . . Joseph Heller about his wild, exuberant first novel, *Catch-22*, and that may go down as the understatement of the publishing year. Not since *The Catcher in the Rye* and *Lord of the Flies* has a novel been taken up by such a fervid and heterogeneous claque of admirers.

Lawyers like it, and so do cartoonists. Poet John Ciardi stayed awake all night to finish Heller's comic extravaganza about a war run by lunatics and

SOURCE: *Newsweek*, Vol. 60 (October 1, 1962), pp. 82–83. Copyright © 1962 by Newsweek, Inc.

a young bombardier whose only target is to keep himself alive. The director of public relations for CARE, Sam Kaufman, was so taken with *Catch* he considered attaching a flyer to all CARE publicity, advising "Send CARE packages to the hungry overseas. They need it. And don't fail to read *Catch-22*. You need it."

Heller has fans at the Rand Corp., the Behavioral Sciences Center at Stanford University, and the Kansas City *Star*. Producer David Merrick likes the zany, unclassifiable novel so much he wants to do a Broadway version. Columbia Pictures has paid $150,000 for the movie rights and hired Heller to write the screenplay.* Anthony Quinn, Jack Lemmon, Ben Gazzara, Paul Newman, and Eli Wallach all want to play the hero, the bombardier Yossarian.

The book obviously inspires an evangelical fervor in those who admire it. Newscaster John Chancellor is so eager to spread the word that he printed up stickers reading "Yossarian Lives" and "Better Yossarian than Rotarian." Father Charles E. Sheedy, dean of the College of Arts and Letters at Notre Dame, was so caught up by *Catch* that he raved about it after a lecture on ethics at the U.S. Air Force Academy, and convinced some less enthusiastic airmen to take another look at the book, which is, of course, about their arm of the service.

Philip Toynbee liked it so much he called it "the greatest satirical work in English since *Erewhon*," and the English liked it so much that within a week of its publication this summer, *Catch-22* became London's No. 1 best seller.

Contagion

Although the novel has sold 40,000 copies in the U.S., it has never made the best-seller lists here, because these are national surveys, and most of the book's sales were in New York. Last week, the novel came out in paperback, making it a virtual certainty that *Catch* will spread throughout the U.S. It has already swept the cocktail-party circuit where *Catch-22* is the hottest topic going and Joe Heller himself is the hottest catch, although he usually declines invitations.

But he is no recluse like J.D. Salinger. "I like Salinger," Heller said last week. "I think he's unique. I love him as a person—because it's impossible to see him. But being alone is appealing only when you're not alone. I need outside disturbances. I draw inspiration from daily embarrassments. If I were in New Hampshire, now, far away from anyone close to me, I would be frightened. I'd go there only if I could be next door to Salinger,

---

* Heller never did attempt the screenplay. See "On Translating *Catch-22* into a Movie," pp. 346–362 of this book.—Eds.

but if I were next door, he would immediately move to Wyoming."

Heller's personality pattern, what his friends call his "wacky-looking sanity," was set sometime during the depression when he was growing up in Coney Island. At 19 he went off to World War II and was stationed on the island of Corsica, as a bombardier like Yossarian.

"I am one of those who benefited from war," said Heller. "If I had not gone to war, I would not have gone to college, and if I had not gone to college, I would not have been a writer. I don't know what would have become of me." As things turned out, he studied at NYU and Oxford, taught English composition for two years at Penn State, then became a full-time advertising copy writer.

The discovery of Louis-Ferdinand Céline and Vladimir Nabokov "literally in the same week" inspired him to start *Catch-22*. "What I got from Céline," he said, "is the slangy use of prose and the continuity that is relaxed and vague rather than precise and motivated; from Nabokov's *Laughter in the Dark*, the flippant approach to situations which were filled with anguish and grief and tragedy. *Catch-22* is really a juxtaposition of life and death. Laughter and loving are life and war is death."

Addict

The first chapter came quickly and was dispatched to New World Writing, which published it under its original title, *Catch-18*. (Later the title was changed to avoid confusion with Leon Uris' forgettable *Mila 18*. Heller says: "I was heartsick. I thought eighteen was the only number.") For two hours almost every night, five nights a week, for seven years, Heller wrote his novel. Once, for two weeks, he quit in disgust, turned to television and other pastimes, finally bored himself stiff. "What do people who are not writing novels do with their evenings?" he asked his wife, and then returned to novel-writing.

What kind of book is it? "A moral book," says the author, "dealing with man's moral dilemma. People can't distinguish [82] between rational and irrational behavior, between the moral and the immoral." Can Joe Heller? "I can really, but it's not easy. It's insane when I think this is a world in which the keepers are as nutty as the inmates. . . ."

This past summer on Fire Island, Heller began making notes for his new novel "about a married man who is working for a large company and who wants to work himself up to the point where he makes a speech at the company's annual convention in Bermuda." Pressed for details, Heller confessed, "It has implications."

He also found time to answer some of his voluminous mail, which includes such letters as the following from one of the eight countries where *Catch-22* is coming out in other languages: "I am translating your novel

Catch-22 into Finnish. Would you please explain me one thing: What means Catch-22? I didn't find it in any vocabulary. Even the assistant air attaché of the U.S.A. here in Helsinki could not explain exactly."

Joe Heller, who knows there is a catch to everything, comments dryly: "I think in Finland the book will lose a great deal in translation." [83]

Anonymous
A Review:
'Catch-22'

We are informed on the jacket of *Catch-22* that the author has attended New York University and Columbia, and has been a Fulbright student at Oxford. He has taught (English, I fear) at Pennsylvania State College and is now a "promotion executive." The term is no doubt a genteelism, less sinister than it sounds, meaning only that Mr. Heller is passing through the *Purgatorio* of the advertising man in his ascent from the *Inferno* of the teacher to the *Paradisio* of the creative artist. His age, thirty-eight in 1961, makes it possible that he served in the Second World War or in Korea, but if so he has found it unnecessary to levy upon personal experience. His war book derives from other war books, the movies, the stage, television, and current fashions in sans-culottism. He worked upon it from 1953. A copyright date of 1955, in addition to that of 1961, suggests that early precautions were taken lest its treasures be rifled. The portrait of the author on the jacket shows a countenance handsome, healthy, and relaxed—perfect icon of *l'homme moyen sensuel*.

Since books not worth reading are not worth reviewing and *Catch-22* is worthless, my review needs justification. I will supply it in conclusion. Meanwhile it may be [155] viewed as a protest against the means by which I was fubbed, an advertisement containing twenty-three testimonials to the superlative quality of Mr. Heller's book. Four of these were anonymous quotes from mass media (*Time, Newsday, Newsweek*, Associated Press) which seemed to support the identified speakers with the voice of the people which is also the voice of God. Of the identified speakers, about half were professional wind-raisers for the publishing industry and its captive journals. I am not bitter about these. To sustain themselves in the

SOURCE: *Daedalus*, Vol. 92 (Winter 1963), pp. 155–165. Reprinted by permission of the publisher. Reprinted by permission of the American Academy of Arts and Sciences, Boston, Massachusetts.

needy world of book-page journalism they must review more books than they read, and no doubt end many a working day with plaintive speculations: surely there must be *some* way of earning an honest living. It was by the nonprofessional enthusiasts that I was, in all senses of the word, sold. One was A. J. Liebling, whom I had assessed as a man not easily exploited. Another was a professor who, by unlucky coincidence, shares a surname with one of Mr. Heller's asinine villains.* I know him to be neither villain nor ass. Indeed none of the testifiers need be thought of as wicked or stupid men. They share in the prevalent confusion which I shall deal with at the end. And they are generous. It may not have occurred to them that, in supporting a raid on my purse and leisure, they were being generous with time and money not their own.

Nelson Algren ("the best"), Orville Prescott ("wildly original"), Robert Brustein ("superlative work"), Merle Miller ("it grabbed me"), Irwin Shaw ("congratulations"), *Time* ("written with brilliance"), Walt Kelly ("a very funny man"), James Jones ("marvelous"), Morris West ("wonderful"), Art Buchwald ("one of the greatest," nota bene, "in a cable from *Paris*"), Alexander King ("wit, grace, and intellectual awareness"), *Newsday* ("wonderful"), Selden Rodman ("devastatingly comic"), Oscar Cargill ("wonderful"), Ernest K. Gann ("the finest"), Harper Lee ("the only war novel"), Associated Press ("something special"), Leo Lerman ("our Swift"), *Newsweek* ("great power"), Maurice Dolbier ("hilarious, raging, exhilarating," etc.), A. J. Liebling ("the best"), Gladwyn Hill ("may become a classic"), Seymour Epstein ("nothing less than a fantastic experience").

The above may not serve to cast me in the role of David against Goliath, but it should prove that I am not striking a man who is down. I must add one more defensive note. Institutional rivalry has nothing to do with my estimate of *Catch-22*. Its author might have passed through my own university as he has through New York University, Columbia, and Oxford, unscathed by education. He is a phenomenon of our times, when a fair percentage of students prepare themselves to shape our culture by proving impervious to culture, and to use the tool of language by acquiring no skill with languages. A writer need not learn to write; he still can make his mark.

Before describing the theme of *Catch-22* I must make this point which I trust will not be considered trifling—that its author cannot write. My page references are designed to let the reader check, if he wishes, the fact that the specimens offered truly exist and are typical of the style of their context. In most of the book the question of style scarcely arises. Its pages [156] are filled with dialogue of the type which television comedians blame

---

* This would be the late Oscar Cargill of New York University.—Eds.

on their "writers," with the skits linked by brief paragraphs in the simple-style-dogmatic of the post-Hemingway era. Flat assertions succeed each other with the engaging rhythm of a slapping screen-door. It is when the author aspires to vivid or "fine" writing that we get a taste of his quality. Journalese emerges as the basic language, whole sentences consisting of clichés punctuated by proper names: "Even though Chief White Halfoat kept busting Colonel Moodus in the nose for General Dreedle's benefit, he was still outside the pale" (pp. 58–59).* Inevitably there follows the car which "slammed to a screeching stop inches short" of something or other. The author's way of breaking the cliché barrier is to supply all nouns with adjectives, frequently in strings: "He was a sad, birdlike man with the spatulate face and scrubbed, tapering features of a well-groomed rat" (22). If "spatulate" still means "broad and flat," it creates certain anatomical difficulties when used in connection with the "tapering features" of a rat; perhaps this is a form of ambivalence. Mr. Heller returns for another look at this face: "He had a dark complexion and a small, wise, saturnine face with mournful pouches under both eyes" (33). Observe the helpful word "both"—serving those of us accustomed to faces with pouches under only one eye. Recalling the curious rat which this character resembled, we trust that the pouches were like the features, tapered, and not like the face, "spatulate," and that they sagged under "both" beady eyes.

Mr. Heller's special genius is for selecting not the wrong word but the one which is not quite right, as when he describes one of his Italian beauties as having "incandescent blue veins converging populously beneath her cocoa-colored skin where the flesh is most tender" (25). Obviously she was well-peopled with veins, but their "converging beneath" her skin leaves us puzzled about where they diverged—surely not, cilia-like, *above* her skin nor yet at her stout whore's heart. In any event she would have been, as all women were to Hungry Joe, "lovely, satisfying, maddening manifestations of the miraculous" (53). As women to Hungry Joe, so alliteration to Mr. Heller. I will leave this matter of style after quoting, without comment, two sentences which Mr. Heller himself might wish to offer in evidence of his "power and commanding skill" (*Newsweek*), his "grace, and intellectual awareness" (King):

That was where he wanted to be if he had to be there at all, instead of hung out there in front like some goddam cantilevered goldfish in some goddam cantilevered goldfish bowl while the goddam foul black tiers of flak were bursting and booming and billowing all around and above and below him in a climbing, cracking, staggered, banging, phantasmagorical, cosmological wickedness that jarred and tossed and shivered, clattered and pierced, and

---

* This and succeeding page references are to the Dell edition (1962) of the novel.—Eds.

threatened to annihilate them all in one splinter of a second in one vast
flash of fire (50).

Along the ground suddenly, on both sides of the path, he saw dozens of
new mushrooms the rain had spawned poking their nodular fingers up
through the clammy earth like lifeless stalks of flesh, sprouting in such
necrotic profusion everywhere he looked that they seemed to be proliferating
right before his eyes (147–48). [157]

Catch-22 is about American aviators based on a Mediterranean island in
1945. The bombardier Yossarian is a reluctant hero who wants to be
grounded but is kept flying ever more missions by his ambitious superior,
Colonel Cathcart, until he resolves to desert to Sweden. The title is explained by the following (and many more) dialogues:

Yossarian looked at him soberly and tried another approach. "Is Orr crazy?"
"He sure is," Doc Daneeka said.
"Can you ground him?"
"I sure can. But first he has to ask me to. That's part of the rule."
"Then why doesn't he ask you to?"
"Because he's crazy," Doc Daneeka said. "He has to be crazy to keep flying
combat missions after all the close calls he's had. Sure, I can ground Orr.
But first he has to ask me to."
"That's all he has to do to be grounded?"
"That's all. Let him ask me."
"And then you can ground him?" Yossarian asked.
"No. Then I can't ground him."
"You mean there's a catch?"
"Sure there's a catch," Doc Daneeka replied, "Catch-22. Anyone who wants
to get out of combat duty isn't really crazy" (46–47).

For readers who have found the above insufficiently explicit, several paragraphs succeed, exploring the subtleties of the term "in all its spinning
reasonableness." The philosophical message of the book is that sane people
are crazy and crazy people sane. The incantatory power of the word
"crazy" is relentlessly exploited, in harmony with those stirring slogans of
our day, Crazy, man, crazy! Mad, Mad, Mad!

The term is finally extended to include all the sly ruses of organized
society, designed to frustrate natural and sensible men like Yossarian, who
asks only to be left alone so that he may feed like the python and try to
match the sexual prowess of the Japanese beetle: "Yossarian gorged himself in the mess hall until he thought he would explode and then sagged
back in a contented stupor, his mouth filmy with a succulent residue" (22).
I omit illustration of how he "bangs" women in rapid succession, but lest

I seem to be acting in restraint of trade, let me certify that *Catch-22* contains as many four-letter words as any rival product and that women are in it only as objects of lust, whether Wacs, nurses, officers' wives, or Italian prostitutes and countesses.

The book tells no story. It alternates serially, by means of the "advanced" technique of fragmented structure, five standard routines: I, Hospital routine, with malingering soldiers and incompetent staff; II, Combat routine, with everything snafu, yet missions accomplished with negligent gallantry; III, Funny fraud routine, involving army supplies and G.I. tycoon; IV, Red tape routine, at training center and headquarters; V, Leave in Rome routine, with orgies. The last is the only one of a type unavailable to television viewers, the elder of whom must console themselves with fond memories of the penny-in-the-slot movie, *Ladies' Night in a Turkish Bath*, where everyone ran around naked.

There are no characters. The puppets are given funny names and features, but cannot be visualized or distinguished from one another except by association with their prototypes. Sergeant Bilko, Colonel Blimp (and Captain Whizbang) [158] are immanent and circumambient, their spirit, like Yossarian in his plane, moving over the face of the waters. The character-names range from the subtly whimsical (General Dreedle) to the mercilessly side-splitting (Milo Minderbinder and Dori Duz, who, as Mr. Heller and his publisher carefully explain, "did"). Alliteration is rife: General P. P. Peckem, Colonel Cathcart, Colonel Cargill, Colonel Korn, Major Metcalf. One character surnamed "Major" has received from his cruel father the given name "Major" and since he is now a Major in the army, he is Major Major Major. He must have picked up a middle name when my attention lagged since one of Mr. Heller's chapters is titled "Major Major Major Major" at which point our laughter becomes uncontrollable. In this world, of course, Texans are bores, Iowans rubes, chaplains feeble, doctors hypochondriac, and officers increasingly contemptible as they rise in rank until we reach generals, who are effete. The copying of every available stereotype, and the failure to find in the whole range of humanity anything new to draw illustrates the author's indifference to people. We can see no one because he has seen no one.

The forms of verbal wit are limited to two. The first consists of self-contradictory statements which may or may not be meaningful. This might be called the Plain Man's Paradox or Everybody's Epigram since the fact that a sally of wit has been attempted is inescapable: ". . . the games were so interesting they were foolish" (9); "Nately had a bad start. He came from a good family" (13); ". . . the finest, least dedicated man in the whole world" (14); "And if that wasn't funny, there were lots of things that weren't even funnier" (17); "Failure often did not come easily" (28); "He was a self-made man who owed his lack of success to nobody"

(28); "He had decided to live forever or die in the attempt" (30); ". . . never sees anyone in his office while he's in his office" (110); ". . . she was irresistible, and men edged away from her carefully" (221); "This . . . old man reminded Nately of his father because the two were nothing at all alike" (250); "He did not hate his mother and father, even though they had both been very good to him" (255). This last, like several others of the hundreds in the book, comes near to being a hit, but Mr. Heller, as usual, kills it by the wrong kind of "milking." He proceeds to lambaste the mother and father for snobbishness. After gazing apathetically at the constant shower of sparks rising from Mr. Heller's "mordant intelligence" (Brustein), we are amazed to come upon this:

"My only fault," he observed with practical good humor, watching for the effect of his words, "is that I have no faults."
Colonel Scheisskopf didn't laugh, and General Peckem was stunned (328–29).

General Peckem and Author Heller are brothers under the skin after all (as are Colonel Scheisskopf and I). The striving for paradox often takes the form of extended statement ending in a "snapper." A review of intellectual attainments will end "In short, he was a dope" (70), or a list of virtuous traits with "I hate that son of a bitch" (19). There is much multiplying of negatives, as in the comment on [159] the farmer paid for not raising crops, which alone might well have been eight years in the making (85–86). It is designed for those who have never had this joke in a large enough portion.

Mr. Heller's other resource is echolalia. This is a device best illustrated in one of its traditional settings, the minstrel show:

Interlocutor: Bones, who was that lady I saw you out with last night?
Bones: Who was that lady you saw me out with last night?
Interlocutor: Yes, Bones. Who was that lady I saw you out with last night?
Bones: That was no lady. That was my wife.

Mr. Heller employs some form of echolalia on every page. Usually it is pointless:

"You're a chaplain," he exclaimed ecstatically. "I didn't know you were a chaplain."
"Why yes," the chaplain answered. "Didn't you know I was a chaplain?"
"Why, no: I didn't know you were a chaplain" (13).

Sometimes it italicizes a joke, on the remote chance that we have not heard it, like the one showing dignitaries so ignorant that they fail to recognize the name of a famous author:

"Well, what did he say?"
" 'T. S. Eliot,' " Colonel Cargill informed him.
"What's that?"
" 'T. S. Eliot,' " Colonel Cargill repeated.
"Just 'T. S.—' "
"Yes, sir. That's all he said. Just 'T. S. Eliot.' "
"I wonder what it means," General Peckem reflected. Colonel Cargill wondered too.
" 'T. S. Eliot,' " General Peckem mused.
" 'T. S. Eliot,' " Colonel Cargill echoed with the same funereal puzzlement (37).

(Could this be what Professor Cargill has in mind when he testifies, "Heller writes the freshest dialogue since the advent of Hemingway thirty years ago"?)

The device sometimes retreats coyly into simple redundance, as in the repeated "Texan from Texas," sometimes rises in triumph to what in balladry would be called "incremental repetition":

"All right, I'll dance with you," she said, before Yossarian could even speak. "But I won't let you sleep with me."
"Who asked you?" Yossarian asked her.
"You don't want to sleep with me?" she exclaimed with surprise.
"I don't want to dance with you."

Then, after a descriptive paragraph, comes:

"All right. I will let you buy me dinner. But I won't let you sleep with me."
"Who asked you?" Yossarian asked with surprise.
"You don't want to sleep with me?"
"I don't want to buy you dinner" (157).

What Mr. Heller prizes most he echoes most assiduously. An all-out effort to describe a "lush" nurse is provided twice on the same page in almost the same words (221–22). There are a number of "Yes, sir—No, sir" sequences, including one where a colonel with "a big fat mustache" is bullying subordinates:

"Don't interrupt."
"Yes, sir."
"And say 'sir' when you do," ordered Major Metcalf.
"Yes, sir."
"Weren't you told not to interrupt?" [160]

This goes on for five pages (77–82). At one point in *Catch-22* a character says of another, "He must be getting delirious. . . . He keeps saying the same thing over and over again" (190). To signalize so any special character in this "contrapuntal masterpiece" (A. J. Liebling) is unfair discrimination. One indubitable advantage of chronic echolalia is that it stretches the book to 443 crown octavo pages, price $5.95.

Nothing is easier than to blast a book, especially a sitting turkey, and, ordinarily, nothing more gratuitous. There will always be vulgar and noisy authors vulgarly and noisily praised, and ill-written, uncreative, and tedious books for which the proprietors can drum up a claque. What gives the present enterprise its special significance is the peculiar kind of pretentiousness involved, and the dislocation in literary and moral standards encouraging this kind of pretentiousness. The appalling fact is that author, publisher, and reviewers seem unaware that the book is destructive and immoral, and are able to add to their economic and other delights in it, gratifying sensations of righteousness. There is the real "catch" in *Catch-22*.

The identity of the book as non-art may be illustrated by a single detail. In the hospital where Yossarian malingers is a so-called "soldier in white" whose limbs are in traction and whose body is swathed in bandages except for holes where he breathes and where tubes enter for intravenous feeding and kidney drainage. Before he dies, this "soldier in white" becomes one of Mr. Heller's comic props. On page 10 we read:

When the jar on the floor was full, the jar feeding his elbow was empty, and the two were simply switched quickly so that the stuff could drip back into him.

In a word, he is being fed his own urine. On page 174 this brutal fancy is repeated, in the usual two sentences where one would do:

Changing the jars for the soldier in white was no trouble at all, since the same clear fluid was dripped back inside him over and over again with no apparent loss. When the jar feeding the inside of his elbow was just about empty, the jar on the floor was just about full, and the two were simply uncoupled from their respective hoses and reversed quickly so that the liquid could be dripped right back into him.

Catch-22, says Orville Prescott, "will not be forgotten by those who can take it." Why should we wish to take it?

The issue here is an artistic, not a moral, one. There is in art, current notions to the contrary, such a thing as decorum, propriety, fitness—a necessary correspondence between matter and mode. No kind of matter is denied the artist, providing he finds the right mode and possesses the right skills. Swift might have been able to adapt the matter of the "soldier in white" to the mode of satire as he adapted the idea of butchering Irish babies for the English meat market in his *Modest Proposal*. Swift's persona is consistent and *serious*, the powerful thrust of the piece deriving from his frightening obtuseness; the material, as it must be in such a risky case, is under perfect control, the intention unmistakable. Heller, *pace* Leo Lerman, is not "our Swift." His conception of satire, if he has one, is that it is any [161] mixture of the repellent and ridiculous, and so he keeps pelting us from his bag of merry japes. Suffering and death are not fit subjects for his mode and talents, and neither is juvenile pimping in Rome. It is not that we are horrified by his "soldier in white." We are a little disgusted and greatly bored. The jokes are there to prevent us from taking the figure seriously, and the figure is there to prevent us from taking the jokes as jokes even if they were good. The result is vacuum. Whatever else it may be, art may not be vacuous.

The adolescent gourmet who wants a mixture of everything at the soda fountain, assuming that if each of ten things is good the ten together will be ten times as good, grows up and consigns such mixtures to the garbage pail. Too many of our newsprint arbiters of taste have not grown up, or have found it expedient to reverse the process. They accept the assumptions which a Mr. Heller accepts and mix their adjectives as he mixes his ingredients: "brilliantly comic—brutally gruesome" (Prescott), "funniest —saddest" (Miller), "uproarious—horrifying" (Shaw). They are put in mind of hypothetical collaborations. Seymour Epstein proposes Dante, Kafka, and Abbott & Costello. I have not, as I trust Mr. Epstein has done, given my days and nights to the study of Dante, but I have read him. Between Dante and Heller I detect no resemblance. Robert Brustein assembles a cast of half a dozen serious and comic authors as the composite Heller, and adds *A Night at the Opera* which, as a matter of fact, is art of a higher order. This is a game all may easily play, and if given time they might have found Heller a fusion of Stephen Crane and P. G. Wodehouse, Shakespeare and Ezra Pound, Louisa May Alcott and James Joyce, St. Paul and Henry Miller. What they fail to see is that plus and minus numerals add up to zero, that the indiscriminate mixture of colors gives not the spectrum of the rainbow but the brown of mud. Their level of critical thinking finds perfect expression in Walt Kelly's ineffable words:

Heller "has quarterbacked a passion play through the left side of the line for all the marbles."

In addition to arbitrary mixture, formlessness and excess are being increasingly accepted as the badge of "true art." Because Heller's book reads as if the pages of the manuscript had been scrambled on the way to the printer, it is viewed as experimental and "modern"—like the work of the painter who squirts colors on the side of a barn with a firehose and thus triumphs in a new "technique." The idea has still failed to penetrate that formlessness is not a new kind of form, and that true modern art is not formless. The ideal of excess is explicitly stated by one of Heller's contemporaries writing of another. Updike in praising Salinger has said that the mark of the true artist is the "willingness to risk excess on behalf of [his] obsessions." Our timid demurrer that a few true artists have risked moderation on behalf of their insights is irrelevant in the present context. The interest of Updike's dictum is the evidence it provides that artistry is being defined in terms of *differentia* and that *genus* is being forgotten. Artistry, we had supposed, was mastery of materials, the ability of certain unusual people to arrange the right things in the right order, [162] words, or sounds, or colors and shapes; but if excess and obsession are its mark, we must revise our notions and accept the fact that membership in the society of artists is wide open. Although Updike and Salinger write far better than he, they will have to admit Heller. Perhaps it should be put the other way around. Salinger was one of those mentioned as incorporated in Heller. Updike did not make the grade.

Those who can mistake non-art for art can mistake immorality for morality. My word immorality applies, of course, to Mr. Heller's book, not his personal character or literary intentions. In assessing the response of the reviewers, I realize that I am dealing with excerpts, but I have made sure that these excerpts predicate; no amount of hedging in the unquoted portions of the critiques would alter the implications. The Associated Press excerpt contains the usual bullying sentence: "If you have no imagination you won't understand it." I have imagination and I understand it. I have observed that *Catch-22* contains trace elements of decency. Mr. Heller avoids scatological and homosexual humor, for which I thank him, and he dedicates his book to his mother, wife, and children. Although during its "heart-stopping moments" (West) my heart beat steadily on, I know where they are supposed to be—indeed, in my initial exposure to the book, was looking for them longingly, desperately. Yossarian sorrows over the death of rear-gunner Snowden in spite of the clever pun "Where are the Snowdens of yesteryear?" and the neat turn given the account of his wound:

Here was God's plenty, all right, he thought bitterly as he stared—liver, lungs, kidneys, ribs, stomach and bits of the stewed tomatoes Snowden had eaten that day for lunch. Yossarian hated stewed tomatoes and turned away dizzily and began to vomit (449).

Yossarian wishes to rescue "Nately's whore's kid sister" from the brothel, even though earlier she has been hilariously portrayed as completely adapted to the environment. The humble family visiting Yossarian in the hospital is kindly, even though they insist on mistaking him for someone else. Although Yossarian is quite the village atheist, Mr. Heller's pile-driver satire comes down less heavily on the chaplain than on other officials, divesting this man of God only of dignity. Mr. Heller's heart is no doubt in the right place; the trouble is with his head and the current notions which have addled it.

Catch-22 is immoral in the way of so much contemporary fiction and drama in being inclusively, almost absent-mindedly, anti-institutional. This quality has become so pervasive that it now evades recognition. The codes of conduct subtending such institutions as marriage and family life are treated casually as if nonexistent or vestigial. Acts of adultery are presented as if it would occur to no one to object, with the betrayed partner usually the unsympathetic party—a natural concomitant of the new literary form of betrothal, not an exchange of vows but getting into bed. Indulgence emerges as a new ideal, with so cleanly a thing as sexuality consistently dirtied by association with ideas of violence, prowess, and proof of normality, and divorce from ideas [163] of procreation or tenderness. By a new kind of stock response, profanity and obscenity are accepted as signature of the literature of the elect, reverberating more loudly in theatres than in bars. Every observant reader must be familiar with the mounting insistence with which he is made to stare at the same graffiti scrawled on different walls. In 1955 as distinct from 1961 the nation was not "ready" for Catch-22.

It now requires considerable temerity to write words like the above; they have become the only kind *unprintable* in literary media. The new conformity is there with its bludgeon, and hordes of hack reviewers ready to step forth valiantly to defend the autonomy of the artist. The question is, where is the autonomy and where are the artists? The lock-step is the lock-step, whether the march is forward or backward. Books are immoral if they condone immoral behavior inadvertently or otherwise. Because legal censorship of seriously intended works is wrong, as most intelligent men agree, it does not follow that moral considerations should be barred from critical discussion. If a book like Catch-22 is offensive, we should say so. Even now aspiring English majors at New York University must be ungirding their loins to "top" the performance of the distinguished alumnus. They are certainly doing so elsewhere. A considerable share of the responsibility lies with educators too tired to fight for their standards of art, taste, and morality, or too flaccid ever to have had any.

Catch-22 is immoral because it follows a fashion in spitting indiscriminately at business and the professions, at respectability, at ideals, at all visible tokens of superiority. It is a leveling book in the worst sense, leveling everything and everyone downward. It is chilling to observe the compulsive love of destruction that has gone into this presumed protest against the destructiveness of war. The only surviving values are self-preservation, satisfaction of animal appetite, and a sentimental conception of "goodness of heart." The "sane" view is live-and-let-live, as if it were as simple as that, and men had never died so that others might live. By stacking the cards so clumsily that they clatter, Mr. Heller is able to demonstrate that Yossarian does right by deserting: "That crazy bastard may be the only sane one left" (114)—except for the other deserter, Orr. Selden Rodman says in his piece, "The preposterous morality of this world passes in review." Observe the grand inclusiveness. Presumably no distinction exists between the morality of the Nazis, who murdered non-Nordic countrymen because they were non-Nordics, and the morality of the Danes, who rescued non-Nordic countrymen because they were human beings— all the morality "of this world" is equally "preposterous." The American effort which Mr. Heller "satirizes" was not a crusade, but some Americans who died in it, perhaps even a few colonels, fought as they did because they hated cruelty. It is easy enough to be "sane" in a simple world of self, where the value of all actions can be judged in terms of personal convenience. Sanity of Mr. Heller's brand was evidently on the increase in Korea, among those who sold out their [164] fellow prisoners for an extra handful of rice.

If it seems that this book is being taken too seriously—just a first book, and one that tries to be funny—have we not been told that it is "an intensely serious work" (Brustein)? When it was more recently advertised, the "sixth printing" was mentioned (with the usual reticence about the size of the printings), but the full-page ads and the promises of dirt and delight have not yet succeeded in jacking it into the best-seller lists in this country. The promoters claim to have done so in England, and this is not implausible. It has an ersatz American quality, like those imitations of hound-dog singing now making British music halls hideous. Europe has always imported our more dubious cultural products, and is in the market for surplus Beatism. Philip Toynbee has boarded the Catch-22 bandwagon—"the greatest satirical work in English since Erewhon." When the publishers run out of American boosters, there will always be an Englishman. The number of printings, six or six hundred, is quite immaterial—the book is what it is. Its author should know that there are some of us who see no distinction between a fraudulent military success like his Colonel Cathcart's and a fradulent literary success like his own.

My final admonitions will be constructive. If Mr. Heller wishes to be a humorist, let him relax. There is more humor, even more satire, in a strip of the cartoon "Peanuts" than in the whole of *Catch-22*. If he wishes to strike a blow against atomic extinction, let him read Elizabeth Thomas's *The Harmless People*. This simple descriptive report might teach him how to be an artist without going into convulsions, and what it is like to be human. Thomas's African bushmen I am willing to strive to save. Heller's Americans make me feel that atomic extinction is inevitable and not especially undesirable. Or if he wants an example of how appalling material can be used as a power for good, let him read Kamala Markandaya's *Nectar in a Sieve*. The author's purely literary endowment may be no greater than his own, although that is hard to conceive, but she has the capacity for selfless absorption in the lives of others, and her book erased in a single evening my prejudice against a people. Incidentally there is a prostitute in this novel whose story might encourage Mr. Heller to think a little about the background of his bouncing Italians. Finally, if he wishes a tip on how words may be artfully repeated, and on how a really good propagandist persuades men to pick up the pieces, let him read the following: "Whatsoever things are true, whatsoever things are honest, whatsoever things are just, whatsoever things are lovely, whatsoever things are of good report; if there be any virtue, and if there be any praise, think of these things." I recommend the words also to his reviewers. [165]

CHRONOLOGY	YOSSARIAN		McWATT	NATE...
	URBAN ASSYRIAN	e	e	... NATE ... CLEVIN ... ISLAN
CIVILIANS — E... is ED MAN	STATIONED IN COLORADO. →MEETS WINTERGREEN →DISCOVERS HOSPITAL - EPISODE OF "SOLDIER WHO SAW EVERYTHING TWICE"			
AVIATION CADET	STATIONED AT SANTA ANA CALIFORNIA. BOMBAR... MEETS CLEVINGER. SCHEISSKOPF WINS PARADES. SLEEPS WITH SCHEISSKOPF'S WIFE		-	CLEVIN FACE... A SAC... FOUND
SHIPPED OVERSEAS TO PIANOSA	FLIES AS A LEAD BOMBARDIER. LATER HE IS DEMOTED TO WING BOMBARDIER, THEN REINSTATED, THEN DEMOTED AGAIN		McWATT IS YOSSARIAN'S PILOT — DUNBAR A LEAD BOMBARDIER IN ANOTHER SQUADRON	NATE... CO-PI... CLEVIN... DUNBAR
CATHCART ARRIVES AS GROUP COMMANDER RAISES MISSIONS	YOSSARIAN HAS 23 MISSIONS WHEN CATHCART ARRIVES AND RAISES THE MISSIONS TO 30.			
FERRARA	GOES OVER THE TARGET TWICE. DESTROYS THE BRIDGE. IS REPRIMANDED BECAUSE KRAFT'S PLANE IS SHOT DOWN THE SECOND TIME AROUND. TO AVERT CRITICISM, YOSSARIAN IS GIVEN A MEDAL AND PROMOTED TO CAPTAIN		McWATT IS YOSSARIAN'S PILOT ON THIS MISSION	
MILO FORMS HIS CARTEL (APRIL)				
ROME CAPTURED (JUNE 4)	..YOSSARIAN ACCOMPANIES NATELY TO HIS GIRL FRIEND'S WHOREHOUSE		DUNBAR GOES TO THE WHOREHOUSE	1. NATE... 2. NATE... BEL... 3. THEY...
BOLOGNA	1. MISSION IS POSTPONED AND EVERYONE IS TERRIFIED 2. YOSSARIAN CAUSES ONE DELAY BY "POISONING" FOOD, ANOTHER BY MOVING THE BOMBLINE. ... 3. HAS A DRUNKEN ROW AT THE OFFICERS CLUB WITH COLONEL KORN. 4. SABOTAGES YOSSARIAN AND MAKES PILOT TURN BACK. MISSION IS A MILK RUN. 5. YOSSARIAN GOES BACK AS A LEAD BOMBARDIER THE NEXT DAY, TAKES NO EVASIVE ACTION, RUNS INTO FLAK. 6. AFTER THE MISSION HE GOES TO ROME ON A REST LEAVE... MEETS		McWATT IS YOSSARIAN'S PILOT ON THIS MISSION	CLEVIN... THAT HAS A... TO T... HIS... NATE... ROME HIS... AND ... OF M...
BETWEEN BOLOGNA AND AVIGNON	LUCIANA. 7. WHILE HE IS ... RAISES MISSIONS TO ... YOSSARIAN RUNS INTO THE HOSPITAL ... 9. LEAVES HOSPITAL ... MISSIONS, + GOES BACK ... ARE RAISED TO 45. HE NOW HAS ...		DUNBAR HANGS AROUND	A... TEL... TO Y... MECH... BRIEF...
AVIGNON	1. YOSSARIAN M... BRIEFING ROOM. NATELY TRIES TO PROTECT HIM. 2. SNOWDEN ... THROUGH THE MIDDLE AND DIES. ... TREATS HIM FOR THE WRONG WOUND			
SNOWDEN'S FUNERAL	1. YOSSARIAN ... FROM THE PLANE NAKED. 2. GOES ... CEMETERY AND SITS IN A TREE 3. STANDS IN FORMATION NAKED TO RECEIVE THE MEDAL HE WON FOR FERRARA		... HELPS ... OUT OF YOSSARIAN WHEN HE EMERGES FROM THE PLANE	
CLEVINGER DISAPPEARS IN A CLOUD	SHORTLY BEFORE CLEVINGER IS LOST, YOSSARIAN ARGUES WITH HIM AT THE OFFICERS CLUB ABOUT WHICH ONE IS CRAZY		DUNBAR ARGUES WITH CLEVINGER THAT LIFE IS ...	CLEVIN... ARGU... YOSS... CRA... HE IS...
YOSSARIAN ENTERS HOSPITAL	YOSSARIAN ENTERS THE HOSPITAL IN DESPAIR OVER CLEVINGER'S DEATH. FAKES A LIVER AILMENT, CENSORS LETTERS WITH WASHINGTON IRVING'S NAME.		DUNBAR IS IN HOSPITAL AS A FRIEND AND FELLOW MALINGERER	CLEVIN... IN A ... IS W...
YOSSARIAN LEAVES HOSPITAL	HE NOW HAS 44 MISSIONS			NATE... IN...
YOSSARIAN TRIES TO BE	1. GOES TO DANEEKA FOR HELP AND IS TURNED DOWN 2. FLIES THREE MORE MISSIONS AND HAS 47. 3. GOES TO CHAPLAIN FOR HELP			

ON FORM

John Wain

A New Novel about Old Troubles

It now seems a certainty that *Catch-22* will pass into literature, i.e., break through the invisible but tough wall that separates the volcanic flow of 'recent books'—mere merchandise to be weighed, transported, labelled and commented on by blear-eyed hacks—from the tiny residue of permanent work that each age deposits. Its reception was ecstatic, and the usual limbs were gone out on; the dust-jacket gives a few samples, for instance that one reviewer called it 'the greatest satirical work in English since *Erewhon*'. I don't think I could go this far, because surely *Animal Farm* is better satire than *Catch-22*: just as poignant, just as far-reaching and inclusive, but much more elegant and economical. Elegance and economy are odd virtues to bring up in connection with *Catch-22*, which rather magnificently spurns both; still, they are virtues nevertheless.

On the other hand, I do agree with Nelson Algren's claim that '*The Naked and the Dead* and *From Here to Eternity* are lost within it'. As a

SOURCE: *The Critical Quarterly*, Vol. 5 (Summer 1963), pp. 168–173. Reprinted by permission of the author.

book about war, written from the viewpoint of the fighting man, it is entirely credible, very moving, and—I expect to find—unforgettable. Most of it is pitched in the key of bitterly exuberant farce, a farce through which fear and *ennui* are always perceptible. But now and again the custard-pies are quietly laid aside, and we are given a deadly serious passage which proves that Mr. Heller, if he had wanted to, could have written a Jones or a Mailer into the ground. (If you happen to have the book by you, and are interested enough to want an example long enough to prove the point and therefore too long to quote in a review, I am thinking of such things as the description of Snowden's death on pp. 446–50.) *

Of course Snowden's death has been mentioned a number of times, and even partly narrated; it is typical of the book's narrative method that we should have to wait till page 446, a bare twenty pages or so from the end, before getting the full details. Broadly speaking, this method is half-way between straight narrative and what the [168] Elizabethans would have called an 'anatomy'. Instead of taking us in a straight line from one point in time to another, the story zigzags considerably, ending up only a very little further on from where it began. A tremendous amount of incident, a huge gallery of portraits, and an ambitiously wide range of emotions and effects lie in between. No wonder this book took eight years to write, and was gestated for eight before that! Thus we are told, for instance, that the hero, Yossarian, one day appeared on parade stark naked. Various comic pseudo-explanations of this are given, but the real reason—that his uniform had been drenched with Snowden's blood and guts on that terrible occasion, that he had peeled it off hysterically, and continued for some time in a state of shock, refusing to wear a uniform again—is held back until we are ready for it. And so on, throughout scores of intertwined episodes. And be it noted that the construction is circular or spiral, like that of *Finnegans Wake*: it opens with Yossarian in hospital, having a conversation with the chaplain, and ends with Yossarian again in hospital and talking to the same chaplain.

This method of scrambling the narrative has one disadvantage at the beginning; it reminds the reader too forcibly of the dozens of other scrambled narratives through which he has had to pick his dazed, irritated way. To a certain kind of modern novelist, regular progression and a clearly-indicated time-sequence add up to an admission of weakness. The reader must be kept guessing, and if the writer's vision of life, his understanding of his characters, are not profound enough to make the reader work hard, then he must be tied up in the plot: information must be kept back, the story must stop, start, and go backwards, till the reader becomes so en-

---

* Page references are to the Dell edition (1962).

grossed in the struggle to make out what is happening that he submissively concedes the book's right to be called difficult, *avant-garde* and 'advanced'. For a few pages, *Catch-22* recalls this familiar annoyance. But only for a few pages. After that, it becomes clear that the method is completely justified. To these bomber-pilots, life does not flow in a regular, unfolding ribbon, experience following on from experience, as it does in even the most tumultuous life in peace-time. It teeters round and round in a continual stalemate. Each time they wait to fly on another mission, everything has to stand still until they know whether or not they are going to survive. The experiences they have in the meantime, all the escapist drinking, whoring and quarrelling, may be intense, but they are static and self-contained. They issue from nowhere and lead nowhere, being enclosed in a stiff cast of anxiety. And this gives us the strong impression that the lives of fighting men are utterly and helplessly different, cut off and set apart from normal lives. Which is, of course, what *erat demonstrandum*.

In the last few pages, the story suddenly shakes itself, gets up and moves. Hungry Joe, who had seemed dementedly immortal, dies. Orr has reached Sweden by paddling on a raft. And all of a sudden [169] Yossarian realizes the carefully planned method behind Orr's madness. Up to that time, Orr had seemed to Yossarian, and therefore to the reader, as no more than a helpless grotesque:

Orr was an eccentric midget, a freakish, likable dwarf with a smutty mind and a thousand valuable skills that would keep him in a low income group all his life. He could use a soldering iron and hammer two boards together so that the wood did not split and the nails did not bend. He could drill holes. He had built a good deal more in the tent while Yossarian was away in the hospital. He had filed or chiseled a perfect channel in the cement so that the slender gasoline line was flush with the floor as it ran to the stove from the tank he had built outside on an elevated platform. He had constructed andirons for the fireplace out of excess bomb parts and had filled them with stout silver logs, and he had framed with stained wood the photographs of girls with big breasts he had torn out of cheesecake magazines and hung over the mantelpiece. Orr could open a can of paint. He could mix paint, thin paint, remove paint. He could chop wood and measure things with a ruler. He knew how to build fires. He could dig holes, and he had a real gift for bringing water for them both in cans and canteens from the tanks near the mess hall. He could engross himself in an inconsequential task for hours without growing restless or bored, as oblivious to fatigue as the stump of a tree, and almost as taciturn. He had an uncanny knowledge of wildlife and was not afraid of dogs or cats or beetles or moths, or of foods like scrod or tripe (321–22).

Just before this description, Orr has made Yossarian an offer: " 'You ought to try flying a few missions with me when you're not flying lead. Just for laughs. Tee-hee.' Orr gazed up at Yossarian through the corners of his eyes with pointed mirth."

Yossarian simply does not bother to consider the idea, Orr being notoriously accident-prone, and it is only in the closing pages that he, and we, realize that Orr has been devotedly practising crash-landing, pancaking on to the water, etc., so as to put himself in a position to get to neutral territory and be interned in comfort. The moment he does realize this, Yossarian experiences a great wave of positiveness, decides that his apparently insuperable problems can be solved if only he is man enough to run away from them, and deserts. Whereupon the story ends.

A war-novel which ends with the desertion of the hero is obviously not heroic, and Catch-22 is in fact a pretty thorough debunking job. Every senior officer who appears in the story is either a maniacal sadist or a blundering oaf, and those characters who show any great zeal for their duties are plainly ticketed as floperoos, duped into playing the game of General Dreedle, General Peckem, Lieutenant Scheisskopf and the rest of the Dickensian crew. We get a pretty fair idea of the book's objectives from the conversation—obviously a set-piece, written in as exposition and not thrown up by the organic life of the story—between Nately and the old man in the whorehouse (p. 250 ff.), of which this is a specimen: [170]

"Well, frankly, I don't know how long America is going to last," he proceeded dauntlessly. "I suppose we can't last forever if the world itself is going to be destroyed someday. But I do know that we're going to survive and triumph for a long, long time."

"For how long?" mocked the profane old man with a gleam of malicious elation. "Not even as long as the frog?"

"Much longer than you or me," Nately blurted out lamely.

"Oh, is that all! That won't be very much longer then, considering that you're so gullible and brave and that I am already such an old, old man."

"How old are you?" Nately asked, growing intrigued and charmed with the old man in spite of himself.

"A hundred and seven." The old man chuckled heartily at Nately's look of chagrin. "I see you don't believe that either."

"I don't believe anything you tell me," Nately replied, with a bashful mitigating smile. "The only thing I do believe is that America is going to win the war."

"You put so much stock in winning wars," the grubby iniquitous old man scoffed. "The real trick lies in losing wars, in knowing which wars can be *lost*. Italy has been losing wars for centuries, and just see how

splendidly we've done nonetheless. France wins wars and is in a continual
state of crisis. Germany loses and prospers. Look at our own recent history.
Italy won a war in Ethiopia and promptly stumbled into serious trouble.
Victory gave us such insane delusions of grandeur that we helped
start a world war we hadn't a chance of winning. But now that we
are losing again, everything has taken a turn for the better, and we will
certainly come out on top again if we succeed in being defeated."

Nately gaped at him in undisguised befuddlement. "Now I really don't
understand what you're saying. You talk like a madman."

"But I live like a sane one. I was a fascist when Mussolini was on top, and
I am an anti-fascist now that he has been deposed. I was fanatically
pro-German when the Germans were here to protect us against the Americans
and now that the Americans are here to protect us against the Germans
I am fanatically pro-American. I can assure you, my outraged young
friend"—the old man's knowing, disdainful eyes shone even more effervescently
as Nately's stuttering dismay increased—"that you and your country
will have a no more loyal partisan in Italy than me—but only as long as
you remain in Italy."

"But," Nately cried out in disbelief, "you're a turncoat! A time-server! A
shameful, unscrupulous opportunist!"

"I am a hundred and seven years old," the old man reminded him suavely.

When Nately points out that Italy, having been occupied by the Germans and currently occupied by the Americans, can't be said to be doing very well in the war, the old man replies, 'Italian soldiers are not dying any more. But American and German soldiers are. I call that doing extremely well'.

And so we come round again to the eternal discussion about values and about honour. 'Who hath it? He that died a Wednesday.' Is the war a just one? Is it worth giving your life for? Personally I [171] have every sympathy with anyone who takes the same line as the old man, that survival is the great test of fitness to survive. On the other hand, I admire and even revere men brave enough to give their lives for a cause they believe in. An out-and-out pacifist book, debunking 'war' on the grounds that 'war' kills people, never seems to me to give the whole picture, though it arouses deep and sympathetic echoes in me. Perhaps these questions are too hard for one person to solve. Certainly Mr. Heller side-steps them. He sets his story at a time when the war is nearing its close, when the Germans, and the Japanese, cannot hold out much longer. At such a time, to fight bravely is merely to serve the interests of the military higher-ups. And since the novel portrays those higher-ups as subhuman nuisances, unfit to clutter the earth's surface, the answer is evident. Yossarian is right to desert, Orr is right to ditch his plane and paddle to Sweden. Still, the nagging questions remain, and Mr. Heller tries rather clumsily to push them back where they can't do any serious harm to his story. In the closing scene, Yossarian has a conversation with Major Danby, one of the very few sympathetic senior officers, in which he justifies himself.

With deliberate amiability he said, "Danby, how can you work along with people like Cathcart and Korn? Doesn't it turn your stomach?"

Major Danby seemed surprised by Yossarian's question.

"I do it to help my country," he replied, as though the answer should have been obvious. "Colonel Cathcart and Colonel Korn are my superiors, and obeying their orders is the only contribution I can make to the war effort. I work along with them because it's my duty. And also," he added in a much lower voice, dropping his eyes "because I am not a very aggressive person."

"Your country doesn't need your help any more," Yossarian reasoned without antagonism. "So all you're doing is helping them."

"I try not to think of that," Major Danby admitted frankly. "But I try to concentrate on only the big result and to forget that they are succeeding, too. I try to pretend that they are not significant."

"That's my trouble, you know," Yossarian mused sympathetically, folding his arms. "Between me and every ideal I always find Scheisskopfs, Peckems, Korns and Cathcarts. And that sort of changes the ideal."

"You must try not to think of them," Major Danby advised affirmatively. "And you must never let them change your values. Ideals are good, but people are sometimes not so good. You must try to look up at the big picture."

Yossarian rejected the advice with a skeptical shake of his head. "When I look up, I see people cashing in. I don't see heaven or saints or angels. I see people cashing in on every decent impulse and every human tragedy."

"But you must try not to think of that," Major Danby insisted. "And you must try not to let it upset you."

"Oh, it doesn't really upset me. What does upset me, though, is that they think I'm a sucker. They think that they're smart, and that the rest [172] of us are dumb. And, you know, Danby, the thought occurs to me right now, for the first time, that maybe they're right."

"But you must try not to think of that too," argued Major Danby. "You must think only of the welfare of your country and the dignity of man."

"Yeah," said Yossarian.

"I mean it, Yossarian. This is not World War One. You must never forget that we're at war with aggressors who would not let either one of us live if they won."

"I know that," Yossarian replied tersely, with a sudden surge of scowling annoyance. "Christ, Danby, I earned that medal I got, no matter what

their reasons were for giving it to me. I've flown seventy goddam
combat missions. Don't talk to me about fighting to save my country. I've
been fighting all along to save my country. Now I'm going to fight a
little to save myself. The country's not in danger any more, but I am."
"The war's not over yet. The Germans are driving towards Antwerp."
"The Germans will be beaten in a few months. And Japan will be beaten a
few months after that. If I were to give up my life now, it wouldn't
be for my country. It would be for Carthcart and Korn. So I'm turning my
bombsight in for the duration. From now on I'm thinking only of me"
(454–55).

I quote the whole of this conversation because it makes clear not only
the central evasiveness of the book, its one serious flaw, but also Yossarian's
rôle as hero. Yossarian is the hero of every modern novel; he is the man
who looks up towards an ideal and sees, thrusting in between him and it,
the phonies, liars and exploiters. 'What does upset me is that they think
I'm a sucker.' And so he is. That's why Yossarian is the hero. Because he's
the fall guy. It runs right through the centre of modern literature, like a
vein in quartz: this conviction that the life we live, in the society we have
made, is a deep swindle, that you can't win if you are handicapped with
decency and humanity: so you concentrate on losing: gracefully, humorously, resistantly, but always losing. That, at any rate, is what the bulk of
Western literature says; and there is plenty of indirect evidence that Eastern literature, if it were free to say anything at all, would say the same
thing. Does this reflect the true state of man in our time? Or is it just the
writer, enmeshed in the world of the technocrat, who sees himself, and
everything he loves, as bound to go down? [173]

W. Scammell
Letter in Reply
to Mr. Wain

Dear Sirs

One of the illustrious names invoked in the blurb of *Catch-22*, and not
mentioned by Mr. Wain, is that of Lewis Carroll; surely *Alice in Wonder-*

SOURCE: *The Critical Quarterly*, Vol. 5 (Autumn 1963), pp. 273–274. Reprinted with
permission of the publisher.

land is a more apt and revealing comparison than *The Naked and the Dead* or *From Here to Eternity*. Mailer and Jones were attempting 'realistic' novels, whereas the distinguishing feature of *Catch-22* is its rich vein of *fantasy*—a fantasy which is, strictly speaking, paradoxical and nonsensical but which is nonetheless (like *Alice*) very much grounded in the real world.

Had Mr. Heller been able to sustain the fantastic world he creates in the first half or two-thirds of the book, and utilised it to make known his darker purpose—if he had been able, in other words, to get across his 'message' through the medium of fantasy—I would be inclined to agree with Mr. Wain that he had written a novel of lasting worth. But in fact Heller fails to do this, and has to resort to crude and vapid moralising, which simply doesn't fit in with what has gone before. Also his 'message' does not appear to be very well thought-out, which leads, as Mr. Wain remarks, to evasion and side-stepping.

The basic fault of *Catch-22* seems to me that it switches back and forth between the 'fantastic' and the 'naturalistic' mode, and so destroys both the tone and the unity of the narrative. Obviously we cannot believe literally in the slapstick world of the first half of the book, where men insult and beat up their superior officers, and every incident takes on the wildly improbable character of a Marx Brothers film. Yet at other times we are required to do just this—as when, for instance, we are finally given the details of Snowden's death.

So long as Mr. Heller continues (in the idiom of the book) to play it strictly for laughs, everything is hunky-dory; in this manner he achieves great things, as in the story of Milo Minderbinder and M & M Enterprises, which is both wildly funny and a superb send-up of the private enterprise ethic. But when he deserts his post and exchanges the Fool's cap for the Preacher's robes, as [273] he does intermittently throughout the second half of the book, he loses both himself and his readers. Worse, he forfeits the Fool's unique privilege of talking meaningful nonsense.

Hampstead, N.W.3   *Yours faithfully,*
                                              W. Scammell [274]

Constance Denni~~......~~

'Catch-22':

A Romance-Parody

When Joseph Heller's *Catch-22* was first published, it received much adverse criticism. Spencer Klaw of the *New York Herald Tribune* thought that the characters of Heller's book were not drawn with enough individuality (xxxviii, October 15, 1961). Granville Hicks said that there were just too many characters to deal with any one in depth and concluded that, in general, the book was too complicated to be comprehended (*Saturday Review*, xliv, October 14, 1961). The book reviewer of *Time* felt that, because of its episodic structure, *Catch-22* was a formless piece of fiction (lxxviii, October 27, 1961). A number of critics thought that Heller's chief weakness was his inability to write humor. They assumed that he intended to write a comedy but failed because he repeated and elaborated on his jokes to the extent that they became more gross than amusing.

Many of the objections to *Catch-22* stem from the fact that critics take this work to be a traditional novel where we expect to find fully developed characters that seem to be reflections of ordinary people in a specific time and place in history. Even though *Catch-22* is set in a specific time and place, its plot structure and characterization have more in common with another genre, the romance. The figures of the romance are flat, idealized types, and its plot is episodic in nature; its heroes undergo numerous trials that often seem repetitious. The traits of the romance evident in *Catch-22* are naturally objectionable to critics who take it to be a traditional novel.

But if this work is treated as a traditional romance, other critical problems arise. The war romance in particular celebrates the ideals of patriotism and courage. The medieval Gawain does not run away from the challenge of battle as Yossarian does. Then Gawain returns home, the hero of his society, because he has restored the values of courage and trustworthiness, but Yossarian escapes to another country. He is not the hero we find in the romance.

It may seem then that *Catch-22* is not in the mainstream of literature

SOURCE: Portions of this article appeared earlier in "The American Romance-Parody: A Study of Purdy's *Malcolm* and Heller's *Catch-22*," *Emporia State Research Studies*, Vol. 14, No. 2 (1965), pp. 42–64. Reprinted by permission of the author and publisher. The present essay was revised especially for this book.

since it fits neither category, the romance nor the novel. Or is this assumption the either/or fallacy?

There is yet another possibility, another genre of long fiction, the romance-parody, described by Northrop Frye in his *Anatomy of Criticism*. According to Frye, the romance-parody is a mixture of genres. It makes use of the structure of the romance but subjects its mythic properties to the world of everyday experience, the world of the novel. When these opposing forces, the mythic and the mundane, meet, their differences result in alarming contradictions and ironies. The ideals of the romance, such as justice, loyalty, and honor become a mockery. Melville's *Confidence-Man*, whose hero uses religious ideals, faith, hope, and charity, to trick his victims or Twain's *Pudd'nhead Wilson*, whose hero makes a mockery of justice in his futile attempt to bring about social order, are just two examples of the romance-parody.

Frye classifies the romance-parody in six phases. The first phase makes use of light satire, comic in nature, to describe a world where values are just beginning to deteriorate. The last phase, the one that applies to *Catch-22*, describes a world where values are deteriorated to the extent that the villains dominate. This is the case when Melville's villainous confidence-man dupes his victims into hell or when Pudd'nhead Wilson by his victory in court destroys the life of the virtuous Tom Driscoll. It is in this phase, Frye notes, that satire recedes to irony; the comic is tinged with tragedy. The mixture of the comic and tragic was used intentionally in *Catch-22*. Heller says:

> I tried consciously for a comic effect juxtaposed with the tragic, working the frivolous in with the catastrophic. I wanted people to laugh and then look back with horror at what they were laughing at.

A study of the mixture of the opposing elements of Heller's work will show that *Catch-22* is typical of the romance-parody.

Catch-22 has more than three dozen characters, and all but the hero are of nearly equal importance. The huge cast of characters presents a cross section of life, and the great variety of characters can only be supported by the romance form which deals with flat characterizations.

The character types of this work are parodies of those found in the American romances. In the upside-down world of *Catch-22*, the characters fall into two categories, the aggressors and the victims. The aggressors are Yankee types who express their American know-how and individuality in a will to power. These naive and arrogant Yankees succeed in bullying those they cannot deceive. Heller's description of the farmer is an example of his satire of the Yankee character:

Major Major's father was a sober, God-fearing man whose idea of a good joke was to lie about his age. He was a long-limbed farmer, a God-fearing, freedom-loving, law-abiding rugged individualist who held that federal aid to anyone but farmers was creeping socialism. He advocated thrift and hard work and disapproved of loose women who turned him down. His specialty was alfalfa, and he made a good thing of not growing any. The government paid him well for every bushel of alfalfa he did not grow. The more alfalfa he did not grow, the more money the government gave him, and he spent every penny he didn't earn on new land to increase the amount of alfalfa he did not produce.

The officers who run the machinery of the war are examples of selfishness and maliciousness. They desire to advance themselves at the expense of the lives of men they command. Heller says of one officer: "Colonel Cathcart had courage and never hesitated to volunteer his men for any target available." Another officer who is foolish enough to beat Major ——— de Coverley at a game of horseshoes is stricken with a severe disease as a result. Milo Minderbinder is the officer in charge of buying for the mess hall, and he uses his office to make quick profits. He believes that war should be run as a business and says, "What's good for the syndicate is good for the country." As boss of the syndicate, Milo is responsible for directing a bombing raid against his own squadron in order to make a profit. General Peckem is described as a man who believes only in himself. He says, "My only fault . . . is that I have no faults." American officers are as dangerous to the American enlisted men as are the Germans. The Germans can be defeated, but the American commanders are too powerful to be undermined, and their evil power will not subside when the war with the Germans comes to an end.

Yossarian and his friends are victims. They are sensitive to the brutalities in the world; they are cheated and maligned and are helpless to do anything about it. They are not aggressive and are, therefore, misfits in a world where only power has value. Doc Daneeka, Hungry Joe, Chief Halfoat, and Orr are a few examples of the long list of misfits who are among Yossarian's friends. Doc Daneeka is "a neat, clean man whose idea of a good time was to sulk." Hungry Joe has "a desolate, cratered face, sooty with care like an abandoned mining town." Chief Halfoat is "a glowering, disillusioned, vengeful Indian." Orr is "an eccentric midget, a freakish, likeable dwarf . . . with a thousand valuable skills that would keep him in a low-income group all his life." The victims are aware of the fact that they are in immediate danger of a violent and meaningless death.

Catch-22 has a double plot, one concerning the aggressors in their struggle to gain power, the other concerning the hero, Yossarian, in his struggle to live. In the plot concerning the aggressors, one American general declares war on another. General Peckem is head of Special Services, and while at that post, he gives Special Services authority over all other branches of the service. Later, General Peckem leaves Special Services and declares war on General Dreedle and obtains the top post as wing commander. Lieutenant Scheisskopf is left to command Special Services when General Peckem transfers out of that branch, but Peckem forgets to void his memorandum giving Special Services the highest command. Peckem defeats Dreedle, only to find that he is under Scheisskopf, who has been promoted to Lieutenant General. Scheisskopf is described as a man who wants war because he loves to wear a uniform and direct parades. When he becomes the top commander, he orders the wing to line up for a parade. The plot concerning the aggressors ends in complete absurdity.

The plot concerning the victims centers around the quest of the hero, Yossarian. Here, the structure of the plot is typical of the romance as defined by Northrop Frye. Frye says that the first stage of the quest presents the hero in a series of minor trials; the second stage, the climax, is the hero's major trial; and the last stage is the hero's elevation to a place of importance in his society. In the parody, however, the third stage is a mock elevation. Yossarian becomes a mock hero when he is awarded a medal and a promotion for being absent without leave.

Yossarian's quest, unlike the romantic quest, is more human than heroic. He wants to stay alive. The first thirty-eight chapters of *Catch-22* present the first stage of Yossarian's quest, a series of episodes in which Yossarian avoids death through every creative measure he can muster. The second stage of the hero's quest, the major conflict, takes place in Chapter 39, "The Eternal City." Yossarian goes absent without leave to Rome to try to save Nately's whore's young sister. He soon realizes that to find the girl is a hopeless task. He is surrounded by devastation and is a helpless bystander in an inferno of hate and destruction. The hero sees a sick world:

> The night was filled with horrors, and he thought he knew
> how Christ must have felt as he walked through the world, like a
> psychiatrist through a ward full of nuts, like a victim through a prison full
> of thieves.

In this climactic chapter, Yossarian learns that there is no justice in the world. He sees a man beating a small boy to death while a sinister crowd looks on, and police beating a man while the man himself, as a matter of form, desperately calls to the police for help. Then Yossarian, who is absent without leave, is arrested by M.P.s, but the M.P.s are polite to Aarfy who has just murdered the maid. At this point, Yossarian recognizes that the good are victims in the hands of malicious forces, overpowering in numbers. In his major trial, in his attempt to save the innocent from being victimized, the hero fails.

The third stage of the romance-parody begins with Chapter 40. This stage presents the mock celebration of the protagonist as hero. Yossarian is brought before Colonel Cathcart and Colonel Korn because he has been absent without leave. Instead of punishing him, the colonels invent a story to make Yossarian a hero. But ironically, he refuses to play the role. Unlike Pudd'nhead Wilson or Melville's confidence-man, he is too noble for heroics. In this respect, he is similar to Don Quixote. Inner freedom is more important to Yossarian. He decides to flee to Sweden where he can govern himself even though he realizes that the journey is long and the risk great.

The circular plot begins with Yossarian's pretending to be sick to escape death at the hands of tyrants, and ends with his flight to Sweden so that he may be free of tyranny. He is like a man forever standing in a sea on melting chunks of ice, forced to jump to a larger piece of ice as it melts.

Yossarian's predicament is typical of the ironic hero in bondage described by Northrop Frye. In this state, the victims are too weak to overthrow the tyrants, and, in the case of Yossarian, his decision to run away does not make his life any more secure. He is typical of the unheroic hero of ironic fiction. The hero seeks a goal that is unattainable: Sweden, a symbolic Eden, cannot be found in a world of meaningless cruelty and violence. Yossarian will never be free from those who seek to destroy him, and death itself will be his only release from the fears he suffers.

The title of Heller's book, *Catch-22*, is taken from an army regulation that is symbolic of inescapable bondage. This regulation is a Fascistic rule which does not let men do what they want to do, but which forces them to do what they do not want to do. Catch-22 states that if a man wants to fly missions, he is crazy and must be grounded, but if he does not want to fly missions and asks to be grounded, he is sane and must continue to fly missions. The Catch-22 regulation also states that no one has a right to examine it or question its validity. Near the end of the book, the military police push the whores out into the street and confiscate their home. The police obtain the authority for this action from the Catch-22 regulation. The old woman who is left to tell Yossarian of the fate of the women says, "Catch-22 says they [the military] have a right to do anything we can't stop them from doing." Yossarian tells her that she should have asked to see the regulation, but she says, "They don't have to show us Catch-22. . . . The law says they don't have to."

In the last chapter of the book, the hero takes an existentialist attitude toward life. Once he assumes full responsibility for himself and disowns military life, his struggle to stay alive becomes a joyful pursuit. This decision is an important change in the attitude of the hero, because, up to this point, he had considered himself a part of a huge military force, and the fact that he had to be nimble to stay alive was nauseous to him. At the end of the novel, the hero celebrates life and decides to fight for it outside the framework of military ranks. When Major Danby warns Yossarian that it is impossible to get to Sweden, Yossarian replies, "Hell, Danby, I know that. But at least I'll be trying." The major also tells Yossarian that his journey will not be a happy one, but the hero replies with exuberance, "Yes it will." Thus, the book ends upon an ironic note: the hero filled with conviction begins a journey that is perhaps futile, but he has reached the existentialist point on the other side of despair, a point of self-fulfillment. He is fulfilling his own convictions, not those of military tyrants, and, for the first time, the hero has true courage.

Even though Yossarian finds inner harmony, unlike the hero of the romance, he can bring no order to his society. It seems past redemption. The values usually celebrated in the war romance no longer exist. Death and patriotism in war are unheroic.

Patriotism in Catch-22 is an absurdity. The high-ranking officials of the American army, fighting for self-interests, are at war with each other. In their struggle for power, the squadron commanders victimize those whom they command by demanding extra missions or by killing those who stand in the way of their progress. Patriotism can only exist when a country has a degree of unity. In Catch-22, the idea that war should be a unified effort, that Americans should fight for other Americans, does not seem to occur to the commanders.

Even the subject of death that traditionally belongs to the tragic modes of literature, especially in the case of the war romance, is parodied in Catch-22. In all cases, death is presented as being absurd and unheroic. In the opening chapter of the book, a soldier, covered in a white plaster cast, is in the hospital ward with Yossarian. The soldier's arms and legs are useless, and his senses are gone. He is fed through the arm from one jar, and the wastes from his kidneys are drained into a jar on the floor. When the jar attached to his arm is emptied, it is switched with the one on the floor in a continuing process. The attempt to save life, when carried to this extreme, is shown to be absurd because, for all practical purposes, the man in the cast is dead.

Heller's parody is most brutal in the episode of Kid Sampson's death. Kid Sampson is spending a pleasant day at the beach with other bathers, when McWatt, who is a practical joker, playfully flies low over the bathers and accidentally hits Kid Sampson. The plane's propeller cuts off Kid Sampson's body at the top of his legs. The description of this macabre incident is told through a grotesque technique of slapstick comedy. Kid Sampson's legs stand alone for a minute, then fall back into the water and turn upside down, revealing the white underside of his feet, while the rest of his body, cut into the size of raindrops, falls in a shower over the rest of the bathers. The incongruity of the comic technique with the tragic subject emphasizes the irony of death. Heller, then, follows up the accidental death with a suicide and a fake death. McWatt, realizing that his playfulness has resulted in death, crashes his plane into a mountain, committing suicide. Sergeant Knight refers to his list of men that are supposed to be on McWatt's plane and, finding Doc Daneeka's name there, subsequently reports him dead. Doc Daneeka, however, is standing beside the sergeant and keeps protesting that he is alive. The army pays no attention to Doc Daneeka's plight because, as far as they are concerned, he is a name that is crossed off their list. The army sends a form letter to Mrs. Daneeka, announcing the death of her husband. The letter, designed to fit every case, points up the absurdity of efficiency that does not consider the personal implications of death. The letter sent to Mrs. Daneeka reads:

Dear Mrs., Mr., Miss, or Mr. and Mrs. Daneeka: Words cannot express the deep personal grief I experienced when your husband, son, father, or brother was killed, wounded, or reported missing in action.

Because of the conflicting evidence of the army's letter and her husband's letters, Mrs. Daneeka, unable to deal with the problem, runs away. The death-rebirth myth is satirized here. A man, supposedly dead, writes letters, but his sudden reappearance doesn't bring a spring celebration traditional to the myth. It only brings terror and disbelief. Doc Daneeka's fake death is reminiscent of a situation comedy with the last scene, the solution, missing.

In *Catch-22*, death is unheroic and meaningless. The heroics of the romance are subjected to the mundane situations of everyday life presented in novels, not romances. Though Heller's work utilizes the flat characterizations and plot structure of the romance, its conventions are parodied. Critics who expect *Catch-22* to imitate life will be disappointed. It doesn't imitate life; it imitates a literary genre, the romance.

Victor J. Milne
Heller's `Bologniad':
A Theological Perspective
on "Catch-22"

Most recent studies of Catch-22 share the assumptions that the novel presents the world as absurd and chaotic, and that Yossarian's desertion reflects the currently widespread sentiment in favor of dropping out of a mad society. Thus Yossarian has been variously presented as an idealistic "puer eternis" who "refuses the traditional journey of learning in manhood," [1] and as the traditional comic rogue-figure who "never tries to change the society that he scorns." [2] Although most critics are agreed on these points, their evaluative judgments run through the whole spectrum from laudatory to condemnatory, and the majority of them register some uneasiness about the moral perspective which they impute to Heller. John Wain, for instance, in a generally favorable review accuses Heller of side-stepping moral issues.[3] However, Wain's strictures are mild compared to those of Norman Mailer and Joseph J. Waldmeir, who link their complaints about the moral vision of the novel with a charge of structural looseness.[4] As well as animadverting on Heller's truly Shandean propensity to digress, Mailer (in common with most other critics) deplores the sudden shift in tone and outlook that sunders the final chapter from the rest of the novel: [50] "Building upon itself the book becomes substantial until the last fifty pages grow suddenly and surprisingly powerful, only to be marred by an ending over the last five pages which is hysterical, sentimental and wall-eyed for Hollywood." [5]

---

[1] Sanford Pinsker, "Heller's Catch-22: The Protest of a Puer Eternis," Critique, VII, ii (1965), p. 151.

[2] Frederick R. Karl, "Joseph Heller's Catch-22: Only Fools Walk in Darkness," Contemporary American Novelists, ed. Harry T. Moore (Carbondale, 1964), p. 139.

[3] John Wain, "A New Novel about Old Troubles," Critical Quarterly, V, ii (1963), p. 172.

[4] Cf. Norman Mailer, "Some Children of the Goddess," Contemporary American Novelists (above), pp. 13–14; and Joseph J. Waldmeir, "Two Novelists of the Absurd: Heller and Kesey," Wisconsin Studies in Contemporary Literature, V, iii (1964), p. 195.

[5] Mailer, op. cit., p. 13.

SOURCE: Critique, Vol. 12, No. 2 (1970), pp. 50–69. Reprinted by permission of the author and publisher.

to the texture of the novel and the epic. In the *Iliad* an undertone of universal pathos is built up by the accumulated effect of the structurally irrelevant descriptions of the heroes' homelands and of the ways in which they came to join the Achaian host, and the end result is that the epic achieves cosmic significance. Heller, too, uses digressions to give his work a universal frame of reference so that war is treated not so much as a problem in its own right but rather as a symbol of the plight of modern western civilization, and this he accomplishes with a fine blend of pathos and comedy, appropriate to his mock-epic form, as, for example, in the digression on Major Major's upbringing and his induction into [53] the army.

Another constant feature of the epic is the elegiac note, heard in the famous passages in *Beowulf* and in Homer's formulaic conclusion to a battle scene—the bodies of the young men are laid in the dark earth far from their homes. Heller introduces the elegiac element with just the degree of grotesque parody appropriate to his inversion of the *Iliad* when Yossarian disrupts Clevinger's educational session with the unanswerable question: "Where are the Snowdens of yesteryear?" (35). The parody of Villon's elegy seems unimportant at this point, but significance accrues to it throughout the novel until in the penultimate chapter the full revelation comes in a scene which is well qualified by its intensity to serve as the ethical center of the whole novel.

Closely allied to the elegiac note is the tragic sense of life in the primary epic. George Steiner holds that the *Iliad* is the prototype of all tragedy, and he affirms that the essence of tragedy is doubt about the rationality and justice of the universe, an assertion "that the forces which shape or destroy our lives lie outside the governance of reason." [7] The *Iliad* taken as a whole may be said to pose this root question of theodicy and to hint at a despairing answer, but none of the characters in the epic ever engages in such radical questioning. In this respect Yossarian goes beyond Achilles to become Job: "Good God, how much reverence can you have for a Supreme Being who finds it necessary to include such phenomena as phlegm and tooth decay in His divine system of creation" (184). The question of the justice of the universe runs like a black thread through the novel, sometimes hyperbolically bitter as above, sometimes unrelievedly tragic, and sometimes transmuted into comedy as when one of the hospital patients observes: "There just doesn't seem to be any logic to this system of rewards and punishment. . . . Who can explain malaria as a consequence of fornication?" (175). In *Catch*-22 the tragic questioning of God's ways to men is prompted above all by the war, by the pointless extinction of one human life after another: "Kraft was a skinny harmless kid from Pennsylvania who wanted only to be liked, and was [54] destined to be dis-

---

[7] George Steiner, *The Death of Tragedy* (New York, 1963), pp. 6–7.

appointed in even so humble and degrading an ambition. Instead of being liked, he was dead. . . . He had lived innocuously for a little while and then had gone down in flame over Ferrara on the seventh day, while God was resting" (56).

Homer's tragedy is intensified because the Olympian gods provide "a comic background to the tragedy below." [8] For example, Ares' complaint to Zeus when he is lightly wounded by Diomedes is comically outrageous in its insignificance following a battle in which scores of warriors stoically accepted death. In *Catch-22* the equivalent comedy is provided by the upper echelons of the military, who are safe from the dangers of combat, and who at all times act as though they had no share in mortality. Just as the gods urge whole armies into battle and doom certain men to death, all the while quarrelling jealously among themselves, so the headquarters staff in *Catch-22*, in the midst of their scramble for status, deliver pep talks and issue the orders that doom men like Nately to an unnecessary death. The parallel between Homer's gods and Heller's senior officers need not be pressed further, except to observe a trace of Zeus' character in General Dreedle, the autocratic but by no means malevolent supreme commander.

One other illuminating parallel between these two literary universes may be developed. Although all the other gods tremble at the words of Zeus almost as much as Colonel Cathcart does at the frown of General Dreedle, neither Zeus nor the Gods as a whole are supreme in the universe. They themselves must submit to the decrees of the *Moirai*, the impersonal fates that rule the cosmos. In the same way, Dreedle, Peckem, Cathcart, Korn and the rest do not really run the microcosm of Pianosa but merely ratify the decrees of Milo Minderbinder and ex-Pfc. Wintergreen. As Colonel Korn explains in a moment of self-revelation, he and the other noncombatant officers are all helpless victims of the competitive ethic: "Everyone teaches us to aspire to higher things, a general is higher than a colonel, and a colonel is higher than a lieutenant-colonel. So we're both aspiring" (435). The competitive ethic is the law decreed by omnipotent capitalism, [55] personified in Milo Minderbinder, who, as his very name indicates, has the power to shackle thought and decent human feelings, and who, Heller makes plain, is to be conceived of as the supreme deity of this insane world: "Milo was the corn god, the rain god and the rice god in backward regions where such crude gods were still worshipped, and deep inside the jungles of Africa, he intimated with becoming modesty, large graven images of his mustached face could be found overlooking primitive stone altars red with human blood" (244). Of course, from a Christian point

---

[8] W. H. D. Rouse, "Preface," *The Iliad* (New York, 1950), p. vi.

of view the pagan gods are no more than devils, and Milo, whose "argosies . . . filled the air" (260), does indeed represent the prince of the powers of the air. As we shall soon see, he is elsewhere unmistakably identified with Satan.

Heller, then, uses the mock-epic form to reject the pre-Christian (and sub-Christian) values of the military-economic complex, whose competitive ethic is another manifestation of the ancient heroic code. Yossarian, a twentieth-century man with a Christian attitude to the sanctity of human life, finds himself—up to the last chapter—plunged into the indifferent pre-Christian universe of the primary epic. The code appropriate to that alien and hostile universe is most nobly expressed in Sarpedon's great speech before his death, where he claims economic privilege and pride of place for himself and Glaukos because of their valor, and he counsels that they take the risks of battle since death is inevitable. Whereas the warriors of the *Iliad* submit stoically to sudden death, Yossarian resolves "to live forever or die in the attempt" (30). Whereas they chiefly prize fame won in battle, Yossarian answers with a negative Colonel Korn's question: "Don't you want to earn more unit citations and more oak leaf clusters for your air medal?" (435). Yossarian categorically rejects the heroic code in his talk, but the definitive disavowal of these outworn values comes in the act of desertion. Thus above all else, the conflict between the competitive ethic and the humanistic Christian ethic determines the literary form of the novel as a "Bologniad," as a mock-epic embellished with comedy and horror, in which a modern Achilles says "baloney" to the [56] demands of a corrupt society with its iniquitous heroic code requiring the sacrifice of human lives.

For the very reason that Yossarian opposes himself to the competitive ethic and its attendant heroic code we cannot view him as the traditional rogue figure who delights us by his impudent, self-centered indifference to conventional morality. Although he is concerned with his personal safety, he wants to save his life in both senses of the phrase. We have observed that Heller makes every effort to show that the desertion is a responsible, moral act; to this we must now add that he is not inconsistent in drawing attention to the moral perplexities involved in Yossarian's choice. Inevitably, because of a passion for oversimplifying moral issues, some critics have failed to appreciate the rightness of Yossarian's decision. Thus Joseph Waldmeir wants Heller to decide univocally in favour of one side of a moral dilemma:

There is nothing wrong with an American novelist being in favor of the Second World War; Heller would in fact be unique if he opposed it. But since he appears to be opposed to it throughout the novel, there is

something wrong with Yossarian, even as Heller's spokesman, mouthing
pro-war sentiments.[9]

Waldmeir is referring, of course, to the conversation between Yossarian
and Danby in which Yossarian clearly desires an American victory over
Nazi Germany even though he is withdrawing from active participation in
the war. Yossarian, however, does not have a choice between absolute good
and absolute evil. Instead he is faced with a choice between two incompatible relative goods—a patriotism that is justifiable because his country
is engaged in a just war and a rebellion against an inhumane system of
exploitation, whereby Cathcart and Korn enjoy their meaningless triumphs
of egotism at the expense of men's lives. The opposition between the two
goods means that each good has an evil inseparably annexed to it. Rebellion against the American system of exploitation involves abandonment
of the struggle against the inhumanity of the Nazi state; support of the
American war effort entails supporting the evil system and being disloyal
to the friends who have suffered under it. Although Heller leaves no doubt
that the American system, which gives so much scope to the [57] petty
oppressors, is still a lesser evil than the frank tyranny of the Nazis, we are
made to feel in the course of the novel that Yossarian must take a stand
against the exploitation that confronts him.

At many points Yossarian argues with Major Major, Clevinger and
Danby the ethical dilemma of submitting to exploitation in order to
further a morally good cause, and all the while the plot of the novel leads
him to the point where the quandary is expressed in its plainest form,
when he is forced to say of those who are in charge of prosecuting the
war against Germany: "They've got all my pals, haven't they?" (45). Just
before Yossarian decisively rejects the odious deal, he relives his gruesome
experience with Snowden, and in his reflections, we have clearly stated the
dominant ethical concern of the novel: one must respect above all else the
sanctity of individual human lives:

It was easy to read the message in his entrails. Man was matter,
that was Snowden's secret. Drop him out of a window and he'll fall. Set fire
to him and he'll burn. Bury him and he'll rot like other kinds of garbage.
The spirit gone, man is garbage (450).

Yossarian has already learned as he tells Danby: "Between me and every
ideal I always find Scheisskopfs, Peckems, Korns and Cathcarts. And that
sort of changes the ideal" (454). Confronted with the appalling physical

---

[9] Waldmeir, *op. cit.*, p. 196.

facts of "liver, lungs, kidneys, ribs, stomach and bits of the stewed tomatoes Snowden had eaten that day for lunch" (449), Yossarian can only
choose the concrete ethic of the inviolability of human life in opposition
to the remote ideal. Moreover, Yossarian remains invincibly loyal to his
ethical judgment. When Dobbs offers still another escape by announcing
that he will kill Cathcart if only Yossarian will say that it is a good idea,
Yossarian cannot bring himself to say that word.

Obviously there is no unequivocally right decision for Yossarian, and we
may say in objection to Waldmeir's criticism that it is neither morally nor
aesthetically justifiable for an author to ignore the complexities of the
ethical problems he raises. If Heller had implied that the question of an
Allied victory in World War II was morally neutral, we should have des-
pised such a shallow view of human affairs, and the lack of [58] dramatic
tension in Yossarian's choice would have rendered the novel boring. Waldmeir's criticism totally misses the mark, but it does perform a valuable service in directing our attention to the moral dilemma of the novel. Although
the novel needs no defence beyond a demonstration that Heller has dealt
faithfully with the moral complexities of his hero's situation, the recognition of the paradox inevitably does prompt the question whether there is a
resolution within the novel. There is some evidence of such a resolution,
and to understand it we must examine the theological background of the
novel—particularly, the concept of guilt.

One of the most important episodes in the novel is Yossarian's stripping
off his clothes to go to Snowden's funeral and to receive his medal. As Sanford Pinsker notes, the incident symbolizes an attempt to return to "primal
innocence." [10] After Snowden has "spilled his secret" Yossarian feels uncomfortable—that is to say, guilty—in his uniform. Amusingly enough,
Yossarian, as a second Adam in naked innocence, rejects temptation in a
ludicrous re-enactment of the story of the Fall of Man. Sitting on what
he calls "the tree of life and the tree of the knowledge of good and evil"
(269), Yossarian is approached by Milo Minderbinder playing the role of
the serpent and offering in place of the fruit a piece of chocolate-coated
Egyptian cotton. The actual temptation is for Yossarian to submit to
absurd exploitation and in doing so to give Milo the encouragement he
wants to take advantage of all the men in his mess halls. The scene is a
highly surrealistic rendering of the central temptation of the novel, which
is offered in more realistic terms by Cathcart and Korn: the temptation for
Yossarian is always that of sanctioning exploitation by submitting to it.

From a theological viewpoint the novel presents exploitation and submission to exploitation as the two great sins. Exploitation, however, need
not involve the imposition of physical hardships; it is better defined in

---

[10] Pinsker, *op. cit.*, p. 152.

Erich Fromm's phrase as "the reification of man." [11] Thus Milo, viewing the men only as a market to be manipulated, exploits them fully as much in providing broiled Maine lobster as in trying to introduce [59] chocolate-coated cotton to the menu. It is in this sense—the denial of humanity—that Milo, or capitalism, requires human sacrifice. The political system, as much as the market place, encourages the process of reification, and it is particularly noticeable in the idealists, Clevinger and Danby. Even though their actions are externally indistinguishable from those of men who have responsibly decided to serve a cause, they have, in fact, reified themselves in accepting the notion that their value resides only in their utility as cogs in the war-machine. The soldier in white, who functions only as part of a pipeline between two glass jars, and of whom life can be predicated only on the basis of a thermometer reading, is the perfect symbol of the reification of man. Yossarian, then, in insisting upon the unique value of his individual life, constitutes a focal point of resistance to exploitation. Milo and Colonel Korn both recognize his importance and treat him as the bellwether whom the rest of the flock will follow. If Yossarian will allow himself to be used in any way, even in accepting the odious deal, none of the others will refuse to fly combat missions.

In stripping off his clothes Yossarian is trying to deny his complicity in the evils of the world. However, in the chapter entitled "The Eternal City" —let us note in passing that Rome is the "Babylon" of the Book of Revelation, the epitome of the worldly lust for pomp and power—Yossarian acknowledges the guilt that he shares with the rest of humanity:

Nately's whore was on his mind, as were Kraft and Orr and Nately and
Dunbar and Kid Sampson and McWatt, and all the poor and
stupid and diseased people he had seen in Italy, Egypt and North Africa
and knew about in other areas of the world, and Snowden and Nately's whore's
kid sister were on his conscience, too. Yossarian thought he knew
why Nately's whore held him responsible for Nately's death and wanted
to kill him. Why the hell shouldn't she? It was a man's world, and she and
everyone younger had every right to blame him and everyone older
for every unnatural tragedy that befell them; just as she, even in her grief,
was to blame for every man-made misery that landed on her kid sister, and on
all other children behind her. Someone had to do something sometime.
Every victim was a culprit, every [60] culprit a victim, and
someone had to stand up sometime to try to break the lousy chain of inherited
habit that was imperiling them all (414).

---

[11] Erich Fromm, "Medicine and the Ethical Problem of Modern Man," *The Dogma of Christ and Other Essays* (London, 1963), p. 126.

In this passage there is (in addition to a modern redefinition of original sin) a significant explanation for the puzzling attacks of Nately's whore: hers is the role of an accuser, almost a comic equivalent of the Eumenides. Interestingly enough, she succeeds only once in stabbing Yossarian, immediately after he commits his one unequivocally loathsome action in agreeing to the odious deal. Her attack is obviously the incident which jolts Yossarian into rejecting the deal: "Goddammit, Danby. I've got friends who were killed in this war. I can't make a deal now. Getting stabbed by that bitch was the best thing that ever happened to me" (456–7). Thus Nately's whore is to be viewed in the latter part of the novel as an allegorical projection of Yossarian's own conscience, which will not let him come to terms with any form of exploitation.

At this point the moral dilemma of the novel is posed in its acutest form. If Yossarian were to accept the deal, he would be guilty towards his friends, who have been exploited by Milo and Cathcart. If he were to desert he would be guilty towards his country and the just cause in which it is engaged. If he were neither to accept the deal nor to desert, he would face a court-martial on trumped-up charges. A superficial application of Christian ethics would suggest that Yossarian could escape guilt by staying to face the false accusation. However, Yossarian's suffering could have no redemptive value for the other victims since, as Danby points out, all without exception will believe the charges. Yossarian's situation raises in a peculiarly acute form the question of passive suffering as against active resistance. By offering himself as a victim, by trying to keep his conscience spotless, Yossarian would really be helping the powerful exploiters of humanity. In other words, excessive scrupulosity can be dangerous, for it can too easily reconcile hope for social justice with a passive submission to the bluff of the authorities that "Catch-22" says "they have a right to do anything we can't stop them [61] from doing" (46). Thus Yossarian's decision to desert enacts Heller's ethical judgment that an individual has no right to submit to injustice when his action will help to maintain an unjust system, for the desertion is a positive moral act calculated to discomfort the exploiters, whereas facing the court-martial would represent a paralysis of the will, a desire to maintain purity of conscience at the cost of inaction.

To understand the problem more clearly and Heller's resolution of it, we must examine two subordinate characters, Chaplain Tappman and Major Major. So far as Catch-22 can be allegorized, we may say that these two represent the Christian virtues as popularly conceived and in particular the disabling "virtue" of excessive scrupulosity. They are both men of good will, and they both submit patiently to all the indignities thrust upon them. Major Major, especially, is characterized by his adherence to the Decalogue and the moral teachings of Christ:

He turned the other cheek on every occasion and always did unto others
exactly as he would have had others do unto him. When he gave
to charity, his left hand never knew what his right hand was doing. He never
once took the name of the Lord his God in vain, committed adultery or
coveted his neighbor's ass. In fact, he loved his neighbor and never
even bore false witness against him (87).

The result of such characteristics is that Major Major and the chaplain
are both exiled from human society and become ineffectual hermits unable to influence the world for good or evil. This is the price exacted by
excessive concern with purity of conscience; one can avoid evil but cannot
do good: "The chaplain was a sincerely helpful man who was never able
to help anyone" (280). In fact, the chaplain has become so paralyzed by
his undeniable virtues that at the end of the novel Yossarian must urge
him: "For once in your life, succeed at something" (460).

Yet a theological solution to the dilemma allows the man of good will
to engage in redemptive action rather than passive withdrawal and suffering. He must act in good faith and then accept the truth that his action
has involved him in guilt. A [62] remarkable verbal parallel in *Catch-22*—
a paradoxical statement of this principle—is applied both to Major Major
and to the chaplain:

He had sinned, and it was good, for none of the documents to which he had
signed Washington Irving's name ever came back (96).

The chaplain had sinned, and it was good. Common sense told him that
telling lies and defecting from duty were sins. On the other hand,
everyone knew that sin was evil and that no good could come from evil. But
he did feel good: he felt positively marvellous. Consequently, it followed
logically that telling lies and defecting from duty could not be sins (372).

There is, of course, a faulty premise in the chaplain's syllogism; every freshman who has been subjected to *Paradise Lost* knows of a considerable body
of opinion which holds that good can come from evil. The original paradox
is true and cannot be explained away: "He had sinned and it was good."
As the chaplain's further reflections demonstrate, one must not infer from
the paradox that one should "sin the more that grace may more abound";
any attempt to deny the genuine sinfulness of sin could result only in the
self-satisfied and self-deceiving hypocrisy of a Milo Minderbinder or a
Colonel Cathcart: "It was almost no trick at all, he saw, to turn vice into
virtue and slander into truth. . . . Anybody could do it; it required no
brains at all. It merely required no character" (372). In other words, one
must learn to dispense with scrupulosity without becoming unscrupulous.

Catch-22 has seemed inconsistent to a number of critics because the theological substructure of the novel is in full accord with the paradoxical insights of classical Protestant thought. On the one hand, Protestant doctrine recognizes the sinfulness of all human endeavour, and on the other hand, it refuses to be seduced into ignoring the imperfect world of becoming in favour of the perfect world of being. On the contrary, Protestant theology insists on activism even though sin inevitably results; the principle is enshrined in Luther's startling maxim, *pecca fortiter*—sin resolutely. The same notion is expounded more thoroughly in a modern Protestant classic, Dietrich Bonhoeffer's *Letters and Papers from Prison*, a work [63] which may be profitably read in conjunction with *Catch-22* as it also comes out of World War II and shows a remarkable affinity in temper to Heller's novel. In analyzing the qualities of the German character which made possible the rise of Nazism, Bonhoeffer blames the typical German virtue of obedience to authority:

The trouble was, he [the German] did not understand his world.
He forgot that submissiveness and self-sacrifice could be exploited for evil
ends. . . . He could not see that in certain circumstances free and
responsible action might have to take precedence over duty and calling. As a
compensation he developed in one direction an irresponsible unscrupulousness,
and in another an agonizing scrupulosity which invariably frustrated
action. Civil courage, however, can only grow out of the free
responsibility of free men. Only now are we Germans beginning to discover
the meaning of free responsibility. It depends upon a God who demands
bold action as the response of faith, and who promises forgiveness
and consolation to the man who becomes a sinner in the process.[12]

What Bonhoeffer calls civil courage and free responsibility are Yossarian's primary virtues and are the virtues most needed in the world of Pianosa.

It would be impossible to summarize Bonhoeffer's complex doctrine of responsibility which forms the core of his ethical thought. Basically, we may say that responsibility involves an acceptance of the need to relate all moral action to the concrete situation of mingled good and evil, and thus it is opposed to a Kantian affirmation of abstract ethical demands which are to be practised universally without regard to the concrete situation. Yossarian recognizes that he must make his choice in the real situation which offers only relative good and relative evil. Any choice will involve sinning against some abstract ethical principle. And according to Bonhoeffer's doctrine a choice such as Yossarian's is justified by God even if the greater evil is unintentionally chosen, for "if any man attempts to escape guilt in responsibility, he detaches himself from the ultimate reality

---

[12] Dietrich Bonhoeffer, *Letters and Papers from Prison* (London, 1959), pp. 137–8.

of human existence" and "sets his own personal innocence above his responsibility for men." [13] Yossarian, then, is the responsible man, in Bonhoeffer's sense, while Clevinger and Danby in their arguments with Yossarian show themselves to [64] be Kantians who cannot understand his reluctance to affirm that an ethical abstraction must be honoured at all times and at all places and under all conditions.

Our theological perspective can be completed only by a consideration of the God of *Catch-22*, the true God who stands in opposition to Milo Minderbinder's demonic claims. One persistent motif in the narrative is the chaplain's progressive loss of faith in God. Like Yossarian the chaplain is led by the spectacle of meaningless death to question the justice of the universe, and after his failure to dissuade Colonel Cathcart from raising the required number of missions, he is ready to disbelieve "in the wisdom and justice of an immortal, omnipotent, omniscient, humane, universal, anthropomorphic, English-speaking, Anglo-Saxon, pro-American God" (293). Why should he believe in such a God? This God has based his reputation on his abilities as a benevolent stage-magician who will always intervene on behalf of a right-thinking, humane Anglo-Saxon, but "there were no miracles; prayers went unanswered, and misfortune tramped with equal brutality on the virtuous and the corrupt" (293–4). The chaplain's "atheism" may be regarded as an essential preliminary condition of true faith; he must reject the anthropomorphic idol invented to ratify the pretensions and prejudices of a particular culture if he is ever to believe in the mysterious Biblical God who impartially distributes temporal blessings and misfortunes. Moreover, the chaplain rejects the anthropomorphic God in his role as the benevolent, grandfatherly deity of popular religion, who is invoked only at funerals to give frightened individuals the cheap and uncertain consolation of a supernatural continuation of their self-centered personalities:

The chaplain felt most deceitful presiding at funerals, and it would not have
astonished him to learn that the apparition in the tree that day was a
manifestation of the Almighty's censure for the blasphemy and
pride inherent in his function. To simulate gravity, feign grief and pretend
supernatural intelligence of the hereafter in so fearsome and arcane a
circumstance as death seemed the most criminal of offenses (279).

As the last quotation indicates, the chaplain never wholly loses faith in God but only in the man-made idol, and when [65] the time comes, he is given a new revelation. The chaplain has rejected the stage-miracles of religious tradition, but he discovers that there is a different kind of mira-

---

[13] Dietrich Bonhoeffer, *Ethics* (London, 1955), p. 210. Cf. all of Chapter VI.

cle. When news of Orr's safe arrival in Sweden reaches Pianosa, he exclaims: "It's a miracle, I tell you! A miracle! I believe in God again" (458). Orr's escape has a quite obvious religious significance, for seen in a theological context, his crash-landing in the Adriatic is a symbolic baptism and the sudden news of his safety gives the whole episode the quality of resurrection following death—a miraculous reversal of the seemingly irrevocable catastrophe.

Orr is an important figure but remains enigmatic up to the last chapter of the novel. To Yossarian he seems a comic figure, a sucker, the prototypal victim of all the forms of exploitation that Yossarian himself protests against. To him Orr is "a freakish, likeable dwarf with . . . a thousand valuable skills that would keep him in a low income group all his life," and he is convinced that Orr needs to be shielded "against animosity and deceit, against people with ambition and the embittered snobbery of the big shot's wife, against the squalid, corrupting indignities of the profit motive and the friendly neighborhood butcher with inferior meat" (321). Yossarian is wrong, of course, because, though seeing the qualities that lie behind Orr's apparent innocence, he does not understand their value. Orr is self-reliant ("a thousand valuable skills"), patient, enduring ("oblivious to fatigue"), and adaptable ("not afraid . . . of foods like scrod or tripe"). Above all, Orr is a doer rather than a contemplative like the chaplain, and he is admirably equipped to survive. The imagery identifies Orr closely with the natural world—he is "a gnome," "a dwarf," "as oblivious to fatigue as the stump of a tree" and has "an uncanny knowledge of wildlife" (321-2). He may be seen as a mischievous and resilient earth-spirit like Puck or as the true embodiment of the seemingly naive but really shrewd and self-reliant archetypal Yankee farmer, of whom Major Major's father is a ludicrous parody. In any case, Orr is the personification of the qualities of intelligence and endurance which make possible the survival of humanity under the worst conditions of oppression and exploitation. While the chaplain engages in futile efforts to [66] reason with Colonel Cathcart, while Yossarian carries on a futile and dangerous revolt, Orr quietly practises the skills that will ensure his survival. Only after Orr has acted can Yossarian grasp the possibility of escape that was and still is open to him, and then he realizes that he must imitate Orr in being "as wise as serpents and harmless as doves":

"Bring me apples, Danby, and chestnuts too. Run, Danby, run. Bring me crab apples and horse chestnuts before it's too late, and get some for yourself."

"Horse chestnuts? Crab apples? What in the world for?"

"To pop into our cheeks, of course." Yossarian threw his arms up into the air in a gesture of mighty and despairing self-recrimination. "Oh, why didn't I listen to him? Why wouldn't I have some faith?" (459)

Throughout the novel, Yossarian, for all the verbal energy displayed in his revolt, has been paralyzed by his moral quandary. In the Snowden episode he was an impotent good Samaritan, and in the chapter, "The Eternal City," he was a Pharisee walking past terrible spectacles of human misery and not daring to aid the victims; only now, with the example of Orr before him, can he perform a positive moral action. The forgiveness of sins promised in baptism has important consequences not only on the eternal level but also on the temporal level in that the consciousness of divine forgiveness can break the neurotic paralysis of the will induced by the fear of sinning. Thus the baptismal symbolism of Orr's escape indicates that Orr's qualities, including his all too human shrewdness, are forgiven, sanctified, and employed in a miracle that has redemptive value for Yossarian and the chaplain. Yossarian then realizes that he must follow Orr —even though it involves him in the sin of withdrawing his resistance to Nazism—because it will help no one if he is put in prison on false charges. The moral effects of Yossarian's action are admittedly almost insignificant; he may be able to help Nately's whore's kid sister, and he will be able to embarrass Cathcart and Korn. Yet this is the only morally valid possibility for Yossarian and he must not shrink from it either to accept the odious deal or to help the exploiters by submitting to martyrdom. However, Heller makes clear that Orr's course of action is not necessarily the proper one [67] for everyone. The chaplain, though similarly freed from his moral paralysis by Orr, does not face the same dangers as Yossarian; while endorsing Yossarian's decision to flee, he realizes that he can and ought to continue the struggle on Pianosa: "If Orr could row to Sweden, then I can triumph over Colonel Cathcart and Colonel Korn, if only I persevere" (461).

This is the God of *Catch-22*. He does not help out men with stage-tricks, but to the man who is willing to act for the sake of righteousness He promises that evil will not ultimately prevail against good. From this theological perspective we can see an explanation for a problem that has troubled several critics—the discontinuity of the last chapter with the rest of the novel. The reason is that nature and grace are discontinuous, as are human wisdom and faith. In the last chapter of the novel Yossarian and the chaplain discard their vision of the pagan universe of the epic for the Christian faith in a God of salvation: "There is hope, after all. . . . Even Clevinger might be alive somewhere in that cloud of his, hiding inside until it's safe to come out" (459).

Just as important as the promise that justice shall prevail is the promise of forgiveness for the sins committed in a sincere pursuit of righteousness. And that is how the novel ends. Yossarian sins in acting morally. He decides as a free and responsible man to resist the exploitation of himself and others in the only way left open to him—by fleeing from it even though the very exploiters do have a valid claim on his conscience. Danby points out the sinful quality of the action and warns Yossarian: "Your conscience will never let you rest" (462). To which Yossarian replies: "God bless it. . . . I wouldn't want to live without strong misgivings" (462). In symbolic terms the last paragraph of the novel reinforces the theme of forgiveness for responsible action with the appearance of Nately's whore, the embodiment of Yossarian's accusing conscience:

> Yossarian jumped. Nately's whore was hiding just outside the door. The knife came down, missing him by inches, and he took off (463).

Yossarian can sin in his pursuit of the kingdom of heaven [68] because he is *simul iustus et peccator.* [69]

Jesse Ritter
Fearful Comedy:
"Catch-22" as Avatar
of the Social
Surrealist Novel

Joseph Heller was skillful enough in structuring formlessness and alogic in *Catch-22* that legions of readers fell away (usually at about Chapter III), baffled by a novel that seemed to go nowhere. That it has gone somewhere, has become for a vast number of young readers a handle on modern reality, is sufficient reason for a study of *Catch-22* that yields to the novel's inner logic and organic structure. Such a study first requires a step back, a perspective that enables us to see *Catch-22* as avatar of a new fictional genre—the *social surrealist* novel. From this, we may swing back to the structure of *Catch-22* to understand more fully the novel's unity.

The social surrealist novel is an extension of the modern ironic mode. Its form is a mixture of picaresque, romance-parody, and anatomy (or Menippean satire), containing elements of surrealism, black humor, the grotesque and tragicomedy, the Absurd, apocalyptic visions, and a semimythic "antihero." Authors of such novels try to present a visionary social

---

SOURCE: This essay was written especially for this book. For an essay by Mr. Ritter on *Catch-22* as black humor, see James Nagel, ed., *Critical Essays on* Catch-22 (Encino, Calif.: Dickenson, 1973).

satire, achieved by extending reality to the point of distortion and by emphasizing the disrelations or discontinuity of the modern world through radical juxtaposition. The earlier emergence of this genre is found in the fiction of Jonathan Swift, Nikolai Gogol, Louis-Ferdinand Céline, William Faulkner, Franz Kafka, and Nathanael West; the genre is displayed in the more recent novels of Günter Grass, Nelson Algren, Ralph Ellison, Ken Kesey, Jakov Lind, James Purdy, Thomas Pynchon, Jerzy Kosinski, and Terry Southern. Other novelists whose techniques anticipated the social surrealist genre are Cervantes, Dostoevsky, Melville, James Joyce, John Dos Passos, and Jean-Paul Sartre.

One of the most salient features of the genre—and *Catch-22*—is a radical irony, irony raised to the level of structure. Northrop Frye's comment on the movement of the ironic mode provides a point of departure: "Irony descends from the low mimetic; it begins in realism and dispassionate observation. But as it does so, it moves steadily towards myth, and dim outlines of sacrificial rituals and dying gods begin to appear in it." [1] The radically ironic vision that informs the social surrealist novel is responsible for outcast heroes of mythical stature, the parody and fusion of conventional literary forms, the structural juxtaposition of unrelated elements, and the bitter mixture of black humor and tragicomedy. The central principle at work here is the tendency to submit romance and illusion to the test of contemporary experience, hence the preponderance of picaresque and romance-parody fictional forms in the works of Heller, Grass, West, Lind, Pynchon, Purdy, and Ellison.

A general comparison of *Catch-22* with Günther Grass' *The Tin Drum* and *Dog Years* will establish the outlines of a genre definition. Both Heller and Grass use the hospital and disease as metaphors for aspects of modern society and existence. Both try to embrace and convey the experience of catastrophe (war) in fiction. Both present heroes with mythic overtones involved in a quest for love and order. Both novelists parody fictional forms and techniques. Both satirize society and human behavior by a process of extension, extending qualities of society and behavior to the point of absurdity. Finally, both novelists convey a sense of values largely skeptical of specific ideology, values expressed by many post-World War II novelists.

Mutant Forms: Surrealism and Naturalism

The social surrealist novelists tend to blend and parody traditional novel forms. This fusion—of the picaresque, romance-parody, and anatomy—extends well beyond *Catch-22* to Thomas Pynchon's *V*, for instance, which

---

[1] *Anatomy of Criticism* (Princeton, N. J., 1957), p. 42.

is picaresque, a parody of the spy novel, romance-parody, anatomy, and a blend of the novel of manners and the novel of ideas (the last two qualities are found often in the social surrealist genre). In *V*, the travels of Benny Profane and Herbert Stencil are a contrapuntal search for the ideal of love. The mysterious V seems to be the victim of international intrigue. Profane's "quest" takes him "beneath the streets" of New York, where he hunts alligators for the Sanitation Department. The elaborate medical descriptions of cosmetic nose surgery and dentistry suggest the fictional anatomy, and the satirical presentation of some inhabitants of New York bohemia, "The Whole Sick Crew," suggests the novel of manners and the novel of ideas.

Northrop Frye defines the romance-parody as a structure which subjects the mythic properties of the romance to everyday experience. We shall see how Frye's definition of the anatomy form applies to *Catch-22*. I have chosen the term "social surrealism" carefully to define the specific quality that sets off *Catch-22* and the novels mentioned here from modern fiction characterized by extreme realist-naturalist objectivity or by the solipsism of interior consciousness. It represents a fusion of the two modern fictional techniques of naturalism and surrealism. I have deliberately selected the term surrealism rather than "expressionism." While both describe an artistic technique which emphasizes subjectivity, dreams, myth, and the grotesque, the German Expressionist dramatists tended to use stridency, rather than humor, for emotional effect.

Ralph Ellison's *Invisible Man* and Nelson Algren's *The Man with the Golden Arm*, *Never Come Morning*, and *A Walk on the Wild Side* are four novels which clearly blend naturalistic, environmental social reality with grotesque figures and surreal, hallucinatory technique. Malcolm Cowley noticed this fusion when he observed that in *The Man with the Golden Arm* the characters are "driven and deformed by conditions beyond their power to change, as in every naturalistic novel since Zola," but Algren does not emphasize that "vast forces are grinding these people down." Algren, said Cowley, emphasizes "the rebellions and lies and laughter by means of which they retain, even the most repulsive of them, some remnants of human pride." [2] Cowley also noted the same technique in Ellison's *Invisible Man* by calling it "another novel that starts with social conditions and ends as a defense of the separate personality. . . . The technique is closer to that of the expressionists: every scene is exaggerated, even caricatured, in order to convey what the novelist thinks is the essential truth about it" (p. 91). Another critic confirms Cowley's judgment by remarking that "Ellison varies from the direct presentation of actuality through brutal nat-

---

[2] *The Literary Situation* (New York, 1954), p. 90.

uralism, to the fantasy and surrealism of writers so disparate as Kafka and Melville of *The Confidence Man.*" [3]

As the social surrealist genre develops, its increasingly bitter humor and hallucinatory presentation of reality in no way diminish the objective presentation of social reality. Referring to Thomas Pynchon's "multiple absurdities" in his description of used cars as the battered, castoff egos of their former owners in *The Crying of Lot 49*, Don Hausdorf insisted that "This may be 'Black Comedy' in its grotesque manipulation of details but it also embodies social protest against dehumanization." [4]

The foregoing qualities provide criteria helpful to us in distinguishing social surrealist from surrealist or expressionist novels (such as Djuna Barnes's *Nightwood*, Hermann Broch's *The Death of Vergil*). These qualities, humor and specialized use of detail, appear significantly in Heller's descriptions of Milo Minderbinder's financial operations: Minderbinder's produce market is catalogued in dizzying detail. First a sense of social reality is established, then we escape from this into a parody of social reality, an explosion of ridiculous reality.[5] We are rooted in the real world—to the point of nightmare.

The Secular Inferno of "Catch-22": Structure as Descending Spiral

Stunned by the catastrophic vision and alternating between laughter and shock, the reader of *Catch-22* may feel that Heller merely flung on paper a chaotic vision of the air war in World War II. The first and subsequent reviewers of the novel agree on one point—that, good or bad, the novel lacks form. Even reviewers and readers reacting favorably often feel that Heller could profitably have pruned and ordered the novel for greater structural effect. Norman Mailer summarized this attitude and articulated the sense of futility any critic feels before the size and range of *Catch-22*, arguing that passages could probably be removed from any part, but concluding that "it would be a virtuoso performance to write a definitive piece on *Catch-22*. It would take ten thousand words or more. Because Heller is carrying his reader on a more consistent voyage through Hell than any American writer before him (except Burroughs . . .), and so the analysis of Joseph Heller's Hell would require a discussion of other varieties of

---

[3] John McCormick, *Catastrophe and Imagination* (London, 1951), p. 130.

[4] "Thomas Pynchon's Multiple Absurdities," *Wisconsin Studies in Contemporary Literature*, VII, 3 (Autumn, 1966), 261.

[5] A not-so-ridiculous reality since Vietnam. In a 1969 radio interview over a San Jose, California, station, Heller observed that he meant to write about World War II but had since discovered that he was writing about Vietnam!

inferno and whether they do more than this author's tour." [6] The *Time* reviewer claimed an "overdose of comic non sequitur" and felt the novel contained an "almost experimental formlessness." [7] Another reviewer asserted that "in general, the book is too complicated to be comprehended." [8] Others believed that Heller did not "have to try so hard to be funny," or that his book is "too grim to be genuinely funny," or that "Heller lacks control and logical center." [9] Yet a careful reading of *Catch-22*, combined with some knowledge of the contours of twentieth-century fiction, reveal a tangible structure and order in the novel. It is simply a different type of structure and order from that to which the novel-oriented reader may be accustomed.

Robert Brustein early hinted a way out of Heller's structural puzzle: "Considering his indifference to surface realism, it is hard to judge Heller by standards of psychological realism (or for that matter, by conventional artistic standards at all, since this book is as formless as any picaresque epic). He is concerned entirely with that thin boundary of the surreal, the borderline between the hilarity and horror which, much like the apparent formlessness of the unconscious, has its own special integrity and coherence." [10] Constance Denniston later demonstrated this coherence by studying James Purdy's *Malcolm* and *Catch-22* as examples of the romance-parody defined by Northrop Frye. Such a view lops off much of *Catch-22*, however; by her definition, *Catch-22* is no more than a war-novel parody. [11] Actually, the novel is not simply the parody of a genre but is a mixture of genres which parody not only fictional forms but many of the patterns of twentieth-century existence as well. [12]

Had Miss Denniston read Northrop Frye more carefully, and had she

---

[6] "Some Children of the Goddess," *Contemporary American Authors*, ed. Harry T. Moore (Carbondale, Ill., 1964), p. 13.

[7] "Good Soldier Yossarian," *Time*, LXXVIII (October 27, 1961), 98.

[8] Granville Hicks, "Medals for Madness," *Saturday Review*, XLIV (October 14, 1961), 32–33.

[9] William Barrett, "Two Newcomers," *Atlantic*, CCLX (January, 1962), 98. Spencer Klaw, "Airman's Wacky War," *New York Herald Tribune*, XXXVIII (October 15, 1961), 8. Hicks, *op. cit.*, p. 33. *Time, op. cit.*, p. 8. Joseph J. Waldmeir, "Two Novelists of the Absurd: Heller and Kesey," *Wisconsin Studies in Contemporary Literature*, V, 3 (Autumn, 1964), 202.

[10] "Logic of Survival in a Lunatic World," *The New Republic*, 145 (November 13, 1961), 11–12.

[11] "The American Romance-Parody: A Study of Purdy's *Malcolm* and Heller's *Catch-22*," *Emporia State Research Studies*, XIV, 2 (December, 1965), 58.

[12] The financial gyrations of Milo Minderbinder, for instance, rather systematically parody specific patterns of free-enterprise philosophy and action. During the recent cyclamate sweetener scare, Pepsico, Inc., took Diet-Pepsi off the market and later announced it was sending a shipload of Diet-Pepsi to the South Vietnamese.

been aware of the rise of a new fictional style forged to encompass the catastrophe of twentieth-century violence and warfare—social surrealism —she might have placed *Catch-22* in the category of the modern *anatomy* as defined by Frye. By viewing Heller's novel as an anatomy, we can see not only an internal unity in the work itself but also a continuation of Menippean satire, reshaped by the modern fictional sensibility. The Menippean satire "presents us with a vision of the world in terms of a single intellectual pattern. The intellectual structure built up from the story makes for violent dislocations in the customary logic of narrative, through the appearance of carelessness that reflects only the carelessness of the reader or his tendency to judge by a novel-centered conception of fiction." [13] Frye charts variations on the tradition from the earlier Roman forms of Menippean satire to Elizabethan and Jacobean borrowings, into fiction through Sterne's *Tristram Shandy*, and on into the twentieth-century versions found in Joyce's *Ulysses* and *Finnegans Wake*, noticing, along the way, the tendency of the modern novel to mix genres. "When we examine fiction from the point of view of form, we can see four chief strands binding it together, novel, confession, anatomy, and romance" (p. 312). In their larger contours, *Catch-22* and the novels mentioned in this study fit the novel-anatomy and the novel-anatomy-romance patterns. This argument should suggest to the student of recent fiction that he be somewhat tentative in castigating formlessness and mixtures of genres. As Frye concludes, "It is the anatomy in particular that has baffled critics, and there is hardly any fiction writer deeply influenced by it who has not been accused of disorderly conduct" (p. 313). Joseph Heller himself made it quite clear that he was deliberately mixing genres when he commented in an interview that "I tried consciously for a comic effect juxtaposed with the tragic, working the frivolous in with the catastrophic. I wanted people to laugh and then look back with horror at what they were laughing at." [14] This "disintegration of form" is characteristic of the ironic mode.

With this in mind, let us review the structural outline of *Catch-22*. The novel presents the events of a medium-bomber squadron in the European theater of World War II, based on the fictional island of Pianosa in the Mediterranean Sea. The novel opens with the protagonist, Captain Yossarian, in the base hospital, recounts the life of the bomber squadron during the span of only a few months, and ends with Yossarian again in the hospital, resolving to desert the Air Force and make his way to Sweden, a neutral sanctuary. The Jonsonian nature of the satire is indicated by the chapter headings; all of the forty-two chapters, except four, are titled with

---

[13] *Anatomy, op. cit.*, p. 310.
[14] "So They Say: Guest Editors Interview Six Creative People," *Mademoiselle*, LVII (August, 1963), 234.

the names of characters involved in the action. Most of the names suggest character traits.

The narrative method can best be described as a modified or *objectified* stream of consciousness. Most of the events are filtered through the consciousness of Yossarian. At times they are objective re-creations of earlier events; at times they are Yossarian's memories triggered by outward events. The hospital is the narrative and thematic center of the novel.

The oblique, spiral effect of the novel's form arises from the circular appearance and reappearance of things and events which are presented with more detail each time around: the hospital, the man in white, Snowden's death, and the dead man in Yossarian's tent. The man in white and Snowden's death comprise two vivid examples of Heller's synecdoche raised to the level of structural element. These objective symbols of the horrors of war and the cruel absurdity of a world filled with suffering haunt Yossarian's consciousness, motivating his actions. Until Chapter XIX, the center of the novel, almost all the narrated events occur in retrospect while Yossarian is in the hospital. Chapter XIX, entitled "Colonel Cathcart," begins the forward movement through time leading to Yossarian's decision to desert. However, within this latter framework previous events are objectively narrated. The ultimate effect of this technique is one of stasis; there is no sense of a Joycean character always *moving through* the present, carrying the past with him; the effect is of an eternal *now*—a fixed, cruel cosmos filled with the fixed venality of the aggressors, both enemy and friend. The world seems a nightmare in which things happen with chaotic rapidity and simultaneity, where the participants are trapped by Catch-22. The structure of the novel is gathered up and dictated by Catch-22, the Absurd law of life which says, ultimately, that "they have a right to do anything we can't stop them from doing." [15] Yossarian, struggling vainly to "stop them" by adopting various stratagems of survival, ultimately flees the whole society. The stasis—the immutable Catch-22 trap—is further intensified by the pervading psychological sensation of *déjà vu* (things seen again). There is an airman in the hospital who "sees everything twice"; Yossarian occasionally mutters "*déjà vu*"; finally, in a bitter epiphany, Dunbar bolts upright and "sees everything twice" in the hospital. With these multiple variations, Heller blends psychological sensation, word play, bitter farce, and structural principle. The critics who missed the unity and simultaneity of Heller's repetitions missed the dense structural unity of the novel.[16]

Finally, Yossarian's struggles provide another configuration to *Catch-22*.

---

[15] *Catch-22* (New York, Dell, 1962). Further references are to this edition of the novel.
[16] For a thorough discussion of *déjà vu* as structural principle, see James M. Mellard, "*Catch-22*: *Déjà vu* and the Labyrinth of Memory," *Bucknell Review*, XVI, 2 (1968), 29–44.

The hero's adventures follow those of the romance-parody: quest (Chapters I through XXXVIII), vision (Chapter XXXIX), and escape (Chapters XL to the end).[17]

The spiral of recurring key events is not prolixity. The bondage of the protagonist is absolute, and the horror of mass killing and mechanized aerial warfare is revealed by degrees as the reader—and Yossarian—becomes more aware of the man in white, the dead man in Yossarian's tent, and the hideous death of young Snowden. Absurdity surmounts absurdity. The absolute power the military holds over the individual soldier in wartime symbolizes by extension the power of death and suffering the world holds over all men everywhere.

Readers unaccustomed to this spiraling narrative form will experience frustration (they are *supposed* to!), expecting at least a straightforward, unified resolution of events as they appear. Events recede, however, as the novel moves off on another narrative tangent. Then events abandoned earlier reappear, perhaps in more detail, perhaps only peripherally. Yet the central event of the novel, Snowden's death, grows in significance. As it grows, Yossarian's motives become clearer. With this event Yossarian had looked into the red wound of horror and meaninglessness. We are told that Yossarian learned Snowden's "secret," but the "secret" is not revealed until the full event is narrated, not until after Yossarian's apocalyptic trip into the wartime wasteland of bombed-out Rome. After this enlightenment, Yossarian understands Orr's oblique secret and Snowden's secret, resolving to make a separate peace. Narrative structure reinforces thematic unity. *Catch-22* is a fiction which slips the bonds of traditional narrative forms as it develops paradox into an encyclopedia of the Absurd, retaining, however, the contours of ironic romance and Menippean satire.

The Genre and a New Sensibility

The sharply divided critical and reader reactions to *Catch-22* are further intensified by the dislocated sensibility of the novel. It is a sensibility characteristic of the social surrealist novel—and such films as *Dr. Strangelove*, *M*A*S*H**, and *Little Big Man*: radical juxtaposition.[18]

Susan Sontag coined the term in *Against Interpretation*, perceiving a widespread sense and use of "radical juxtaposition," derived from surreal-

---

[17] Denniston, *op. cit.*, pp. 54–55.

[18] Indeed, *Catch-22* and its sensibility contribute greatly to the generation gap—the gap between those attuned and those not attuned to the deep ironies of modern life. In a discussion of *Catch-22*, Nelson Algren recently commented to this writer that "the kids who really understand Heller also understand and admire Lord Buckley and Lenny Bruce. They go together."

ism, in much of avant-garde art. She spoke of surrealism as "a mode of sensibility which cuts across all the arts in the twentieth century. There is a Surrealist tradition in the theatre, in painting, in poetry, in the cinema, in music, and in the novel. . . . The Surrealist tradition in all these arts is united by the idea of destroying conventional meanings, and creating new meanings or counter-meanings through radical juxtaposition (the 'collage principle')." [19] Ranging afar, she suggests that the process of free association practiced by psychoanalysis is also radical juxtaposition, concluding that "One may also see a kind of involuntary collage-principle in many of the artifacts of the modern city: the brutal disharmony of buildings in size and style, the wild juxtaposition of store signs, the clamorous layouts of the modern newspaper, etc."

Radical juxtaposition plus the comic becomes radical irony in the social surrealist film and novel. In the passage just cited, Miss Sontag points out that "there is something comic in modern experience as such, a demonic, not a divine, comedy, precisely to the extent that modern experience is characterized by meaningless mechanized situations of disrelation."

Radical juxtaposition, then, is a form of ironic commentary on the disrelations and alogic of modern existence—on the Absurd. Such commentary, however, requires an echoing sensibility in the reader or viewer—a fairly comprehensive frame of reference against which we judge the vision of Heller and the social surrealists. Northrop Frye has made a helpful observation here in writing that an ironic frame of reference "is the negative pole of the allegorical one. Irony presents a human conflict which, unlike comedy, a romance, or even a tragedy, is unsatisfactory and incomplete unless we see in it a significance beyond itself, something typical of the human situation as a whole." [20] What is important for our purposes is to grasp the fact that a dominant characteristic of the modern fictional sensibility has become a structural principle in the novel. For Joseph Heller in *Catch-22*, radical juxtaposition is a multileveled rhetorical device for expressing the Absurd.

A Grammar of the Absurd

Much of modern literature is devoted to portraying the Absurd, or the failure of rationalist expectations.[21] Heller's relentless use of radical juxta-

---

[19] *Against Interpretation* (New York, 1966), pp. 269–270.
[20] "The Road to Excess," *Myth and Symbol*, ed. Bernice Slote (Lincoln, Neb., 1963), p. 14.
[21] In an operational sense, "absurd" here simply refers to ridiculous or irrational human behavior; the "Absurd" in this study is that condition defined by Albert Camus as "this confrontation between the human need and the unreasonable silence of the world. . . . [T]he Absurd is not in man (if such a metaphor could have a meaning)

position in *Catch-22* intensifies our sense of the Absurd to the point of hallucination. The nonexistence of things or the topsy-turvy nature of reality is expressed by the non-sequitur arguments, the instantaneous reversals, and the metaphysical negatives scattered throughout the novel. Yossarian, for instance, often goes to the officer's club because "it was truly a splendid structure, and Yossarian throbbed with a mighty sense of accomplishment each time he gazed at it and reflected that none of the work that had gone into it was his" (p. 19). Horror jostles hilarity, absurdity jostles logic, that which exists seems not to, and that which doesn't exist seems to. Yossarian refers to the "dead man in his tent" so consistently that the company clerk begins using the same term. "In reality, he was no such thing. He was simply a replacement pilot who had been killed in combat before he had officially reported for duty" (p. 111). Officially he is still alive; his personal effects remain in Yossarian's tent, a constant reminder of the anonymity of death in war and of military inefficiency. Doc Daneeka, on the other hand, is declared dead after supposedly crashing with McWatt's plane. He protests vainly; after his wife collects on his government and private insurance policies, he wanders about the squadron, disconsolately trying to prove his existence.

Sometimes the metaphysical negatives illustrate the truth of absurdity; sometimes they simply telescope the relationship between human motive and act and satirize human behavior. Much of the arrogance and illogic of military and civilian behavior are presented through juxtaposition. Colonel Cargill, General Peckem's troubleshooter, was a marketing executive before the war. "Colonel Cargill was so awful a marketing executive that his services were much sought after by firms eager to establish losses for tax purposes. . . . He was a self-made man who owed his lack of success to nobody" (p. 28). Major Major Major Major's father was a farmer who specialized in alfalfa, "and he made a good thing out of not growing any. . . . The more alfalfa he did not grow, the more money the government gave him, and he spent every penny he didn't earn on new land to increase the amount of alfalfa he did not produce" (p. 85). It is significant that these forms of argument and behavior tend to cluster in the first half of the book; they recede after situational illogic and social absurdity are established. As the horror of war advances, the social satire diminishes. The absurd gives way to the Absurd.

Image patterns abound which generally reinforce either the Absurd (found in the lists of disease and hospital metaphors) or Yossarian's deeply

---

nor in the world, but in their presence together." (*The Myth of Sisyphus*, trans. Justin O'Brien, [New York, 1959], pp. 16, 23.) The distinction between the two terms is ignored by many critics.

rooted sexuality, his life force (his mind and senses become a riot of sexual sensation whenever he thinks of the female). Grotesque metaphors are frequent, such as when a road is described as "knotted" and as lying "like a broken suspender between the hospital and the squadron" (p. 21). The squadron pilots, after fifty missions, "were grotesque, like useless young men in a depression. They moved sideways, like crabs" (p. 27). Heller's parody of absurd behavior frequently takes the form of dizzying lists, such as when he reels off the incredible varieties of goods with which Milo Minderbinder barters, buys, sells, bribes, and speculates.

The frequent instantaneous reversals of action are a narrative extension of Heller's technique of radical juxtaposition. The island is surrounded by a "placid blue sea . . . that could gulp down a person with a cramp in the twinkling of an eye and ship him back to shore three days later, all charges paid, bloated, blue and putrescent, water draining out through both cold nostrils" (p. 18). The most shocking event in the novel occurs in the middle of an idyllic lull in the war, when the fliers are frolicking and bathing in the nude on the beach: McWatt's light-hearted buzzing of the beach and swimming raft on his return to Pianosa on the mail run, inadvertently slicing Kid Sampson in two just above the trunk and spattering the bathers with Sampson's blood and gore.

This selective jumble of paradox and non sequitur creates a tonality heard by one critic as "pitched in the key of bitterly exuberant farce." [22] The novel is no traditional surrealist private fantasy. Men laugh and die. Colonel Cathcart orders the chaplain to hold group prayers before missions so he can gain favorable publicity in the States. Men fall into the quiet blue Mediterranean and die. Captain Aardvaark rapes an Italian girl and throws her out the window to die; Yossarian is arrested in the same room for being AWOL. Social surrealism in modern fiction is a rhetorical strategy forged to embrace and convey a sense of the Absurd, the grotesque disrelations, and the collective violence of our world.

Midway Through Life's Journey, He Fell Waking into Catch-22

To Leibnitz and the deists of the Enlightenment, the universe was a wondrously rational, smoothly running machine operating by a set of natural laws; to Goethe and the poets of the Romantic Movement, the universal principle was life, growth, and organic unfolding; to modern writers such as Joseph Heller, the universe is Catch-22, and Catch-22 is "the universe's enigmatic and immensely cruel joke: the cosmic catch, the given steel trap

---

[22] John Wain, "A New Novel About Old Troubles," *Critical Quarterly*, V, 2 (Summer, 1963), 168.

in human affairs." [23] Since Heller's method is grounded in defensive laughter, however, Catch-22 is tragicomic; it designates both human folly at which we can laugh and human suffering before which we can only shudder. Yossarian's first encounter with Catch-22 is simply a warning; it brushes past him in basic training. Yet he knows the ultimate enemy is the Absurd which, somewhat like Schopenhauer's will, manifests itself in the world and in human form. Before Clevinger's court-martial in basic training, Yossarian had tried to warn him about military logic:

> "You haven't got a chance, kid," he had told him glumly. "They hate Jews."
> "But I'm not Jewish," answered Clevinger.
> "It will make no difference," Yossarian promised, and Yossarian
> was right. "They're after everybody."
> Clevinger recoiled from their hatred as though from a blinding light. These
> three men who hated him spoke his language and wore his uniform, but
> he saw their loveless faces set immutably into cramped, mean lines of
> hostility and understood instantly that nowhere in the world,
> not in all the fascist tanks or planes or submarines . . . not even among all
> the expert gunners of the crack Hermann Goering Antiaircraft Division
> or among the grisly connivers in all the beer halls in Munich and
> everywhere else, were there men who hated him more (p. 83).

Clevinger—and Yossarian—have momentarily glanced behind the mask of Catch-22. Later, Catch-22 appears only as a manifestation of military logic. Doc Daneeka initiates Yossarian into this mystery when he tells Yossarian he can't ground Orr because Orr is crazy. Catch-22's metaphysical symmetry embraces all the paradoxes of human reason and behavior. It merely

> specified that a concern for one's own safety in the face of dangers that
> were real and immediate was the process of a rational mind. Orr was
> crazy and could be grounded. All he had to do was ask; and as soon as he
> did, he would no longer be crazy and would have to fly more missions. Orr
> would be crazy to fly more missions and sane if he didn't, but if he was
> sane he had to fly them. If he flew them he was crazy and didn't
> have to; but if he didn't want to he was sane and had to. Yossarian was moved
> very deeply by the absolute simplicity of this clause of Catch-22 and
> let out a respectful whistle.
> "That's some catch, that Catch-22," he observed.
> "It's the best there is," Doc Daneeka agreed (p. 47).

---

[23] R. W. B. Lewis, "Days of Wrath and Laughter," Trials of the Word (New Haven, 1965), p. 227.

Here it is a military regulation, yet the universal possibilities are clearly suggested. By Heller's method of extension, Catch-22 comes to designate all absurdity, therefore, from human to cosmic. Even the old woman in the house invaded by the MP's in Rome refers to Catch-22. " 'Catch-22,' the old woman repeated, rocking her head up and down. 'Catch-22. Catch-22 says that they have a right to do anything we can't stop them from doing' " (p. 416). When Yossarian asks her if the Army had read the law to her, she replies that the law says they don't have to. " 'What law says they don't have to?' 'Catch-22.' " Yossarian tries to puzzle it out: "Catch-22 did not exist, he was positive of that, but it made no difference. What did matter was that everyone thought it existed, and that was much worse, for there was no object or text to ridicule or refute, to accuse, criticize, attack, amend, hate, revile, spit at, rip to shreds, trample upon or burn up." (p. 418)

Ultimately Yossarian is initiated into the Absurd death mysteries of Catch-22; as the term implies, there is no *escape*. To be human and mortal is to be caught—and helpless. Yossarian had tried to comfort the horribly wounded Snowden. One facet of the event recurringly haunts Yossarian—Snowden's faint, repeated whimper "I'm cold. I'm cold." When Snowden's entrails spilled out on Yossarian and on the plane floor, Yossarian, in a variation on Homeric divination,

gazed down despondently at the grim secret Snowden had spilled all over the messy floor. It was easy to read the message in his entrails. Man was matter, that was Snowden's secret. Drop him out a window and he'll fall. Set fire to him and he'll burn. Bury him and he'll rot like other kinds of garbage. The spirit gone, man is garbage. That was Snowden's secret. Ripeness was all (p. 450).

The initiation is completed. Yossarian's world is circumscribed by Catch-22, from military regulations to Snowden's death. Earlier, while in a state of anesthetic delirium in the hospital, he told a Colonel MD he was "born on a battlefield . . . in a state of innocence" (p. 440). Theme and technique unify as Catch-22 grows before our eyes like a cancer. The oblique narrative presses this malignancy upon us. As the novel progresses, Catch-22 enlarges, the soldier in white reappears in more detail, Snowden's death is more fully explained, and all of Yossarian's travels have culminated in the surrealist, apocalyptic journey through what is described in black humor as the "Eternal City" (Chapter 39).

Catch-22 itself draws together, then, the radical juxtaposition of absurd humor and Absurd tragedy. It prevents even a rational presentation of the world in ordered terms. Norman Mailer puts it this way: "The crisis of reason is that it can no longer comprehend the modern world. Heller demonstrates that a rational man devoted to reason must arrive at the conclusion that either the world is mad and he is the only sane man in it, or . . . the sane man is not really sane because his rational propositions are without existential reason." [24]

Alan Cheuse

Laughing on the Outside

The shock of the news that a novel we care about has gone into production as a film is something like the pain we feel upon hearing that our first girl friend is getting married to some joker we know in our bones can only lead her to ruination.* If it is only a novel we flirted with that has been seduced by a yokel with lots of cash we move quickly from sadness to the harsh business of pointing out that even while we enjoyed her she possessed those qualities which led to her bad end. If it was not the way she saw the world, her ideas about life, then it might have been the way she dressed or the way she spoke or the way she wore her hair which seems so disagreeable now. Somehow, with the news of her new union, all those annoying traits, to which we had so readily acquiesced in order to take our pleasure, become clear.

Now that Joseph Heller's famous *Catch-22* has been turned over to Hollywood those of us who were cajoled into agreement about the book by chuckling veterans and drooling reviewers have a second chance, like Yossarian, the novel's mythic protagonist who was unsure about his target on the first bomb-run over the bridge at Ferrara and went back a second time to blow it up, to express our doubts about the novel before the touts of Hollywood hawk it as the Most Best Fillum Yet, and the memory of the book settles comfortably in our minds as another of those Great novels we will have to come back to some day.

Since most of the novels we respect have gone through the Hollywood

---

[24] "Some Children of the Goddess," *op. cit.*, pp. 14–15.

SOURCE: *Studies on the Left*, Vol. 3 (Fall 1963), pp. 81–87. Reprinted by permission of the author.

* Cheuse refers to the original sale of the movie rights to *Catch-22* to Columbia, which planned to have Richard Brooks direct the film. Paramount later bought the rights and eventually Mike Nichols directed. For details, see "On Translating *Catch-22* into a Movie," pp. 346–362 in this book.—Eds.

machine and emerged minus their heart, head and balls, it may seem illogical to argue that the novel is a bad one because it has been chosen to be immortalized on film. It does, however, have an especially good chance of becoming a real stinker of a movie since the director is Richard Brooks, the man who made *The Robe*, and if one may take the chance to cast a dissenting vote alongside the yeas of the mixed grill of Heller partisans (Nelson Algren, James Jones, [81] Robert Brustein of the *New Republic*, Orville Prescott of the *N. Y. Times*) it must be said that Heller has tied the noose around his novel with his own hand. Not because he has signed away the film rights, but, rather, because his book, beneath the tough, flashy comic mask, is a truly sentimental novel.

What greater cause than Humanity, the real hero of the novel lurking behind the empty, paste-up figure of Yossarian (who has no past, no family, no vocation except that of a seeing-eye dog for the reader in the blind-mad world Heller has concocted), could have prompted such a grotesque popular front as Norman Mailer and Orville Prescott, both of whom agree that this is a book for the ages? Another reading of the novel, admittedly with much malice aforethought, resulted in the discovery of a flaw which must have engendered the spiritual collusion between Algren *et al*, ex-flier Ernest K. Gann ("Wonderful. The finest piece of hilarious satire I have ever read.") and the man who filmed that forgettable history of the early Christian Church by Lloyd C. Douglas. Sadly, one discovered that the strain of sentimentalism on the part of the author is as deep and destructive to the novel as his artist's sense of construction is right.

Because of the humor and because Heller is in control of his characters (and cunningly, rather than artfully, withholds the revelation of the key scene until late in the work) it is easy and, at times, a pleasure to be fooled by this novel. There is much rich confusion and comedy to keep us from noticing, at least the first time around, the clanking of his philosophical machinery and the unattractiveness of his prose. Unlike the modern "war" novels which have stayed with us—*The Naked and the Dead, From Here to Eternity, The Gallery*—Heller's book is not in the realist tradition. His ideas do not rise out of the action of the book as those of Mailer, Jones and John Horn Burns *seem* to do, allowing the reader to assign moral value to seemingly natural actions of characters he accepts in his imagination as real people. Most of Heller's characters are prejudged, and fiercely so, in a grand satiric manner; because of the nature of the themes and characters satirized—the war, the military power-elite—we find ourselves on Heller's side despite a serious drawback to the comedy, the purportedly pathetic undercurrent of the threat of senseless death.

The book fails as coherent fiction at the intersection of the comic and the tragic, precisely in the area where its heart lies. For, with the exception of one scene, "The Cellar," the reader can only abstract from the novel the idea that the comedy and the pathos should be complementary. The air base on an imaginary island off the coast of Italy with its insane bomber squadron is reminiscent of Swift's Laputa, an isle floating in the clouds, fueled by the folly and desperation of the world below. But where Swift's satire grows fiercer with each new scene, the initial force of Heller's satire is dissipated by the intrusion of his sentimental attitude toward life, grinding the fiction to a halt and revealing a visionary island raised [82] up only on stilts. One way of seeing this is through his prose.

Most of the novel is a series of comic incidents involving Yossarian's efforts to avoid flying more bombing missions to the mainland, and these incidents almost always turn into a kind of *pas de deux* for two madmen. Here is Yossarian and the company doctor on Catch-22:

> "You're wasting your time," Doc Daneeka was forced to tell him.
> "Can't you ground someone who's crazy?"
> "Oh, sure. I have to. There's a rule saying I have to ground anyone who's crazy."
> "Then why don't you ground me? I'm crazy. Ask Clevinger."
> "Clevinger? Where *is* Clevinger? You find Clevinger and I'll ask him."
> "Then ask any of the others. They'll tell you how crazy I am."
> "They're crazy."
> "Then why don't you ground them?"
> "Why don't they ask me to ground them?"
> "Because they're crazy, that's why?"
> "Of course they're crazy," Doc Daneeka replied. "I just told you they're crazy, didn't I? And you can't let crazy people decide whether you're crazy or not, can you?"

The language is simple and direct. Heller has drawn the speech of two simple men and melded it into a conversation imitating the rhythm of the entire novel—simple honesty butting up against the deadly logic of total power. If there is an explanation for what makes us laugh with these verbal merry-go-rounds, it is the hopeless repetition of the simple plea and its continual refutation by power which leads us on to the point where we think change is possible and then slaps us back. The above conversation is, I think, a fair sample of the kind of verbal humor most prevalent in the novel. Here is its conclusion:

> Yossarian looked at him soberly and tried another approach. "Is Orr crazy?"
> "He sure is," Doc Daneeka said.
> "Can you ground him?"
> "I sure can. But first he has to ask me to. That's part of the rule."

"Then why doesn't he ask you to?"

"Because he's crazy," Doc Daneeka said. "He has to be crazy to keep fly-ing combat missions after all the close calls he's had. Sure, I can ground Orr. But first he has to ask me to."

"That's all he has to do to be grounded?"

"That's all. Let him ask me."

"And then you can ground him?" Yossarian asked.

"No. Then I can't ground him."

"You mean there's a catch?"

"Sure there's a catch," Doc Daneeka replied. "Catch-22. Anyone who wants to get out of combat duty isn't really crazy."

This flat tone, along with the absurd extension of normal conversation, is prevalent throughout the novel:

The middle-aged big shots would not let Nately's whore leave until they made her say uncle.

"Say uncle," they said to her.

"Uncle," she said.

"No, no. Say uncle."

"Uncle," she said.

"She still doesn't understand."

"You still don't understand, do you? We can't really make you say uncle unless you don't want to say uncle. Don't you see? Don't say uncle when I tell you to say uncle. Okay? Say uncle."

"Uncle," she said.

"No, don't say uncle. Say uncle."

She didn't say uncle.

"That's good!"

"That's very good."

"It's a start. Now say uncle."

"Uncle," she said.

"It's no good."

"No, it's no good that way either. She just isn't impressed with us. There's just no fun making her say uncle when she doesn't care whether [83] we make her say uncle or not."

"No, she really doesn't care, does she? Say 'foot.' "

"Foot."

"You see? She doesn't care about anything we do. She doesn't care about us. We don't mean a thing to you, do we?"

"Uncle," she said.

Humorous? Yes, and these small sequences hold up upon a second and further readings. Accompanying this kind of humor are many comic set-pieces—the briefing room before a bomb-run, the officers' club, the trips to Rome—and character sketches in which the routine of the air base and the men in power are brutally satirized. The best of these narratives, the most sustained ironic writing in the novel, describes the rise to power of Milo Minderbinder, a mess-hall officer, who builds a vast trading empire in both the allied and enemy camps. The action of his ascent—he creates an illusory corporation in which every man has a "share," and even bombs his own airfield when the Germans give him a good price for it—is an analogue for the verbal humor in which any one word, item, or action may take on total power and rule the rhythm or the plot under the aegis of the totalitarian contract, Catch-22. As Heller describes the pennants won by the best marching squadron:

Like Olympic medals and tennis trophies, all they signified was that the owner had done something of no benefit to anyone more capably than everyone else.

The war, the army, the world of Catch-22, is *completement fou*. Heller tries to enhance this idea by describing the world in terms of what he calls "modern art," which seems to be a mixture of surrealist and cubist techniques: Clevinger "looked to Yossarian like one of those people hanging around modern museums with both eyes together on one side of a face"; and "Milo had a long, thin nose with sniffing, damp nostrils heading sharply off to the right, always pointing away from where the rest of him was looking"; and, "The words on the blue neon sign surprised him mildly for only an instant. Nothing warped seemed bizarre any more in his strange, distorted surroundings. The tops of the sheer buildings slanted in weird, surrealistic perspective, and the street seemed tilted." When Yossarian begins to understand Catch-22, in all its "spinning reasonableness," he sees

an elliptical precision about its perfect pairs of parts that was graceful and shocking, like good modern art, and at times Yossarian wasn't quite sure that he saw it all, just the way he was never quite sure about good modern art.

Heller's theme is simple: the only road to sanity leads out of the mad world of war and Yossarian, when his creator considers the madness sufficiently described, is made to seek a separate peace. Yossarian's personal rebellion is not a new theme but, because of the slapstick presentation, it seems new. Yet just as Yossarian is not "quite sure about good modern art," Heller is never quite sure of his language.

When he is not building a comic scene, by sentence after sentence of flat conversation, funny in its total composition, when he is not satirizing an outlandishly patriotic colonel or an avaricious junior officer, [84] the prose seems forced and unnatural to the action. In describing physical action he becomes wordy, uses adjectives excessively ("Everyone ran in a sluggish stampede, shooting tortured, horrified glances back, filling the shadowy, rustling woods with their frail gasps and cries."), when people are not described as figures done by Picasso or Léger the prose teeters on the edge of cliché ("She would have been perfect for Yossarian, a debauched, coarse, vulgar, amoral, appetizing slattern . . ."), and the large word is used when the small word might have served ("a chaotic bus depot . . . echoing with the snarling vituperations of unshaven bus drivers . . .").

There was only one catch and that was Catch-22, which specified that a concern for one's own safety in the face of dangers that were real and immediate was the process of a rational mind. Orr was crazy and could be grounded. All he had to do was ask; and as soon as he did, he would no longer be crazy and would have to fly more missions. Orr would be crazy to fly more missions and sane if he didn't, but if he was sane he had to fly them. If he flew them he was crazy and didn't have to; but if he didn't want to he was sane and had to. Yossarian was moved very deeply by the absolute sincerity of this clause of Catch-22 and he let out a respectful whistle.

Something of the madness of the conversational humor still lingers in this flatly worded descriptive paragraph because of the manner in which the sentences lash back upon themselves, emblematic of the paradoxical Catch-22. The combat sequences are less interesting since the humor is replaced by Heller's great concern for Man in war:

The B-25s they flew in were stable, dependable, dull-green ships with twin rudders and engines and wide wings. Their single fault, from where Yossarian sat as a bombardier, was the tight crawlway separating the bombardier's compartment in the plexiglass nose from the nearest escape hatch. The crawlway was a narrow, square, cold tunnel hollowed out beneath the flight controls, and a large man like Yossarian could squeeze through only with difficulty. . . . There was a time of tension then, a time of waiting with nothing to hear and nothing to see and nothing to do but wait as the antiaircraft guns below took aim and made ready to knock them all sprawling into infinite sleep if they could.

Late in the novel, after the death of Yossarian's friend Nately, a death brought about by the catch which says he must fly as many missions as the colonel wills him to, Yossarian returns to Rome to bring the news to Nately's girl, a stoic streetwalker. When he sees the city this time it is not as a pleasure-palace for airmen on leave but, tempered by his mission, the city is viewed as morally shattered, not "appetizing," anymore, but rather, merely "debauched, coarse, vulgar and amoral." In a key passage which is there to prepare for his final decision to desert he thinks a sermon at us which reads, for all its sentiment, like a sixth-grade pamphlet on irony:

What a lousy earth! He wondered how many people were destitute that same night even in his own prosperous country, how many homes were shanties, how many husbands drunk and wives socked, and how many children were bullied, abused or abandoned. How many families hungered for food they could not afford to buy? How many hearts were broken? How many suicides would take place that same night, how many people would go insane? How many [85] cockroaches and landlords would triumph? How many winners were losers, successes failures, rich men poor men? How many wise guys were stupid? How many honest men were liars, brave men cowards, loyal men traitors, how many sainted men were corrupt, how many people in positions of trust had sold their souls to blackguards for petty cash, how many never had souls? How many happy endings had unhappy endings? How many straight-and-narrow paths were crooked paths? How many best families were worst families and how many good people were bad people? When you added them all up and then subtracted, you might be left with only the children, and perhaps with Albert Einstein and an old violinist or sculptor somewhere. Yossarian walked in lonely torture, feeling estranged.

Sad that, in a novel so passionate and brilliantly comic about the ideas and people whom he detests, the author is unable to write eloquently, or even passing fair, outside of the comic scenes. However much we care about the ideas presented in a novel we must be *made* to care through the art of the fiction. When Heller writes so naively and so poorly that the ideas upon which the novel depends read almost like parody it is difficult to care about his novel. He is *so* sincere that he trips over his own prose and the novel falls with him.

Take, for instance, the characterization of the chaplain, one of the few whom Heller *consciously* declines to ravage with his satire:

It was already some time since the chaplain had first begun wondering what everything was all about. Was there a God? How could he be sure? Being an Anabaptist minister in the American Army was difficult enough under the best of circumstances; without dogma, it was almost impossible. . . .
Doubts of such kind gnawed at the chaplain's lean, suffering frame insatiably. *Was* there a single true faith, or a life after death? How many angels *could* dance on the head of a pin, and with what matters *did* God occupy himself in all the infinite aeons before the Creation? Why *was* it necessary to put a protective seal on the brow of Cain if there *were* no other people to protect him from? *Did* Adam and Eve produce daughters? These were the great, complex questions of ontology that tormented him. Yet they never seemed

nearly as crucial to him as the question of kindness and good manners. He was pinched perspiringly in the epistemological dilemma of the skeptic, unable to accept solutions to the problems he was unwilling to dismiss as unsolvable. He was never without misery, and never without hope.

Besides all this, we are told he missed his wife and children; he blushes when he thinks about sleeping with his wife.

Just as in the combat scenes, he cannot find a prose to handle the pathos; when he deals with the above character, and others (Orr, Nately, Luciana) for whom he feels compassion, he can never free himself from the bounds of satire. He can destroy, but when he offers something in place of that which he destroys his prose becomes limp and pedestrian, generated by a position of affirmation which comes from *outside* the characters and the action, a sentimental affirmation.

To get his man Yossarian out of the war Heller concocts an existential "secret," a pithy philosophical nugget he had been holding back from Yossarian and the reader for almost the entire length of the novel:

Yossarian was cold, too, and shivering uncontrollably. He felt goose pimples clacking all over him as he gazed down despondently at the grim [86] secret Snowden had spilled all over the messy floor [of the plane]. It was easy to read that message in his entrails. Man was matter, that was Snowden's secret. Drop him out a window and he'll fall. Set fire to him and he'll burn. Bury him and he'll rot, like other kinds of garbage. The spirit gone, man is garbage. That was Snowden's secret. Ripeness was all.

This "secret" is Yossarian's escape clause from Catch-22 and the novel ends shortly afterwards with his decision to desert the air force and try to make his way to a neutral country. Sorry to say it, but the prose reads like those pamphlets we find in model airplane kits; only the subject matter is different.

Heller tips his hat to Sartre at the conclusion of the novel: Yossarian, like Orestes in the last scene of *The Flies*, is escaping *into* responsibility, pursued by Nately's whore, a furious young lady who is out to get him with a knife (her man has died, we are supposed to assume, because of Yossarian's indifference). But Heller's allegiance is only superficially aligned with existential thought; he would have used any means to get Yossarian out of the war. He tipped his hand on the first page of the novel with Yossarian's "love at first sight" for the chaplain, and once we know where his heart lies we can see that lurking beneath the abundant comedy is not pathos, but overbearing sentimentality voiced in dull, dull prose—which will soon appear in cartoon form in our neighborhood movie houses. [87]

Eric Solomon
From Christ in Flanders to 'Catch-22':
An Approach to War Fiction

Simone Weil in her brilliant study "The Iliad, or the Poem of Force" perceives that violence "obliterates anybody who feels its touch. It comes to seem just as external to its employer as to its victim." In a world of despair and destruction the only possibility of relief is spiritual: "A monotonous desolation would result were it not for those few luminous moments scattered here and there throughout the poem, those brief, celestial moments in which man possesses his soul." For Homer and for Joseph Heller, for the sublime and for the ridiculous, for the epic and for the mock epic, the idea of war has yoked together black illogic with a gleam of religious hope.

Joseph Heller's Catch-22, published in 1961, sixteen years after the end of the World War II the book delineates and ridicules, culminates a tradition of bitterly ironic war fiction. In Catch-22 the major elements common to nearly all war fiction are presented and mocked. Like the Fabrizio of Stendhal's The Charterhouse of Parma, Heller's Yossarian loses his innocence through attempts to comprehend the madness of battle; like the Pierre of Tolstoy's War and Peace, Heller's protagonist discovers the cruelty of death in battle; and like the Frederick Henry of Hemingway's A Farewell to Arms, Yossarian makes his separate peace. What makes Catch-22 differ from its twentieth-century predecessors, with the possible exception of The Good Soldier Schweik, is its coruscating humor. And paradoxically this wild laughter makes Heller's novel even more despairing than the work of his contemporaries who have written about war in our time—than Norman Mailer and Irwin Shaw, than John Ashmead and Van Van Praag, than James Jones and John Hersey.

While Catch-22 is funny, the humor, as Philip Toynbee has remarked, resembles the script of a Marx brothers film as it might have been written by Kafka. The novel's mood is apocalyptic, in the tradition documented by R. W. B. Lewis in his "Days of Wrath and Laughter"; "the perpetual and lunatic Armageddon of Catch-22" is close to the despair of American

SOURCE: Texas Studies in Literature and Language, Vol. 11, No. 1 (Spring 1969), pp. 851–866. Reprinted by permission of the author and publisher.

novelists of hopelessness such as Mark Twain and [851] Nathanael West. Heller's work is distinguished, however, by its final possibility of faith, what I can only call a Christian ethic, inverted perhaps, but still Christian. Here, Heller approaches the mode of World War I writing, the mixture of appalled disbelief and intransigent nostalgia. But *Catch-22* is a reduction of World War I tone and style, just as the second war seemed less artistically controllable and, to some, more morally confusing in its final stages. [852]

. . .

From my mother's sleep I fell into the State,
And I hunched in its belly till my wet fur froze.
Six miles from earth, loosed from its dream of life,
I woke to black flak and the nightmare fighters.
When I died they washed me out of the turret with a hose.

RANDALL JARRELL, *The Death of the Ball Turret Gunner*

The nature of *Catch-22* defies easy critical categories. The idea of a comic war novel is in itself paradoxical, and Heller's willful distortions of time and structure as well as his buckshot approach to political and social satire cover his tracks as serious novelist. He has admitted that *Catch-22* is "about the contemporary regimented business society," and the novel does take on most of the contemporary targets of black humorists. Heller mocks and inverts business ethics in his broad satiric attacks on the venal mess officer, Milo Minderbinder, who cheats and steals to the obsessive motto "What's good for M & M Enterprises is good for the country"—even to the extent of bombing his own men and stealing morphine from their kits. Heller sustains broad satiric attacks on oil claims, public relations, psychiatry, racism, loyalty oaths, and security trials; he employs the military setting to scoff at American pseudo ideals of sportsmanship, success, patriotism, and morality. Indeed, his parodic technique is finally aimed at the Protestant Ethic and the American Dream themselves.

The method of Heller's fiction, however, is not only that of heavy, broad American satire similar to that employed, say, by Mark Twain [859] in *The Gilded Age* or Ring Lardner in *The Big Town*. Heller appropriately casts his novel in the tone of G.I. Humor, the exaggerated, despairing, self-mocking humor best associated with the cartoons of Bill Mauldin. Yossarian's credo becomes one of the set phrases of the G.I., "When in doubt —bug out." He is in doubt about a war that seems aimed at him (the normal military paranoia, perhaps), but he stays with this war until it is nearly over, until victory is assured, flying more missions, after all, than any of his fellow pilots. Yossarian bugs out of the power structure, controlled by the self-serving, personally ambitious war leaders that would kill him for their own profit. Toward the end of his experience with military expediency and chicanery, Yossarian makes the distinction that protagonists of war fiction from Dos Passos through Faulkner insist upon: " 'What have you and Colonel Cathcart got to do with my country? You're not the same.' "

Heller writes of war in the available rhetoric of contemporary philosophy. The problems of time, identity, phenomenology, alienation, and, above all, illogic provide his intellectual framework. The novel has been called immoral * because, unlike most of his predecessors in the tradition of war fiction, Joseph Heller ordinarily makes us laugh where our expectations call for tears. His view is that war forces an absurd world; thus in revolting against what *is* revolting, in the Swiftian agony, macabre exaggeration turns pathos to humor. Therefore, even though the novel fits its broad range of characters into Dantesque circles of rage and despair, their evil or loss is sardonic not tragic.

Heller shows four types of characters. There are the purely corrupt, ambitious men who use their fellow humans: Cathcart and Korn, Dreedle and Peckem, Cargill, Scheisskopf, Black, Whitcomb, Aarfy. At the opposite end of the spectrum are the outsiders, good men caught and for the most part destroyed by the system—Nately, Chief White Halfoat, Hungry Joe, McWatt, Danby, the chaplain. Yossarian is at once of them and above them, for in his ultimate revolt he becomes their leader and, by refusing to fly any more missions, saves the remnant. But he can only save a few, like the chaplain and Major Danby, for Yossarian knows just how many death has undone: " 'They've got all my pals, haven't they?' " The third group of characters are predators also, but they are so outrageously comic, and largely aware of their rapacity, that they are less than evil: Milo, Wintergreen, Doc Daneeka, even Clevinger, Major Major Major and Major ——— de Coverley. The fourth category carries the novel's most profound meaning; these are the dead who never were alive in the pages of the book: the unknown soldier named Mudd who is doomed to anonymity since he was killed before his name was officially on the roster, yet who had time to leave his [860] equipment, his identity, in Yossarian's tent ("Yossarian knew exactly who Mudd was. Mudd was the unknown soldier who had never had a chance, for that was the only thing anyone ever did know about all the unknown soldiers—they never had a chance. They had to be dead."); Kraft, whom Yossarian kills in the second bombing run that earns him a medal; Snowden, whose death in Yossarian's arms over Avignon is referred to again and again in the novel as raising the overwhelming eschatological question answered at the book's close. All these missing characters are summed up in the invisible soldier, swathed in bandages and fed intravenously—who may not exist at all. Lastly, there is Orr, Yossarian's little

---

* In "A Review: *Catch-22*," pp. 27–39 in this book.—Eds.

roommate, the accident-prone pilot who fits into no category. He, too, poses a major question—why he stuffs chestnuts in his cheeks—and, again, when Yossarian can answer he will know what is truth and need neither wait nor jest.

As the humor turns to horror within the novel's rhythm, we should notice the second part of Heller's own statement about *Catch-22* quoted above. He writes about contemporary business society, to be sure, but it is "depicted against the background of universal sorrow and inevitable death." In the manner of an earlier war's great novels, *Catch-22*, I would argue, is seriously religious.

Chaplain Tappman represents official religion. He is a good man who is, however, both ineffective and victimized. The novel opens and closes with confrontations in the hospital between Yossarian and the chaplain. At the start the chaplain is confused by the bombardier's attempts to avoid combat; at the end he actively assists Yossarian's flight to freedom. Between these two events the saintly chaplain has his faith shaken by the realization that only lies can save him, by his exile into the wilderness in a tent, by his confrontation with Colonel Cathcart's attempt to use public prayers for a tight bomb pattern as a way of getting publicity in the *Saturday Evening Post* (a plan that is dropped only when the colonel realizes that officers and enlisted men, according to the chaplain, pray to the same God), and by his trial and persecution as a subversive. Although the chaplain wants to uphold his Anabaptist faith, the antireligion of victims like Dunbar shakes his belief. Dunbar can calmly remark, " 'There is no God,' " or hold the views that God has forgotten about men, or is simply resting. For the chaplain, after Dunbar has disappeared and Sampson and Nately have been killed, despair and a sense of responsibility for others' deaths are overwhelming. He is saved by Yossarian, whom earlier the chaplain felt he had met, somewhere, and whom the chaplain mistakes for Christ in a comic vision when Yossarian perches naked in a tree.

Heller carefully prepares the way for the concept that Yossarian must [861] be considered a version of Christ. Like Faulkner's Joe Christmas or Silone's Pietro Spina, Yossarian is, of course, a mock Christ, corrupt, self-serving, sexually amoral. Yet he is fighting for life. In his early military career, Yossarian is sufficiently naïve to believe that "God was on his side, he had been told, and God, he had also been told, could do whatever He wanted to." By the time that he has taken upon himself the guilt for Kraft's death, the death that brings Yossarian the Distinguished Flying Cross, he has become the "nemesis" to the anti-Christ Colonel Cathcart: ". . . perhaps there were not really three Yossarians but only two Yossarians, or maybe even one Yossarian. . . ." In his trinitarian role Yossarian no longer heeds the chaplain's advice to trust in God; he becomes for Dobbs, who wants to murder Colonel Cathcart, a God figure, for Dobbs cannot kill without Yossarian's permission. Yossarian is wounded in the groin, he opposes social wrongs—" 'Misery depresses you. Ignorance depresses you. Violence depresses you. Slums . . . Greed . . . Crime . . . Corruption depresses you.' "—but, most important, he fights death: "Death was irreversible, he suspected, and he began to think he was going to lose."

Joseph Heller makes explicit the relation of his mock hero to a mock Christ. The key to Yossarian's identification is the death of Snowden, an event that counterpoints the entire narrative and that is finally described in detail toward the book's end. There is both a comic and a tragic version of Snowden's influence on Yossarian. Revolted by the fact that the guts of the dying man have been splattered all over Yossarian's uniform, he refuses to wear any clothes at all. During Snowden's funeral Yossarian sits naked in a tree and observes the ceremony. Milo Minderbinder—the moneylender, the pagan god ("Milo was the corn god, the rain god and the rice god . . . deep inside the jungles of Africa . . . large graven images of his mustached face could be found overlooking primitive stone altars red with human blood . . .")—tries to tempt Yossarian to return to uniform, to war, and to believe in Milo's magic that would transubstantiate cotton into candy. Yossarian is quite conscious that "with Snowden smeared abundantly all over his bare heels and toes, knees, arms and fingers," someone must redeem this death. To Milo the tree is a chestnut tree, to Yossarian it is a cross: " 'It's the tree of life . . . and of knowledge of good and evil, too.' " Yossarian who has already been bound to the crosslike plane—with his suffering apparently renewed eternally as the missions continue to be extended—has had his normative faith in man's immortality destroyed over Avignon, the city where Christianity suffered its grave doubts as two Popes struggled for power, in the manner of generals Dreedle and Peckem.

The evil General Dreedle, naturally, does not recognize the naked [862] Yossarian when he gets his medal, but the good chaplain, seeking direction, looks up from Snowden's bier and turns Yossarian and Milo into a mythic vision of Christ and Satan. Already convinced that he had met Yossarian before, on an occasion "momentous and occult," and guilty because he has denied him recently and always, "in some remote, submerged, and perhaps even entirely spiritual epoch in which he had made the identical, foredooming admission that there was nothing, absolutely nothing, he could do to help him," the chaplain views Yossarian in the tree and distorts Yossarian into Jesus. "An Angel from heaven or a minion from hell? . . . two men, actually, since the first had been joined shortly by a second man clad in a brown mustache and sinister dark garments from head to toe who bent forward ritualistically along the limb of the tree to offer the first man something to drink from a brown goblet. . . ."

The chaplain's vision of Yossarian is comic and absurd. Yossarian's vision of the wounded and dying Snowden is tragic and obsessive. Yossarian pleads, " 'Oh, God! Oh, God, oh, God,' " and he tries to comprehend Snowden's secret, to read the message in his entrails. Snowden's words are hidden—" 'I'm cold' "—as is his wound. Yossarian bandages the thigh wound but misses the essential wound in Snowden's side. The novel culminates in horror as we finally learn what happened over Avignon in the last of the many references to the scene. We discover why Yossarian's question had no answer: " 'Where are the Snowdens of yesteryear?' " Snowden's insides slither onto the floor, and Yossarian watches the guts pour out in ghastly detail ("Here was God's plenty") and can hardly comfort the dying man with apples: " 'There, there,' Yossarian mumbled mechanically. . . ." He has a naturalistic interpretation of Snowden's secret, one typical of most negative war fiction. "Man was matter. . . . Drop him out a window and he'll fall. . . . Bury him and he'll rot like other kinds of garbage. The spirit gone, man is garbage."

Such a negative, solipsistic approach—"That was the secret Snowden had spilled to him on the mission to Avignon—they were out to get him" —fits the conception of Yossarian as alienated Everyman. He is trapped in a mad world of the seven deadly sins: Gluttony (the lavish food and drink in the mess halls), Avarice (Milo), Lechery (a world of brothels), Sloth (Doc Daneeka), Pride (the generals and colonels), Envy (their competition), and Wrath (the war itself). To save himself as well as others, he must go through his dark night of the soul to discover not only others' responsibility for his plight but his own guilt.

The dark ending of *Catch-22* is not really a mood change from the wild humor of most of the book, for the ideas of death and of Yossarian [863] as ineffective scapegoat-rebel pervade the novel. After the death of Nately, the innocent American boy type, Yossarian fails to comfort Nately's whore, just as he failed, using the same words, with Snowden. With his soul in jeopardy, Yossarian makes a hellish night journey through a blasted Rome. This harrowing of hell, as it were, discovers in the eternal city every conceivable kind of cruelty and inhumanity. But the Yossarian who wanders the unreal city streets is no longer simply afraid. He has been attacked by Nately's whore until he is "bleeding everywhere." He has reversed the military ethic by strapping on a gun and walking backwards to avoid ambush and flying more missions. Through his *non serviam* he has gained disciples; the men who previously shunned his antipatriotism now support his revolt, but only in the dark. When Yossarian flies to Rome, he accepts the blame for Nately's death, takes on the mantle of guilt. "Yossarian thought he knew why Nately's whore held him responsible for Nately's death and wanted to kill him. Why the hell shouldn't she? It was a man's world, and she and everyone younger had every right to blame him and everyone older for every unnatural tragedy that befell them. . . . Every victim was a culprit, every culprit a victim, and somebody had to stand up sometime ["A man could stand up"] to break the lousy chain of inherited habit that was imperiling them all."

Now as he wanders through the wrecked brothel, Yossarian understands the absurd military world ruled by Catch-22, the illogic of force that kills, destroys joy and life. "Catch-22 did not exist, he was positive of that, but it made no difference. What did matter was that everyone thought it existed, and that was much worse, for there was no object or text to ridicule or refute. . . ." In other words, Catch-22 does not exist, and Yossarian is its nonprophet. Yet such was the image the age of war demanded. For pages Heller takes Yossarian through a world of pain, populated by cold and hungry beggars, starving mothers, a soldier in convulsions, an intellectual hauled away by the police, a dog and later a child being beaten—all the Freudian nightmare images of our times. "The night was filled with horrors, and he thought he knew how Christ must have felt as he walked through the world. . . ." Death is not his obsession now—it passes by him in the form of a cowled monk, and he doesn't notice—the suffering, not just the absurdity of life, is his burden. Aarfy gratuitously commits murder, however, and Yossarian is arrested for lacking a pass; Catch-22, the absurd, is still operative.

The Cathcarts and Korns play out their Satanic roles. They tempt Yossarian, offering him safety—life—in return for his betrayal of his comrades-in-arms. And Yossarian is tempted to accept their offer, to go home quietly rather than continue his revolt publicly, to indicate that [864] acquiescence to power brings its own reward; he is saved from sin by the burden he previously accepted—when the knife of Nately's whore catches him in the side. In the hospital he sees no salvation. To accept the colonel's offer would be betrayal: " 'Christ, Chaplain! Can you imagine that for a sin? Saving Colonel Cathcart's life?' " Yossarian could not save Kraft, or Snowden, or Mudd, or Nately, or Hungry Joe, or Orr who drowned when his plane crashed, or Clevinger who disappeared into a cloud. Yossarian sees only the high command cashing in when he looks up, and he wants " 'heaven or saints or angels.' " Although " 'this is not World War I' " and these Germans are evil, his mission as defender of the faith should have been long since completed. The Christian paradox seems operable to Major Danby, who advises Yossarian to let them send him home, for the choices of vegetating in the hospital, flying more missions, or attempting to desert would surely lead to failure. Yossarian, for his part, realizes that acceptance of Catch-22 is doom: " 'It's a way to lose myself, Danby.' " He must save himself outside of the system in order to subvert it, or he will gain life at the expense of his soul. At the bleakest moment of "no hope at all," the chaplain bursts in with the news that saves—Orr lives. He has survived his plane crash and rowed in a tiny raft to Sweden. The chaplain

is convinced of divine intervention, " 'A miracle! I believe in God again.' "
Yossarian, however, believes in man.

He understands what Orr sought to tell him by the various parables. Orr
stuffed his cheeks with chestnuts to pretend to be something he was not;
he hired a whore to hit him on the head with her shoe to put him out of
combat; and, all else failing, he practiced crash-landing on each mission, he
learned how to use a raft—all to save himself. Orr the pragmatic tinker
follows the true American standard of self-reliance. The paradoxes culminate in his achievement of the Swedish heaven of rationality. Wise as
Lear's fool, he tries to be his brother's keeper, but while Yossarian can accept the gift of Orr's stove, the prospect of flying with a crash-prone pilot
eludes him, even when Orr "on both knees" tells Yossarian that the smart
move would be to fly with the little pilot. Yossarian's only response is,
" 'Are you trying to tell me something?' "

Orr tells him that, revers'ng the Christian paradox, in an anti-Christian
world of war, by saving yourself you *can* save your soul, and others. Previously Yossarian had emulated a dying soldier, in order to malinger in the
hospital, until "his talented roommate died, and Yossarian decided that he
had followed him far enough." His subsequent roommate is more talented
and can lead to life. Orr (the name is a pun on "rock") is the Peter who
understands about loaves and fishes better than his master. Like Huck
Finn, whom he resembles in many ways, [865] Orr improvises morality, is
ready to go to hell, and discovers heaven; baptized by the sea journey, having fallen to rise again, Orr provides the answers to all Yossarian's questions. One cannot retreat to the hospital (Dunbar) or to prayer (the chaplain) or to isolation (Major Major Major) or to self (Milo). A man must
prepare and endure, discover his own freedom without dehumanizing
others, accept his own guilt and his own grace. Then the world becomes
possibility, and even Clevinger may someday fly out alive from his cloud.
Man is only matter (to sustain the hospital image) if one accepts Catch-22.

Like the hero of Ralph Ellison's *Invisible Man*, Yossarian admits his
own humanity and jumps up from underground. He will go to Rome and
in the Eternal City suffer the little child, Nately's whore's sister, to come
unto him. After his frustrating tour of duty as prophet in a false world of
combat that wanted none but strange gods ("Why do ye not understand
my speech?"), Yossarian realizes that he must fight alone ("He who is not
with me is against me"). He runs *to* responsibility, leaps from the slough
of despond, having been washed in the blood of the lamblike Snowden
and crucified by the bombing missions ordered by a corrupted society. Like
Ignazio Silone's protagonist, who is not a saint but who is for liberty, Joseph
Heller's nonhero answers the question posed by a half century of war fiction
by ending Yossarian's World War II with the beginning of his war against
war. [866]

ON STRUCTURE

James L. MacDonald
I See Everything Twice!:
The Structure of Joseph Heller's
"Catch-22"

"I see everything twice!" today's college student scrawls on the last page of his bluebook to signify that he had a bad day. "You've got flies in your eyes," he mutters at the campus policeman or the dormitory prefect. "Where are the Snowdens of yesteryear?" he asks, referring to a friend who has flunked out, been drafted, or suddenly made the Dean's List after two years on probation.

The use of the quotations testifies to the impact *Catch-22* has made since its publication in paperback just over four years ago. Like *The Catcher in the Rye, Lord of the Flies,* and *A Separate Peace,* Joseph Heller's novel has become one of those books which college students take up as their own, from which they draw the slogans which are meaningful to them in relation to the established power structures they live under.

I suspect, however, that students admire *Catch-22* for the wrong reasons. Though the book is in tune with the restlessness and rebelliousness of the times, and though the "Catch Cult" rightly praises its black humor and

SOURCE: *University Review,* Vol. 34 (Spring 1968), pp. 175–180. Reprinted by permission of the publisher.

its anarchic (even pacifist) tendencies, it is not merely a book which reflects and forms current college opinion. It is a novel, and it seems time to discuss it as a novel: to examine, in some detail, its formal values.

On a first reading, *Catch-22*—switching its focus from one character to another, whirling crazily through a hodgepodge of slapstick antics, bizarre horrors, grotesque anecdotes, and aimless digressions—may well make the reader try to rub the flies out of his eyes and wonder where the Snowdens of yesteryear or any year fit in. But close analysis reveals that Heller is a highly sophisticated, conscious artist who carefully manipulates the diverse and seemingly divisive elements of the novel to achieve structural unity: that discernible pattern which gives the reader a firm sense of the time, place, and thematic relevance of each unit in the novel, so that he knows where he is at each point in relation to where he has been before.

Ironically, the reader's bewildered "I see everything twice!" provides the key to the relation of the parts to the whole, what Chaplain Tappman calls "*Déjà vu*": "For a few precarious seconds, the chaplain tingled with a weird, occult sensation of having experienced the identical situation before in some prior time or existence. He endeavored to trap and nourish the impression in order to predict, and perhaps even control, what incident would occur next, but the afflatus melted away unproductively, as he had known beforehand it would. *Déjà vu*. The subtle, recurring confusion between illusion and reality that was characteristic of paramnesia fascinated the chaplain, and he knew a number of things about it." [1]

This is a remarkably clear description [175] of the method Heller employs. Obviously, he is not dealing with this "characteristic of paramnesia" scientifically; but he is using the phenomenon as the basis of the novel's structure. Out of the welter of digressions, flashbacks, and anecdotes, he constructs his narrative and contrives thematic patterns so that the reader has the experience of seeing everything twice—the sensation which the chaplain calls "*Déjà vu.*"

"*Déjà vu*" is, first of all, an explanation of and a reason for Heller's narrative construction. An artificial chronology of the novel's action can be worked out: the action proper begins with Yossarian's training in Colorado; it proceeds through his combat missions over targets like Avignon and Bologna, and the death and disappearances of his comrades; it is marked by Milo Minderbinder's rise to power and the raising of the missions from forty to eighty; and it culminates in Yossarian's refusal to fly any more missions, his discovery of the real meaning of Catch-22, and his desertion.

The actual narrative, however, is not chronological. Heller—like Proust, Joyce, Virginia Woolf, and Faulkner—is the heir of Henri Bergson: he

---

[1] Joseph Heller, *Catch-22* (New York, 1962), p. 209. Subsequent references to this, the Dell edition, will appear in the text.

does not view time as something dependent on and made relevant by the artificial orderings of the clock or the calendar; rather he regards it as something governed and made tangible by the consciousness of the individual, his situation, and his memory. The past operates in the present by forming the individual's apprehension of the present, coloring and outlining each significant moment.

Thus Heller begins the novel in the middle of things, just beyond the mid-point of Yossarian's career as a bombardier when, in the hospital after flying forty-four of the required fifty missions, he meets the chaplain. From this point on, the action alternates between what happened before the opening of the novel, and what happens after it. Heller interweaves past and present, the past action continually crowding into the present. A character or situation in the present is outlined; then, through free association with some aspect of the character or situation, an event from the past, in the form of an anecdote, a digression, or a flashback, sweeps into and obliterates the present. This event, in turn, frequently merges with or flashes off to still another event. The past event, however, is seldom related as one complete, coherent unit. Rather the reader learns of it partially, in disjointed fragments: he has the "sensation of having experienced the identical situation before," the desire to "trap and nourish the impression," and the frustration of seeing "the afflatus" melt "away unproductively." Only tentatively and gradually can he reconstruct it, place it in relation to other events in time, and understand its significance.

The story of Snowden's death exemplifies Heller's technique. In Chapter Four, the reader learns the bare facts, that "Snowden had been killed over Avignon when Dobbs went crazy in mid-air and seized the controls away from Huple" (35–36); but then the account shifts to the intrigues of Colonels Cathcart and Korn. In the following chapter the incident is recalled, and the reader learns that Dobbs had broken radio silence with a plea to help Snowden, who lay dying in the back of the plane; but then the incident is dropped. It is not taken up again until [176] Chapter Twenty-One, where some of its significance is hinted at: during the story of how Yossarian stood naked to receive the Distinguished Flying Cross, Captain Wren explains that " 'A man was killed in his plane over Avignon last week and bled all over him. . . . He swears he's never going to wear a uniform again' " (223).

In the following chapter the reader discovers that "Yossarian lost his nerve on the mission to Avignon because Snowden lost his guts," hears Snowden's plaintive "I'm cold," and sees him "freezing to death in a yellow splash of sunlight near the new tail gunner lying stretched out on the floor . . . in a dead faint" (230–231); but again the account shifts, this time to the story of Dobbs' plan to murder Colonel Cathcart. In similar fashion, additional information about the death of Snowden is supplied in subsequent chapters. Not until the second-last chapter of the novel, however, is the whole story reconstructed. In the hospital, Yossarian—bathed in an "icy sweat" which reminds him of Snowden—recalls the entire event and remembers "Snowden's secret" that "Man was matter," that "the Spirit gone, man is garbage" (445–450).

One can describe the novel's overall construction, then, as an interplay between present narrative and the cumulative repetition and gradual clarification of past actions. The interplay portrays, dramatically, the manner in which the characters apprehend their world, and shows the impact of the past on their present attitudes and actions. Each moment in the present flashes their minds back to fragmentary images of past events which influence their behavior so heavily. The reader's gradual and partial realization of the nature and significance of past events matches those "weird . . . sensations" which the chaplain characterizes as *Déjà vu.*

Déjà vu further provides the basis for the method Heller uses to contrive the thematic patterns of the novel. He manipulates the characters, events, and situations into elaborate parallels which, through comparison and contrast, clarify and illustrate the novel's central themes. He thereby gives the reader the sensation of seeing everything at least twice, of "having experienced the identical situation before" because it parallels other situations or is related to others thematically.

Heller carefully sets two worlds in opposition to each other: the world of those in power, and the world of their victims. Revolving the action around that "subtle, recurring confusion between illusion and reality" which the chaplain notes, he centers the themes of the novel on the question of human identity. By a series of parallels, he clarifies the concerns and attitudes of both groups. Those in power attempt to succeed within an artificial system by adhering to its ethics, which reduce human beings to abstractions, statistics. Their victims attempt to preserve their identities by rebelling against the system—either through parody, or outright defiance.

The official attitude of those in power is outlined very clearly by the doctor who persuades Yossarian to pose for the parents of the dead Giuseppe as their son:

"They [the parents] didn't come to see me," Yossarian objected. "They came to see their son."

"They'll have to take what they can get. As far as we're concerned, one dying boy is just as good as any other, or just as bad. [177] To a scientist, all dying boys are equal" (187).

For "scientist" the reader might well substitute "bureaucrat" or "officer" (or "Scheisskopf," the name signifying the role of all officers), or simply "those in charge." This is the official attitude: those in charge view all human beings as "dying boys," statistics, means to an end. Employing the crews as their pawns, they wage a constant battle for position and glory. Heller illustrates the attitude by paralleling the motives and methods of the officials along the entire scale of army rank.

The novel is marked by a series of bids for power, which the reader sees again and again. At the highest level of rank is the struggle between Generals Dreedle and Peckem. Just below it is the rivalry between Colonels Cathcart and Korn, with Cathcart's ambitions epitomizing the irrationality and pedantry of those who attempt to rise in the system. Cathcart treats all crews—"dying boys"—alike: he raises their missions and volunteers the squadron for the most dangerous assignments, not to help win the war, but to attain glory and promotion. His letter of sympathy, in the jargon which marks all the official communiqués in the novel, typifies his attitude:

> Dear Mrs., Mr., Miss, or Mr. and Mrs. Daneeka: Words cannot express the deep personal grief I experienced when your husband, son, father or brother was killed, wounded or reported missing in action (354).

On a lower level there are Captain Black's loyalty oath crusade and the plots of the C.I.D. men. Finally there are Gus and Wes, who treat all patients alike, painting their gums and toes purple and forcing laxatives down their throats, regardless of the ailment. Triumphant over them all, of course, is Milo Minderbinder, whose Enterprises virtually make him ruler of the world, who regards whole armies as means to his end, impartially contracting to bomb both the Allies and the Axis for the profit of the syndicate.

The victims of the officials are bewildered and virtually helpless. They live in a world which, in keeping with the attitudes and actions of the officials, is irrational and inexplicable. As the warrant officer with malaria complains, " 'There just doesn't seem to be any logic to this system of rewards and punishment.' " (175)

There is no real logic within a system manipulated by those who have the right of Catch-22 which says " 'they have a right to do anything we can't stop them from doing.' " (416) Thus Major Major Major becomes, almost automatically, Major Major Major Major and, by official whim, is made squadron commander; the dutiful Major Metcalf is shipped to the Solomon Islands to bury bodies; Dunbar is "disappeared"; the patriotic Clevinger and the innocent Chaplain are ruthlessly interrogated; Chief White Halfoat is the victim of the government and the land-grabbers;

Yossarian is arrested for being in Rome without a pass while Aarfy, the murderer, goes free.[2]

All the dying men are treated alike and all men—in war—are dying. The dying, the dead, have no real identity—only official status. Death and life are merely matters of official routine: the question is decided, not through recourse to reality, but by reference to [178] official lists and records.

The parallel incidents involving the soldier in white, Mudd, and Doc Daneeka typify the predicament. It is impossible to tell whether the soldier in white is dying or dead: wrapped up in plaster and gauze like a mummy, he is no more than a helpless unidentifiable victim. Equally helpless are Mudd (whose name signifies his fate) and Doc Daneeka. Mudd, the dead man in Yossarian's tent, was killed in combat over Orvieto; but according to official army records he is alive because he never officially reported for duty. Doc Daneeka, in reality, is alive; but according to official lists he is dead because he was officially listed, though not really present, in the crew of the plane which McWatt flew into the mountain. Heller explicitly links the three victims, indicating the deliberate parallelism he sets up.

Yossarian complains that " 'Anybody might be in' " that case of plaster and gauze that is the soldier in white: " 'For all we know, it might even be Mudd!' " (174) Later, Sergeant Towser laments that "now he had *two* dead men on his hands—Mudd . . . who wasn't even there, and Doc Daneeka . . . who most certainly was there and gave every indication of proving a still thornier administrative problem for him." (350)

The problem the victim faces in maintaining his identity centers most obviously on Major Major Major, whose identity is fixed by a perverse practical joke: "It was a harsh and stunning realization that was forced upon him at so tender an age, the realization that he was not, as he had always been led to believe, Caleb Major, but instead was some total stranger named Major Major Major about whom he knew absolutely nothing and about whom nobody else had ever heard before. What playmates he had withdrew from him and never returned, disposed, as they were, to distrust all strangers, especially one who had already deceived them by pretending to be someone they had known for years. Nobody would have anything to do with him." (87)

His identity determined by the official list—the birth certificate—Major Major Major is abandoned by all. He has no real identity of his own; his fellow officers suspect that he is Henry Fonda. He becomes the perpetual

---

[2] Of course there is the inevitable backfire, when Scheisskopf is inexplicably made a Lieutenant General, ends up in charge of Special Services, and is thereby in command of everything.

outcast, one whose very existence is dubious. Finally he retires into bizarre seclusion, completely withdrawn from the squadron: he can only be contacted in his office when he is not there; when he is there, no one is permitted to enter.

Major Major Major's actions reduce the official attitude to absurdity, parodying it by turning it upon itself. Throughout the novel, the victims—and Major Major Major must be numbered among the victims, even though he is a high-ranking officer—attempt to preserve themselves by adopting masks designed to thwart the official attitude, to take advantage of the I.B.M. mentality of those in charge. Both Major Major Major and Yossarian pose as Washington Irving when they carry out official duties. Major Major Major takes the pose further by signing himself as Irving Washington, John Milton, or Milton John on official documents. Yossarian, in order to remain safe and secure in the hospital, adopts the identities of Warrant Officer Homer Lumley, Giuseppe, and A. Fortiori.

These masks belong to a pattern of acts of rebellion against the system, [179] some comic, others deadly serious. As the novel progresses, the victims, growing more and more aware of the menace of the system, carry gestures of rebellion to the point of outright defiance. Yossarian—with the chaplain the moral conscience of the novel—is most blatant in defiance of the system: his moaning during the Avignon briefing, and his query " 'Where are the Snowdens of yesteryear?' "; his insistence that there is a dead man in his tent; his nakedness after the Avignon mission and during the presentation of the medal; his efforts to halt the Bologna mission by putting soap in the squadron's food and moving the bomb line; his repeated requests to be grounded, his final refusal to fly any more missions, and his desertion. The system, as such, cannot be lived with. It cannot be changed. It cannot be thwarted, beyond a certain point. The only way to overcome Catch-22 is to run away from things—to commit an act of treason, desertion in the face of the enemy. All of the action and the events of the novel point to this conclusion.

Throughout Catch-22, then, Heller is using Déjà vu as the basis of the methods by which he achieves structural unity. Constructing a narrative interplay between the past and the present, contriving elaborate parallel repetitions of and variations on his central themes, he enables the reader to say, with Yossarian, " 'I see everything twice!' " He creates the discernible, ordered pattern which is of the very essence of art. [180]

James M. Mellard
`Catch-22`:
Déjà vu and the Labyrinth
of Memory

"I see everything twice!" the soldier who saw everything twice shouted when they rolled Yossarian in.

"I see everything twice!" Yossarian shouted back at him just as loudly, with a secret wink.

"The walls! The walls!" the other soldier cried. "Move back the walls!"

"The walls! The walls!" Yossarian cried. "Move back the walls!"

One of the doctors pretended to shove the wall back. "Is that far enough?"

The soldier who saw everything twice nodded weakly and sank back on his bed. Yossarian nodded weakly too, eying his talented roommate with great humility and admiration. He knew he was in the presence of a master. His talented roommate was obviously a person to be studied and emulated. During the night, his talented roommate died, and Yossarian decided that he had followed him far enough.

"I see everything once!" he cried quickly.[1]

Overlooked in the enthusiastic furor over *Catch-22* is Joseph Heller's extension of modern fictional techniques, and, thus, his contribution to "a new novel," though different from the one Robbe-Grillet recommends. The method, to use Heller's [29] own label, is *déjà vu*—a term meaning "already seen" that suggests something of the delusive experience, hallucinatory quality and disjunctive expression of reality in *Catch-22*. The term, familiar in medicine and to philosophers such as Bergson, appears several times in the novel. In Chapter XXV, for example, the chaplain asks Yossarian, "Have you ever . . . been in a situation which you felt you had been in before, even though you knew you were experiencing it for the first time?" Yossarian nods yes, but when asked if he has that feeling now, "Yossarian shook his head and explained that *déjà vu* was just a momentary infinitesimal lag in the operation of two coactive sensory nerve centers that com-

---

[1] Joseph Heller, *Catch-22* (New York, 1961), Chapter XVIII. Throughout this text Roman numerals in parentheses refer to chapters in *Catch-22*.

SOURCE: *Bucknell Review*, Vol. 16, No. 2 (1966), pp. 29–44. Reprinted by permission of the author and publisher.

monly functioned simultaneously." Yossarian, not then ready to understand the full significance of that "lag," defines it in purely physiological terms, but to the chaplain it has enormous philosophical significance, for it is concerned both with physical perception and metaphysical understanding, with what the chaplain feels is "the effort to rip away at last the voluminous black folds shrouding the eternal mysteries of existence." And the "lag" has yet another significance for the reader, for in the unfolding of the story it creates a discontinuity between a character, a symbol, a narrative event, and its meaning. Hence, like the character called "The Soldier Who Saw Everything Twice" (XVIII), whose plight Yossarian emulates, one "sees" twice, at least, everything that has importance, but for a reader, as for the chaplain and, eventually, Yossarian, the "lag" is between the *seeing* and the *understanding*. A reader is thus also like the character, caught in one of Yossarian's circular arguments, who says in desperation, "Yes, now I see. But I still don't think I understand" (VII).

Operating within the minds of the invisible narrator, the created characters, *and* the reader, then, much like the Joycean techniques of epiphany and narrative disjunction that apparently influenced Heller, the method of *déjà vu* "proclaims" the writer's "absolute need of the reader's cooperation, an active, conscious, *creative* assistance." [2] Thus, frequently, readers find themselves in the psychological quandary of Yossarian in his journey through Rome, or in the hospital talking to the chaplain, or of the chaplain himself, who "for a few precarious seconds, . . . tingled with a weird occult sensation of having experienced the same situation [30] before in some prior time or existence. He endeavored to trap and nourish the impression in order to predict, and perhaps even control, what incident would occur next, but the afflatus melted away unproductively, as he had known beforehand it would. *Déjà vu*" (XXV). Just about everything in *Catch-22* is introduced as if one *had* seen it before, so one tries to trap and nourish impressions as they occur—for example, the images of the dead man in Yossarian's tent, of Snowden dying in back, the naked man sitting in the tree, of the soldier in white, of Clevinger's plane disappearing into a cloud, of Orr working on the tiny valve or paddling a big yellow life raft with a tiny blue oar. But like the chaplain's, a reader's afflatuses melt away, too, leaving behind questions and images. Because it raises questions that must be answered, however, Heller's essentially lyrical method forces the recurring images to accumulate meanings until their full significance, their essence, is finally perceived. Hence, as Northrop Frye comments about Kierkegaard's "repetition," Heller's *déjà vu* "means, not the simple repeating of an experience, but the re-creating of it which redeems or awakens it to life." [3]

---

[2] See Alain Robbe-Grillet, *For a New Novel* (New York, 1965), p. 156.
[3] *Anatomy of Criticism* (Princeton, N.J., 1957), p. 345.

A method that seems to lead only to needless repetition and redundancy, *déjà vu* is actually neither simply repetitive nor redundant but is rather complexly incremental and progressive, for the examples of *déjà vu* of character, thematic motifs, and events that Heller offers one move inevitably toward completion and resolution. Consider the way the method, somewhat in the manner of Proust's or Joyce's use of what Joseph Frank calls "spatial form," affects the meaning of characters of whom one sees a sequence of "pictures" or images spaced over a long period of time. Even on a relatively low level of thematic seriousness, characters such as Chief White Halfoat and Captain Flume generally expand in significance. In Chapter V, for example, one learns of Halfoat's threats to murder Captain Flume in his sleep and of his prophecy that he himself will die of pneumonia; in the next chapter, one learns of Flume's great fear of Halfoat and his hermit-like retreat into the woods to live, where, in Chapter XII, he is discovered to be living, ill-kempt and in ill-health; in Chapter XXV, one learns of the chaplain's encounter with Flume, now the [31] "mad hermit," in the woods and his taking Flume's words, that he will return before winter, as the words of a prophet; then, finally, in Chapter XXXII, one finds that Halfoat "felt cold and was already making plans to move up into the hospital to die of pneumonia. Instinct told Chief White Halfoat it was almost time. His chest ached and he coughed chronically. Whiskey no longer warmed him. Most damning of all, Captain Flume had moved back into his trailer. Here was an omen of unmistakable meaning." All this seems comically absurd—and it is—but at the end of the sequence one has the overwhelming sensation that Halfoat *will* die, for behind the comic absurdity of these two characters is the discovery of a strange world of tragic consequences. No better illustration of this discovery may be found than in the recurring references to Hungry Joe, to his self-defeating lusts for women and for making photographs of nudes, his chronic nightmares (III), his dreams of a cat sleeping on his face (VI), or his comic fight with Huple's cat, after which "he went to bed victorious and dreamed again that Huple's cat was sleeping on his face, suffocating him" (XII). Such idiosyncrasy seems humorous enough until one learns in Chapter XLI that Hungry Joe "died in his sleep while having a dream. They found a cat on his face." As a consequence of the method of *déjà vu*, then, many characters like these, including Major Major, Dunbar, Doc Daneeka, and Major ———— de Coverley, who look at first only like insignificant figures of comic idiosyncrasy, become at last meaningful figures of ironic obsession or compulsion.

A thematically more important aspect of Heller's technique may be seen in the treatment of characters like the soldier in white, the dead man in Yossarian's tent, and Kraft, all of whom are handled in a rhythmical way parallel to E. M. Forster's use of "expanding symbols" (E. K. Brown's term). One hears very early (I) about the soldier in white, but he is not fully depicted until many chapters later: "The soldier in white was constructed entirely of gauze, plaster and a thermometer, and the thermometer was merely an adornment left balanced in the empty dark hole in the bandages over his mouth early each morning and late each afternoon by Nurse Cramer and Nurse Duckett right up to the afternoon Nurse Cramer read the thermometer and discovered he was dead" (XVII). The dead man in Yossarian's tent is mentioned [32] first in Chapter II, early in Chapter III and late in the same chapter, and again late in Chapter IX, but it is only in Chapter X that one learns his name is Mudd, and in Chapter XXIV that he was actually killed in a flight over the bridge at Orvieto, and that it is not he but his gear that Yossarian refers to as the dead man in his tent. Kraft, on the other hand, is associated with the run over the bridge at Ferrara during which Yossarian, flying lead bombardier, took his squadron of six planes over the target not once, but twice, destroying the bridge and winning a medal and promotion but losing Kraft and his crew.

Kraft, the dead man in Yossarian's tent, and the soldier in white, like the more concrete characters of Halfoat, Flume, Hungry Joe, et al., take on added meanings as mention of them recurs, but the meanings (with apologies to Cassirer) are more symbolic than actual, for they come to represent forms of death and responsibility—two of the most important subjects in *Catch-22*. Moreover, a recognition of the meaning of these symbolic characters contributes to the development of Yossarian, the novel's central character and consciousness. Kraft, for example, makes Yossarian aware of death, *violent* death, just as the dead man in his tent is a constant reminder of its presence, but Kraft also makes Yossarian aware of his moral responsibility in the war. Thus, although Kraft is introduced quite early (VI), the most meaningful details of his death do not appear until Chapter XIII, where it is revealed that Yossarian "killed Kraft and his crew" but was uncertain how he was supposed to feel about him and the others, "for they had all died in the distance of a mute and secluded agony at a moment when he was up to his own ass in the same vile, excruciating dilemma of duty and damnation." The medal and the promotion given to Yossarian are emblematic of the official attitude toward Kraft's death, but Yossarian himself begins to feel both a responsibility and a guilt that prepare him for his criticism of Milo Minderbinder, who denies *any* responsibility for his role in the death of the man in the tent, this despite his having masterminded the bombing run over the bridge at Orvieto. Hence for Yossarian, Mudd becomes a concrete symbol for Milo's generalized *ir*responsibility. The soldier in white, on the other hand, epitomizes for Yossarian the "neater," more delicate and tasteful death he can expect in the hospital, one for [33] which even the responsibility is difficult to determine, though "now that Yossarian looked back, it seemed that Nurse Cramer, rather than the talkative Texan, had murdered the soldier in white; if she had not read the thermometer and reported what she had found, the soldier in white might still be lying there alive" (XVII). Although he, along with Kraft and Mudd, represents a form of the responsibility that must accompany any potential "decision to terminate," the "excruciating dilemma of duty and damnation" that faces every soldier, perhaps every man, the soldier in white nonetheless represents a death that seems less personal, less threatening than those more violent forms, until, rhythmically, he *reappears* for the last time (in Chapter XXXIV) and terrifies the hospital's inmates even more than death outside. For besides being unsure that the man in the bandages even exists, they cannot be certain that his death is *not* the responsibility of some official act, like Nurse Cramer's, some *official* "decision to terminate," a "disappearance" like Dunbar's and Major Major's and Major ——— de Coverley's, or a bureaucratic "death" like that of Doc Daneeka, who is physically alive but technically dead because he was supposed to be on a plane that crashed killing all the crew. Ultimately, therefore, this kind of death, for which even the *living* such as Cathcart, Korn, Black, Dreedle, Peckem, and Scheisskopf are discovered to be representatives, is even more to be feared than death by violence.

Like the characters, both real and symbolic, who gradually gain in significance, a thematic concept such as Catch-22 also changes in meaning as it recurs. Presented in the first chapter as if one had seen it before ("Catch-22 required that each censored letter bear the censoring officer's name"), it is somewhat more fully defined in Chapter V, where Doc Daneeka explains to Yossarian why he cannot ground men like Orr, who is thought to be cracking-up: "There was only one catch and that was Catch-22, which specified that a concern for one's own safety in the face of dangers that were real and immediate was the process of a rational mind. Orr was crazy and could be grounded. All he had to do was ask; and as soon as he did, he would no longer be crazy and would have to fly more missions. Orr would be crazy to fly more missions and sane if he didn't, but if he was sane he had to fly them. If he flew them he was crazy and didn't have to; but if he didn't want to he [34] was sane and had to." The absurd law that, according to Northrop Frye, must often be overcome in a comic plot, Catch-22 is itself as delusive, as hallucinatory, as *déjà vu*, for while at one moment Yossarian can see "it clearly in all its spinning reasonableness," its "elliptical precision," "its perfect pairs of parts" that are "graceful and shocking, like good modern art," at other times Yossarian "wasn't quite sure that he saw it all, just the way he was never quite sure about good modern art."

There are other, though not frequent, references to Catch-22 and its manifold clauses. The most important view of Catch-22 comes near the end of the novel, however, when Yossarian, making his way through the nightmare world of "The Eternal City" (XXXIX) in search of Nately's whore's kid sister, encounters an old woman who tells him that "all the poor young girls" with whom they had once cavorted are gone—driven into the streets by American M.P.'s and Italian *carabinieri:*

"What right did they have?"
"Catch-22."
"*What?*" Yossarian froze in his tracks with fear and alarm and felt his whole body begin to tingle. "*What* did you say?"
"Catch-22," the old woman repeated, rocking her head up and down. "Catch-22. Catch-22 says they have a right to do anything we can't stop them from doing."

Yossarian questions the old woman further but learns only that Nately's whore and the kid sister are also gone, "chased away with the rest." Yossarian, however, reaches a significant conclusion about the absurd law: "Catch-22 did not exist, he was positive of that, but it made no difference. What did matter was that everyone thought it existed, and that was much worse, for there was no object or text to ridicule or refute, to accuse, criticize, attack, amend, hate, revile, spit at, rip to shreds, trample upon or burn up." As a consequence of his understanding, Yossarian has begun to prepare himself for the final confrontation with the "law." In the chapter (XL) entitled "Catch-22," Yossarian is offered a "little deal" by Colonel Cathcart and Colonel Korn if he will desist from his one-man rebellion against flying more missions. The catch this time, Korn tells him, is that Yossarian has to like them: "Like us. Join us. Be our pal. Say nice things about us here and [35] back in the States. Become one of the boys." If he will like them he can be sent home, after another promotion and medal, to make speeches "for morale and public-relations purposes." But Yossarian, finally realizing that the "catch" means a moral if not a physical death, rejects the "little deal," though sorely tempted, and makes his only viable choice among flying more missions, a court-martial and desertion: he makes a decisive leap beyond the realm of the circular—and encircling—principle and heads for Sweden to join his friend Orr.

It is the very close relationship between the kind of story being told and the method of *déjà vu* that actually justifies the method in *Catch-22.* John Wain, the English novelist-critic, has said that Heller's method is relevant because things are held back until readers are ready for them and because it fits the facts of a flyer's life: "To these bomber-pilots, life does not flow in a regular, unfolding ribbon, experience falling on from experience, as it does in even the most tumultuous life in peace-time." [4] However, a better explanation for the disjunction of narrative, the seeming chaos, lies neither

---

[4] "A New Novel About Old Troubles," *Critical Quarterly,* V (1963), 169.

in its fidelity to the external facts of a flyer's life nor to the needs of a reader. Rather, it is the protagonist's *moral* life, his *inner*-life, his *psychological* needs that account for the novel's delaying tactics. The protagonist of *Catch-22* is John Yossarian, a bombardier in the 256th Bomber Squadron, and the narrative center of the novel is Yossarian's painful recognition of his own mortality and personal involvement, his acceptance of individual guilt and a need for a new set of values. He takes a long time to discover these things, for with himself he plays "censor games" like those he plays with the letters of the enlisted men while he is in the hospital and engages in what one of his doctors calls the "business of illusion." It is, therefore, Heller's identification with Yossarian's mind, his ego-consciousness, that explains and realizes the method. Because the ego is caught, as it were, between the super-ego, or society, on one side, and the id, the individual's repressed desires, needs, or memories, on the other, Heller's novel can be felt to move in as many as three directions: (1) outward toward the social expressions of authority found in the satire of figures like Dreedle, Cathcart, [36] Korn, Black, et al.; (2) still outward, but toward the symbolic expression of universal archetypes; and (3) inward, or downward, toward the structure of the personal unconscious and the meaning of repressed individual experience. In Yossarian's narrative, the two figures who centralize these varied movements are Milo Minderbinder and a "strangely familiar kid" named Snowden.

One critic has said that "Heller could have used Milo Minderbinder, the soldier businessman who profits so heavily from the non-sense of the war, to crystallize a direction and purpose for the book," but argues that Milo is "far too outlandish a character, far too preposterous and overdrawn to contribute to any sort of social criticism." [5] Viewed outside the context of the novel as it progresses, such criticism might be valid. But as one reads about Milo in the course of the novel itself, one must recognize that he does crystallize at least one of the directions and purposes of the book. Through Heller's technique, the delayed revelation, the incremental repetition, of *déjà vu*, one is led, even tricked, into accepting the reality of Milo and of exploits that show both the possibilities for and the failure of a major aspect of American culture. It is his recognition of what Milo stands for that forces Yossarian to reject untrammeled private enterprise, a utilitarian business ethic, and the entire moral super-structure of American capitalism itself.

One first hears of Milo, the pilot *cum* mess officer, at the end of Chapter II, where Yossarian learns that he is away "in Smyrna for the fig harvest," but forty pages pass before one learns *why* Milo has gone there for the fig

---

[5] Joseph J. Waldmeir, "Two Novelists of the Absurd: Heller and Kesey," *Wisconsin Studies in Contemporary Literature*, V (Autumn 1964), 195.

harvest: he has used Yossarian's letter from Doc Daneeka that orders the mess officer to give Yossarian all the dried fruit and fruit juices he wants. Seeing the letter a splendid way to get extra goods for reselling, Milo thus uses Yossarian to begin his fantastic career. There are many hints about the stages of that career, hints about his buying up of the entire Egyptian cotton crop and his bombing of the squadron, but the full details of even the early stages are not given until midway through the novel, in a chapter describing Yossarian's and Orr's harried journey with Milo through his kingdoms. To their astonishment, they discover that Milo has parlayed [37] Yossarian's letter into a vast empire called M & M Enterprises, of which "everyone has a share." Milo has become Mayor of Palermo and most of the other towns in Sicily, which he has made the world's third largest exporter of Scotch, become Major Sir Milo Minderbinder in Malta, Vice-Shah in Oran, the Caliph of Baghdad, the Imam of Damascus, and the Sheik of Araby: "Milo was the corn god, the rain god and the rice god in backward regions where such crude gods were still worshipped by ignorant and superstitious people. . . . Everywhere they touched he was acclaimed with honor . . ." (XXII). But like a tragic hero, Milo reaches too far, and on the return journey through Cairo, he "cornered the market on cotton that no one else in the world wanted and brought himself promptly to the brink of ruin" (XXII). In order to extricate himself from the cotton crisis, Milo, who now has his own air force of planes plying the world for goods for the mess halls of the American armies in Europe, contracts with the Americans to bomb the German-held bridge at Orvieto and with the Germans to defend the bridge with antiaircraft fire against his own attack—both on a cost-plus-six per cent agreement and, from the Germans, a thousand dollar bonus for each American plane shot down. And, sharp trader that he is, Milo manages to get both governments to do the jobs contracted for— after all, they did have the men and materials on hand. So "in the end Milo realized a fantastic profit from both halves of his project for doing nothing more than signing his name twice" (XXIV). Heartened by this coup and still pressed by the Egyptian cotton, Milo contracts next with the Germans to bomb the American squadron, for which he was still mess officer. But this time he went too far, and there was an intensive investigation: "Not one voice was raised in his defense. Decent people everywhere were affronted, and Milo was all washed up until he opened his books to the public and disclosed the tremendous profit he had made. He could reimburse the government for all the people and property he had destroyed and still have enough money left over to continue buying Egyptian cotton" (XXIV). With that kind of profit on the books and the fact that everybody has a share of M & M Enterprises, of course Milo is exonerated completely.

Milo is exonerated, that is, by everyone except Yossarian. And [38] it is the scene in which Yossarian rejects Milo that becomes the center of gravity of the novel, for in that scene occur the keys to Heller's method, the pivotal point in Yossarian's development, and the images of the death and birth that give the narrative its shape and significance. The scene is presented from two separate points of view, Yossarian's and the chaplain's, the one giving the personal meaning of the encounter and the other suggesting its archetypal significance. When Heller focuses on Yossarian, who is sitting peacefully and nakedly in a tree, one sees clearly enough that the bombardier has finally rejected Milo's arguments justifying the casualties that occur as a result of his business schemes. To Yossarian, Milo's crimes against humanity, like those of governments, armies, and corporations, are really too huge for comprehension, but his crime against one individual, Mudd, the dead man in Yossarian's tent, is enough to particularize Yossarian's disillusionment with his friend, whom he has more or less unwittingly launched on his career. Despite the fact that everyone has a share of Milo's syndicate (including Mudd), Yossarian has begun to feel that neither this nor his protests that he wasn't even there can obviate Milo's responsibility for the man's death, and his remarks to Milo switch from a tone of awed admiration to one of disillusioned sarcasm as he "advises" him to bribe the government to buy his cotton and to tell everyone that "the security of the country requires a strong domestic Egyptian-cotton speculating industry" (XXIV). In the end, therefore, Yossarian refuses Milo's invitation to "come with" him in his business and to sanction his offering of chocolate-covered cotton to the world.

When Heller focuses on the chaplain, who had been conducting Snowden's funeral during the same time, the archetypal form of the encounter is fully revealed. The chaplain's view of the scene, presented in flashback, is interwoven with his concern for memory and perception, vision and hallucination, the various seeings—*presque, jamais,* and, particularly, *déjà vu* —and his curious "feeling that he had met Yossarian somewhere before the first time he *had* met Yossarian lying in bed in the hospital" (XXV). Though the chaplain never identifies Yossarian as the naked man in the tree, he at least suspects that their first "meeting" was on some occasion "far more momentous and occult" [39] than that in the hospital, was "a significant encounter . . . in some remote, submerged and perhaps even entirely spiritual epoch in which he had made the identical, foredooming admission that there was nothing, absolutely nothing, he could do to help him" (XXV). And it is in connection with the "enigmatic vision" of the naked man in the tree, "the most extraordinary event that had ever befallen him" (XXV), that the chaplain brings up with Yossarian the phenomenon of *déjà vu,* though the chaplain fears that not even *déjà vu* is flexible enough to include his "vision." As the chaplain wonders about it—"was it a ghost, then? The dead man's soul? An angel from heaven or a minion from hell?"—some of the archetypal symbolic potential begins to emerge, a potential that is more clearly suggested when Heller writes that "The possibility that there really had been a naked man in the tree—two men, actually, since the first had been joined shortly by a second man clad in a brown mustache and sinister dark garments from head to toe who bent forward ritualistically along the limb of the tree to offer the first man something to drink from a brown goblet never crossed the chaplain's mind" (XXV).

Putting these details in their place with Yossarian's ironic reference to the tree as the "tree of life" and the "tree of the knowledge of good and evil," one must finally recognize the dual purposes of the scene, taking place as it does on the third day after Snowden's death and the third day of Yossarian's nakedness. On the one hand, it certainly represents Yossarian's "temptation" by Milo, the Jungian "shadow" in his "sinister dark garments" and the Christian Satan, identified with the serpent, who "inches" up the tree, "hisses" at Yossarian, and breathes fire, albeit a "virtuous fire." For Yossarian, this confrontation is the first real step in his moral regeneration. As C. G. Jung writes in "Aion: Contributions to the Symbolism of the Self":

The shadow is a moral problem that challenges the whole ego personality, for no one can become conscious of the shadow without considerable moral effort. To become conscious of it involves recognizing the dark aspects of the personality as present and real. This act is an essential condition for any kind of self-knowledge, and it therefore, as a rule, meets with considerable resistance. Indeed, self-knowledge as a psychotherapeutic measure [40] frequently requires much painstaking work extending over a long period.[6]

Jung's comment here is almost a description of Yossarian's development; it is therefore hardly surprising that, after Milo, near the end of the novel, has been absorbed by the socioauthoritarian structure (he joins forces with Wintergreen, Cathcart, Korn, et al.), he should be replaced, in Yossarian's delusive vision in the hospital for the last time, by another shadowy figure saying, "We've got your pal, buddy." For Yossarian to have gone with Milo (or with Cathcart and Korn, when they make him their offer of a "little deal") is to suggest that the *shadow* has gotten him too, just as it has Dunbar and Major Major. To know and yet to deny the shadow is to know and affirm one's moral being.

If the rejection of Milo represents the birth of moral consciousness, the death of Snowden and the simultaneous regression of Yossarian to naked-

---

[6] Quoted from *Psyche & Symbol: A Selection from the Writings of C. G. Jung*, ed. Violet S. de Laszlo (New York, 1958), p. 7.

ness represent for the latter a death and a rebirth of self. Of particular concern here, then, is the way the method of *déjà vu* forces both reader and
character beyond meanings they might see only half through the novel to
the final meanings in Snowden's death, meanings that are implicit in Yossarian's experiences from the start but that, like those around Milo, are
able to push only slowly and tortuously out of memory into consciousness.
As it must, the recognition of Snowden's full meaning parallels both the
moral and archetypal patterns of death and birth; for through Snowden,
Yossarian comes to an awareness not only of the fact of death but also of
the possibility for life—for himself and for others.

That Snowden has particular significance for Yossarian is suggested in
the first appearance of the name in a question Yossarian asks at an indoc-
trination session: "Where are the Snowdens of yesteryear?" he asks an
instructor, parodying Villon's question in French, "*Où sont les Neigedens
d'antan?*" and "ready to pursue him through all the words in the world to
wring the knowledge from him if he could . . ." (IV). But he gets no
answer this time, although the reader gets the information that Snowden
had been killed over Avignon, and one suspects that the pursuit of that
knowledge of Snowden will be for Yossarian a [41] long and tortuous *rite
de passage*. Later, in the midst of an explanation for Yossarian's great skill
at directing the plane's evasive action, we are told that Yossarian has not
yet "resigned" himself to the idea that he was going to die; and for a moment, there is an abrupt descent into the memory of "the pitiful time of the
mess on the mission to Avignon when Dobbs went crazy in mid-air and
began weeping pathetically for help" for the bombardier. But Yossarian
is the bombardier, so he yells he is all right, and Dobbs begs, "then help
him, help him." And the chapter concludes with the oft-recurring line:
"And Snowden lay dying in back" (V). The next time the name recurs,
Yossarian is in the hospital because "being in the hospital was better than
being over Bologna or flying over Avignon with Huple or Dobbs at the
controls and Snowden dying in back." To Yossarian, "there was none of
that crude, ugly ostentation about dying that was so common outside the
hospital. They did not blow up in mid-air like Kraft or the dead man in
Yossarian's tent, or freeze to death in the blazing summertime the way
Snowden had frozen to death after spilling his secret to Yossarian in the
back of the plane" (XVII). At this time one learns that Snowden had
whimpered "I'm cold . . . I'm cold," and Yossarian had tried to comfort
him with, "There, there . . . There, there." And shortly after this one
learns part of what Snowden's secret is, the part that causes Yossarian to
spend so much time in the hospital, to become so proficient at directing
the plane's evasive actions, and, eventually, to refuse altogether to fly combat missions and to walk around backwards with a forty-five in hand so

that no one can slip up on him from behind; the secret "Snowden had spilled to him on the mission to Avignon" was that "they were out to get him; and Snowden had spilled it all over the back of the plane" (XVII).

There are other recurrences to Snowden's death, both by Yossarian and other characters on whom the incident also has a tremendous effect. Through Doc Daneeka's point of view, one sees the state of shock Yossarian is in when he gets off the plane, stark naked, after the mission. Through the chaplain's point of view, one sees the rather frozen, pictorially depicted scene around Snowden's grave, when Milo slithers up the tree to sit with the still naked Yossarian. And from Yossarian [42] himself one gets a gradually accumulating series of details concerning his passage out of the nose section, through the labyrinthine crawlway, "up over the bomb bay and down into the rear section of the plane where Snowden lay on the floor wounded and freezing to death in a yellow splash of sunlight . . ." (XXII). But it is not until the penultimate chapter that one learns the full details of Snowden's death and the entire secret that he spilled, and it comes only after Yossarian's nightmare journey into the "Eternal City," after Milo had caused his friend Nately's death, a love-death struggle with a "terrible mother" in Nately's whore, the offer of the "little deal" by Cathcart and Korn if he will desist from his rebellion and be shipped quietly home, a nearly fatal stabbing by Nately's whore, and after visits by the shadowy dream-figure saying, "We've got your pal, buddy" (XLI). In this chapter, entitled "Snowden," the novel comes full circle, with Yossarian again talking to the chaplain as he had been in Chapter I, and one finally learns the full text of Snowden's message: "Man was matter, that was Snowden's secret. Drop him out a window and he'll fall. Set fire to him and he'll burn. Bury him and he'll rot. . . . The spirit gone, man is garbage. That was Snowden's secret. Ripeness was all."

As a result of Snowden's *full* message, Yossarian goes beyond the belief in mere existence to find a life in a belief in "The Spirit," the essence, of man. But, obviously, existence does precede essence, and to fulfill the latter one must insure the former. Thus, caught, as one has seen, between the Scylla of court-martial and the Charybdis of Catch-22, Yossarian makes his "leap" of faith and lights out for Sweden, behind Orr, his mentor, but, like Huck Finn, ahead of the rest.

It is the strategy of Yossarian's retreat to Sweden that creates the most vexing problems for most readers of the novel, bringing under scrutiny as it does both the values of American society and culture and of Yossarian. Read in one way, conservatively, shall we say, the retreat is an egocentric denial of social responsibility, but read in another way, radically perhaps, it is an existential act of individual affirmation. To date there has not been much of a middle, liberal, position; for how can Yossarian's leaving for Sweden be both an individual affirmation and an affirmation of American culture? According to Joseph Campbell, one can reconcile [43] such contradictions simply by seeing the rejection of society as a birth *from* rather than a denial of it; society therefore becomes "a fostering organ," a kind of exterior "second womb," "wherein the postnatal stages of man's long gestation . . . are supported and defended," and the individual simply becomes himself and, thus, fully human.[7] Hence, Yossarian's rite of initiation—his experiences with Kraft and Mudd and the soldier in white, Nately and the whore and her kid sister, and Milo and Snowden—is, as one has seen, a "second birth," and Yossarian, following in the footsteps of just about every major hero of American literature, becomes "truly the 'twice born,' freed from the pedagogical devices of society, the lures and threats of myth, the local *mores*, the usual hopes of benefits and rewards." [8] Having proved himself and, in a sense, his society by fulfilling yet another form of the American dream, Yossarian achieves his freedom and his maturity, ready now to become, like Nately and the chaplain, a "father" in his own right as he sets out to find the "kid sister" who reminds him of a lot of other "kids"—Snowden, Huple, the boy in the streets of Rome, Sampson, Dobbs, Kraft, Mudd—in order "to try to break the lousy chain of inherited habit that was imperiling them all" (XXXIX). Consequently, *déjà vu* in *Catch-22* applies not only to the images of the external world of social consciousness, the eternal world of the archetype, and the internal world of the personal consciousness; the narrative these images create also applies to a universal myth, the myth of the journey into the underworld, the labyrinth, the heart of darkness. In the novel, therefore, *déjà vu* involves both form and content, for not only is it the material that creates but also it becomes the method that penetrates this labyrinth of memory. [44]

---

[7] "Bios and Mythos: Prolegomena to a Science of Mythology," in *Myth and Literature*, ed. John B. Vickery (Lincoln, Neb., 1966), p. 20.
[8] *Ibid.*, p. 21.

Jan Solomon
The Structure of
Joseph Heller's
'Catch-22'

On the whole, the reviewers and critics who judged *Catch-22* in the fall
and winter of 1961 were not entirely enthusiastic. One observation common
to favorable and unfavorable notices alike was that *Catch-22* lacked structure. According to *Time*: "Heller's talent is impressive, but it is also undisciplined, sometimes luring him into bogs of boring repetition. Nearly
every episode in *Catch-22* is told and retold." [1] In *The New York Times
Book Review* repetition is again noted: "its material is repetitive and monotonous." Further, the novel "gasps for want of craft and sensibility"; in
fact, "the book is no novel." [2] *The New Yorker* echoes the "no novel" judgment: *Catch-22* "is not really a book. It doesn't even seem to have been
written; instead it gives the impression of having been shouted onto paper." [3] The more favorable reviews as well expressed some uneasiness about
the form. Orville Prescott tempered his admiration by commenting that the
book was "not an entirely successful novel" and "not even a good novel by
conventional standards." [4] But Robert Brustein's review-essay on *Catch-22*
is most instructive. Despite his enthusiasm for and his unique insight into
Heller's novel, Mr. Brustein too charges *Catch-22* with formlessness: "Considering his indifference to surface reality, it is absurd to judge Heller by
standards of psychological realism (or, for that matter, by conventional
artistic standards at all, since his book is as formless as any picaresque epic)."
Formlessness in this case is not to be considered a weakness and the charge
is dismissed as being inconsequential in regard to a novel worthy of being
described as "one of the most bitterly funny works in the language." [5]
    While the success of *Catch-22* was not immediate, the novel soon began

[1] *Time*, October 27, 1961, p. 97.
[2] Richard G. Stern, *The New York Times Book Review*, October 22, 1961, p. 50.
[3] Whitney Balliett, *The New Yorker*, December 9, 1961, p. 247.
[4] Orville Prescott, *The New York Times*, October 23, 1961, p. 27.
[5] Robert Brustein, *The New Republic*, November 13, 1961, pp. 13, 11.

SOURCE: *Critique*, Vol. 9, No. 2 (1967), pp. 46–57. Reprinted by permission of the
author and publisher.

to gain in importance. The English publication of [46] the book in the spring of 1962 brought very favorable notices and within one week it was first on the English best-seller list.⁶ Soon *Time* was including paragraphs on Heller in its occasional reports on the literary scene, and even *Vogue* printed his picture above some coy copy and under the puzzling title of "The New Veers." Popular articles on the absurd in American fiction were incomplete without a consideration of *Catch-22*.⁷ Finally, *Heller* became an entry in the Twentieth-Century American section of the *PMLA Annual Bibliography* with a scattering of articles in the professional journals listed beneath it. Arrived, admired, and analyzed, *Catch-22* is now something of an institution; there are no more comments on its formlessness. The novel has been accepted as some sort of gifted example of what in literature must be thought to approximate the drip-and-smear school of modern painting. But *Catch-22* is a novel, and fine, formless novels are a rare species. A careful examination of Heller's novel reveals not only that it has form, but that this form is carefully constructed to support the pervasive theme of absurdity, in fact to create its own dimension of absurdity.

The most significant aspect of the structure of *Catch-22* is its chronology. Behind what appear to be merely random events lies a careful system of time-sequences involving two distinct and mutually contradictory chronologies. The major part of the novel, focussed on Yossarian, moves forward and back from a pivotal point in time. Yossarian, like many other anti-heroes of modern fiction from Leopold Bloom to Moses Herzog, lives in a world dominated not by chronological but by psychological time. Yossarian's time is punctuated, if not ordered, by the inexorable increases in the number of missions and by the repetitious returns to the relative safety and sanity of the hospital where, "they couldn't dominate Death . . . but they certainly made her behave." ⁸

While the dominant sequence of events shifts back and forth from the present to the past treating any period of time as equally present, equally immediate, a counter-motion controls the time of the history of Milo Minderbinder. Across the see-saw pattern of events in the rest of the novel Minderbinder moves directly forward from one success to the next. In the solid fashion of nineteenth-century fiction, he begins the novel as a hard-working young hopeful dreaming of a syndicate and ends wielding [47]

---

⁶ As reported by R. Walters in *The New York Times Book Review*, September 9, 1962, p. 8. See also Howard Taubman, *The New Statesman*, June 15, 1962, p. 871; and *The Spectator*, June 15, 1962, p. 801.

⁷ *Time*, February 1, 1963, pp. 82–84; *Time*, February 12, 1965, pp. 94–95; *Vogue*, January 1, 1963, p. 112; *The New York Times Book Review*, June 6, 1965, pp. 3, 28, 30.

⁸ Joseph Heller, *Catch-22* (New York, 1962), p. 170. All other page references to *Catch-22* will be noted parenthetically in the text.

absolute power. Independently, each chronology is valid and logical; together, the two time-schemes are impossible. By manipulating the points at which the different systems cross, Heller creates a structural absurdity enforcing the absurdity of character and event in the novel.

Examining first the part of *Catch-22* dominated by Yossarian, we find a fairly complex chronology. The novel opens at a point midway in the development of the situation, so that "past" events, those preceding the opening scene, must be revealed to the reader. These past events are slowly unfolded as the "present" action progresses, but they are not related through conventional flashbacks. At first numerous, brief references to an event are inserted into the current action; then somewhat fuller allusions; and finally, for each specific important episode, a fairly extended direct narration. This method of weaving past and present time is, of course, what has been labeled repetition. These episodes are never related with any sense of their having become distant in time, but are told with freshness and immediacy, suggesting the effect they continue to have on Yossarian. Since any scene in the novel seems equally "present," all sense of chronological relativity is denied to the reader who thus fails to attain any solid vantage point in time. The sense of time is undermined and with it one hold on the rational.

The network of present and past events builds toward a psychological effect in Yossarian, and in the reader. With the gradual unfolding of such "past" events as The Glorious Loyalty Oath Crusade and The Great Big Siege of Bologna develops the tension that reaches its peak at the end of the novel in the scene of Snowden's death. The negation of the significance of chronology is particularly apparent here; the critical event of the novel—Snowden's death and the revelation of "his secret"—actually occurs some months before the opening of the book.

Time, in this complex system of narration, is marked out for us by two closely linked devices, Yossarian's stays in the hospital and the continual raising of the number of missions. Yossarian's constant retreats to the hospital enforce the reversal of values in the world of Pianosa, where the hospital represents the high-water mark of the safe and the reasonable. These escapes mark as well the stages in Yossarian's insubordination; each self-imposed hospitalization is a response to the raising of the required number of missions. Insubordination, the refusal to [48] play the game, has begun in the "past" time of the novel. After the death of Snowden, Yossarian goes naked rather than wear a uniform stained by Snowden's mortality. Naked, he attends Snowden's funeral, and naked, he receives a medal. But the acts of insubordination toward the end of the novel become increasingly dangerous to authority. Yossarian refuses to fly further missions, a decision he enforces by walking backwards and carrying a gun. His penultimate gesture of revolt takes him AWOL to Rome, and at last he deserts. The psychological development of revolt in Yossarian significantly does not depend on the actual chronology of the events. The cause and effect pattern of increased missions and flights to the hospital is the first indication of rebelliousness the novel presents. The more absurd and intense insubordination of nakedness predates any of Yossarian's Pianosa hospitalizations; yet, although it is alluded to early in the book, it is not fully recounted until Chapter 24, more than halfway through the novel, where it fits into the pattern of Yossarian's growing psychological unrest. The events do make a pattern, not in terms of chronology but in terms of the order in which they are related. Again the significance of real time is negated.

In Yossarian's final insubordination, his desertion, chronology and the narrative order of events combine. The chronological order of events has brought Yossarian into dangerous conflict with Colonels Cathcart and Korn. Thus, present events motivate him. But past events are equally forceful, for at this point in the novel the death of Snowden is narrated in full and horrible detail. Snowden's death occurred months before, but it is described at the end of the novel so that it may have its ultimate effect in the ultimate action of the novel, the desertion. There is, of course, psychological validity; past events can motivate present actions, but more important is the insistent denial of the typical novelistic convention which locates causes in immediately antecedent events.

In the structural economy of *Catch-22*, the raising of the missions and Yossarian's flights to the hospital not only serve the psychological development of Yossarian but also permit us to follow the time-scheme of the novel. When the novel opens, the missions have been raised to 45 and Yossarian has responded by escaping to the hospital on the pretext of his liver condition. This opening hospital scene admits the reader to the history of [49] Yossarian *in medias res* and at the same time initiates certain key events such as Yossarian's friendship with the chaplain, the creation of Washington Irving, mysterious signer of letters and documents, and the appearance of The Soldier in White. Driven from the ward by a cheerful Texan, Yossarian returns to duty, only to find the missions raised to 50; he flees once more to the hospital. When he leaves the hospital again, the action proper of the novel begins.

In the first three or four chapters references to past events reveal that many of the novel's most significant episodes have already taken place. Avignon and Ferrara have been bombed. All the "Great" and "Glorious" events have occurred: The Glorious Atabrine Insurrection, The Glorious Loyalty Oath Crusade, and The Great Big Siege of Bologna. Furthermore, Snowden, Kraft, and Clevinger, as well as other less significant characters have already died. For two-thirds of the novel, about 300 pages, the disclosure of these past events forms a considerable part of the texture of narration; the last third of the novel moves steadily forward at an increased pace directly relating the events of the present.

Catch-22 falls into three nearly equal parts separated by the rhythmic repetition of hospital scenes. In the first section, although the narration dwells primarily on the past, a few events do occur in the present to advance the action somewhat. The missions are raised from 45 to 50 and to 55, at which point Yossarian goes to Major Major Major Major with his grievance. When Yossarian finally manages to see this elusive figure, he is offered the option of flying only milk-runs. Yossarian turns the offer down, foreshadowing his similar refusal of the Colonels' deal at the end of the novel. This kind of narrative rhythm is another of Heller's structural devices, and we see it again when Yossarian flees from the terrors of the Bologna mission to a Rome populated by soldiers and whores, a flight to be repeated at the climax of the novel.

In the first section of *Catch-22* primary attention is paid to introducing us to the major characters of the novel and to adding more information of past events to the framework of knowledge being built around Yossarian and Pianosa. Occasionally in the early chapters past events are told in the form of extended straight narration, not, however, any of the events occurring on Pianosa, but only those histories that took place in the more distant [50] past: Yossarian and Clevinger at Santa Ana (particularly the trial of Clevinger) and the biography of Major Major Major Major. Otherwise, by hints and allusions we receive some information about Avignon, Ferrara, Bologna and about the interpersonal affairs of the men on Pianosa: Orr and Appleby and the ping-pong fight, the war between Flume and Chief Halfoat, the fistfight between Huple's cat and Hungry Joe. Not until the end of this section does the narration tend to concentrate on one major past event, The Great Big Siege of Bologna. The first third of the novel ends with the second run over Bologna and Yossarian's night in Rome with Luciana, after which, on returning to Pianosa, he finds the missions raised to 40. Yossarian rushes to the hospital.

The second passage of hospital scenes, beginning with Chapter 16, marks the division between the first two sections of the novel and establishes circularity and repetition by bringing together several points in time. Yossarian leaves the hospital after ten days, but again the missions are raised, now to 45, and again he returns. The manipulation of time has brought us back to the opening of the novel: Yossarian in the hospital with the missions at 45.

Chapter 17 is entitled "The Soldier in White" and now further grotesque description magnifies the horror of his symbolic depersonalization. From this series of hospitalizations the narrative moves back in time to others. Reference is made to Yossarian in North Africa with venereal disease. A passage follows about Yossarian's first hospitalization, a form of malingering that began back at Lowry Field, where Yossarian so much enjoys spending Thanksgiving in bed that he attempts to remain there by imitating the symptoms of The Soldier Who Saw Everything Twice. As a result, when this soldier dies, Yossarian is forced into impersonating him for the benefit of his visiting family. The device of exchanged and confused identities will, like The Soldier in White, recur.

The second section of *Catch-22* is again approximately 150 pages, or one-third of the novel, and again appears framed in hospital scenes. This section contains somewhat more action in the present time. The problems of the chaplain with Colonel Cathcart, Corporal Whitcomb, and the Washington Irving Investigation are developed. Then, as the missions are raised to 60, Dobbs conceives his plan to kill Colonel Cathcart. In Rome more [51] attention is paid to the whores and to the old man with whom a frustrated Nately passionately debates the principles of the American dream. Past events in this section focus primarily on the events of Avignon, the moaning at the briefing, Snowden's death (still given in only fragmentary detail), and Snowden's funeral with a naked Yossarian in attendance in a tree. Since Avignon preceded Bologna, the events most concentrated on in the first section, we have yet another denial of chronology.

Yossarian, at the end of this second section, returns to the hospital, not this time as a malingerer but as a casualty. He has been wounded as a result of Aarfy's poor navigation on returning from Parma. At this point, the issue of confused identities is repeated. Dunbar has become A. Fortiori, a feat accomplished by taking over A. Fortiori's bed. Dunbar suggests that Yossarian drive one Lumley, a lower-ranking soldier, out of his bed, thereby assuming Lumley's identity. This action has unfortunate ramifications; Yossarian, certified at last by the hospital psychiatrist as crazy enough to be sent home, is jubilant. The orders arrive; they are for A. Fortiori.

In the final section of the novel, which, except for the full narration of the death of Snowden, concentrates on events in the present, the tempo of horrors increases. The chief officers become even more self-seeking and incompetent. Lt. Scheisskopf arrives from California, soon becomes a General, and takes over Special Services from General Dreedle at the moment when Special Services takes over the control of combat. More of Yossarian's fellows die, and their deaths are more bizarre. McWatt buzzes the raft and cuts Kid Sampson in half; guilt drives McWatt to fly his plane into a mountain. Doc Daneeka, supposedly on that plane, dies on paper, a death that proves just as effective as a more mortal end. Chief Halfoat dies of pneumonia, as predicted, and Hungry Joe smothers under Huple's cat. New young soldiers arrive and commit the weirdest of murders by removing the effects of the dead man, Mudd, from Yossarian's tent. Even Orr, shot down again, is missing. As the missions sky-rocket to 80, the chaplain is arrested and questioned about Washington Irving in a scene that repeats the earlier mad trial of Clevinger. Dunbar "is disappeared," and finally Nately dies, his whore becoming a ubiquitous assassin threatening Yossarian.

In the increased pace of the final section there is an additional [52] reminder of the hospital. The careful rhythm is not disrupted although it is not Yossarian who is hospitalized but Nately whose nose Yossarian has broken in a wild Thanksgiving revel. All morality is corrupted now as even the chaplain appears in the hospital with "Wisconsin shingles," finding at last the delights of sin in his malingering: "The chaplain had sinned, and it was good." (372) Most disturbingly, there appears in the ward another Soldier in White, another faceless, featureless, characterless mummy absorbing liquid through one tube and evacuating liquid through a second tube attached to the first. Neither the soldiers nor the reader can be sure that it is not the same spectral soldier who appeared at the opening of the novel.

Finally, Yossarian's rebellion takes a more aggressive form; wearing a gun and walking backwards, he refuses to fly. He goes AWOL to Rome where, after passing like an important Dante through the Eternal City which has become a modern Inferno, he finds that Aarfy has murdered a maid. The M.P.s arrive and arrest not Aarfy, the murderer, but Yossarian, the AWOL soldier. When the Colonels offer Yossarian and themselves an out, an opportunity for him to return home and to advertise the goodness and intelligence of his officers, Yossarian wavers, accepts, and then, attacked by Nately's whore, is hospitalized. The novel ends as it began, in the hospital. Here Yossarian learns of Orr's escape to Sweden and the reader learns the details of Snowden's death. Yossarian turns down the deal, as he had turned down Major Major Major Major's earlier offer, and deserts.

The chronology of the Yossarian portion of the novel, then, moves between present and past from the point at which the novel opens, marking off divisions in the novel by returns to the hospital, and creating ever-increasing tension through the narrated order, not the actual chronology, of events. *Catch-22* is not simply an anti-novel in the sense that it avoids the more simple and direct chronological and causal chain of events that makes up the traditional novel. Heller is interested as well in presenting us with his particular vision of the absurd and he accomplishes this too through the time-structure of the book.

The absurd is structurally expressed through the confrontation of the psychological time in which Yossarian's history is told and the chronological time in which Milo Minderbinder's history [53] is told. Minderbinder is introduced to us after Yossarian is released from the hospital at the beginning of the novel, that is, *after* many of the events in the novel have taken place, notably after Avignon and the death of Snowden and after

The Great Big Siege of Bologna. Minderbinder enters the novel at the very outset of his career, when he has just been made mess sergeant and when, on first meeting Yossarian, he talks of "the syndicate I'd like to form someday." (68)

Heller, however, begins immediately to confuse the two chronologies. As we are told that Minderbinder is just starting out, so we are also presented with a series of past events, mentioned early in the novel, that include some of Minderbinder's more infamous exploits, the bridge at Orvieto—when Milo's planes attacked and Milo's guns defended—and Milo's bombing and strafing of his own squadron on Pianosa. The incompatibility of the chronological and causal relationships of events is apparent at once; for these sinister exploits are explained as the necessary economic results of the financial embarrassment occasioned by Minderbinder by his cornering the world cotton market. Since Milo's plunge into cotton cannot have occurred when we first meet him, obviously neither Orvieto nor the bombing of the squadron can have yet taken place. In the narrative order of events Heller makes this quite clear; the cornering of the cotton market is related in Chapter 22, the bombing of the squadron in Chapter 24. Nevertheless, the network of references to events preceding the opening of the novel deliberately confounds the time-sequence.

A great deal seems to hinge on the actual time of the cornering of the cotton market in relation to other events, but Heller avoids establishing this time. His technique here depends on the subtle manipulation of transitions. He presents us with an event which is placed in the time-scheme of the novel; then he compares this to a second event, one which we cannot place in relation to the time of any other happening. The rhetoric of comparison conceals the shift. Finally, the reader shuttles back and forth between events unable to tell which came first.

In the instance of the cotton market, we are told of Dobbs' eagerness to kill Colonel Cathcart as a result of the missions having been raised to 60. Since the missions establish relative time in the novel, there is no difficulty. Dobbs' emotional condition at this time is then compared to Orr's at the time when [54] Orr and Yossarian joined Milo on a tour. This buying trip takes them to Cairo and to the ticker-tape machine which introduces Minderbinder to cotton. The confounding of our time sense is subtly accomplished, and we cannot know whether this tour preceded or followed the period when the missions were raised to 60.

Dobbs was in even worse shape than Hungry Joe, who could at least fly missions when he was not having nightmares. Dobbs was almost as bad as Orr, who seemed happy as an undersized, grinning lark with his deranged and galvanic giggle and shivering warped buck teeth and who was sent along for a rest leave with Milo and Yossarian on the trip to Cairo for eggs when Milo bought

cotton instead and took off at dawn for Istanbul with his plane packed to
the gun turrets with exotic spiders and unripened red bananas. (234)

This narrative sleight-of-hand conceals the fact that Heller is building a
chronological impossibility. For the cotton caused the bombing of the
squadron and the bombing of the squadron is related as one of the events
preceding the opening of the novel—at 45 missions—as preceding, in fact,
The Great Big Siege of Bologna (see page 32), while in fact Milo only
initiates his career when the novel begins, shortly after Bologna.

The irreconcilability of the two chronologies serves the effect of absurdity,
and the two time-schemes operate to enforce thematic considerations, principally the repudiation of the business ethic. The separate time-lines of the
novel exist simultaneously, moving, like lines of polyphonic music, into
occasional shocking dissonance. As Yossarian develops increasing rebelliousness through events of past and present, so Minderbinder increases his
financial empire step by chronological step. The dissonance sounds when
a step in Milo's success occurs simultaneously with the relating of an event
in the "past" time of Yossarian's story. The dissonances, moreover, tend
to fall at moments when one of Minderbinder's greatest successes coincides
with one of the more grotesque moments in the decay of Yossarian's world.
The logic of connection between cynical success and moral decay super-
sedes the logic of chronology.

Heller's technique becomes most apparent in two scenes which bring
together Milo's progress and the details of Snowden's death and funeral.
Chapter 24 tells of the funeral with Yossarian naked in a tree. He is joined
in the tree by an [55] immaculately attired Minderbinder, who wants Yossarian to taste his latest ingenious attempt to unload the now chocolate-
covered cotton. Of course, the chronology is impossible; Minderbinder was
not mess officer, was not apparently even on Pianosa, at the time of
Avignon and Snowden's death. Nevertheless, the logic is inescapable, the
symbolic juxtaposition of death and business.

"Look at that!" [Minderbinder] exclaimed in alarm. . . . "That's a fu-
neral going on down there. . . ."
Yossarian answered him slowly in a level voice. "They're burying that kid
who got killed in my plane over Avignon the other day. Snowden."
"What happened to him?" Milo asked in a voice deadened with awe.
"He got killed."
"That's terrible," Milo grieved, and his large brown eyes filled with tears.
"That poor kid. It really is terrible." He bit his trembling lip hard, and his voice
rose with emotion when he continued, "And it will get even worse if the
mess halls don't agree to buy my cotton." (270)

More significantly anachronistic and more markedly cynical is the juxtaposition of Minderbinder and Snowden when the details of Snowden's death are finally revealed. The details are horrible, and Yossarian's humanity, his revulsion at the sight of Snowden, his careful binding of the wrong wound, only draw the agony finer. To Snowden's continued complaint of cold, Yossarian murmurs comfort, and at last, reaching for the morphine, finds that there is none.

There was no morphine in the first-aid kit, no protection for Snowden against pain but the numbing shock of the gaping wound itself. The twelve syrettes of morphine had been stolen from their case and replaced by a cleanly lettered note that said: "What's good for M & M Enterprises is good for the country. Milo Minderbinder." (446)

The chronological illogicality fades into insignificance beside the appropriateness of the final example of Milo's rapacity and the cruel impersonality of the now enormous syndicate. Heller makes his final thrust with the revelation of Snowden's secret: "Man is matter." Men (Yossarian, Snowden, Nately, Clevinger, and the others) make their tentative way through a complex pattern of past and present; there is no possibility of progress, only the [56] near certitude of death. But Milo Minderbinder moves consistently, inexorably forward—against nations, against wars, against time itself.

The conclusion of *Catch-22* is frequently criticized, and the third section of the novel, with its comparatively straight-forward narration of present events, undoubtedly lacks the force of the earlier sections. The optimism, even the euphoria, of Yossarian's desertion is also difficult to accept. Nevertheless, Yossarian's flight is fitting, even necessary. Minderbinder can build an empire in the world of the novel, the microcosm of Pianosa; for his success depends on the venality and self-interest of others. Milo faces no moral dilemmas. He operates according to the accepted ethics of Pianosa, the sanctity of business, and he avoids the one deadly sin, doing business with the Communists. For Yossarian, the world of Pianosa becomes the world of impossible alternatives in which he must either betray himself by playing along with the Colonels or face court-martial and prison. Even though Yossarian is innocent, he will be proven guilty, because "They can get all the witnesses they need simply by persuading them that destroying you is for the good of the country." (453) "The good of the country," the ultimate sanction of Minderbinder's ethics, is turned against Yossarian. There is no percentage and not even any valor in remaining to fight this offense against justice and morality, for there are no more moral imperatives in this world and no more concepts of justice. The slogans alone remain and even the slogans have been bought up by M & M Enterprises. [57]

Doug Gaukroger
Time Structure in 'Catch-22'

The most striking feature of *Catch-22* [1] is the novel's unusual structure, more specifically its time structure. The rapid changes between events back and forth in time with seemingly little regard for the reader's ability to follow the action clearly has confused some and delighted many. Therefore, it seems strange that in the eight years since the novel's publication only one article has appeared (*Critique*, 1967) which attempts to examine its intricate chronological structure. This article by Jan Solomon sought to illuminate the structure and sort out to some extent the juxtaposed and carefully disordered time sequence of *Catch-22*.[2] Unfortunately, Mr. Solomon's article is flawed by a number of grave textual errors and misreadings; so grave in fact as to subvert entirely his main thesis. I hope to refute points put forth in the Solomon essay, and following this, to lay out for the first time the events in the novel in their proper chronological order. This latter step is, I feel, made necessary by two considerations. First, it offers an alternative to Mr. Solomon's faulty interpretation of the time structure. Second, it will facilitate an examination of some minor inconsistencies which appear in the novel.

A brief summary of Mr. Solomon's thesis and his arguments in support of it will be necessary before we begin to examine and ascertain its validity. He begins by telling us that he is going to examine the novel's form and that the form is most heavily influenced by the time structure. [70]

A careful examination of Heller's novel reveals not only that it has form, but that this form is carefully constructed to support the pervasive theme of absurdity. . . .

---

[1] Joseph Heller, *Catch-22* (New York, 1962). All subsequent references are to this edition.

[2] Jan Solomon, "The Structure of Joseph Heller's *Catch-22*," *Critique*, IX, 2 (1967), 46–57 [and pp. 122–131 in this volume].

SOURCE: *Critique*, Vol. 12, No. 2 (1970), pp. 70–85. Reprinted by permission of the author and publisher.

The most significant aspect of the structure of *Catch-22* is its chronology. Behind what appears to be merely random events lies a careful system of time-sequences involving two distinct and mutually contradictory chronologies. The major part of the novel, focussed on Yossarian, moves forward and back from a pivotal point in time. Yossarian, like many anti-heroes of modern fiction from Leopold Bloom to Moses Herzog, lives in a world dominated not by chronological but by psychological time. Yossarian's time is punctuated, if not ordered, by the inexorable increases in the number of missions and by the repetitious returns to the relative safety and sanity of the hospital. . . .

While the dominant sequence of events shifts back and forth from the present to the past treating any period of time as equally present, equally immediate, a counter-motion controls the time of the history of Milo Minderbinder. Across the see-saw pattern of events in the rest of the novel Minderbinder moves directly forward from one success to the next. . . . Independently, each chronology is valid and logical; *together, the two time-schemes are impossible.* By manipulating the points at which the different systems cross, Heller creates a structural absurdity enforcing the absurdity of character and event in the novel.[3] (italics mine)

This thesis, then, states that Yossarian and Milo Minderbinder, while they appear and interact together throughout the novel, actually exist in two different time structures and that it is (at times) impossible for these two time structures to meet. It is further claimed that two events in the novel could not possibly have occurred: the first is Milo climbing the tree to join the naked Yossarian who is watching Snowden's funeral (pp. 267–74), and the second involves the missing syrettes of morphine (in the B-25's first-aid kit when Yossarian tries to treat Snowden's wound) which have been replaced by signs reading, "What's good for M & M Enterprises is good for the country. Milo Minderbinder" (p. 446). These two events are impossible because Milo supposedly does not arrive on Pianosa until Yossarian's hospital visit, described in Chapter I of the novel at the time when Yossarian had 38 missions to his credit.[4] Yossarian, by this reading, does not meet Milo until shortly after this hospital visit. But this particular hospital stay did not occur until after the Avignon mission and Snowden's death and funeral. How then could Yossarian talk to [71] Milo in the tree at a

---

[3] *Ibid.*, pp. 47–48.
[4] It should be noted that time in the novel is regulated by the number of missions flown by Yossarian and by the number of missions required by Colonel Cathcart. Yossarian never quite reaches the required number; each time he comes close the limit is raised by another five missions. Thus, during the hospital visit described in the opening chapter, Yossarian has completed 38 missions (p. 165) and the official number of required missions is 40. By the time he leaves the hospital and returns to fly his remaining two missions, however, the limit has been raised to 45.

time prior to their first meeting? How could Milo have stolen the morphine for his syndicate when his syndicate had not yet been formed? Such obviously impossible events are explainable only as conscious devices used by Heller in an effort to cause the structure of the novel to coincide with and "support the pervasive theme of absurdity, . . . and to create its own dimension of absurdity." [5]

If all the smoke-screening found in the notions of the two time sequences, the "psychological time" of Yossarian and the "chronological time" of Milo Minderbinder, is cleared away we find that Solomon's article relies totally on two "facts" which he has gleaned from his textual analysis. One is that Yossarian does not meet Milo until after the hospital visit and that Milo has not yet begun his syndicate. The other "fact" is the impossibility of determining at which point in the chronology Yossarian and Orr join Milo on the buying trip which results in his cornering the world cotton market. If these two assertions are disproven and it is shown that Yossarian met Milo before Snowden's death, that the cotton market cornering took place before Avignon, then arguments for an impossible time sequence crumble.

Let us begin by taking a look at Yossarian's first meeting with Milo which Heller describes in Chapter VII and attempt to determine whether it actually did take place after the hospital visit described in Chapter I, when Yossarian had 38 missions.

"What's this?" Milo had cried out in alarm, when he came upon the enormous corrugated carton filled with packages of dried fruit and cans of fruit juices and desserts that two of the Italian laborers Major ———— de Coverley had kidnapped for his kitchen were about to carry off to Yossarian's tent.

"This is Captain Yossarian, sir," said Corporal Snark with a superior smirk. Corporal Snark was an intellectual snob who felt he was twenty years ahead of his time and did not enjoy cooking down to the masses. "He has a letter from Doc Daneeka entitling him to all the fruit and fruit juices he wants."

"What's this?" cried out Yossarian, as Milo went white and began to sway.

"This is Lieutenant Milo Minderbinder, sir," said Corporal Snark with a derisive wink. "One of our new pilots. He became [72] mess officer *while you were in the hospital this last time.*" (pp. 61–62; italics mine)

Milo, then, became mess officer and hence began planning his syndicate while Yossarian was "in the hospital this last time." Nothing in this statement, nor in any statement before or after, would suggest that "this last

---

[5] Solomon, *op. cit.*, p. 47.

time" refers to the opening hospital scene. The handling of the chronological structure in Chapter VIII gives the impression that all events are equally present in time, and thus a superficial reading makes it appear that Yossarian does indeed meet Milo for the first time after his hospital visit at 38 missions. A closer reading, however, reveals that this conclusion is unjustified and that in reality Chapter VII offers no clue at all as to when the first meeting did take place. Later I hope to demonstrate that while one cannot determine *exactly* when Yossarian and Milo first met, one can show that they did indeed meet before 38 missions, probably at a time previous to The Great Big Siege of Bologna.

If one assumes that Milo's career did not begin until after he first met Yossarian at the time when Colonel Cathcart was demanding 45 missions, then two events (the missing morphine over Avignon, and Snowden's funeral), both of which involve a wealthy Milo in some way, are rendered chronologically impossible because they occur prior to the time of the 45 missions. These two alleged chronological impossibilities, then, are said to "serve the effect of absurdity, while the two time schemes operate to enforce thematic considerations, principally the repudiation of the business ethic." [6] Excluding the fact that one cannot prove that Yossarian first met Milo at the time of 45 missions (when Yossarian had 38 missions), a large number of other events involve Milo before this time. If only two events were out of time, as has been suggested, a case might be made for a dual time scheme; however, *all* the events involving Milo occurred at a time prior to the period of 45 missions. This suggests to me either that Heller made a colossal error in his plotting or that Solomon is guilty of overlooking or misreading a great number of events in *Catch-22*. I believe the latter to be the case and the only real impossibility [73] in the time sequence is Solomon's interpretation of it. Heller repeatedly states in the novel that Milo was doing his dirty work long before Yossarian's hospital visit of Chapter I when he had 38 missions. Let us look at some examples.

At the time when Yossarian first meets Milo (p. 61), Milo asks Yossarian if he knows why Corporal Snark has been demoted.

[Milo speaking] "Incidentally, do you happen to know why he was busted to private and is only a corporal now?"

"Yes," said Yossarian. "He poisoned the squadron."

Milo went pale again. "He did what?"

"He mashed hundreds of cakes of GI soap into the sweet potatoes just to show that people have the taste of Philistines and don't know the difference between good and bad. Every man in the squadron was sick. Missions were cancelled." (p. 65)

---

[6] *Ibid.*, p. 55.

Actually there were two poisonings. This is the first and occurred during the missions to Ferrara (p. 20) before Milo arrived on Pianosa. The second poisoning occurs during The Great Big Siege of Bologna when Milo had already been made mess officer.

"Please find out from Corporal Snark if he put laundry soap in the sweet potatoes again," he requested furtively. "Corporal Snark trusts you and will tell you the truth if you give him your word you won't tell anyone else. As soon as he tells you, come and tell me."

"Of course I put laundry soap in the sweet potatoes," Corporal Snark admitted to Yossarian. "That's what you asked me to do, isn't it? Laundry soap is the best way."

"He swears to God he didn't have a thing to do with it," Yossarian reported back to Milo. (p. 128)

Milo, apparently, became mess officer between the two poisonings, as he did not know about the first but had become mess officer by the second. The second poisoning occurred during The Great Big Siege of Bologna when Yossarian had 32 missions and the Colonel wanted 35 (p. 169). Bologna occurred before the Chapter I hospital visit when Yossarian had 38 missions; yet here we have Yossarian talking to Milo both before and during the second mess hall poisoning which happened a full six missions previous to the time they supposedly met. [74]

Solomon's further assertion that,

A great deal seems to hinge on the actual time of the cornering of the cotton market in relation to the other events, but Heller avoids establishing this time. . . . This buying trip takes them to Cairo and to the ticker-tape machine which introduces Minderbinder to cotton . . . we cannot know whether this tour preceded or followed the period when the missions were raised to 60.[7]

also proves quite false. On the contrary, we *can* accurately establish the time when Yossarian, Orr, and Milo flew to Cairo and cornered the cotton market. The reader has merely to turn to pages 125–126 and examine the conversation between Yossarian and Wintergreen. Wintergreen, who is in competition with Milo, comes to Pianosa "to learn if it was really true about Milo and the Egyptian cotton" (p. 125). While Wintergreen is on Pianosa, Yossarian begs him to save the squadron from the fate of flying to Bologna.

---

[7] *Ibid.*, pp. 54–55.

Yossarian suddenly seized his [Wintergreen's] arm. "Couldn't you forge some official orders on that mimeograph machine of yours *and get us out of flying to Bologna?*" (p. 126; italics mine)

Milo bought the Egyptian cotton, then, just before The Great Big Siege of Bologna which was at the time of 35 missions when Yossarian had flown 32. This means that Milo bought the cotton before Mudd was killed at Avignon, and not afterward as we have been led to believe.

Another misreading is found in Solomon's statement that "Since Avignon preceded Bologna . . . we have yet another denial of chronology." [8] The Avignon mission did *not* precede Bologna; it was flown about three weeks and perhaps four missions later. Yossarian's thirty-second mission was the second mission to Bologna after which he fled directly to Rome (p. 156). We learn that Snowden is also in Rome at the time Yossarian trips over his duffel bag, just before he finds the maid in the lime-green panties (pp. 137, 168). If Snowden is still alive at this time, the only conclusion that can be drawn is that the Avignon mission must have been flown after Bologna, probably during the six missions Yossarian flew between hospital visits at 32 and 38 missions.

Many other examples show Milo going about the business [75] of building an empire long before the time he supposedly arrived on Pianosa. Milo begins his air empire by tempting Major ———— de Coverley with visions of a fresh egg frying in fresh butter (p. 139). Major ———— de Coverley disappears when Yossarian moves the bomb-line during The Great Big Siege of Bologna which, as we have seen, is some time before Yossarian allegedly meets Milo. Clevinger wonders how Milo can buy eggs at seven cents in Malta and sell them at a profit on Pianosa for five cents (p. 69), yet Clevinger is dead two and one half weeks before Milo supposedly starts his empire (p. 176). At the time of 70 missions, just after Thanksgiving, we find that Milo has been overseas for eleven months (p. 378). Yet it is stated that "Minderbinder . . . was not apparently even on Pianosa, at the time of Avignon and Snowden's death," [9] which occurred about the middle of the summer. Milo is mentioned in connection with The Great Loyalty Oath Campaign (p. 119) which was broken up my Major ———— de Coverley; therefore, it must have taken place before Bologna. Milo secretly feeds both Captain Flume and Major Major when they go into hiding, which is long before the period of 45 missions. We find that "April had been the best month of all for Milo" (p. 257). His mess hall ventures are going strong in the spring, yet he is not supposed to have been made

---

[8] *Ibid.*, p. 52.
[9] *Ibid.*, p. 56.

mess officer until the summer. If we add all these "chronological impossibilities" to the three already noted, there seems to be little doubt that Milo *was* around long before the time of 45 missions.

That it cannot be shown for certain that Milo was just beginning his career at the time of 45 missions, plus the fact that Heller clearly shows us that Milo's fortunes were booming long before this time, demonstrates quite amply that any theory which posits two juxtaposed time schemes developed to further the sense of absurdity is false. On the contrary, I believe a time scheme for the novel is possible in which all events follow quite logically one upon the other. With one or two minor exceptions, chronological paradoxes are quite rare in *Catch-22*. The following is a summary of the events of the novel in what I believe to be their proper chronological order.

Yossarian talks to Wintergreen at Lowry Field, Colorado [76] (p. 108). We learn that sometime after this, Wintergreen strikes a waterpipe while digging holes as punishment for going A.W.O.L. The water is rumored to be oil, and Chief White Halfoat is kicked off the base and eventually ends up on Pianosa as a replacement for Lt. Coombs who was killed in Kraft's plane when it was shot down during the second bomb-run over Ferrara. We also learn that Milo bombs the squadron seven months after Wintergreen strikes water.

Yossarian is a private at Lowry Field (p. 181). He discovers the hospital as a sanctuary when he enters it to escape calisthenics. Here he first learns to fake a liver condition. He spends ten days in the hospital, then fourteen more under quarantine with the soldier who saw everything twice. Yossarian imitates this soldier's symptoms for one more day but quits when the man dies. Before he leaves the hospital Yossarian must take the place of Giuseppe, the dying soldier, whose parents have come to visit him (pp. 188–191). This hospital stay coincides with Thanksgiving, and Yossarian resolves to spend all his Thanksgivings in a hospital.

One full year later we find Yossarian taking officer training in California under Lieutenant Scheisskopf (pp. 69–72) and spending Thanksgiving in bed with Scheisskopf's wife, arguing about God. We learn of Scheisskopf's passion for parades (p. 72) and Clevinger's experiences with the "Action Board" (pp. 76–82).

Yossarian, Appleby, and Kraft fly from Puerto Rico to Pianosa and become involved in The Splendid Atabrine Insurrection (p. 109). Yossarian first refused to take his malaria pill in Puerto Rico and ten days later, Appleby, immediately upon arrival on Pianosa, tries to report Yossarian to Major Major, only to find that the Major is in hiding.

Yossarian begins flying missions under Colonel Nevers. When he has flown 17 missions Yossarian enters the hospital with a case of clap.

Hungry Joe had finished flying his first twenty-five missions during the week of the Salerno beachhead, when Yossarian was laid up in the hospital with a burst of clap he had caught on a low-level mission over a Wac in bushes on a supply flight to Marrakech. Yossarian did his best to catch up with Hungry Joe and almost [77] did, flying six missions in six days, but his twenty-third mission was to Arezzo, where Colonel Nevers was killed, and that was as close as he had ever been able to come to going home. The next day Colonel Cathcart was there, brimming with tough pride in his new outfit and celebrating his assumption of command by raising the number of missions required from twenty-five to thirty. Hungry Joe unpacked his bags and rewrote the happy letters home. (p. 54)

Much important chronological information is to be gleaned from this paragraph. Yossarian and Hungry Joe seem to begin flying at approximately the same time under Colonel Nevers when the required number of missions was 25. Yossarian has a total of 17 missions when he enters the hospital; Hungry Joe, who continues flying, reaches 25 during this time. Discharged from the hospital, Yossarian flies six more missions in six days for a total of 23 when Colonel Nevers is killed. Colonel Cathcart takes over and raises the required number to 30.

One of the first acts of Colonel Cathcart upon taking command is to volunteer the group for Ferrara, where ". . . his men had flown nine missions . . . in six days and the bridge was not demolished until the tenth mission on the seventh day, when Yossarian killed Kraft and his crew by taking his flight of six planes over the target a second time" (p. 141). A great many problems with time surround these Ferrara missions. We know that they occurred after Yossarian had 23 missions because they were ordered by Colonel Cathcart who assumed command at that time (p. 54). We also know that they occurred before the First Mission to Bologna which would have been Yossarian's thirty-second mission had he not aborted it. ("By the time of the mission to Bologna, Yossarian was brave enough not to go over the target even once . . ." p. 144.) It is obvious that Yossarian did not fly all the missions to Ferrara as there were ten flights in all and Yossarian could have flown a maximum of eight (24–31 inclusive). This would mean that the final successful mission to Ferrara was Yossarian's thirty-first, though if he flew less than his possible maximum of eight, then it might have been his [78] thirtieth or twenty-ninth. The squadron was first poisoned by Corporal Snark during the Ferrara missions (p. 20), an event Milo has not heard of so he could not have been on Pianosa at this time (p. 65). When Corporal Snark poisons the squadron again during The Great Big Siege of Bologna (p. 128), Milo is already mess officer during The Siege. This, however, conflicts with Corporal

Snark's remark to Yossarian, that Milo was made mess officer while Yossarian was "in the hospital this last time" (p. 62). This is plainly not the hospital visit at 17 missions necessitated by the clap, nor is it the hospital visit at 32 missions which occurred *after* Bologna. As far as we can determine there is no hospital visit in between. Were it not for this remark by Corporal Snark, we would assume that Milo had joined the squadron shortly after the Ferrara missions, and the chronology would follow plausibly. Similarly, were it not for the single reference (p. 20) made by Yossarian to the food first being poisoned during Ferrara, we might assume the poisoning occurred very early, even before Yossarian got the clap. This would allow Milo to have been made mess officer while Yossarian was "in the hospital this last time." Indeed, when Yossarian refers later to the first poisoning, he says to Milo: ". . . every man in the squadron was sick. Missions were cancelled" (p. 65). This does not sound like Ferrara where ten missions were flown in seven days. It is difficult to see how any missions were cancelled when ten were flown in a single week.

There is a definite conflict in time as regards this whole business of Yossarian's releases from the hospital, the first food poisoning, Milo's promotion to mess officer, and the Ferrara missions. It is, of course, impossible to say for certain whether Heller deliberately included this conflict in the novel or whether it was an oversight. There seems to be no artistic demand for the two conflicting statements of Yossarian, or for Corporal Snark's reference to Milo's promotion, so the whole matter might be interpreted as a slight slip in plotting. After all, the book was written and re-written, old episodes dropped and new episodes inserted over a seven-year period, and this business of the food poisoning during Ferrara may [79] be an example of an event which has been changed or should have been changed during the book's final editing. Another example of this may be the puzzling statement by Yossarian after Ferrara when he suggests that Colonel Cathcart give him a medal because, "You gave one to Hungry Joe when he cracked up that airplane by mistake" (p. 143). As the only mention of Hungry Joe crashing a plane, this may be a reference to an event which Heller decided at some period in his editing to leave out, and the statement of Yossarian's is all that remains.

Major Major's retreat from the world also presents some problems in chronology. When Yossarian and Appleby arrive on Pianosa from Puerto Rico, Appleby's first action is to report Yossarian to Major Major because he will not take his Atabrine tablets (p. 109). Major Major, however, is in hiding and Appleby cannot see him because, as Sergeant Towser tells him, "Major Major never sees anyone in his office while he's in his office." This contradicts the account of Major Major's actions preparatory to his going into seclusion. Major Major drops out of sight some time after he is appointed Squadron Commander by Colonel Cathcart; however, Colonel Cathcart does not take over the squadron until Colonel Nevers dies at the time when Yossarian has completed 23 missions. It is, therefore, impossible for Major Major to have already gone into hiding when Yossarian and Appleby first arrive on Pianosa. This inconsistency may be merely a detail which escaped Heller's notice, but I am inclined to view it as an inability on his part to resist placing the priggish and officious Appleby in a position where he can be humiliated by Sergeant Towser.

The next series of events occur during The Great Big Siege of Bologna which is central to the novel. The long, nerve-eroding wait for the dreaded flight to Bologna is important to the character development and motivation of Yossarian. He has lost his bravery over Ferrara and thus feels more keenly the sense of doom which pervades the base. A number of events occur during The Siege. Yossarian moves the bomb-line (p. 123), which causes Major ——— de Coverley to fly to Florence and [80] disappear (p. 135) and enables General Peckem to get a medal because he "was the only officer with sufficient initiative to ask for it" (p. 124). Chief White Halfoat first decides to die of pneumonia at this time (p. 131). Corporal Snark prolongs the wait by poisoning the fliers again (p. 128). Hungry Joe goes to pieces and tries to kill Havermeyer and a day later has a fistfight with Huple's cat (p. 134). Milo, Orr, and Yossarian fly to Cairo, and Milo corners the cotton market (p. 234). In order to pay for all the cotton which begins piling up in the warehouses, Milo is forced to take contracts from both sides to bomb and defend the bridge at Orvieto, and later takes a second contract from the Germans to bomb his own squadron. Yossarian sees Wintergreen about Milo's Egyptian cotton (p. 125). Yossarian has a fight with Colonel Korn over the Lepage glue gun (p. 128). Orr is holidaying in Rome during The Siege and during the actual mission is on a rest leave after he ditched his plane over Genoa (p. 147). It is never specifically mentioned how long The Great Big Siege of Bologna lasts. As time in the novel is measured only in terms of the number of missions flown, the length of periods when missions are not being flown is impossible to determine. I believe Heller is deliberately vague in his treatment of The Siege in order to avoid the necessity of being specific about the order and chronology of all the events which occur during this time.

Yossarian aborts the mission to Bologna by tearing out the wires in his intercom (p. 145). Bologna proves to be a milk-run (p. 148). The second run to Bologna encounters heavy flak, and Yossarian is reduced to a quivering hulk by Aarfy, who won't get out of the hatch way and keeps prodding Yossarian in the ribs (pp. 151–156). This was Yossarian's thirty-second mission.

Yossarian runs to Rome and finds Lucianna (p. 156), then loses her (p. 169). When he returns to base he finds that the required number of missions has been raised.

"Forty missions," Hungry Joe announced readily in a voice lyrical with relief and elation. "The colonel raised them again."

Yossarian was stunned. "But I've got thirty-two, goddammit! Three more and I would have been through." [81]

Hungry Joe shrugged indifferently. "The colonel wants forty missions," he repeated.

Yossarian shoved him out of the way and ran right into the hospital. (p. 169)

Yossarian stays in the hospital for ten days, comes out and flies six more missions for a total of 38, then runs right back into the hospital when Colonel Cathcart raises the required number to forty-five. A number of important events occur during these six missions between hospital visits: the Avignon mission in which Snowden is killed is flown (he is alive in Rome [p. 168] but dead by this second hospital visit at 38 missions [p. 170]); Clevinger disappears (p. 176); Yossarian receives his medal for the Ferrara mission (p. 223) and sits naked in the tree watching Snowden's funeral (pp. 268–273).

During the hospital visit at 38 missions Yossarian first meets the Chaplain (p. 7), and also the soldier in white. The whole business of forging Washington Irving's signature and the subsequent investigations of the C.I.D. begin at this point. Yossarian and his friends are eventually driven out of the hospital by the friendly Texan, and Orr tells Yossarian about his apple cheeks and the whore who kept hitting him over the head (pp. 23–25). Yossarian flies six more missions and Colonel Cathcart raises the required number to 50.

"Fifty missions," Doc Daneeka told him, shaking his head. "The colonel wants fifty missions."

"But I've only got forty-four!" . . .

"Fifty missions," he repeated, still shaking his head. "The colonel wants fifty missions."

Yossarian flies four more for a total of 48 but the Colonel raises the required number to 55.

Yossarian slumped with disappointment. "Then I really do have to fly the fifty missions, don't I?" he grieved.

"The fifty-five," Doc Daneeka corrected him.

"What fifty-five?"

"The fifty-five missions the colonel now wants all of you to fly." (p. 60)

Yossarian goes to see Major Major about grounding him when he has 51 missions. Major Major offers him an opportunity to fly only milk-runs, but

Yossarian turns him down (p. 106). After seeing Major Major, Yossarian goes to Doc [82] Daneeka to be grounded. Doc Daneeka refuses to help and advises Yossarian to fly the remaining four missions so that he will be in a stronger position when he refuses to fly any more. Yossarian decides to fly the remaining missions, but before he reaches 55 Colonel Cathcart raises the number to 60 (p. 194). The season is now late August (p. 203). At this time, Dobbs comes to Yossarian's tent with a plan to kill Colonel Cathcart (p. 232), and the Chaplain reports to the Colonel about the prayers before missions which the Colonel hopes will get his picture in *The Saturday Evening Post*, and leaves with a plum tomato (p. 194).

Yossarian is wounded in the groin on the weekly milk-run over Parma and is hospitalized (p. 296). While Yossarian is in the hospital, Orr makes his last practice crash-landing off the coast of Marseilles during the second mission to Avignon (p. 315). In the hospital Yossarian has his experiences with Major Sanderson, the psychiatrist (pp. 303–312). He is visited by Dobbs who again tries to enlist his help in killing Colonel Cathcart (p. 308). A. Fortiori gets Yossarian's medical discharge while he and Dunbar are returned to combat (p. 312).

When Yossarian comes out of the hospital, the required number of missions is still 60. He tries to enlist Dobbs' help in killing Colonel Cathcart, because he has scheduled another mission to Bologna, but Dobbs now has completed his 60 missions and refuses (p. 315). Orr finishes his stove and asks Yossarian to fly with him on the mission to Bologna. Yossarian refuses and Orr disappears on that flight (p. 325).

After Orr's disappearance, Yossarian almost kills McWatt when McWatt flies too low returning from a practice mission (p. 342). During this time Yossarian begins taking Nurse Duckett to the beach. Just after McWatt frightens Yossarian by flying too low on a practice mission, he flies low over the raft at the beach and chops Kid Sampson in half and then flies himself into a mountain (pp. 347–349). Colonel Cathcart is so upset by the deaths of McWatt and Kid Sampson that he raises the number of missions to 65 (p. 349). When he hears that Doc Daneeka is also "dead," he raises the number to 70 (p. 350). "Yo Yo's" roommates move in within [83] forty-eight hours of McWatt's and Kid Sampson's deaths (p. 355). Yossarian runs to Rome and rescues Nately's whore from the generals (pp. 360–368).

Thanksgiving night Sergeant Knight shoots up the camp and Yossarian breaks Nately's nose, sending him to the hospital (p. 370). Yossarian, Dunbar, Hungry Joe, and the Chaplain check in as patients to visit him (p. 371). The soldier in white returns, pandemonium breaks out, and Dunbar "is disappeared" (p. 376).

Yossarian and Nately both finish their 70 missions (p. 383). Nately is afraid that he will be sent home, and thereby lose his whore, if he does not volunteer to fly more than 70 missions (p. 377). Colonel Cathcart wants to raise the required number to 80, but he is afraid the men won't fly any more (p. 383). He figures that if he "can get just one of the regular officers to fly more, the rest will probably follow" (p. 383). Milo tells him about Nately and Colonel Cathcart is overjoyed.

> "But Nately will fly more!" Colonel Cathcart declared, and he brought his hands together in a resounding clap of victory. "Yes, Nately will fly more. And this time I'm really going to jump the missions, right up to eighty, and really knock General Dreedle's eye out. And this is a good way to get that lousy rat Yossarian back into combat where he might get killed." (p. 383)

The next day, Yossarian cannot find Nately in time to persuade him not to fly and thus present a solid opposition to the increased number of missions. They all fly the mission to Spezia and Dobbs and Nately are killed (p. 385). This is Yossarian's seventy-first and last mission. From this point on, Yossarian refuses to fly any more missions, and the climactic chapters which follow are plainly chronological and need not be summarized at this point.

After spending such a great deal of time proving (what in any other novel would be taken for granted) that the chronological structure of *Catch-22* is indeed possible, one must face the question as to why Heller spent so much effort in obfuscation. The answer is, I believe, twofold. The most obvious is the effect created by treating all events as equally present. The intent is to confuse the reader's sense of order and to upset [84] his basic assumptions regarding proper form and structure. The unorthodox treatment of time in *Catch-22* is both parallel to, and prepares the reader for, the unorthodox treatment of the subject matter. It is only fitting that a novel which deals with an apparently absurd and confused world should be written in an apparently absurd and confused style.

The second reason for Heller's obfuscation concerns itself mainly with numerous events occurring during The Great Big Siege of Bologna. By being vague (or even obtuse) as to the length of The Seige, Heller is able to deal with a large amount of humorous material, from a satiric treatment of a loyalty crusade to jokes about a Lepage glue gun, without the necessity of trying to locate events specifically in time. Heller does not need to develop an impossible time scheme to create a sense of absurdity and confusion in his novel; he achieves this effect better by obscuring and twisting a chronological structure which is both plausible and logical. [85]

Howard J. Stark

The Anatomy of 'Catch-22'

In Chapter XX, approximately halfway through *Catch-22*, Chaplain A. T. Tappman experiences a "weird, occult sensation," the phenomenon of *déjà vu*.[1] Technically, the chaplain is a victim of Korsakow's syndrome, the condition in which temporal order is disrupted because of psychological causes, resulting in a confused comprehension of the succession or duration of events. It is the chaplain's fascination with the perplexities of *déjà vu* and its alternate forms, *jamais vu* and *presque vu*, that provides the key to the structural method and pattern of the novel. Throughout, the novel projects in a profusion of scenes and images the "subtle, recurring confusion between illusion and reality" that has so bewildered the chaplain. Moreover, it is from this subtle manner in which structure is organized and manipulated that the novel develops theme and meaning, its "achieved content."[2]

To achieve this effective relationship between theme and structure, between form and content, Heller makes use of structural devices basic to the Theatre of the Absurd: the juxtaposing of incongruities—the comic with the tragic, the grotesque with the farcical, the real with the illusory; the renunciation of time as an ordering factor; the failure of language as an effective means of communication; the use of the ludicrous and the illogical as standards of moral or ethical behavior; and the depiction of the deep-seated feelings of frustration and anguish. As Martin Esslin expresses it, the structure of an absurd drama is the key to the play's meaning:

---

[1] Joseph Heller, *Catch-22* (New York: Dell, 1962), p. 209. All references are to this edition and will be cited hereafter in the text.

[2] Mark Schorer, "Technique as Discovery," in *Critiques and Essays on Modern Fiction*, ed. John W. Aldridge (New York: Ronald Press, 1952), p. 67. Schorer states that "modern criticism has shown us that to speak of content as such is not to speak of art at all, but of experience; and that it is only when we speak of the *achieved* content, the form, the work of art as a work of art, that we speak as critics. The difference between content, or experience, and achieved content, or art, is technique."

SOURCE: This essay was written especially for this book. For a study of *Catch-22* as the ultimate irony, see Mr. Stark's essay in James Nagel, ed., *Critical Essays on Catch-22* (Encino, Calif.: Dickenson, 1973).

The whole play is a complex poetic image made up of a complicated pattern of subsidiary images and themes, which are interwoven like the themes of a musical composition, not as in most well-made plays, to present a line of development, but to make in the spectator's mind a total, complex impression of a basic, and static, situation. In this, the Theatre of the Absurd is analogous to a Symbolist or Imagistic poem, which also presents a pattern of images and associations in a mutually interdependent structure.[3]

Esslin's point is that structure controls the emotional and intellectual impact of a play through the ordering of the scenes and images, arranging them into a certain sequence of imagistic perceptions atomized and juxtaposed to create tension, suspense, and, ultimately, understanding. The significance of this discordant kind of arrangement is that it reflects more accurately the themes and content of a work. In discussing the content of an "absurd" drama, Esslin states that "there is an immense difference between artistically and dramatically valid nonsense and just nonsense." [4] What makes an "absurd" drama a work of art, according to Esslin, is the quality and complexity of the images, "the skill with which they are combined and sustained," and, most important of all, "the *reality* and *truth* of the vision these images embody." [5] Because the primary concern of the Theatre of the Absurd is the essence and reality of the human condition, it uses discordance as the most descriptive way of presenting the discrete aspects of contemporary life. Time and the orderly arrangement of events, for that reason, are not visualized as a logical, continuous flow from past to present to future; instead, everything is present tense because modern man no longer views or relates in a concrete way to life in a sequential manner. For Esslin, then, the Theatre of the Absurd is "a theatre of situations as against a theatre of events in sequence" [6] in which man is forced to face the antinomy of his condition in a world tending toward entropy.

In the same vein, Joseph Frank in "Spatial Form in Modern Literature" states that modern literature is moving in a direction where one is intended to apprehend a literary work "in a moment of time, rather than a sequence." [7] Frank contends that the complete understanding of a literary work cannot be achieved until all scenes and images have been brought together and seen in their proper relationship and from the proper perspective. Because spatial form engages and bombards one's sensory re-

---

[3] Martin Esslin, *The Theatre of the Absurd* (Garden City, N.Y.: Doubleday, 1961), p. 294.

[4] *Ibid.*, p. 309.

[5] *Ibid.*, p. 311.

[6] *Ibid.*, p. 294.

[7] Joseph Frank, *The Widening Gyre* (New Brunswick, N.J.: Rutgers University Press, 1963), p. 8.

sponse in an irrational or disjunctive manner, there is a tendency to become lost, confused, or misled. One must, therefore, wait for the structural pattern to work itself out in order to see the complexity of the literary work and to understand "its structure, texture, and impact," its "achieved content."

In *Catch-22*, Heller uses structure as both Esslin and Frank define its function, setting up a pattern of images and scenes arranged in a nonsequential manner and which take on meaning only after being brought together and seen in their proper relationship and from the proper perspective. In its pattern, the novel flows from one isolated scene to another, from one isolated image to another, from one "immobilized time-area" to another. As this movement occurs, it reveals a structure that on the surface appears to be incongruous and illogical, which is, however, precisely the design of the novel. *Catch-22* does not explain, analyze, or argue situations or causes; it effectively presents the absurdity of modern life through the careful juxtaposing of seemingly incongruous scenes and images. Thus, the incongruous and illogical disappear as the function of structure becomes clear, and as the significance of the structural pattern solidifies, meaning begins to take shape.

On its simple narrative level, *Catch-22* moves in a straight line, covering approximately seven months: from summer to late fall in 1944. Entwined into the narrative level, however, is a psychological free association of ideas type of plot development which explodes the simple narrative and takes the novel through a frenetic three-year time period. Although the narrative plot development may not always be immediately discernible, it is clearly indicated throughout by numerous clues, such as the number of missions Yossarian has flown or by references to seasonal changes. The chronology of the narrative plot, however, is purposely obfuscated by the associational digressions which continually juxtapose the past with the present and fuse these scenes and images into a single comprehensive image: a grotesque picture of the absurd condition of modern life.

Consequently, the reader, like the chaplain, has the uneasy feeling that he has gone through an experience before; and so he has, for the novel returns again and again to the same scenes and images—*déjà vu*—or to contrasting scenes and images which only give the illusion of being different from those previously seen—*presque vu, jamais vu*. This spatializing of form effectively removes the distinctions between past and present and between various locations to emphasize the psychological relationship between events and ideas.

The scenes and images in the novel, then, can be divided into three types: those in which there is a static recurring image, *déjà vu*; those in which there is a shifting recurring image, *presque vu*; and those in which there is an illusory recurring image, *jamais vu*.

The static recurring image is one that does not change its form, meaning, or identity throughout the novel. The soldier in white, Snowden, and the dead man in Yossarian's tent are examples of static recurring images because their symbolic value is consistent and immediately recognizable. Although the shifting recurring image maintains the same meaning throughout the novel, the characters and places are constantly changing. For example, the trial scenes between Clevinger and the fat colonel, Yossarian and the fat colonel, and the chaplain and the fat colonel fit this pattern because the scenes produce the same idea but use different people and situations to do so. The various scenes set in different hospitals, the bombing raids to Avignon, Bologna, and Ferrara, Milo's bombing of the squadron, and his flights for the syndicate are all shifting recurring images. In the same way, Dreedle, Peckem, Scheisskopf, Cathcart, Korn, Cargill, and Moodus are components of the same incompetent yet effective bureaucracy, along with the hospital doctors.

The illusory recurring image, though, is more difficult to see at first; not only are there different people involved, but the idea being expressed seems different also. The scenes that focus on Nately's conversation with the old man in the Roman bordello, Yossarian's conversation with the army psychiatrist, and Yossarian's encounter with Milo in the Garden of Eden scene during Snowden's funeral all depict the same themes. In the same way, Doc Daneeka after his death, Yossarian when impersonating the dead soldier, and Snowden wrapped in his white parachute are illusory recurring images for the soldier in white. Another illusory recurring image is Orr, the only major character in the novel without his own chapter. There is the suggestion that Orr, like the soldier in white, may not physically exist, that he, too, is the personification of an illusory ideal.

The three types of imagistic scenes, then, serve to juxtapose physically isolated events and meld them into a psychological continuum. What emerges is the realization that there is no difference between the bizarre and the realistic, the ludicrous and the grotesque; what emerges is the awful awareness that the grisly treatment of Snowden's death is no more terrifying than Doc Daneeka's ridiculous demise. The three types of imagistic scenes, when compared reflexively, vividly demonstrate that under every absurd, inane, farcical, ludicrous image and scene lies Kurtz's penetrating comment: "The horror! the horror!"

The frame in which these three types of scenes fit, the novel itself, can be divided into three main sections: Chapters I through XVIII, XIX through XXV, and XXVI through XLII. During the first two sections, the reader is exposed to a seemingly confused, disordered, hodgepodge, a complexity of turmoil, pandemonium, and lunacy. And so he is, for the rapid movement of the narrative through Chapter XXV is intended to overwhelm the reader, to stun him with the fierce, comic onslaught that comes tumbling from the pages.

The first section of the novel, in which the actual time lapse of four weeks is glossed over, covers a two-year period and establishes the mood, tone, and themes of the novel as a whole. Like Yossarian's non-existent liver condition, the supposed contrast between reality and illusion is emphasized in these chapters as the narrative oscillates from scene to scene. The misleading nature of the surface impression of the novel begins with the opening words: "It was love at first sight. The first time Yossarian saw the chaplain he fell madly in love with him" (p. 7). The first time Yossarian saw the chaplain, however, he "just took it for granted he was either another doctor or another madman" (p. 12). What follows the exaggerated first lines appears to be a series of short, comic, *non sequitur* scenes depicting the inane activities of a group of not really sick men. No one is in the hospital because of war injuries; instead, like the captain with a "mosquito bite on the ass" from making love or Yossarian's pain in the liver, the hospital presents a world where everything is a few notches out of kilter, as symbolized by Yossarian's temperature always being two degrees above normal and Doc Daneeka's always being two degrees below. From Yossarian's psychologically revealing assaults on the letters he has to censor to the doctor's wild, insensible assaults on the dying colonel, the narrative unrolls in a humorous manner, carefully underplaying the serious implications of the scenes.

Starting with Chapter II, the narrative begins running quickly in kaleidoscopic fashion through a series of frenetic scenes. Chapter II starts with a dissolve to the past for a scene in the officers' club, returns to the present to introduce some members of the squadron, cuts back to the officers' club again, and ends in the present, picking up Yossarian's return from the hospital, which is seen again at the start of Chapter III, but from another angle. The absurd dialogue between Yossarian and Orr during the first part of Chapter III provides a stream-of-consciousness fade to a scene in the past, which ends with a sharp cut to the present before moving through several short flashes showing the ludicrous behavior of various staff officers. The narrative then cuts to the past to disclose the inanity of a bombing mission, dissolves from this past to another past and another aspect of a bombing mission, and then jumps on cue to the present for the preposterous scene in which Havermeyer, the lead bombardier, attacks the mice in his tent with dum dum bullets fired from the .45 automatic he has stolen from the dead man in Yossarian's tent.

The pattern of mixing slow fades or glides with quick cuts is repeated through the next four chapters, with scenes shifting from present to past to present, from parody, ridicule, caricature, from the absurd and the incongruous, to terrifying, petrifying realism. Chapters VIII and IX, however, interrupt the narrative flow to lampoon the philosophical dilemma of "necessity" and "circumstance," mocking and burlesquing justice, military life and protocol, farm subsidies, un-American activities, love, sex, God, mother, and patriotism—repeating, in essence, the ideas and images of the first seven chapters, déjà vu, just presenting them in another way.

The focal point of Chapters X to XV is the bombing mission to Bologna. This event takes place in the past and is constantly being interrupted as the narrative keeps switching to other events to offer contrasting images. Chapter XVI carries on the absurdity of the preceding six chapters, switching from men in war to men in love, both just as anguished and ridiculous. The narrative returns to the present in Chapter XVII to repeat almost all of Chapter I and in greater detail the soldier in white scene, to develop further Yossarian's reasons for rushing to the hospital, and to mull once more the philosophical complexities of death, duty, and disease. Chapter XVIII takes the narrative back to Yossarian's aviation cadet school days and his impersonation of a dead soldier, his discovery of hospital duty, his affair with Lieutenant Scheisskopf's wife and their discussion of God, values, and other diseases. Chapter XVIII repeats the ideas of Chapter XVII, which is an enlargement of Chapter I.

With Chapter XVIII, then, the first section of the novel circles back to the beginning and closes. During this movement, the narrative has been establishing major themes through structure by repeating scenes and images echoing the confusion between reality and illusion, between the absurd and the grotesque. The montage of static, shifting, and illusory images in this section conveys forcefully impressionistic scenes frozen in their own instant isolated time and space yet interchangeable to the degree that they all mirror the same irrational view of existence.

The second section of the novel continues in the same vein as the first. Because the narrative time lapse in Chapters XIX to XXV is just one day —actually the morning and afternoon of one day—the manner in which Heller is employing the free association of ideas technique can be seen more clearly. These scenes, however, no longer seem a disparate mulching of unrelated events, as much of the material has already been covered in the first section.

Chapter XIX opens with a caustic character delineation of Colonel Cathcart and then develops the confrontation between Cathcart and Chaplain Tappman. This encounter echoes the theme of "necessity" and "circumstance," as seen in Chapter VIII, and ridicules the efficiency of the two men, both symbols of leadership and both victims of circumstances neither can control nor handle. Like Clevinger's "To die or not to die," Doc Daneeka's death, Major ——— de Coverley's disappearance, Dreedle's ouster, Milo's success, or Scheisskopf's coup d'état, man as a victim of circumstance is treated in a humorous fashion as the scenes in this section of the novel digress and spin-off to repeat the idea from Chapter XVII: "There just doesn't seem to be any logic to this system of rewards and punishment" (p. 175).

Humiliated by Colonel Cathcart in Chapter XIX, Chaplain Tappman returns to his tent where, in Chapter XX, he is subjected to another browbeating, this time from his assistant, Corporal (later Sergeant) Whitcomb. Chapter XXI picks up Colonel Cathcart as he was last seen in Chapter XIX: "The chaplain's first mention of the name *Yossarian!* had tolled deep in his memory like a portentous gong" (p. 214). Suddenly, the colonel is recalling a series of events, and in each one a Yossarian was involved: the man who bombed the bridge at Ferrara was Yossarian; the man who moved the bomb line before the mission to Bologna was Yossarian; and the man who had stood naked in the ranks to receive his Distinguished Flying Cross was Yossarian. The scene ends with Colonel Cathcart in a muddle, feeling that he will never make general. This thought triggers a transition to General Dreedle, and the narrative dissolves from Cathcart to Dreedle and then to the scene in which Dreedle awards a medal to a naked man, from which it then fades to a new scene, the one which uncovers the reasons behind Yossarian's nakedness: the briefing for the Avignon mission.

The briefing session turns into a comic debacle as Yossarian begins moaning at the sight of General Dreedle's nubile nurse, at the sight of the "rolling, ripened triangular confluences of her belly and thighs . . ." (p. 225). The pandemonium of this scene is carried into the first scene of Chapter XXII, which is a short, flak-filled sequence of the mission to Avignon, during which Snowden loses his guts and Yossarian his nerve. The bedlam of this mission is carried into the next scene, as Dobbs concocts a wild scheme to murder Colonel Cathcart. This scene establishes the transition for a time and place shift to the past for the details of Milo Minderbinder's wild odyssey through the Mediterranean on a secret mission: to buy eggs at five cents apiece to be fried in real butter at the squadrons' mess halls while Kraft, Coombs, and Mudd are being fried over the targets for nothing, while the ripened confluences of Snowden's belly and thigh are being ripped open and Yossarian moans anew.

Chapters XIX to XXV use static, shifting, and illusory imagistic scenes to repeat thematic ideas started earlier. The "necessity-circumstance" theme in this section of the novel, the horns of the dilemma on which both Colonel Cathcart and Chaplain Tappman have been squirming, is the same "vile, excruciating dilemma of duty and damnation" that Yossarian "was up to his own ass in" during the mission to Bologna sequence. It is Yossarian's job to be killed, ex-P.F.C. Wintergreen tells him, just as it is Wintergreen's job to "unload these Zippo lighters at a profit" (p. 126) and Colonel Cathcart's job to keep raising the number of missions and be promoted to general. It is the crux of the dialogue between Nately and the diabolical, lecherous old man in the Roman bordello in Chapter XXIII. The seedy, unprincipled, "hundred and seven" year-old man enthroned like a satanic deity in the bordello reminds Nately very much of his father because the two are "nothing at all alike." As an illusory image for Nately's father, a Brooks Brothers WASP, the sordid old man expresses views which are anathema to Nately's traditional, patriotic ideals: ". . . anything worth dying for," he tells Nately, "is certainly worth living for," and imagine a man "risking what little life he has left for something so absurd as a country" (p. 253). The old man has managed to survive because he will not be a victim of circumstance. Like Yossarian's response to Clevinger's ours-is-not-to-wonder-why-ours-is-but-to-do-or-die attitude before he disappeared into a plane-devouring nimbus—"it doesn't make a damn bit of difference *who* wins the war to someone who's dead" (p. 127)—the old man's argument calls attention to the absurdity of an existence in which man blindly follows the concepts of a questionable necessity, moral or ethical, and then falls victim, ironically, to circumstance, as with General Dreedle:

He had no taste for sham, tact or pretension, and his credo as a professional soldier was unified and concise: he believed that the young men who took orders from him should be willing to give up their lives for the ideals, aspirations and idiosyncrasies of the old men he took orders from. (p. 222)

Dreedle, however, falls victim to General Peckem's campaign to place all combat units under Special Services. All moral and ethical questions concerning "necessity" and "circumstance" are neatly answered in Chapter XXIV when Milo shows the tremendous profit "free enterprise" has made in the name of the syndicate from contracting with the Germans to bomb Colonel Cathcart's squadron. The necessity for Milo's actions are well-documented and legally defensible, for a contract is a contract, and those who were injured in the raid were just part of the overall scheme, like Snowden. Snowden provides the transition to the last scene in the chapter, which is a garishly mixed picture of the bizarre, ludicrous, macabre, and angelic. This scene is a parody of the temptation scene in the Garden of Eden, with Yossarian sitting naked in the tree of life and knowledge watching Snowden's funeral while Milo, sitting next to him attired in his dark business uniform, bewails his economic misfortunes and tries to tempt Yossarian with chocolate-covered cotton.

Chapters XXIII and XXIV also present several scenes which are illusory images for one in the Bologna sequence. Yossarian's perch in the tree at Snowden's funeral recalls the image of Doc Daneeka "roosting like a melancholy buzzard" below the sign nailed to the medical tent: "CLOSED UNTIL FURTHER NOTICE. DEATH IN THE FAMILY." (p. 112) The wet, moldy atmosphere during the Bologna mission suggests T. S. Eliot's "April is the cruelest month," which is parodied in Chapter XXIV: "April had been the best month of all for Milo" (p. 257). The Bologna mission, Milo's buying spree, and the syndicate's bombing mission all take place in April. The portraits of Captain Black and Major —— de Coverley in Chapters XI and XIII personify the abstract ideals Nately and the old man debate and suggest the relationship between Nately's old man and the old man.

Chapter XXV continues directly from Chapter XX and is a fitting close for the second section of the novel. As the chaplain puzzles over complex questions of ontology and epistemology, his thoughts wander to the night Colonel Cathcart tried once again to throw him out of the officers' club, pause in a lovely parody of Shylock's "Am I not a man" speech, drift to his wife and children, and then recall the vision of the naked man he had seen sitting in the tree (or were there two men) during Snowden's funeral. Spurred by his sense of inadequacy, the chaplain rushes off once again to assert himself with Colonel Cathcart. What follows is reminiscent of a Keystone Kops comedy chase, as the chaplain plunges and scurries back and forth between his tent and the squadron area in his futile quest, finally ending up in Colonel Cathcart's office where he gets the odd sensation he has experienced a situation like this once before: "*Déjà vu* again" (p. 289).

Throughout Chapter XXV, the chaplain has been worrying over the significance of values and the meaning of man's existence. He has been concerned with reality and illusion and the phenomenon of *déjà vu*. What the chaplain questions, what he fears may be the "*illusion* of an illusion," is what Heller has been carefully orchestrating and illuminating through structure: "the subtle, recurring confusion between illusion and reality" that twists every scene, transfigures every image into another state, another dimension. The static, shifting, and illusory recurring images that annihilate time and space destroy surface impressions and plumb deeply into the substrata of the novel to force new meanings to the surface, to bring order and a new understanding out of the seeming chaos of life.

Structurally, the onrushing confusion in the second section of the novel reflects the deep-seated anxiety that permeates the atmosphere and manifests itself in the racking agony of men in an irrational world, one in which the horror and decimation of man and his values becomes so grotesque and incomprehensible that life is reduced to a vicious, ludicrous expression of human nature. Men's actions, which at first seem incredible, suddenly take on a frightening appearance: the fiery torment of an absurd reality.

The third section of the novel seems more drawn out than it really is. Consisting of a three-month period, from September to late November, the last section of the novel compresses time and concentrates on a limited number of events. Although the rapid oscillation that characterized the first twenty-five chapters is curtailed, there is no abatement in the free association of ideas technique, as this method still provides the impetus for the narrative. Working from themes and images established in the first two sections, the last seventeen chapters widen the scope of the novel and extend the meaning and significance of these points, building carefully to the final paragraphs where structure and content coalesce into a unified, finished statement—the "achieved content."

Chapter XXVI begins as though it were continuing on in the same manner as the previous chapters, but after a few pages Heller brings the narrative to the present where it continues for the remainder of the novel, except for the four times Snowden appears. From Nately's bored whore's heroic indifference to Aarfy's inability to recognize difference, the narrative moves from the past to the present through a semi-comic, flak-filled scene: the supposed milk run to Parma, during which Yossarian is wounded. For the remainder of this chapter and all of Chapter XXVII, the action takes place in the base hospital again. The return to the base hospital repeats a pattern from the first section of the novel, as both sections one and three open and close in the base hospital. Although section two opens and closes in Colonel Cathcart's office, there is no difference between the motives, ideals, ethics, or methods of the base doctors and Colonel Cathcart. Both the doctors and Colonel Cathcart are illusory images whose theatre of operations reflect the same theme of debased standards and values.

The tone of Chapters XXVI and XXVII is one of levity giving way to absurdity, as the narrative traces Yossarian's anguished yet carefree involvement with the nurses, his encounter with a psychiatrist, and his attempt once again to dissuade Dobbs from killing Colonel Cathcart. After the psychiatrist attests that Yossarian is crazy and then sends Lieutenant Fortiori home because he thinks Yossarian is Fortiori, Yossarian goes back to combat because, as Doc Daneeka tells him, "Who else will go?" (p. 314). The involvement of Lieutenant Antony F. Fortiori at this point in the narrative is significant in that *a fortiori* is a term used in logic "to denote an argument to the effect that because one ascertained fact exists, therefore another, which is included in it, or analogous to it, and which is less improbable, unusual, or surprising, must also exist." [8] Because Yossarian was in Fortiori's bed, he is Fortiori. Yossarian is crazy; therefore Fortiori is sent home. Because Milo made a profit bombing his own squadron, the wanton killing and wounding of men and the destruction of valuable material is excusable as it helps the war effort and relieves the taxpayers'

---

[8] Henry Campbell Black, *Black's Law Dictionary*, Fourth Edition by the Publisher's Editorial Staff (St. Paul, Minn.: West Publishing Company, 1951).

burden. Doc Daneeka is listed on the flight log of McWatt's plane, and McWatt's plane has crashed; therefore, Doc Daneeka is dead. Examples of this type of perverse logic are like the records attesting to Doc Daneeka's death: Lieutenant Mudd was killed before he was officially checked in; therefore, he never existed. Yossarian is awarded a medal for bombing the bridge twice; Milo buys eggs for seven cents and sells them at a profit for five cents; the chaplain is guilty or he would not be on trial. In its logical simplicity, *a fortiori* is another way of defining Catch-22:

Orr was crazy and could be grounded. All he had to do was ask; and as soon as he did, he would no longer be crazy and would have to fly more missions. Orr would be crazy to fly more missions and sane if he didn't, but if he was sane he had to fly them. If he flew them he was crazy and didn't have to; but if he didn't want to he was sane and had to. (p. 47)

Structurally, the introduction of *a fortiori* is made at the appropriate time and in the appropriate place: the base hospital, which as Yossarian says is controlled by either madmen or doctors. Coming at the beginning of section three, just after the narrative has returned to the present and settled down, *a fortiori* clarifies and justifies the rationale behind the method of juxtaposing scenes and images. Throughout the first two sections, seemingly dissimilar events have been compared or blended together to show analogous relationships. From Chapter XXVII on, the absurdity depicted in the first two sections, and the logic behind it, is expanded and exploited in a forceful manner as each new scene echoes a previous one and extends the distorted logic almost beyond comprehension.

Chapter XXVIII starts with a reversal—Yossarian's attempt to persuade Dobbs that Colonel Cathcart must be killed—and then slides into a long scene between Yossarian and Orr about values and existence and the conundrum brought up several times before: why was the whore hitting Orr over the head with her shoe? The chapter ends with Orr's disappearance at sea. In Chapter XXIX, *a fortiori*-Catch-22 moves on in relentless conquest. First, Special Services begins its takeover of military operations; second, military operations become totally pointless or have almost nothing to do with the war. Both General Peckem's military maneuvers and the briefing session for a raid on a small mountain village show the complete collapse of reason and logic and establish the senseless and incredible as the basis for all judgments and actions. At this point, neither "circumstance" nor "necessity" has any meaning: the question is moot.

Chapter XXX develops languidly, capturing the men's sense of isolation, alienation, and frustration and showing, through Yossarian's brief affair with Nurse Sue Ann Duckett, the temporary solace that comes from a physical relationship. The mood of this scene is soon shattered by the horror of McWatt's killing Kid Sampson by buzzing too closely the raft near the beach. This scene is followed by the absurdity surrounding Doc Daneeka's disappearance and the bonanza that comes to his wife after his "death." As "records attesting to his death were pullulating like insect eggs and verifying each other beyond all contention" (p. 353), the bureaucratic system begins churning with a blind efficiency that moves through scenes at first comic, then farcical, then preposterous, then grotesque, and then horrendous. This totally absurd situation culminates in Chapter XXXI with Mrs. Daneeka's new-found wealth and status as a war widow. In several ways, Chapters XXX and XXXI replay in imagistic scenes Chapters X to XV, the mission to Bologna sequence.

Picking up in tempo, Chapters XXXII to XXXIX present swift, unrolling juxtaposed scenes of death, isolation, insanity, alienation, horror, and absurdity. There is the efficient and effective eviction of the dead man from Yossarian's tent in Chapter XXXII; Yossarian's loneliness and the boisterous naked generals in Chapter XXXIII; the riotous Thanksgiving Day feast and the return of the soldier in white in Chapter XXXIV; the partial takeover of the world by Milo and Nately's death in Chapter XXXV; the chaplain's trial in Chapter XXXVI; the installation of General Scheisskopf as military commander in Chapter XXXVII; and Yossarian's rebellion, Major Major's disappearance, Nately's whore's vendetta, and the cleansing of the bordello in Chapter XXXVIII.

Each of these scenes has been echoing previously presented scenes and ideas but adding to them a new thought: the strident grotesqueness and absurdity shown no longer seems illogical or abnormal. Suddenly, the more insane a situation or idea becomes, the more normal it seems. This point is emphasized in Chapter XXXIX, Yossarian's walk through the grotesque, ambiguous absurdity of a Roman night. Although he has been in Rome several times before, Yossarian now realizes that "Rome was in ruins." The "Eternal City," the symbol of Western man's philosophic, moral, and artistic ideals, is "off balance," where "nothing warped seemed bizarre anymore," where grotesque symbols of humanity patter through the shimmering, sulphurous, surrealistic atmosphere. As Yossarian walks past drunken and convulsive soldiers, deformed civilians, children in "drugged misery," as he walks through the rain- and blood-splattered streets, past inviting neon signs—"TONY'S RESTAURANT. FINE FOOD AND DRINK. KEEP OUT" —past the dry water fountain, he witnesses scene after scene of pain, stupidity, indifference, decay, deformity, hate, and mutilation. And as he walks past a man beating a small boy, he has the feeling that "he had witnessed that same horrible scene sometime before. *Déjà vu?*" But the nightmare in which he finds himself turns from one kind of absurdity to another when the M.P.s arrest him for being AWOL, ignoring Aarfy's rape and murder of the plain maid in the officer's apartment.

Every grotesque and absurd image and scene in the novel is mirrored in Chapter XXXIX. From Milo's blind, burning fixation—"Let me go. I've got to smuggle illegal tobacco" (p. 420)—to Aarfy's outraged comment about the girl he has pushed out the window—"She has no right to be there. It's after curfew" (p. 428)—Rome is a city peopled with soldiers in white, Doc Daneekas, Natelys and Dunbars, Cathcarts and Korns, with a never-ending parade of tortured, hideous, repulsive, insensitive human shells who stumble animal-like through the Plutonian night. Only Orr and the old man from the bordello are missing. Orr has disappeared, and the old man is dead, killed by the impossible logic of the Catch-22-*a fortiori* combine that his relativistic approach to life could not fathom. Caught in this same dilemma is Captain John Yossarian, who wants "to break the lousy chain of inherited habit that was imperiling them all" (p. 414). And through Chapters XL to XLII he struggles to make a meaningful decision regarding his life and his relationship to society.

In Chapter XL, Yossarian accepts Colonel Korn's deal, a "despicable deal" that will save his life and send him home a hero. All he has to do is "Like us. Join us. Be our pal." All Yossarian has to do is practice the philosophy of the old man and Milo. But in Chapter XLI, lying in the base hospital, wounded by Nately's whore, Yossarian relives Snowden's death and comes to understand one part of an important message; he realizes what Snowden was telling him before Snowden became a soldier in white covered "with white nylon sheets":

Man was matter, that was Snowden's secret. Drop him out a window and he'll fall. Set fire to him and he'll burn. Bury him and he'll rot like other kinds of garbage. The spirit gone, man is garbage. That was Snowden's secret. Ripeness was all. (p. 450)

Like Edgar's cry in *King Lear*—"Ripeness is all"—and Hamlet's advice—"The readiness is all"—Yossarian realizes that man cannot live like the old man or Colonels Cathcart and Korn, that being a "pal," joining the syndicate is no way out of the hell of the "Eternal City." But there is no way out for Yossarian, either, until he receives the second part of the message: Orr has rowed to Sweden. Spurred by the knowledge that man must be ready and ripe, that Orr "knew what he was doing every step of the way," Yossarian makes his decision and jumps. Thus the novel closes the same way it opened: with Yossarian leaving the hospital. Only this time, he asserts, he is running to his responsibilities; he is not returning to the madness of the Catch-22 world to gorge himself in Milo's mess halls, to seek empty solace in the arms of a Luciana or Nurse Duckett, or to get killed for the glory of Colonel Cathcart. This time he was striking out for freedom and sanity, for a meaningful life in a new Eden.

As leitmotifs, Snowden's message and Orr's conundrums have been haunting Yossarian. Over and over they have appeared, weaving in and out enigmatically, major strains of *déjà vu*. Structurally, as the novel progresses and builds, it works toward the denouement in Chapter XLII. Only after the mad, terrifying world of Catch-22 has been presented in all its grotesque splendor can Yossarian assess the significance of these messages, messages which answer the cry that has echoed through the novel—"Why?" "Why me?"—the timeless cry of men in anguish and despair.

It is Job's cry, Oedipus' cry, and the cry of Hamlet and King Lear. It is the cry of Milton's Samson, Melville's Ahab, and Dostoevsky's Karamazovs. It is the cry that has permeated contemporary fiction, drowning out all other sounds and taking on an even more plaintive tone, for contemporary man has had to find the answer for himself. Because the modern world is no longer predicated on the idea that the universe is a rational, ordered place in a great chain of being, the contemporary hero can find no solace in the Gods of Job, Oedipus, or Milton. The conception of self-identity in relation to a stable world that once gave comfort to man is not applicable today. Living in a world in which everything has become absurd, contemporary man must find a way to live freely with self-respect amid absurdity.

Catch-22 is a statement about this situation, about contemporary man's relationship to the world he inhabits. It presents a world in which the loss of values, the sense of alienation, and the failure of meaningful communication are accepted conditions; it presents a world in which the aware man exists in a state of anguish, bitterness, frustration, and despair. *Catch-22* echoes the existential cry of man—"Why?" "Why me?"—and then twists it maliciously as it answers "Why not?"

What makes Heller's novel unique among other contemporary novels is the extent and complexity of structure and technique. The range and subtlety of the devices allow him to show absurdity through images and forms of absurdity, through the language and tone of absurdity. His use of spatial form, cinematographic techniques, free association of ideas, multiple point of view, ambiguity, recurring image pattern, and multiple level symbolism create an overpowering effect. But *Catch-22* goes beyond just capturing the form of absurdity; it moves toward a metaphysical statement about reality and truth in the contemporary world and suggests a means for living in this world.

The absurd vision of life Heller presents has within it a statement of hope. For once the illusions that have trapped and held contemporary man have been identified and destroyed, then he can live freely by coming to terms with the world he lives in, by coming to terms on his own terms. Heller's message is that man can live in an absurd world by wiping the glaze of illusion from his eyes and seeing clearly, by maintaining his own moral integrity, his own honor, his own freedom.

ON THEME

Frederick R. Karl
Joseph Heller's 'Catch-22':
Only Fools Walk in Darkness

What we yearn for in the post-war generation is fiction that seems "true" —or suggests whatever passes for truth—in its specifics as well as its generalities. While we all agree that the older great writers still move us profoundly, their vision in its particulars cannot appeal to us: Dostoyevsky was a reactionary, religious fanatic; Conrad, an anti-liberal; Lawrence, for blood, not social action; Mann, a disillusioned nationalist; Hesse, a mystic who recommended asceticism. We are still obviously affected by their psychological vision of man and the world, but repelled by what they offer in return, disturbed by the fact that they do not seem one of us. Perhaps because we have so assimilated their vision, we no longer turn to them for advice. They offer only a diagnosis, not a course of action true in its details. We read them with admiration, respect, even involvement. What they say is intensely true. But when we turn away from their printed pages, we face

SOURCE: Harry T. Moore, ed., *Contemporary American Novelists* (Carbondale, Ill.: Southern Illinois University Press, 1965), pp. 134–142. Copyright © 1964 by Southern Illinois University Press. Reprinted by permission of Southern Illinois University Press.

a different world. They are too idealistic for us. They want too much change, and at best they offer only spiritual rewards.

On the other hand, a novel like *Catch-22*, trailing recollections of Joyce, Nathanael West, and early, "funny" Céline, speaks solidly to those who are disaffected, discontented, and disaffiliated, and yet who want to react to life positively. With its occasional affirmations couched in terms of pain and cynical laughter, it makes nihilism seem natural, ordinary, even appealing. The very zaniness [134] of its vision constitutes its attraction even to those who have compromised with most of the absurdities it exposes.

Catch-22 obviously appeals to the student, who beneath his complacency and hipster frigidity is very confused and afraid. It appeals to the sophisticated professional—the educator, lawyer, professor—who must work at something he cannot fully trust. It appeals to the businessman, who does not really believe that his empire primarily serves the public good. It certainly appeals to all the new professionals—the advertisers, publicity men, television writers—whose world is little different from the absurd one Heller presents.

Wartime life on Pianosa—whatever the veracity of its details—is a replica of life within any organization. Whether one is a lawyer, teacher, doctor, judge, union member, white-collar worker, or writer attached to a magazine, advertising agency, newspaper, or television station, he finds himself in a similar kind of world. It is not simply a neurotic reaction to his surroundings that gives one this sense of absurdity: the absurdity is an actual fact, the consequence of many conflicting interests interacting and creating a world unfit for the individual.

This point is of course true of all good service fiction, but it is particularly true of *Catch-22*, beginning with its catchy title, its sense that the individual must always relinquish part of himself to the organization which chews him up and then eliminates him. Most people try to prevent becoming waste matter. The novel appeals to all those who want the good life and nevertheless reject its particularities, or even fear defining them. Beneath the surface, all its avid readers are afraid that "life"—whatever it is—is dribbling away from them in ways they can never dam. Calling themselves social animals, and arguing that every individual must be part of society, they hate society and distrust any individual who is a social animal.

For those who find given life nauseating, frustrating, and demeaning— that is, our sane citizens—*Catch-22* provides, at least temporarily, a moral, affirmative way out. So far do people diverge from their public image that their [135] frustrated longings often consume their entire existence. They may wish to do right, but are compromised by the wrongness of their situation. They see themselves as defeated victims, but are forced to carry themselves as victors. They want to love, but find that hate is more sophisticated, and viable. They want to pursue self, but are admonished and shamed into embracing the public good. They desire to aid society, but are warned that only a fool puts self last. They wish for authenticity, good faith, decency, but find that inauthenticity brings immediate and often sensational results. Trying to believe, they more frequently are mocked by the very forces they desire to accept. Wishing to embrace the great world, they find themselves successes in the little.

What American novel of the last decade has spoken better to this type of individual—perhaps to all of us?—than *Catch-22*? Its surface extravagance masks a serious purpose: that in an impossible situation, one finally has to honor his own self; that in an absurd universe, the individual has the right to seek survival; that one's own substance is infinitely more precious than any cause, however right; that one must not be asked to give his life unless *everybody* is willing to give *his*.

It is the latter point—a kind of Kantian categorical imperative applied to survival—that has generally been neglected. When Yossarian decides that his life does count, he is making a moral decision about the sanctity of human existence. Life must not be taken lightly, either by others (military men, business manipulators, world leaders) or by oneself. Yossarian is a hero by virtue of his sacred appraisal of his future. To himself he is as valuable as a general or a president. Since he is so valuable, he has a right, an inviolable right, to save himself once he has done his share of the world's dirty business. The individual must consider himself supreme. What could be more democratic, American, even Christian!

Heller's point is always moral. The fact that many outraged readers saw Yossarian as immoral, cowardly, or anti-American simply indicates what falsely patriotic hearts [136] beat sturdily beneath seemingly sophisticated exteriors. Yossarian is a great American—if we must have this point—an American of whom we should all be proud, even if Heller makes him an Assyrian (at times he seems like a young Turk hiding behind an Armenian name).

The morality, in fact, both implied and stated, is somewhat pat. Despite the presence of so many seemingly "evil" characters, Heller believes implicitly in the goodness of man. Even the former (Cathcart, Dreedle, Milo, *et al.*), however, are not really evil in any sinister way: rather, they simply react to the given chance, the proffered opportunity. They could be professors, or even ministers. They are men on the make, and such is the quality of modern life—*all* men are waiting for their chance. There are millions of Eichmanns, Hannah Arendt tells us. Yossarian is a Jesus among the money-lenders, without the mean sense of righteousness of a potential Messiah.

Yossarian is the man who acts in good faith, to use Sartre's often-repeated phrase. In Yossarian's situation—one in which war has turned all men into madmen—people float uneasily in a foreign world where human existence is feeble, contradictory, and contingent upon an infinity of other forces. Nothing, here, is certain except the individual's recurring assurance of his own response. All he can hope to know is that he is superior to any universal force (man-made or otherwise), and all he can hope to recognize is that the universal or collective force can never comprehend the individual. The only sure thing in a swamp of absurdity is one's own identity. "I think, therefore I am" has never seemed truer, distorted though Descartes' phrase may have become in the twentieth century.

Accordingly, the true hero of our era is the man who can accept absolute responsibility. He must act alone, and his faith—not in God, but in himself—must be good, honest, pure. If, as Nietzsche said, all the gods are dead, then man must become mature enough to assume the role. Yossarian's decision that life must pre-empt all other considerations is precisely this moral act of responsibility. In [137] choosing life, Yossarian shows himself to be reflective, conscious, indeed free. All the others are slugs living in the swampy depths of self-deception; not bad men necessarily, they are simply unaware, and unaware they cannot be free.

When Yossarian strikes for freedom at the end of the novel (the fact that it is Sweden demonstrates Heller's concern with the good society made by good men), his act symbolizes more than defiance, certainly not cowardice. He has done his duty—Heller is careful to keep before us Yossarian's many missions (the word itself indicates a high calling). He has shown his responsibility to society at large, and has given his physical energy and his nervous sweat. Now he must seek a meaningful life, try to make order out of chaos. He must overcome nausea. In this respect, Sweden seems like Paradise: sane people, plenty of good sex, a benevolent government, jolly drunkenness. In Sweden, the individual seems to have a chance, what Yeats felt in part about his mythical Byzantium.

It is no more immoral for Yossarian to seek Sweden than for Yeats to have searched for Byzantium. Both places indeed are more a state of mind than a real place. We can be sure that when Yossarian reaches Sweden, he will be disappointed, even frustrated. Not all the tall, blonde women will capitulate, not all the people will be sane; the government will even expect him to work, and liquor will be expensive. Yet Sweden remains valid as an idea—one certainly has the right to seek it as an alternative to death. It may prove a false Eden, but man in his desperation may still desire Paradise. It is a mark of his humanity that he does.

There is, except for Sweden, really no community that Yossarian can join. An open character in a closed society, he must shun everyone to retain his identity: appear naked among the clothed, refuse to acquiesce to ill-motivated orders, avoid love while seeking sex, reject a mission that is no longer his. In virtually every situation, he is alone—his name, his racial origin, his integrity all indicate his isolation. Like an ancient hero rather than a modern [138] *schlemiel*, he goes through his solitary ordeal, and the ordeal, as Heller presents it, is eminently worthwhile: to defy death in the name of reason and life.

A good deal of the humor of the novel derives from Yossarian's very openness in a society closed to authenticity and good faith. When an open character—responsive, sensitive, decent—throws himself upon a closed society—unresponsive, fixed, inflexible—very often the result can be tragic. What keeps Yossarian comic, however, is the fact that he never tries to change the society he scorns; he is quite willing to accept its absurdity if it will leave him alone. Never a revolutionary, rarely a rebel, unintentionally a hero, only occasionally a young Turk, Yossarian is more often a rank conformist. The only sanity he desires is his own, not the world's; the only joys he seeks are those he can himself generate; the only rewards he covets are the compensations, not of glory, but of full lips, breasts, and thighs. He is more Sancho than Don. The comedy of Yossarian is the comedy of a romantic, Rousseauistic natural man forced to do the dirty work of the world.

Yet this twentieth-century natural man is "with it," not against it. He is able to adapt to the forces that would otherwise destroy. He retains his naturalness (integrity, sexual balance, coolness) in situations that have frustrated and smashed men more rebellious and affirmative than he. What both impresses and dismays us is Yossarian's adaptability; his views do not cause rigidity, and without rigidity there can be only personal comedy. Tragedy is always "out there," involving those who try to fight the system or those who are trapped by a system they never understood (Clevinger, Nately, Snowden). Like Yossarian, Milo is of course comic because he *knows* about the system; he is the very fellow who masterminds systems.

The two extremes Yossarian must avoid include the avarice and egoism of Milo and the innocence and naïveté of Nately ("new-born") and Snowden (pure whiteness). As Heller presents the alternatives, a person must be in the know in all the particulars of life or else he cannot be true to himself. Only a fool walks in darkness. Yossarian is an [139] honest man because Yossarian understands that the way to righteousness is through balance: he must assure his own survival without the help of others. Thus, Heller condemns both Nately and Milo; the latter obviously stands for a base, commercial acquisitiveness, while the former attempts to be Jesus Christ in a situation that calls for an instinctive sense of survival.

Those who have felt the tragic overtones of the novel often find it difficult to place its tragic center. Clearly, *Catch-22* is not simply a comic novel full of puns, high jinks, slapstick, witty dialogue, and satirical asides. It has these in abundance—perhaps, on occasion, in overabundance—but its purpose and execution are fully serious, what we feel in Saul Bellow's work, to mention a contemporary American whom Heller comes closest to. At the center of the tragedy is Heller's awareness of a passing era, an era that perhaps never existed but one that might have if people and situations had gone differently. Heller's is the nostalgia of the idealist—such a writer's style is usually jazzed-up, satirical, somehow surrealistic—the idealist who can never accept that moral values have become insignificant or meaningless in human conduct. This heritage, what we find in Nathanael West, early Céline, and a whole host of similar writers, derives from the tragic undertones of Ecclesiastes with its monody against vanity, egoism, hypocrisy, folly—those qualities which have, unfortunately, become the shibboleths of the twentieth century.

Heller's recoil from these false qualities takes the form of his attack upon religion, the military, political forces, commercial values—as C. Wright Mills indicates, the whole power formation of a country successful in war and peace. What is left is the only true thing remaining for all men —sex: healthy, robust, joyful sex. Not love—Heller carefully draws the distinction—for love means entanglements and involvements that will eventually lead to phoniness. It is not so curious that love itself falls victim to a society in which true feeling had better stop at orgasm. Heller's non-treatment of love is of course indicative of his [140] attitude, not of an inability: love is martyred amidst people whose every feeling is promiscuous. To expect more from them, even from Yossarian, is to accept their folly as truth.

The nightmarish scenes of Catch-22 which convey its tragic sense culminate in the cosmic nightmare of Chapter XXXIX, "The Eternal City." Once glorious, Rome is now a "dilapidated shell," as though modern Goths and Vandals had destroyed everything in their path; or as if a modern God had visited his wrath upon it. The monuments are shattered, the streets contain surrealistic nightmares, the people seem the husks and shards of humanity. All values are overturned, all hopes and dreams made valueless; sanity itself becomes a meaningless term. Everything visible—an emblem of what lies beneath—is off balance, out of key. The center of western religion is godless. Here we have Heller's immoral world, a scene from Hieronymus Bosch's Hell, in which Aarfy can freely rape and kill while Yossarian is picked up for lacking a pass. Caught in such a dark world, Yossarian can only run toward the light. If he stays, he will—like Milo and the others—eat and sleep well at the expense even of those who share his ideals.

An early version of Catch-22 was itself much more nightmarish in its development than the published book. Evidently strongly influenced by Ulysses, Heller had originally tried to make the narrative typically Joycean: that is, full of intermittent streams of consciousness and involutions of time. Further, he suggested the narrative through recurring symbols of devastation and doom, eliminating in several places orthodox plot structure.

As a consequence, the reader who missed the significance of the symbols—and they were by no means clear, even peripherally—was lost in a surrealistic forest of words from which there was no escape. Added to the stream, the symbols, and the involutions of time was an impressionistic treatment of characters and events, a half-toned, half-tinted development that seemed neither to go forward nor to remain still. [141]

For the final version, Heller retained in its entirety only the first chapter of the original and then in part straightened out both the narrative line and the character development. Words themselves became a kind of language midway between evocation and denotation; at its worst, the language overextends itself, but at its best it suits Heller's zany, absurd world. So often misunderstood, his language would not of course fit a rational theme—it is itself an attempt to convey a world beyond the logic of the word.

For Heller, the war is a perfect objective correlative, as it was for Hemingway in *A Farewell to Arms*. Both, however, are war novels only in limited ways. The war gave Heller, even more than it did Hemingway, the community against which Yossarian can operate. The military becomes an entire society, looming so large that it casts its shadow on the horizon and blocks out everything beyond. Such is the nature of the curse, and it is this —the indefinable character of what one is a part of—that Heller can exploit. The war or the military (not the enemy) provides the conflict, makes anything possible. The norm is no longer any determinable quality: each action gives birth to a norm of its own. Unlike the fixed roles that people assume in civilian life, in war they hide behind masks (uniforms) and redefine themselves, like the protean creatures in Ovid's *Metamorphoses*. Here, Yossarian—the ancient Assyrian, the modern Armenian, but really a wandering New York Jew—can give vent to his disgust and revulsion, and through laughter show us that our better selves may still turn up in Sweden. [142]

Minna Doskow

The Night Journey
in 'Catch-22'

Sanford Pinsker in his article on *Catch-22* characterizes Heller's hero as a *puer eternis*.[1] As a result, he sees Yossarian refusing the "traditional journey of learning in manhood,"[2] and the ending of the novel becomes Yossarian's escape from reality to Sweden, a kind of never-never land. Although Yossarian may be innocent, as Mr. Pinsker claims, at the beginning of the novel, and his belief that he can work within the establishment using their rules for his own ends is incredibly naive, he does, I believe, learn better, and after his symbolic journey to the underworld, represented by his trip through the dark streets of Rome, he comes to a new recognition of the meaning of his experience and reaches a new knowledge in the hospital after his near death, achieving what one could perhaps call an informed innocence. His flight to Sweden is not an escape but an alternative as he himself tells us: "I'm not running *away* from my responsibilities. I'm running *to* them."[3] Thus, a definite and meaningful pattern of action emerges from the novel, and one which is startlingly similar to the archetypal pattern that characterizes classical epic or romance. Heller's hero, like those of *The Odyssey, The Aeneid* and *The Divine Comedy*, is involved in a struggle with an alien force which he must and eventually does overcome in order to survive. He too reaches a crisis in his struggle, undertakes a journey to the underworld, emerges with new knowledge, and is finally victorious, prevailing against the forces marshalled against him. From the outset of the novel, Yossarian struggles against a hostile establishment and the code it maintains for controlling the society it rules, that is, Catch-22, the principle of power which states "they have a right to do anything we can't stop them from doing." (416) However, the confrontation reaches its climax and emerges most clearly and intensely in the night journey

---

[1] Sanford Pinsker, "Heller's *Catch-22:* The Protest of a *Puer Eternis,*" *Critique*, VII (Winter 1964–5), 150–162.
[2] *Ibid.*, p. 151.
[3] Joseph Heller, *Catch-22* (New York, 1962), p. 461. All quotations and page references are from the Dell edition.

SOURCE: *Twentieth Century Literature*, Vol. 12 (January 1967), pp. 186–193. Reprinted by permission of the publisher.

episode of the last chapters, and in the action that follows from it. A close analysis of these chapters (39–42) will show how Yossarian through his participation in the archetypal pattern of the descent and renewal of the romance hero achieves his new perception which culminates quite logically in his flight to Sweden.

When Yossarian goes AWOL to Rome in an attempt to save the kid sister of Nately's whore, we witness a crisis in his continuous battle with the establishment. In his previous conflicts with those forces, Yossarian was consistently foiled by Catch-22. However, his absolute and unconditional refusal to fly any more [186] missions after Nately's death indicates a new and complete break with the code Catch-22 typifies. In the subsequent trip to Rome his efforts are not only directed at saving his own life, but also those of future generations represented by the still virginal twelve-year-old sister. "Every victim," he tells us in explaining his action, "was a culprit, every culprit a victim, and somebody had to stand up sometime to try to break the lousy chain of inherited habit that was imperiling them all." (414) He is out to break the "mind-forged manacles" that imprison men. While this enemy is far different from the medieval dragon or classical monster whom the romantic hero must overcome, yet it is equally menacing to human life, can prove equally fatal, and Yossarian must overcome it in order to achieve his own renewal.

As he plunges into Rome, a city of universal destruction, Yossarian begins his symbolic descent to the underworld. At first he tries to enlist the aid of the authorities in control. But his initial naive attempt to work with the Roman police is blasted by their essential indifference and by Milo Minderbinder's preference for black-market tobacco profits to the salvation of little girls. Yossarian, realizing that the police will not help him, then begins the journey on his own. However, since it is a journey born out of pure frustration it is cast in a somber and ironic rather than a truly romantic mode. He has already learned that he can expect no help from the police, and before his journey is over he will further discover that the police themselves are the enemy and that he must protect himself from them.

His emergence from the police station leaves him at the bottom of a hill in a "dark tomblike street," obviously suggestive of an entrance into the underworld with its murky atmosphere smelling of death. However, it is not an otherworldly or spiritual hell but the hell that man has created both spiritually and physically here on earth that Yossarian enters. And what the reader sees as he accompanies Yossarian on his harrowing night journey through the labyrinthine streets of this Roman hell is:

all the shivering stupefying misery in a world that never yet had provided enough heat and food and justice for all but an ingenious and unscrupulous handful. (421)

Nevertheless, the striking atmosphere of misery and pain leads to the inevitable comparison with hell which becomes more relevant and forceful as Yossarian travels further along the streets encountering sickness, hunger, poverty, sadistic cruelty and coercion and viewing an entire gallery of mutilated bodies and warped souls.

The pervasive gloom through which Yossarian travels resembles Dante's City of Dis or Homer's City of Perpetual Mist in its absence of penetrating light. In scene after scene of his journey, from the yellow light bulbs that "sizzled in the dampness like wet torches" (421) immediately outside the police station, to the "ghostly blackness," and "dense impenetrable shadows of a narrow winding side street," (423) through the "drizzling, drifting, lightless, nearly opaque gloom," (426) the darkness remains impenetrable. Even the apparent sources of light cannot shatter the gloom. The yellow light bulbs do not enable Yossarian to look around him, and the "flashing red spotlight" (423) attached to the M.P.'s jeep only adds a lurid glow to the picture of the young lieutenant in convulsions. Nor [187] do the amber fog lights of the ambulance which is used to incarcerate the helpless victims of the police light up the scene, and even the street lights themselves appear as "curling lampposts with eerie shimmering glare surrounded by smoky brown mist." (423) The only exception, the piercing white light of Tony's restaurant, is expressly forbidden to the ordinary inhabitants of Rome and to Yossarian as well and is clearly marked "KEEP OUT."

Not only is Yossarian cast into a world without light, but the city itself appears strangely distorted and out of perspective. "The tops of the sheer buildings slanted in weird surrealistic perspective and the street seemed tilted." (421) The lampposts seem to curl, and together with the mists the shadows succeed in "throwing everything visible off-balance." (423) The shimmering uncertainty of forms helps to upset Yossarian's equilibrium and enhance the unearthly quality of the scene through surrealistic distortion.

Even the elements conspire to intensify the hostile and bizarre nature of the setting. From the outset Yossarian finds himself pelted by a frigid rain, exposed and vulnerable, denied shelter and forced to huddle for warmth and protection against the raw night. Moreover, the rain does not, as might be expected in another region, cleanse what it touches, but only besmirches it. Thus the street is "rain-blotched," (423) the mist is "smoky brown," (423) and Yossarian stumbles upon "human teeth lying on the drenched glistening pavement near splotches of blood kept sticky by the pelting raindrops poking each one like sharp fingernails." (424) The rain lends this street a bloody luminescence intensifying the gory and grotesque scene, and the drops themselves seem to sharpen the probing cruelty.

The distortion of the visible world surrounding Yossarian is accompanied by an equal distortion of all that is audible. Just as the yellow bulbs outside the police station lend the street an eerie light, so do the sizzling sounds they emit echo the effect. However, the most common sounds that Yossarian hears as he travels through the streets of Rome are human cries, the sobs and screams of the victims of hell. The scream of the child being beaten, the sympathetic weeping of a woman in the crowd, the "snarling, inhuman voices" (423) of the spectators, the cries of the women being raped begging "Please don't," or in drunken variation "Pleeshe don't," (423) the scream of the man being clubbed by the police, "Police! Help! Police!" (415) all swell the chorus of pain, the cacophony of hell. In addition, the accents of the torturers are also audible and add to the clamour. We hear the hellish accents of the M.P.'s who mock and jeer at the suffering young lieutenant in "raucous laughter." (423)

Even inanimate objects take on the disturbing characteristics of their surroundings. Announcing its arrival with jangling clamour, the ambulance is distorted into an engine of torture, not a vehicle of mercy, and it comes not to aid the soldier with the mutilated mouth, but to incarcerate the screaming civilian who clasps his books to him in an uneven struggle with the club-wielding policemen arresting him. The fountain which Yossarian hopes will help guide him out of hell is dry, and becomes a perfect symbol of the aridity and barren aspect of the surrounding wasteland. The "haunting incongruous noise" (423) that [188] Yossarian hears of a snow shovel scraping against a rain soaked street adds a weirdly surrealistic note suggesting the meaningless and endless labor of some modern Sisyphus.

The labor of hell is characteristically unproductive, endless and pointless. Thus, the labor represented by the sound of the scraping shovel is adapted to its location as is the aimless action of the six soldiers trying to help the epileptic young lieutenant. In their well-intentioned impotence they only succeed in moving him from car hood to sidewalk and back again achieving nothing. The realization of the futility of their attempts to alleviate his pain and help their friend and of the inevitable isolation of the suffering man cause "a quiver of moronic pain [to] spread from one straining brute face to another." (422) Their effort is unproductive and his isolation remains unaffected.

The only actions that yield results in hell are cruelty and coercion. While the soldiers are powerless to relieve the suffering of their sick friend, the M.P.'s can mock it and so intensify it. And, in the same way, the sympathetic woman is powerless to stop the man from beating his dog and must retreat "sheepishly with an abject and humiliated air" (424) from the sadist's stick which can easily be turned against her. The crowd watching the child being beaten has already recognized the limits of action, and thus no one moves in even a futile attempt to stop the beating. No one here still hopes to avert the surrounding cruelty, and the sympathetic only weep "silently into a dirty dish towel." (424)

As Yossarian proceeds further and further into hell on his journey, he witnesses a progression in the inhumanity and brutality that surrounds him. The figures he sees become more horribly maimed, the mutilation becomes more inclusive and extensive, and the possibility for action more limited. The imagery proceeds in a crescendo of distortion and pain until it excludes all possibility of redemption or love, and even the futile attempts to help that he observed toward the beginning of his journey are absent. Yossarian, much like Dante in his progress through the Inferno, thus passes through the various levels of hell necessary for his final emergence as a new person having learned his proper course of action on the verge of entering a new realm. Moreover, accompanying the progression in Yossarian's surroundings, is a progression in Yossarian's own role in the action, again necessary if he is to learn from his hell journey.

Although Yossarian is, from the beginning, haunted by his surroundings and feels compassion for the souls he sees in torment, he is not an integral part of the hell he walks through. He is an alien observer proceeding in "lonely torture, feeling estranged," (422) isolated although not insulated from his surroundings. He feels a sense of his own difference and of alienation from those around him.

. . . he thought he knew how Christ must have felt as he walked through the world, like a psychiatrist through a ward full of nuts, like a victim through a prison full of thieves. (424)

The perception fills him with dread and he tries to escape from the world surrounding him. However, despite his efforts to flee, there is no escape until he has gone through all of hell and until his isolation too has been broken down. In spite of all his efforts not to see and not to hear what is around [189] him, he cannot avoid the sights and sounds of torment, and each turning only takes him farther into the labyrinthine hell of the Roman streets. Even when he sights a familiar landmark, the dry fountain, which he believes will guide him to the officers' quarters, he manages only to come upon another instance of brutality: the man beating the dog. Unlike Raskolnikov, whose dream this scene reminds him of, Yossarian cannot dispel the terror by awakening. The nightmare world is his reality and he must go on in this world observing repeated torments until he recognizes this and recognizes his own involvement in that world as well.

Only after Yossarian comprehends the warning shout uttered by one of the victims of the police:

"Police! Help! Police!" . . . a heroic warning from the grave by a doomed friend to everyone who was *not* a policeman with a club and a gun and a mob of other policemen with clubs and guns to back him up. (425)

when he recognizes the forces that control the world for what they are, does a distinct change occur in his role. For the first time in his journey, Yossarian ceases to be the alien observer isolated from his surroundings. He feels the threat extended to himself as well as to the others around him, identifying him somewhat with them. He also recognizes a direct possibility for action, a distinct opportunity to help the old woman of eighty with the bandaged ankles who is chasing the burly woman half her age. But he responds in the same way as the other inhabitants of hell. Like the passive crowd watching the beating of the child, he does nothing. His failure to act identifies him more closely with the shade-like victims he has observed, and now he no longer observes the action from outside but from within it. This change in his role makes him flee not in dread this time, but in shame since he recognizes his identity with those around him and shares their guilt. Thus, "he darted furtive, guilty glances back as he fled in defeat." (426) He, like all the other inhabitants of Rome, has given in to the forces in control and is defeated since he has allowed the principles ruling hell to rule him as well. Brought to acknowledge that "mobs with clubs were in control everywhere," (426) he also now admits that he has neither the power nor the will to oppose them. This explicit recognition of his defeat foreshadows his later capitulation to the colonels (the ruling minions of that enormous and organized "mob with clubs"—the army) who embody the extension of the ruling principle in the hellish world beyond Rome.

Yossarian, no longer separated from the world around him, is tortured in the same way as the figures he has passed. The only image that he can salvage from the picture of universal corruption is the memory of Michaela, the plain, simple-minded and hard working maid who served in the officers' apartment and who had somehow retained her innocence amid her savage surroundings. His rush towards her is a last attempt to save himself from complete despair. However, only her violated and mutilated body lying on the pavement is there to welcome him, "the pitiful, ominous, gory spectacle of the broken corpse." (427) Aarfy has already raped and murdered her. Thus, the one apparent departure from the picture of universal deformity and perversion has become the sacrificial victim of that deformity and perversion. [190] The demonic distortion that has corrupted the world culminates in the image of Michaela's maimed body, the rape and killing of the one girl associated with the army who was not a whore, and the final resolving chord in the demonic crescendo that has been building throughout the journey is sounded.

In a further change of role which reiterates his position at the inception
of the journey, Yossarian, no longer the observer, no longer passive, challenges the world around him in a last appeal for justice and order, for the
vindication of humane ideals. He shouts: "you can't take the life of another
human being and get away with it, even if she is just a poor servant girl."
(428) It is inevitable that this appeal be denied by the forces in control.
Thus, morality is finally and completely turned inside out; moral law or
justice has completely degenerated into rule through naked power; the
"mobs with clubs" are in full control, and "mere anarchy is loosed upon
the world." As the agents of retribution are heard on the stairs and Aarfy
slowly turns green in anticipation of punishment, Yossarian's absurd hope
that order will be restored to the chaos he has been wandering in all night
is blasted. The "two large brawny M.P.'s with icy eyes and firm sinewy unsmiling jaws" (429) who appear act in perfect consistency with hellish
logic and with Catch-22.

They arrested Yossarian for being in Rome without a pass.

They apologized to Aarfy for intruding and led Yossarian away between
them, gripping him under each arm with fingers as hard as steel manacles. (429)

As if to emphasize the metamorphosis of humane law into its demonic
opposite, the M.P.'s no longer retain even their superficial humanity; their
flesh having turned to steel, they resemble unyielding machinery rather
than men.

After Yossarian has personally experienced the rule of the demonic principles as well as observed their universal application, he consents to become
a part of this rule. Thus, as his actions in relation to the old woman of
eighty have intimated, he accepts Colonel Korn's and Colonel Cathcart's
"odious deal," knowing it is disgusting and deceitful. At this moment he is
rechristened with a hellish name, taking on a new and appropriate identity.
"Everyone calls me Yo-Yo!" (440) he tells us, accepting a name he once
found noxious.

When he accepts the colonels' deal after his return from Rome, Yossarian is for the first time in the novel in complete harmony with his environment. He has joined in the devilish conspiracy that holds sway over the
world and whose undisguised sinister image has been evident throughout
the novel, although most clearly and intensely seen in the night journey
episode. Having then sunk into hell itself, no longer resisting its influence
but becoming part of it, a lost soul himself, Yossarian approaches the absolute depths of the abyss and glimpses a demonic phantom. This is the
"strange man with the mean face," the "spiteful scowl," the sharp fingers,
the "nasty smirk" and "malicious laugh" who eludes Yossarian's grasp and
will only say, "We've got your pal, buddy. We've got your pal." (442) Nor
will he elucidate when Yossarian, with a flicker of sardonic humor on Hel-

ler's part, inquires "What the *hell* are you talking about?" (445) (Italics are Heller's.) However, we must remember that Yossarian is still [191] anesthetized at the moment of his vision. Thus, his physical state of induced unconsciousness partially accounts for his new submissive attitude. It also corresponds to his spiritual or moral state in which consciousness has as well been put to sleep temporarily, as exemplified in his acceptance of the "odious deal." In this state he can see the devil without really recognizing him or perceiving the meaning of his message. The vision is nevertheless vital to any new perception Yossarian will be able to achieve after the both literal and figurative anesthesia wears off.

After his vision, Yossarian once more rebels and refuses the colonels' deal. He emerges, in this way, from unconsciousness and from the abyss into whose depths he had to descend before his renewal or resurrection could occur. Just as Dante descends into the nethermost region of hell, passes Satan himself, and uses the devil to pull himself out of hell, so Yossarian uses his Satanic vision to extricate himself from his hell in order finally to approach a place where there still is hope. In both cases the contact with the devil is mandatory. As Virgil tells Dante, "There is no way/ but by such stairs to rise above such evil." [4]

After he passes the devil whose words recall Snowden's death to him, Yossarian glimpses the truth which gleams from the haunting memory: "The spirit gone, man is garbage." (450) He now realizes that it is necessary to retain some other quality along with the mere existence that he has been struggling to preserve since the beginning of the book and that he had guaranteed through his "deal." Armed by his recent experience in hell and his emergence from it through the recognition of what life means, he has once more achieved the strength to say no to the tyrants in control. "I'm not making any deals with Colonel Korn," (450) he tells us. Unlike his earlier instinctive rebellion, his new denial is informed by the experience of the depths of hell and by his new recognition. Only through his exploration of the abyss has he reached the perception which may lead to his eventual salvation. And it is possible salvation that is offered by Yossarian's projected plan of flight to Sweden. Perhaps it is only Purgatory that Yossarian will gain (as Dante does at this point in his progress), but it is a world where life is at least possible.

Yossarian now realizes that accepting the colonels' deal would be, in his words, "a way to lose myself," (456) would be, that is, his own damnation through complete surrender to the demonic powers in control. But what he is searching for is a way to "save" himself (to use his own words again) in a world that both he and Major Danby, the university professor turned army officer, agree contains "no hope." (458) This last phrase is reiterated

---

[4] Dante Alighieri, *The Inferno*, trans. John Ciardi (New York, 1954), Canto XXXIV, 11, pp. 83–84.

throughout their entire discussion of escape so that we can hardly fail to think of the cardinal feature of hell and also of the motto that Dante tells us is inscribed over the gates of hell. In addition, Heller's language heightens our awareness of the scene's implications. The words "lose," "save," and "no hope" echo rather forcefully the conventional religious language describing the soul's struggle for salvation. From the latter we know that hell is a place of no hope and that it is a spiritual state as well as a geographical location. We know that the lost soul goes to hell and conversely, that hell is the condition of the lost soul. And finally, we know that the [192] soul can only achieve salvation by recognizing evil and resisting or overcoming it. It is obvious how appropriately this describes Yossarian's progress in the novel, shown most clearly in the chapters just discussed.

Thus, Yossarian's departure for Sweden is the concrete external representation of his spiritual renewal that expressed itself first in his recognition of man's nature and in his subsequent refusal of the "deal." As Yossarian knows, Sweden is no paradise or utopia; there are no such things in the world this novel depicts. In escaping to Sweden, Yossarian also recognizes that he is "not running away from responsibilities," (461) but toward them, that salvation entails responsibility, and that he will have to be ever-vigilant in order to remain free of the demonic powers of the world he is forsaking. Thus he leaves taking the necessary risks and exulting in the new feeling of freedom and hope that he now has. If it is a miracle as the chaplain claims, then it is a miracle achieved through Yossarian's own will and conscience and one which leaves him open to ambush and knife attack from such characters as Nately's whore. It is she who marks his departure from the demonic realm, his crossing of the gulf, she who is herself caught in the endlessly repeated and repeatedly unsuccessful actions characteristic of hell, and who thus represents the threats that Yossarian will have to overcome on his new course. [193]

Jim Castelli
'Catch-22' and the New Hero

Perhaps more than any other book, Joseph Heller's *Catch-22* has captured the absurdities and frustrations of a generation; too few people realize,

SOURCE: *The Catholic World*, Vol. 211 (August 1970), pp. 199–202. Reprinted by permission of the author and publisher.

however, that despite its apparently freewheeling nature, it is worked out with Joycean precision and, more importantly, that this sense of order is ultimately symbolic of the life-style advocated by Heller and personified by the character of Yossarian. Frederick Karl has told us that the original manuscript of *Catch-22* was written with the same degree of symbolism and mythological structure as *Ulysses*, but that Heller changed the final version to avoid confusing too many readers ("Joseph Heller's *Catch-22*: Only Fools Walk in Darkness," *Contemporary American Novelists*, Southern Illinois University Press, 1965).*

Heller basically shows us a world in which we are forced to question the very nature of sanity. Sanity is presumed to be the ability to live with society and with the first principles of society, but if those first principles are actually false, then adhering to them is not sanity, but insanity, for the end result may be the loss of life or freedom. Authority, duty, patriotism are all called into question and Heller shows us that when those in authority lack intelligence or morals, as is the case with Yossarian's commanding officers, obeisance to that authority can only be self-defeating. A perfect example of this is seen when Yossarian is interviewed by the hospital psychiatrist: the doctor notes that Yossarian is incensed at the thought that he may be killed at any moment during the war; that he is upset by ignorance, hypocrisy, violence, injustice; and that he is consequently crazy. Yossarian and the reader can see that Yossarian certainly isn't the crazy one.

Frederick Karl notes that:

Wartime life on Pianosa—whatever the veracity of its details—is a replica of life within any organization. Whether one is a lawyer, teacher, judge, or union member, white collar worker, or a writer attached to a magazine, advertising agency, newspaper, or television station, he finds himself in a similar kind of world. It is not simply a neurotic reaction to his surroundings that gives one this sense of absurdity: the absurdity is an actual fact, the consequence of the conflict of many different interests interacting and creating a world unfit for the individual.

To think of *Catch-22* as humor or satire is to oversimplify; it is actually the New Journalism at its best. We can understand this better by looking at one example of *Catch-22*, which Robert Brustein defines as "the unwritten loophole in every law which empowers the authorities to invoke your rights whenever it suits their cruel whim; it is, in short, the principle of absolute evil in a malevolent, mechanical, and incompetent world." Yossarian's roommate, Orr, has discovered that he can be grounded by a doctor who will certify that he is crazy:

---

* See pp. 159–165 in this volume.—Eds.

There was only one catch, and that was Catch-22, which specified that a concern for one's safety in the face of dangers that were real and immediate was the process of a rational mind. Orr was crazy and could be grounded. All he had to do was ask; as soon as he did he would no longer be crazy, and would have to fly more missions. Orr would be crazy to fly more missions and sane if he didn't, but if he was sane he had to fly them. If he flew them he was crazy and didn't have to; but if he didn't want to he was sane and had to. (47)

A new type of hero is needed to cope with this kind of a world. Yossarian has been called an anti-hero, but Vance Ramsey has seen how this is a misnomer: "He (Yossarian) is in short the kind of character the term 'anti-hero' should have been reserved for. Many who are given this title are simply 'non-heroes'—weak, ineffectual men, little more than anguished consciousness. Yossarian is aggressively and even belligerently anti-heroic, and in his anti-heroism is a direct challenge to the values and ideals which the world claims to hold" ("From Here to Absurdity," *Seven Contemporary Authors*, Austin, 1968). [199]

Yossarian's "new heroism," like the more traditional kind, features a reliance on self above all else, but his priorities have been reordered; he values human life more than honor, duty, and glory, the values we are told are heroic. (This is re-enforced in the exchanges between Nately and the old man who runs the whorehouse in Rome: Nately claims that it is better to die on one's feet than live on one's knees, but the old man tells him that he has it backwards—"It is better to *live* on one's feet than die on one's knees. *That* is the way the saying goes." He also points out that "There are thirty or forty countries in this war. Surely they can't all be worth dying for.")

Yossarian displays a concern for people throughout the whole book, whether it is in questioning the nature of a God who would create a world with pain in it, or in trying to save Nately's whore's kid sister from the ruins of Rome. J. P. Stern notes that when Yossarian is trying to save the torn Snowden and is "shocked to the outer limits of his sanity by the spectacle of a man dying slowly in his arms, good old Aarfy (Yossarian's crewmate whose insensitivity allowed him to rape and murder an innocent girl without pangs of conscience) notices nothing. . . ." Situations such as these make it unnecessary for Mr. Heller to engage in a close psychological inspection of Yossarian's mind ("War and the Comic Muse: *The Good Soldier Schweik* and *Catch-22*," *Comparative Literature*, Summer 1968).

There is a great similarity between the actions of Yossarian and those urged by "Situation Ethics." In *Situation Ethics*, Joseph Fletcher describes the three approaches to morality: the *legalistic*, in which everything must be fitted into pre-existing and supposedly eternal rules; the *antinomian* (literally "against law"), which sees no continuity in history and amounts to anarchy; and the *situational*. Fletcher tells us that the situationist "enters into every decision-making situation fully armed with the ethical maxims of his community and its heritage, and he treats them with respect as illuminators of his problems. Just the same, he is prepared in any situation to compromise them or set them aside *in the situation* if love seems better served by doing so." The only criterion for the situationist is agapaic love, love for all of mankind; only when this is served can a decision be a correct one.

The chief argument against Situation Ethics, and against Yossarian's final decision to refuse to fly anymore and to flee to Sweden, is the question "What if everybody did it?" While a first reaction might be that if everyone did as Yossarian did, there would be no wars, Fletcher answers on a more universal level: "There is no human act, no matter how lovingly willed, which could not lead to evil if the circumstance were of a certain pattern—and to say 'universal only for exactly similar situations' is to run away from the variety of life . . . [the 'generalization argument' is] one of the maneuvers designed to discredit personal responsibility and leave law in control. It is fundamentally an anti-situationist gambit. It is a form of obstructiveness, a delaying tactic of static morality."

Heller is very careful to point out that, while Yossarian is rightfully suspicious of his superiors all along, he is aware of his obligations, is the best navigator at Pianosa and believes that Hitler must be defeated; we are also constantly reminded of his number of missions, and we realize the other connotations of the word. Yossarian makes his decision not to fly anymore only when he sees that to do so will not further the war effort, since Germany is on the brink of defeat, but will serve only to add to the glory of his superiors and endanger the lives of more men. Yossarian throughout has recognized the need for some type of system, for he knows that the alternative is the barbarism of Aarfy.

Yossarian breaks out of the system only when he finds it a threat to his humanity to do otherwise: this aspect of Yossarian's personality is perceived by Mike Nichols, who [directed] the film version of *Catch-22*—"I think of it as a picture about dying and about where you get off and at what point you take control over your life and say, 'No, I won't. *I* decide. *I* draw the line.' "

The morality of Yossarian's final decision is described by Karl:

[*Catch-22*'s] surface extravagance masks a serious purpose: that in an impossible situation, one finally has to honor his own self; that in an absurd universe, the individual has a right to seek survival; that one's own substance is infinitely more precious than any cause, however right; that one must not be asked to give his life unless everybody is willing to give his.

It is this latter point—a kind of Kantian categorical imperative applied to survival—that has generally been neglected. When Yossarian decides that his life does count, he is making a moral decision about the sanctity of human existence. Life must not be taken lightly, either by others (military men, business manipulators, world leaders) or by oneself. Yossarian is a hero by virtue of his sacred appraisal of his future. To himself he is as valuable as a general or a president. Since he is so valuable he has a right, an inviolable right, to save himself once he has done his share of the world's dirty business. The individual must consider himself supreme. What could be more democratic, more American, even Christian! [200]

And Yossarian is ultimately Christian. We discussed the Joycean nature of the book; there is every reason to believe that Heller intended to show us many parallels between Yossarian and Christ. First, there is Yossarian's name, which J. P. Stern tells us is "an Assyrian stem with an Armenian ending and echoings of the name of Jesus." This must be important when we consider Heller's almost morality play name symbols: Orr, who rows to Sweden and who presents an alternative; the all-American boy Appleby; Scheisskopf; Dori Duz, who did; and the animalistic Aarfy.

The book is given a definite mythological dimension by the fact that it escapes time. Two separate time schemes are involved; the psychological time of Yossarian, as events are presented at the times they are important to Yossarian's psychological development, not at the times they occur; and the traditional, chronological time of Milo Minderbinder, whose career progresses linearly, page by page, from the time he is introduced. There are many occasions when Milo is found with Yossarian at a time when he had not yet been introduced. This serves to add to the contrast between the personalist Yossarian and the money-hungry Milo, who represents capitalism. One of the anachronistic incidents concerns the time Milo bombs his own men and avoids punishment by disclosing the huge profit he had made on the deal.

In addition to his contrast to the demonic Milo, Yossarian is given a mythological dimension by several subtle references; early in the book he likens himself to Superman and other mythological heroes; when Nately's death is the last straw that leads to his decision to stop flying, Colonel Korn remarks "Who does he think he is, Achilles?", referring to the Greek hero's action after the death of his best friend Patrocles. Colonel Cathcart has consistently raised the number of missions the men had to fly to gain glory which he hoped would make him a general.

Korn again links Yossarian to the mythological when he tells him, "The men were content to fly as many missions as we asked as long as they thought they had no alternatives. Now you've given them hope, and they're unhappy. The blame is all yours." The similarity to the exchange between Christ and the Spanish Inquisitor in *The Brothers Karamazov* is apparent, and here Yossarian is linked with the revolutionary side of Christ who was crucified, above all, for being a political threat to rulers who manipulated the people.

Chapter XXXIX, "The Eternal City," describes the wanderings of Yossarian through Rome in search of Nately's whore's kid sister, and has been compared by M. Doskow to the archetypal descent for purposes of purification into hell of Aeneas, Odysseus, and Dante ("The Night Journey in *Catch-22*," *Twentieth Century Literature*, January, 1967).*

As Yossarian passes through Rome, the center of Western Religion, we are struck by the godlessness of the situation; the only reminiscence of God comes in the growing parallel between Yossarian and Christ:

> The night was filled with horrors, and he thought he knew how Christ must have felt, as he walked through the world, like a psychiatrist through a ward full of nuts, like a victim through a prison of thieves. What a welcome sight a leper must have been! (424)

The fact that Yossarian was trying to save a girl who hated him, and whose sister had tried to kill him, might have been taken as another Christ-like act, but there is more involved:

> Yossarian thought he knew why Nately's whore held him responsible for Nately's death and wanted to kill him. Why the hell shouldn't she? It was a man's world and she and everyone younger had the right to blame him and everyone older for every unnatural tragedy that befell them; just as she, even in her grief, was to blame for all the man-made misery that landed on her sister and all other children behind her. Someone had to do something sometime. Every victim was a culprit, every culprit a victim, and somebody had to stand up and try to break that lousy chain of inherited habit that was imperiling them all. (414)

Like Christ, Yossarian seems to take the responsibility for all of men's sins and atone for original sin; his call to responsibility is every bit as strong, as he hits out at man's inadequacies which allow him to be victimized by Catch-22. When Yossarian reaches the whorehouse, he finds the girls gone, the old man dead and learns from the old woman that it was all the work of the MP's who had thrown the girls out into the street and probably frightened the old man to death, using their only justification as Catch-22 —"Catch-22 says they have a right to do anything we can't stop them from doing." (416) Yossarian is enraged:

---

* See pp. 166–174 in this volume.—Eds.

Catch-22 did not exist, he was positive of that, but it made no difference. What did matter was that everyone thought it existed, and that was much worse, for there was no object or text to ridicule or refute, to accuse, criticize, attack, amend, hate, revile, spit at, rip to shreds, trample upon, or burn up. (418) [201]

Heller has shown us that man is a victim of "inherited habit" which makes him obey authority, no matter what the situation; he has shown us that those in authority do *not* always know what they are doing and, that when they do, their intentions may be less than honorable. This is best seen when Major Danby briefs the men on bombing missions over an innocent Italian village; he tells them that their superiors must know what they're doing, but in reality the superiors had conceived the bombing mission on a whim to bring back an aerial photograph of a "tight bomb pattern."

The conclusion to be drawn from this is that most of man's man-made misery is his own fault, stemming from his failure to stand up for his humanity and question what is going on around him. He has been lulled into accepting what is as reality, and adherence to this reality as sanity; accordingly his actions have been insane. Yossarian's actions seen in the light of Situation Ethics, his contrast with Milo and all he represents, his courage, and his similarities to Christ make him the perfect example of the "new hero," a man capable of restoring true sanity to the world.

Doskow notes that, in leaving for Sweden to join Orr, "Perhaps it is only Purgatory Yossarian will gain . . . but it is a world where life is at least possible. . . ." Faced with the alternative of denying his conscience either by flying more missions or by getting out of danger by mouthing false praises of his superiors, or facing a court-martial, Yossarian chooses to fly to Sweden, but he tells Danby:

I'm not running *away* from my responsibilities. I'm running *to* them. There's nothing negative about running away to save my life. You know who the escapists are, don't you, Danby? Not me and Orr. (461)

The escapists are those who shun responsibility in favor of being told what to do by those in power; Erich Fromm in *Escape From Freedom* tells us that the responsibility called for by freedom is too big a burden for many people, and it is their search for someone to tell them what to do that is the greatest invitation to Fascism.

In this vein Robert Brustein notes:

Yossarian's obsessive concern for morality not only makes him *not* morally dead, but one of the most morally vibrant figures of recent literature—and a giant of the will beside those weary, wise and wistful prodigals in contemporary novels who always accommodate sadly to American life.*

Yossarian does indeed offer a categorical imperative applied to survival: his actions, Situation Ethics and Christ's mission all point to the same conclusion—man's life is sacred, the one thing he must keep and shape in his own way, without the imposition of authority. Yossarian knows that without order there is anarchy and chaos, but that within order, there is still a point where a man must say "No."

The example of Yossarian, like that of Christ, is not an easy one to live up to, but there is much wisdom in Doctor Stubbs' appraisal of Yossarian: "That crazy bastard may be the only sane one left." (114) [202]

Douglas Day
'Catch-22':
A Manifesto for Anarchists

We must throw away our Salingers and Goldings now, all of us chasers after literary fashion: Joseph Heller's *Catch-22*, published a year ago and—until the recent appearance of William Burroughs' *Naked Lunch*—surely the wildest book of the decade, is what the cognoscenti like this year; and we won't be *in* at cocktail parties before long if we can't allude to it with that air of smug familiarity so offensive to non-litterateurs. We might not like it, but we had better pretend to do so; for who dares now to dislike a novel that is totally anti-Establishment? And that is precisely what *Catch-22* is. Seen through the eyes of a patriot like, say, Lieutenant Colonel John Glenn, it would appear to be a sort of perverted Boy Scout's Oath of a novel: it is untrustworthy, disloyal, unhelpful, unfriendly, discourteous, unkind, cheerless, unthrifty, craven, unclean, and irreverent.

Nelson Algren has called *Catch-22* "the best American novel to come out of anywhere in years." David Merrick (according to a full-page advertisement for *Catch-22* recently placed in *The New York Times* by Simon and Schuster, the book's publishers) wants to do a Broadway version of it.

---

* See his "The Logic of Survival in a Lunatic World," on pp. 6–11 of this volume.—Eds.

SOURCE: *Carolina Quarterly*, Vol. 15 (Summer 1963), pp. 86–92. Reprinted by permission of the publisher.

Columbia Pictures has paid $150,000 for the movie rights, and hired Heller to write the screenplay. Art Buchwald has made his debut as critic by calling it "one of the greatest war books." And one nameless enthusiast has entered into the spirit of *Catch-22* by acclaiming it as "the wittiest book since *Beowulf*, the cleverest since *Paradise Lost*." On the strength of all this adulation, *Catch-22*'s paperback publishers have seen fit to print 700,000 copies of it, and presumably are now sitting back to await the imminent collapse of the Salinger-Golding balloons. [86]

They may have to wait longer than they would like, however; for the book's popularity has so far not spread very far beyond two or three metropolitan areas in the United States (and London, where, to be sure, *Catch-22* led best-seller lists for some time), and is not likely to go much further.

Even if the public does make something of *Catch-22*, moreover, all but the most undisciplined of literary critics will despise it. How, academicians will ask, could Heller have spent eight years in writing it? It is certainly derivative—a great part of it is obviously out of William Saroyan by Max Shulman. It seems poorly edited, repetitive, and overlong. It is hopelessly confused in mood, shifting irrationally and irresponsibly from sneering cynicism to the most banal kind of sentimentality (how trite to write a novel the major premise of which is that killing is bad and that we all ought to love one another!), from the rawest and most explicit realism to mad flights of surrealism. Most critics of fiction will be unable to classify *Catch-22*, so they will probably end by scorning it.

In a way they will be right, because *Catch-22* is not, strictly speaking, a novel at all. It is, rather, what scholars like Northrop Frye would define as an *anatomy*, or *satire*—a mixed bag, a hash, a work which is characterized by a great variety of subject matter, a strong interest in ideas, and a disinclination to be bound by the customary logic of narrative. *Catch-22* belongs to a genre developed and perfected by Petronius, Apuleius, Rabelais, Swift, Voltaire, and Sterne; and the reader who tries to judge it by a novel-centered conception of fiction will indeed find little to please.

What, briefly, is *Catch-22* about? It is on its literal level a fiction about the Second World War in Europe—specifically, about a group of American medium bombers operating over Italy in 1943–44. Among its leaders are men whom Lieutenant Colonel Glenn would find entirely admirable: there is iron-clad Colonel Cathcart, who bravely demands sixty missions of all his crews when other groups are flying only forty; there is Captain Appleby, a fair-haired youth from Iowa, and a truly splendid ping-pong player, who believes in God, Motherhood, and the American Way of Life; there is Captain Havermeyer, a lead navigator who never hesitates to risk his own life (and whose cheeks are perpetually flecked with bits of good old American peanut brittle); there is Captain "Aarfy" Aardvaark, a good fraternity man and a protector of virtuous women; and there is Milo Minderbinder, the conscientious squadron mess officer, who will do anything to keep his charges well-fed.

A thorn in the sides of all these paragons is Heller's protagonist, Captain Yossarian, who is so abject a misfit that his [87] psychiatrist must say to him: "You have no respect for excessive authority or obsolete traditions. You're dangerously depraved, and you ought to be taken outside and shot!" Yossarian, who gradually emerges as almost the only sane man in a world gone crazy, does not like the war; he takes the whole business as a personal affront, as an indignity not to be tolerated. He does not like Colonel Cathcart because Cathcart assigns extra missions only to attract attention to himself; he does not like Appleby because Appleby is moronic (which is to say that he does what his superiors tell him to do); he does not like Havermeyer because Havermeyer risks not only his own life, but everyone else's as well; he does not like Milo Minderbinder because Minderbinder is making a good thing, financially, out of the war (to put it mildly); and he especially despises Aardvaark for his blithe—and murderous—disregard for the lives of all those who would not have been socially acceptable to his fraternity.

Judged by the standards of the Establishment, Yossarian is an anarchist: he rages not only against the Germans and Italians who are trying to hit him with their flak, but also against the government that has put him in the air to be hit by flak. "The enemy," as he says, "is anyone who's going to get you killed, no matter *which* side he's on." The real foes for Yossarian are all the congressmen, generals, Cathcarts, Applebys, and Havermeyers who seem to be part of a conspiracy to endanger his life; and his war against them is the real focus of action in *Catch-22*. No tactic is too grand for Yossarian, and none too petty. He comes to open rebellion against his superiors, but he is just as willing to spend days snarling up the squadron's censorship program (one day he pares down all the letters he must censor by removing from them all their adjectives and adverbs; the next day he blacks out all *a*'s, *an*'s and *the*'s; then he proscribes all signatures and salutations, leaving the texts untouched; and finally he turns one letter into a frantic love message, which he signs with the name of the group chaplain), or sitting naked on a tree limb to signify his disaffiliation. If God offends him, Yossarian lets God know how he feels about it. When a Mrs. Scheisskopf (Heller's fun with names often inclines to the sophomoric) defends the Lord, Yossarian explodes:

"And don't tell me God works in mysterious ways. . . . There's nothing mysterious about it. He's not working at all. He's playing. Or else He's forgotten all about us. That's the kind of God you people talk about—a country bumpkin, a clumsy, bungling, brainless, conceited, uncouth hayseed. Good God, how much reverence can you have for a supreme being who finds it

necessary to include such phenomena as phlegm and tooth decay in [88] His
divine system of creation? What in the world was running through that
warped, scatological mind of His when He robbed old people of the power
to control their bowel movements?"

Obviously, Yossarian's revolt is not just against the U. S. Government and
the ruthlessness of capitalist exploitation (although he has a lot to say about
these), but against something much larger. Yossarian is, finally, the Natural Man trying to live the Simple Life in the midst of a world driven mad
by the complexities of its systems. *Eros* and *agape* dominate him: he is a
dedicated lecher, and next to sex he loves best peace, serenity, and his fellow
men. He is, in short, Holden Caulfield grown up into a randy, hairy-bellied,
linty-naveled satyr; and he loves his life too much to tolerate its being
jeopardized. The Establishment's judgment is correct: Yossarian *is* an
anarchist, and one of the most extreme sort—no government, whether
earthly or divine, is tolerable to him.

Yossarian has friends, but none on the side of the incredibly boorish
philistines who govern the war. There is Orr, his squirrel-cheeked roommate, who paddles his life raft to Sweden and safety; there is Dobbs, who
wants Yossarian to join him in a plot to assassinate the colonel; there is
Huple, a good pilot in spite of the fact that he is only fifteen; and there are
assorted other outcasts—whores, nasty old men, neurotics, and drunks, all
devoted to life and squarely against Authority in any form.

If *Catch-22* sounds like a mass of tastelessness and vulgarity, so it is. But
surely no critic in our aggressively emancipated era would have the nerve to
condemn a work simply because it struck him as morally offensive, unless
he were willing to be charged with being guilty of F. R. Leavisim. And,
besides, it may be that tastelessness and vulgarity are perhaps the most
suitable vehicles for the transmission of Heller's undoubtedly strong sense
of moral outrage. When a body falls from a hotel window to land "with
a hideous *plop!* on the sidewalk and die disgustingly there in public like
an alpaca sack full of hairy strawberry ice cream, bleeding, pink toes awry,"
we are naturally shocked by the gruesome—and somehow ludicrous—apt-
ness of the simile; but we are also shocked (and here is Heller's real reason
for the simile) that human beings, with all their capacity for happiness
and dignity, should end so ignominiously, in such shameful positions.

I have perhaps so far failed to suggest that *Catch-22* is, in addition to
being an outraged cry against the System, often a wildly funny book. But
its humor is of a rather special, barbaric type. Time and again one finds
himself hee-hawing over Heller's [89] absurdities, only to be jerked up
sharply by the realization that he is snickering at pain, insanity, and violent
death—surely not customary objects of humor in a society supposedly
governed by principles of mercy and compassion. And Heller's favorite

device is to make sudden and unexpected transitions from the bawdiest kind of farce, into scenes of unrelieved somberness, grotesquerie, and tragedy—and then back again just as quickly to farce, until the reader's responses are hopelessly confused.

In one of *Catch-22*'s most shocking incidents, for example, Yossarian is grappling on the beach with a nurse as one of the squadron's bombers playfully buzzes a group of swimmers. One of these, a silly young boy named Kid Sampson, leaps up from his raft as if to touch the low-flying plane just as it dips low over him, propellers churning:

> There was the briefest, softest *tsst!* filtering audibly through the shattering, overwhelming howl of the plane's engines, and there were just Kid Sampson's two pale, skinny legs, still joined somehow at the bloody truncated hips, standing stock-still on the raft for what seemed a full minute or two before they toppled over backward into the water finally with a faint, echoing splash and turned upside down so that only the grotesque toes and the plaster-white soles of Kid Sampson's feet remained in view.

The audience of *Beowulf* would possibly have been able to laugh unashamedly at Kid Sampson's ghastly end, but modern readers unusually demand that horror and humor be kept distinct, so that they will know clearly when it is time to shudder, and when time to guffaw. Heller cares nothing for our sense of fastidiousness or our sense of decorum, however; and our initial reaction to this sort of thing is to feel resentment at having our responses toyed with in such a cavalier fashion: we are all set to recoil from the bloody scene, our eyes averted—but then we realize that there is something so preposterous about those two skinny, lonely legs and those white soles upended that we cannot help snickering again. The careful reader will eventually come to see that Heller's technique here is far from irresponsible. The point he wishes to make is that our world is not neat and symmetrical, but bizarre and absurd; and that because of this it is impossible to make clear-cut distinctions between horror and humor. The word "absurd" above is the key: Heller's satire seems in many ways more closely related to the drama of Ionesco, Beckett, and Genet than to modern fiction (although one is often reminded by it of works by Burroughs, John Hawkes, and—in its milder moments of farce—even Kingsley Amis). Like all [90] of these, Heller's fundamental note is one of despair; and like all of these, Heller's despair wears an ironic grimace.

The sometimes rather forced silliness of *Catch-22* often obscures this somber note; but the despair is always there, ready to strike us when we least expect it. We learn early in the work, for example, that a bombing run he had made over Avignon has some special meaning for Yossarian. Beyond the knowledge that this flight had been even more chaotic than most, we are at first unaware of what had made it unique. Then, in a process very much like incremental repetition, the truth gradually unfolds: Yossarian's memory turns more and more frequently back to the Avignon flight; and each time it does, Heller relates the incident again, with seemingly only minor changes in each version. Finally, near the end of the book, we learn the reason why the mission had been so traumatic for Yossarian: after the completion of the bombing run he had crawled back through his plane's fuselage to aid a wounded crewman, Snowden, and had found that the man was mortally wounded.

Yossarian ripped open the snaps of Snowden's flak suit and heard himself scream wildly as Snowden's insides slithered down to the floor in a soggy pile and just kept dripping out. A chunk of flak more than three inches big had shot into his other side just underneath the arm and blasted all the way through, drawing whole mottled quarts of Snowden along with it through the gigantic hole in his ribs it made as it blasted out. . . . Here was God's plenty, all right, he thought bitterly as he stared—liver, lungs, kidneys, ribs, stomach and bits of the stewed tomatoes Snowden had eaten that day for lunch.

There is no snickering here; only consternation, horror, and revulsion. After this scene, it would be difficult to blame Yossarian for refusing to fly more missions—which is just what he does.

There is no law to prevent an author from juxtaposing his comic with his tragic elements, certainly—such a technique can find any number of noble precedents, both in fiction and in drama. One does feel justified, however, in assuming that the author wants his material taken seriously when he presents it seriously, without any traces of irony or levity; and we must ask ourselves just what we are accepting when we take Yossarian to our bosoms. When we strip away all the bawdry, all the wild exaggeration, all the horseplay from Catch-22, we are left with a book the hero of which is motivated as much by a desire for self-preservation as by a love for his fellow men. Yossarian, let us state it bluntly, is a coward, a man who throws away all honor, [91] sense of moral obligation, and self-respect in a frantic campaign to escape a death that would seem meaningless to him. He is fey and lovable, yes; but we could never consider him a man of stature sufficient enough to make a tragic hero.

Not, that is, if we are seeing him through the eyes of the Establishment. But if we accept Yossarian's—and Heller's—premises (War is madness; only a fool becomes caught up in madness willingly; therefore sane men will flee from war), then Yossarian, by refusing to sacrifice himself to the insane and unspeakably ruthless machinery of war, is truly noble.

Catch-22, as I predicted earlier, probably will never be taken up very enthusiastically by a large segment of the public: in spite of its surface hilarity, it is too strong a pill for most. Moreover, *Catch-22* is technically speaking a far from perfect work. It is a blowzy, careening, cliché-ridden, fly-specked sort of monstrosity, even when seen as a satire and not as a novel. Fascinating as they all are, there are simply too many incidents, and the really crucial ones do not stand out as they should. Worse, Heller often sails off into surrealistic excesses which soon exist for their own sakes, to the detriment of whatever flimsy unity the work might otherwise have possessed. Worst of all, however, is his tendency to milk his jokes until they are pulled completely out of shape. And, as I have noted, the book is devoid of any sort of restraint or taste (assuming, as perhaps we ought not, that war is capable of being treated tastefully). But Heller somehow manages to get away with it all, which makes him justified by "Catch-22," in Heller's world an unwritten but ubiquitous law, the tenor of which is that anyone has a right to anything he can get away with. [92]

G.B.McK.Henry
Significant Corn: 'Catch-22'

You have got to pull the democratic and idealistic clothes off American utterance, and see what you can of the dusky body of IT underneath. [D. H. LAWRENCE]

I don't claim to have found any dusky bodies in Joseph Heller's *Catch-22*, since it's more a matter of pulling off various other garb to find the democratic idealism. It's a best seller with something in common with the "absurdist" line of *avant-garde* literature; and with that combination perhaps we are right to be suspicious of what is underneath.

We ought to be wary also of the growing influence of the film on the novel. Like most best sellers, *Catch-22* reads at times like a film script; between the lines one senses "pan," "close-up," "tracking shot." Such novels tend to be constructed in scenes, and scenes highly visualized, characters and gestures are observed from the outside, with a sort of cinematic consciousness. Thus the resources of the language may not be fully employed. The temptation to go for a highly-focused "intensity" of experience may

SOURCE: *The Critical Review*, Vol. 9 (1966), pp. 133–144. Reprinted by permission of the author and publisher.

be greater than the desire to explore it. Both the big Hollywood best sellers and the more shyly popular little English novels (like A *Kind of Loving* and *The L-shaped Room*) have the same net effect: we can dramatize ourselves into a world where (however bloody it is) everything comes out all right and our small sins are forgiven. The tragedy of such modern tragedies is that inevitably someone else gets hurt for our sins, some insignificant character on the edge of the drama, and we can have our cake and eat it too. As an example of the "cinematic novel," *Catch-22* shows both the compelling energy of the cinema and the limitations of that world.

The relationship of *Catch-22* to the "absurdist" line of writers is less important than its relationship to popular entertainment, but it should be noticed. The book naturally suggests the word "absurd" in a way that, say, the plays of Beckett and Ionesco don't; it is a "tragi-farce," and Yossarian is its anti-hero—that is, cowardice is substituted for the conventional virtues of courage and loyalty and equated with sanity; and his final "heroic" action is to run away:

> "They're trying to kill me," Yossarian told him calmly.
> "No one's trying to kill you," Clevinger cried.
> "Then why are they shooting at me?" Yossarian asked.
> "They're shooting at *everyone*," Clevinger answered. "They're trying to kill everyone."
> "And what difference does that make?" . . .
> Clevinger really thought he was right, but Yossarian had proof, because strangers he didn't know shot at him with cannons every time he flew up in the air to drop bombs on them, and it wasn't funny at all.

However, as the unavoidable ironic and rational pointedness of this shows, Yossarian's "sanity" is given a definite positive force. While the philosophy of this book is one of rejection of the world, it has none of the "My God, they stink!" attitude about it that tends to appear in "absurdist" literature. If the vision is often surrealistic—[133]

Yossarian crossed quickly to the other side of the immense avenue to escape the nauseating sight and found himself walking on human teeth lying on the drenched, glistening pavement near splotches of blood kept sticky by the pelting raindrops poking each one like sharp fingernails. Molars and broken incisors lay scattered everywhere. He circled on tiptoe the grotesque debris and came near a doorway containing a crying soldier holding a saturated handkerchief to his mouth. . . .

—it is precisely and vividly so. It is not simply a pretty *effect;* the precision defines Yossarian/Heller's acute awareness of the suffering of the world.

The insistence is comparable with parts of Dickens; but still it is a *vision,*
a bit of film. There is an essential unreality, which is not found in Dickens,
involved by its self-consciousness.

Catch-22 also recalls Dickens in that we have the same mixture of the
ingredients of popular entertainment, humour, melodrama, sentiment
(Heller adds sex)—pure corn—with more solid significant stuff. We have
(at first sight at any rate) a similarly two-dimensional, larger-than-life-and-
twice-as-natural pop-eyed vision of the universe. In Heller's case, an apparently chaotic world is found to revolve around fundamental principles
of greed, fear, and violence, its occupants split into two camps of "crazy"
and sane that correspond roughly with the Dickensian goodies and baddies,
exploiters and exploited. The clear similarities are in the characterization—
vivid caricatures, living, yet also showing elements of the stereotype. Heller's way of naming and introducing them, determinedly flat, also has
affinities with Dickens:

General Peckem was a general with whom neatness definitely counted. He
was a spry, suave and very precise general who knew the circumference of the
equator and always wrote "enhanced" when he meant "increased."

But Heller's style derives less from Dickens than from the brighter
American journalism. His language is less flexible than Dickens's. It is
standard American, in the quasi-succinctness, the corner-of-the-mouth
toughness, and the generosity with adjectives. He employs crisp, clean,
terse sentences for his humorous, ironic, or dramatic impact, and long
sentences accumulating images to build up climaxes (it is all rather consciously manipulated):

And there was no time for Yossarian to save himself from combat once Colonel
Cathcart issued his announcement raising the missions to eighty late that
same afternoon, no time to dissuade Nately from flying them or even to conspire
again with Dobbs to murder Colonel Cathcart, for the alert sounded suddenly
at dawn the next day and the men were rushed into the trucks before a decent
breakfast could be prepared, and they were driven at top speed to the briefing
room and then out to the airfield, where the clitterclanking fuel trucks were
still pumping gasoline into the tanks of the planes and the scamping crews
of armorers were toiling as swiftly as they could at hoisting the thousand-pound
demolition bombs into the bomb bays.

Apart from giving the basic impression of haste, the breathlessly long [134]
sentence is also organized to recall the parts played by Nately and Dobbs,
with particular relevance, for we find their planes collide:

His wing broke off at the base, and his plane dropped like a rock and was almost out of sight in an instant. There was no fire, no smoke, not the slightest untoward noise. The remaining wing revolved as ponderously as a grinding cement mixer as the plane plummeted nose downward in a straight line at accelerating speed until it struck the water, which foamed open at the impact like a white water lily on the dark-blue sea and washed back in a geyser of apple-green bubbles when the plane sank. It was over in a matter of seconds. There were no parachutes. And Nately in the other plane was killed too.

We are involved in a wash of words and dropped (like the plane described) tersely and dispassionately on to the climax. In the rush, particular images (like the cement mixer) tend to be lost and to contribute nothing more than a vague sensation. To this extent the writing (not inappropriately, however) is out of control. It is shock tactics, but in context remarkably effective. For the shock thus generated is immediately localized in the chaplain who appears in the succeeding chapter. A progression of images, like snippets out of a newspaper, recalls and emphasizes his obsessive fear of death and injury, working up to a surprisingly unaffected, unjournalistic revelation of his emotion:

The chaplain made fists of his hands to keep them from shaking as they lay in his lap. He ground his teeth together and tried not to hear as Sergeant Whitcomb chirruped exultantly over the tragic event.

The simplicity of this is deceptive; here, the quality of the writing appears in the way the rightness of "chirruped" exposes Whitcomb's shallow conventionality ("tragic event").

The richness of *Catch-22* lies mainly in the complexity with which the fates of the characters are linked to apparently minor and farcical events. Nately's death means little unless it is recalled that he is the nice, naive son of the American aristocracy who fell in love with a whore because of her infinite apathy, who has just succeeded in getting her to respond, and must therefore fly more missions to stay in Italy to be with her, and who would (probably) never have been killed if she had said "uncle" in the right tone of voice (which she couldn't, being apathetic) to the bigwigs from whom Nately, Dunbar, Yossarian and Hungry Joe rescued her so that she finally got a good night's sleep. Dobbs's history is similarly involved but less important. These intricate causal sequences only just become apparent at about this point in the book; and here we see that they lead to crucial events providing the clue and the climax to Heller's view of the world, wherein he (*via* Yossarian) is fighting an increasing tragic despair.

Even the old tricks borrowed from popular entertainment, like double-take and crossed trains of thought, are there to reflect the insecurity and confusion of life that are an integral part of Heller's concept:

"That's a fine thing," General Dreedle growled at the bar . . . [135] "That's really a fine thing when a man of God begins hanging around a place like this with a bunch of dirty drunks and gamblers."

Colonel Cathcart sighed with relief. "Yes, sir," he exclaimed proudly. "It certainly is a fine thing."

"Then why the hell don't you do something about it?" . . . "Aren't you the one who ordered him to come here?"

"No, sir, that was Colonel Korn. I intend to punish him severely, too."

"If he wasn't a chaplain," General Dreedle muttered, "I'd have him taken outside and shot."

"He's not a chaplain, sir," Colonel Cathcart advised helpfully.

"Isn't he? Then why the hell does he wear that cross on his collar if he's not a chaplain?"

"He doesn't wear a cross on his collar, sir. He wears a silver leaf. He's a lieutenant colonel."

"You've got a chaplain who's a lieutenant colonel?" inquired General Dreedle with amazement.

"Oh, no, sir. My chaplain is only a captain."

"Then why the hell does he wear a silver leaf on his collar if he's only a captain?"

"He doesn't wear a silver leaf on his collar, sir. He wears a cross."

"Go away from me now, you son of a bitch," said General Dreedle. "Or I'll have you taken outside and shot!"

Catch-22 is a masterpiece of "pace," the technique of farce. Life is bewildering; impossible things happen that simply issue into more impossible things. In farce, people find themselves in embarrassing situations, and in devising ways to extricate themselves, are ironically tangled in even more awkward situations and so on until everything is finally resolved by a *deus ex machina*, or things reach such a climax of impossibility that the show just has to stop. In *Catch-22* the basic remorseless logic of farce is made monstrous by the inclusion of death. But its *deus ex machina* ending is, we shall see, a severe limitation: the fates, or facts of life, are apparently inescapable until Orr, superficially an idiot, provides Yossarian with the inspiration to make his break for freedom.

A good example of the Kafka-esque power which the possibility of death and suffering gives to Heller's farce can be found in the sequel to the scene already quoted—Nately's death and its effect on the chaplain. At the pitch of his grief the chaplain is arrested and led away to a farcically melodramatic interrogation, faced with the usual equipment for brainwashing and torture. The scene both employs and satirizes the devices of the thriller, but it cuts deeper in its consistent pointlessness. The chaplain is accused of forging a meaningless name to unimportant documents and stealing a plum tomato from Colonel Cathcart:

"Why should a superior officer give you a plum tomato, Chaplain?"
"Is that why you tried to give it to Sergeant Whitcomb, Chaplain? Because it was a hot tomato?"

Heller cannot resist the joke. Most of the time, as in this case, the pun heightens the intense absurdity of the scene. Sometimes, however, as in the similar interrogation of Clevinger much earlier, it is a joke for a joke's sake; Heller is being clever and loses track, and the effect dwindles to facetiousness. But never for long; in the scene with Clevinger, the motive force is rapidly brought to our attention explicitly: [136]

It was all very confusing to Clevinger. There were many strange things taking place, but the strangest of all, to Clevinger, was the hatred, the brutal, uncloaked, inexorable hatred of the members of the Action Board, glazing their unforgiving expressions with a hard, vindictive surface, glowing in their narrowed eyes malignantly like inextinguishable coals. . . . They had hated him before he came, hated him while he was there, hated him after he left, carried their hatred for him away malignantly like some pampered treasure after they separated from each other and went to their solitude.

Clevinger is the highly educated but rather naive, nice intellectual type. He is a "dope" because he is always trying to find rational answers to Yossarian's unanswerable questions, trying to justify his inherited conventional values in the face of Yossarian's simple but infuriating logic. His initial mistake is to try to exercise his constitutional rights. His fate is perfectly calculated: he disappears into a cloud. He is hated because he has a "mind," and the brutish officers who interrogate him are the agents of a stupid and greedy world which cannot tolerate questioning intelligence in any form. The spectacle of the officers going away to hate Clevinger is not only exaggerated and funny but also savagely real. But Clevinger is not simply innocent sensitivity trampled on by brute force; it is his narrow philosophy of loyalty to democracy that makes possible a world where the subtler and more realistic attitude of Yossarian is regarded as madness. Thus the farcical interrogation grimly sums up the nature of contemporary America—the dream of perfect democracy and the reality of crude and destructive military and financial power. This theme is echoed and expanded throughout the book.

The chaplain's case is deeper and more complicated than Clevinger's.

His grief after Nately's death transcends his personal concern for his friends and involves him in the "human condition." But one needs to remember that he is presented to us initially as a stock type, a farcical formula: ridiculously timid, bullied by his aide Sergeant Whitcomb, uncertain of his faith, bewildered by military life, and tormented with apparently mystical experiences that he can't fathom. His inquisition arises from his own timid sensitivity and humanity. He feels guilty for Nately's death, and the guilt is projected in the dream-like interrogation, not because he is in any way causally responsible for it, but because he is one of the few who are sensitive to the violence and suffering of the world and therefore one of the few who could be expected to do anything about it. He is also acutely aware of the ambiguity of his own position, his combined cowardice and safety. But his basic farcical characteristics preclude his being a member of some élite of the super-sensitive condescending to clods. Thus the accusations against him—assuming a false name, intercepting confidential documents, stealing a plum tomato—are in a symbolic way perfectly relevant, the case presented is just, and he is guilty—of doing nothing, of moping. This is the only system of justice discernible in a world dominated by Catch-22, the most general formulation of which is that "they" have a right to do anything you can't stop them from doing: the philosophy of power. The chaplain goes away in a righteous rage of determination to take positive action, but is immediately [137] stumped by the bland logic of Colonel Korn (which appropriately is not so different from Yossarian's):

"Colonel Korn, I want to talk to you about the crash this morning. It was a terrible thing to happen, terrible!"

Colonel Korn was silent a moment, regarding the chaplain with a glint of cynical amusement. "Yes, Chaplain, it certainly was terrible," he said finally. "I don't know *how* we're going to write this one up without making ourselves look bad."

"That isn't what I meant," the chaplain scolded firmly without any fear at all. "Some of those twelve men had already finished their seventy missions."

Colonel Korn laughed. "Would it be any less terrible if they had all been new men?" he inquired caustically.

This brief illustration may suggest how closely and relevantly the novel is organized. All the major characters carry their formulae with a remarkable variety of wit and force, and also point insistently to the major theme of the novel: the meaningless savagery of contemporary civilization. It is good satire, emphasizing the grim brutality of the world while maintaining the high-spirited madness of farce. Each character shows a different aspect of the civilization under attack, the whole range embracing a wide variety of social levels and attitudes. Milo Minderbinder is an obvious and Dickensian case: the young, charming capitalist genius whose only loyalty (except for a conveniently sacrificed attachment to Yossarian) is to private enterprise—his own—who quite logically justifies the bombing of his own squadron by disclosing the enormous profit. And the world worships him. A more interesting example is the thick-skinned Aardvaark, who is also American to the core. For most of the novel Aarfy is a sort of buffoon; he says placidly "What? I can't hear you," as Yossarian, wounded, panics in the nose of the aeroplane. But his infuriating insensitivity is a part of his physical existence:

Punching Aarfy was like sinking his fists into a limp sack of inflated rubber. There was no resistance, no response at all from the soft, insensitive mass, and after a while Yossarian's spirit died and his arms dropped helplessly with exhaustion. He was overcome with a humiliating feeling of impotence and was ready to weep in self-pity.

Yossarian's reaction is significant: he cannot defeat this insensitivity with violence (nor, as we find out, with reason); what is unresponsive (unlike Clevinger) cannot be defeated.

Towards the end Aarfy takes on a different light, providing the climax and epitome of Yossarian's surrealistic vision of the "eternal city" containing nothing but violence and suffering. Aarfy has raped a girl so plain and innocent that none of the other men want her, held her prisoner for two hours, and then thrown her out of the window.

Yossarian's heart pounded with fright and horror at the pitiful, ominous, gory spectacle of the broken corpse. He ducked into the hallway and bolted up the stairs into the apartment, where he found Aarfy pacing about uneasily with a pompous, slightly uncomfortable smile. Aarfy seemed a bit unsettled as he fidgeted with his pipe and [138] assured Yossarian that everything was going to be all right. There was nothing to worry about.

"I only raped her once," he explained.

Yossarian was aghast. "But you killed her, Aarfy! You killed her!"

"Oh, I had to do that after I raped her," Aarfy replied in his most condescending manner. "I couldn't very well let her go around saying bad things about us, could I?"

"But why did you have to touch her at all, you dumb bastard?" Yossarian shouted. "Why couldn't you get yourself a girl off the street if you wanted one? The city is full of prostitutes."

"Oh, no, not me," Aarfy bragged. "I never paid for it in my life." . . .

"You've murdered a human being. They *are* going to put you in jail. They might even *hang* you!"

"Oh, I hardly think they'll do that," Aarfy replied with a jovial chuckle, although his symptoms of nervousness increased. He spilled tobacco crumbs unconsciously as his short fingers fumbled with the bowl of his pipe. "No, sirree. Not to good old Aarfy." He chortled again. "She was only a servant girl. I hardly think they're going to make too much of a fuss over one poor Italian servant girl when so many thousands of lives are being lost every day. Do you?"

"Listen!" Yossarian cried, almost in joy. He pricked up his ears and watched the blood drain from Aarfy's face as sirens mourned far away, police sirens, and then ascended almost instantaneously to a howling, strident, onrushing cacophony of overwhelming sound that seemed to crash into the room around them from every side. "Aarfy, they're coming for you," he said in a flood of compassion, shouting to be heard above the noise. "They're coming to arrest you. Aarfy, don't you understand? You can't take the life of another human being and get away with it, even if she is just a poor servant girl. Don't you see? Can't you understand?"

"Oh, no," Aarfy insisted with a lame laugh and a weak smile. "They're not coming to arrest me. Not good old Aarfy."

All at once he looked sick. He sank down on a chair in a trembling stupor, his stumpy, lax hands quaking in his lap. Cars skidded to a stop outside. Spotlights hit the windows immediately. Car doors slammed and police whistles screeched. Voices rose harshly. Aarfy was green. He kept shaking his head mechanically with a queer, numb smile and repeating in a weak, hollow monotone that they were not coming for him, not for good old Aarfy, no sirree, striving to convince himself that this was so even as heavy footsteps raced up the stairs and pounded across the landing, even as fists beat on the door four times with a deafening, inexorable force. Then the door to the apartment flew open, and two large, tough, brawny M.P.s with icy eyes and firm, sinewy, unsmiling jaws entered quickly, strode across the room, and arrested Yossarian.

The scene has its roots in the gangster film, complete with sound effects. There are the sirens, spotlights, whistles, footsteps and so on, and the detail, like Aarfy's fidgeting with his pipe, has the intensely visual, focused, close-up power of a film scene. The type of scene—"goody" trying to convince "baddy" of his guilt and to break him down as the police arrive—is from corny melodrama. The difference, apart from Yossarian's sadistic, self-righteous "joy," is that Aarfy's insensitivity *is* broken down (up to a point); he succumbs to the incapacitating fear that Yossarian suffered when Aarfy wouldn't listen; but, in the pure logic of the novel, he succumbs [139] *irrationally*, for (as it turns out) *his* faith in the world-order is justified, he has no cause to worry. His insensitivity is human, but it smashes the conventional values represented here by Yossarian ("You killed a girl") and focused in the "broken corpse" of the girl. Why *should* they worry about a poor servant girl when so many lives are being lost? (What is justice?) What difference does it make who is killed, except to the victim? It is Yossarian's Falstaffian argument all over again. One might call it the philosophy of paranoic pacificism. *I* don't want to die, therefore nobody should die. If anybody is killed, it is that individual rather than another, and it is an unjust world. As the world is unjust, why shouldn't they arrest *Yossarian?* He is as guilty as anyone else. And, for the continuity does not stop there, why shouldn't they (as they do) march him off at an increasing pace in a multiplying squad of towering, jack-booted Military Police who terrify him more and more, to Colonel Cathcart's office where he is genially told, "We're sending you home"?

The power and the quality of *Catch-22* lie there—it just doesn't stop, it won't let you alone. So strong are the conventions of popular literature upon which it is based that one is always expecting or hoping that justice will scream around the corner at last. If Aarfy were arrested, or Yossarian court-martialled, one could say that there are order and justice in the world after all. But that doesn't happen in this best seller. This effect is accurately sustained until the last chapter, though a slight tailing-off begins with Yossarian's decision that Catch-22 does not exist and that its force is simply that everyone thinks it does. As Yossarian points out, that means that there's nothing to attack, not that his weapons are too slight to hurt it. But Heller has made Catch-22 a natural part of the world he creates, the final absurdity that prevents any escape. If Catch-22 really existed, Yossarian could not succeed in defying it; if it doesn't exist, his defiance has no meaning. Throughout the book the impression is built up that Yossarian must fail, and probably die—his own logic demands it. But here, as we shall see more clearly later, Heller is beginning to look for a way out.

At its best, the book shows Yossarian's search for a viable justice failing because responsibility for particular suffering cannot be attached to individuals any more than responsibility for the "human condition" can; futile suffering *is* the human condition. Everybody (including Yossarian) is out for himself; if anyone is guilty, everyone is, just as everyone has a share in Milo's "syndicate." Thus nearly all the deaths (except of anonymous people) have an accidental quality, almost unrelated to the war, like the collision that kills Nately and Dobbs. There remain the few innocents caught up in the mess—the girl Aarfy kills, the dead man in Yossarian's tent, Kraft, Snowden, Nately's whore's kid sister—all the direct objects of Yossarian's pity, until in the "eternal city" chapter (where he is identified simultaneously with Raskolnikov and Christ) Yossarian/Heller tries to take on the whole burden of suffering humanity.

Nobody knows why these things happen, they just do. The causal sequences are too intricate to be expressed chronologically; hence the disconnected, [140] roundabout construction of the novel. Colonel Cathcart raises the number of missions the men have to fly; so many men, like Nately, subsequently die. But not necessarily *because of* this: as Korn points out, would it have made any difference if the number of missions had not been raised and other men had been killed instead? It is a double-edged remark; the men are cannon-fodder, the individual life is of no significance, but somebody has to do the job. Similarly somebody has to give the orders. The circle of self-interest (even by running away Yossarian does not escape it) cannot be broken; but why should it? *Catch-22* demonstrates that responsibility (and therefore justice, and the whole moral world) cannot be explained by cause and effect. It is a simple point, but one we need reminding of often enough; and Heller avoids the traps of the narrowly psychological novel. There is none of the vain, persistent self-analysis, the triviality of the psychological approach. There is nothing pathological about it.

Responsibility dissociated from causality: it is the way children think. Heller's war is a monstrous game. It is a small boy's vision of the world (based on comics and Biggles*) turned nasty. The child faces reality in ways that the adult forgets in his consistent attributing of responsibility to cause; Heller recaptures these as in the beautifully boyish feeling in this, for example:

"Murderer," Dunbar said quietly.
The Texan looked up at him with an uncertain grin.
"Killer," Yossarian said.
"What are you fellas talkin' about?" the Texan asked nervously.
"You murdered him," said Dunbar.
"You killed him," said Yossarian.
The Texan shrank back. "You fellas are crazy. I didn't even touch him."
"You murdered him," said Dunbar.
"I heard you kill him," said Yossarian.
"You killed him because he was a nigger," Dunbar said.
"You fellas are crazy," the Texan cried. "They don't allow niggers in here. They got a special place for niggers."
"The sergeant smuggled him in," Dunbar said.
"The Communist sergeant," said Yossarian.
"And you knew it."

What Dunbar and Yossarian accuse the Texan of is sheer fabrication in the terms of the adult world; the truth is in the Texan's fearful guilt—after all, why not? He alone being nice and pally has pressed his narrow platitudes about patriotism upon everybody. That is, he is playing the game; Yossarian and Dunbar are being anti-social. While the whole protest of the book

---

* Biggles is Captain James Bigglesworth, fictional hero of a series of flying adventures written for young readers by the English writer W. E. Johns.—Eds.

("It made sense to cry out in pain every night") is in the tone of the child-ish "It's not fair! It's not fair that *I* should suffer!", there is nothing im-mature in the way this is explored as a possibly valid attitude to life.

The game, the conventional idea of war and life, is cheerfully satirized, but both the target and the joke at its expense are ruined by the presence of the sheer fact of death. The novel is obsessed with mortality and presents it, in its tragi-farce mode, with rare impact. Against the war-film [141] back-ground of bombs dropping and aeroplanes going down in flames are the individual and particular deaths around which the novel and Yossarian's consciousness revolve. Death is omnipresent and an ugly thing, and we are never allowed to forget it, for all the comedy, from the first chapter. There we meet the soldier in white, an unidentifiable borderline between life and death; and there is also an ominous dream-vision, unconnected to any fur-ther events, of a colonel distastefully coughing blood (no one knows what is wrong with him) mourned by a mysteriously beautiful girl. The story develops through a series of deaths and disappearances (Yossarian has to pretend to be dying at one stage so that he can be mourned) to the final blows of Nately, Kid Sampson and McWatt, and Yossarian's complete recollection (so far evaded) of Snowden. In Havermeyer, the fearlessly moronic bombardier who is contrasted sharply with Yossarian, we have a microcosm: his hobby is blasting field mice to bits with a .45.

I have emphasized the film-like quality of *Catch-22*. The characters and events appeal mainly to the eye or to the mind; one doesn't think of them having guts and livers. Hence the necessity to remind us of the facts. Yet even the broken corpse of the raped maid and the teeth on the footpath are images, brilliant and surrealistic, photographed with accuracy and honesty, but images. Heller's conception of life is restricted because death cannot be grasped in a two-dimensional vision. And since any satisfactory idea of justice or moral responsibility, to give meaning to the chaos, is ex-cluded from the world as he presents it, it is necessary for him to go beyond that world, to understand death. What does it mean? Neither Yossarian nor Heller wants to believe that death is simply the cessation of existence that it appears to be in the film vision. They have to break out of this narrow conception of the world, and the only way appears to be through death. Yossarian likes the hospital because death there is cleaner, and he is irritated by the "now-you-see-me-now-you-don't" sort of death outside. Clevinger and Orr simply disappear; "tsst" and all that's left of Kid Sampson is a ridiculous pair of legs. Heller's honesty shows us the men subsequently going to peer out at the decaying stumps on the beach, "like perverts," as if the meaning will suddenly appear. For even the gruesome details of Kid Sampson's death are not complete—there is still no dying. And so the story comes to Snow-den (although his death is earlier in time) as Yossarian/Heller is attracted to this truth of guts and liver, trying to penetrate the mystery. If American man is going to break out of the tormentingly self-conscious narrowness of his vision he must grasp death in his consciousness, possess it—the perfect democracy of it. It is not the morbid philosophizing of a Hamlet ("to this favour must she come"—there is something vindictive in that) but rather a question of *knowing* death as one might be said to "know" war or sex. Which of course is impossible.

Yossarian bent forward to peer and saw a strangely colored stain seeping through the coveralls just above the armhole of Snowden's flak suit. Yossarian felt his heart stop, then pound so violently he found it difficult to breathe. Snowden was wounded inside his flak suit. Yossarian ripped open the snaps of Snowden's flak suit and [142] heard himself scream wildly as Snowden's insides slithered down to the floor in a soggy pile and just kept dripping out.

There is a thrill of conscious excitement in "Yossarian felt his heart stop" indicating what is in fact going on here. He *heard himself* scream; his real involvement is not there at all, this is a conventional gesture. "He forced himself to look again. . . ." Not much force involved; but he must absorb the facts. Heller has now become completely identified with Yossarian, dramatizing himself in the centre of the picture.

Here was God's plenty, all right, he thought bitterly as he stared—liver, lungs, kidneys, ribs, stomach, and bits of the stewed tomatoes Snowden had eaten that day for lunch. Yossarian hated stewed tomatoes and turned away dizzily and began to vomit, clutching his burning throat.

These, then, are the facts; but the stewed tomatoes are a means of evading the issue (whatever that is), although they ironically recall the chaplain's unfortunate experience; and the vomit, like the scream, is "only to be expected." One suspects that the liver, lungs, and so on are also a means of evasion; for, having got to the point (as he thinks) Heller moralizes:

It was easy to read the message in his entrails. Man was matter, that was Snowden's secret. Drop him out a window and he'll fall. Set fire to him and he'll burn. Bury him and he'll rot, like other kinds of garbage. The spirit gone, man is garbage. That was Snowden's secret. Ripeness was all.

The quotation from *Lear* is not important, except to lend an air of tragic authority. The meaning of the scene is utterly different. What Heller/Yossarian is left with is "The spirit gone. . . ." He is no further on. "Where are the Snowdens of yesteryear?" he torments Clevinger earlier in the book, later in the story. The raw facts are no answer.

He has been trying to see into the other side of death, like Dunbar crazily staring into the black hole that does duty for a mouth for the soldier in white. Is there anything inside? The image there is absurdly right. But to have an obsession for the knowledge of the mystery of life and death, and to be left with Snowden's stewed tomatoes!—it is not surprising that Yossarian goes round without his uniform (a conscious charade—"this is what I really am") abdicating from responsibility altogether, and finally runs away. He must go away and be a goody-goody after what he has "seen."

Hence the explanation in the final chapter of Yossarian's attitudes and final decision is completely glib and false: it is implied that he has *really* been a loyal American all along.

> "Between me and every ideal I always find Scheisskopfs, Peckems, Korns and Cathcarts. And that sort of changes the ideal."
>
> "You must try not to think of them," Major Danby advised affirmatively. "And you must never let them change your values. Ideals are good, but people are sometimes not so good. You must try to look up at the big picture."
>
> Yossarian rejected the advice with a skeptical shake of his head. "When I look up, I see people cashing in. I don't see heaven or [143] saints or angels. I see people cashing in on every decent impulse and every human tragedy."

Heller even builds in his defence against those who might argue that the solution of the book is escapist:

> "But you can't just turn your back on all your responsibilities and run away from them," Major Danby insisted. "It's such a negative move. It's escapist."
>
> Yossarian laughed with buoyant scorn and shook his head. "I'm not running away from my responsibilities. I'm running to them. . . ."

But this is quite meaningless.

Yossarian's inspiration is brought by the chaplain: the news of Orr reaching the haven of Sweden paddling a rubber dinghy from Italy. We have been carefully prepared for this, but it is still a *deus ex machina*. And the chaplain, who struggled tragically with his conscience earlier, and who now also has the inspiration to fight back, is made to look ridiculous in his final heroic decision, and the farce has nothing of the earlier content. Thus the whole power and logic of the book (which it must be admitted are sufficient to carry us with enthusiasm over the ending at first reading) are dissipated, and we are left with the best-seller ending: noble democracy in the form of Yossarian will not submit to the selfish bosses, but will muddle through in the end. It is the old democratic idealism with a new twist. And so the book stops, for what more is there to say?

Catch-22 shows us the kind of power cinematic visualization can have:

its satire has energy and variety, and at the same time the book comes near to realizing some of its tragic possibilities. But the full implications of tragedy can't be contained in this vision; and Heller, partly aware of the limitation, compromises his brainchild with the conventional view that if you're brave enough, you can stand it; only other people get hurt (Nately, Kid Sampson, McWatt and Snowden have all disappeared by the end), and you can pity them. [144]

Robert Protherough
The Sanity of 'Catch-22'

There is a catch for critics too, which runs something like this: if nobody reads a new book it doesn't require attention, but if everybody reads it then it must clearly be too popular to merit criticism. The two million paperback sales, the fifteen-million-dollar film-of-the-book, the intoxicated early reviewers crying "masterpiece!" and the *Observer*'s claim "the greatest satirical work in English since *Erewhon*" have been accompanied by the almost total neglect of Heller's work by English critics. Instead it is continually being pushed into a slot, bracketed with a film like *M*A*S*H** or a book like *Slaughterhouse 5*. Nearly ten years later, it is perhaps time to argue that *Catch-22* is not just another fading large-scale novel-of-the-war ("attitudes to war have shifted . . . since Mr. Heller's novel came out in 1961"—John Coleman, *New Statesman*, 18 September 1970), not even an anti-war book which John Wain says "never seems to me to give the whole picture" (*Critical Quarterly*, Vol. v, No. 2), not simply part of a once fashionable Tom-Lehrer-style black-satire movement, not the chaotic, anarchic fantasy going nowhere that so many reviewers seemed to find it. For me, the value and interest lie not in the book's craziness but in its cold sanity. The view of the work which I am proposing is that *Catch-22* is clearly organized, operating in the established traditions of English satire, working towards a positive conclusion, and only in a limited way concerned with the war in its dissection of a whole range of contemporary attitudes and its queries about human nature and purpose.

SOURCE: *The Human World*, No. 3 (May 1971), pp. 59–70. Reprinted by permission of the publisher, The Brynmill Publishing Company Limited, 130 Bryn Road, Brynmill, Swansea, SA2 0AT England.

It may be best to begin with the most limited of the issues: the structure of the novel. Some readers claim to have found the book virtually unreadable because it is so disorganized, confused and episodic. Reviewers and critics have used phrases like "chaotic structure" with "interchangeable" episodes (J. J. Waldmeir), "scrambled narrative" (John Wain), "illogical, formless" (*Books and Bookmen*). Others have defended the novel by claiming that it is only confused and chaotic because it mirrors the disorganization of a muddled society at war. It would be easy to support such a case by pointing out that the traditional satiric form of the innocent in a corrupt world (Fielding, Swift, Voltaire) rejects linear, causal development in favour of episodes held [59] together by a dominating theme. However, I would reject the initial premise of formlessness and argue that *Catch-22* is, in fact, highly organized and carefully structured.

The book is based on a cyclic pattern of continually repeated motifs which may make little impact on their first appearance, but progressively develop in meaning each time that they appear with additional information or seen through other eyes. A simple experiment with the episodes involving, say, Scheisskopf or Nately's whore will indicate that they are not, as Waldmeir contends, interchangeable; there is development which depends upon earlier stages having been read; significant detail is added in a systematic order; the effect upon the reader is calculated and progressive. Two of the recurrent motifs are of particular importance. Until the very end of the book one lies outside it in the past and one ahead of it in the future. The two draw continually closer together, and the point of their meeting is the climax of the book. At that point, instead of living in a continual present the protagonist (and presumably the reader) finally discerns a connection between past, present and future, and takes decisive action. This point will later be discussed in some detail. For the reader, the two motifs occur as problems. The questions we want answered are, in simple terms: (1) What exactly happened to Snowden? (2) What is Orr up to, and what will happen to him? Details accumulate about both and in Heller's structure it is noticeable that attention alternates from one to the other. Eventually the fullest revelation about Snowden comes in the penultimate chapter, the final clarification about Orr's intentions in the last chapter.

The reader's understanding and enjoyment of the book depend largely on the ability to establish points of contact, to synthesize information put into different mouths, very much as we do in actual life. The forty-two chapters are almost all named after characters on whom attention is centered to varying degrees, and only the last after Yossarian himself. Others are named after crucial moments in his development (XII—Bologna; XXXIV—Thanksgiving; XXXIX—The Eternal City). The cyclic pattern means that it is only the end of the book that gives meaning to the beginning, but this does *not* mean that end and beginning are the same, or that the construction is circular, beginning and ending at the same point, as John Wain argues. This is made clear in the way in which Heller's satire works: essentially he lures us into stock attitudes, into laughing at what we take to be comedy or farce, and then rubs our noses in the reality of what has amused us so much. This is the satiric pattern of the book as a whole, and also of the individual parts of it.

The central theme is a stock one of satiric narrative: the progress [60] of a crazy/sane hero (born "in a state of innocence," as he claims in a fearful but significant pun on p. 440* and sitting in "the tree of life . . . and of knowledge of good and evil, too," p. 269) through illusions and temptations towards understanding. As in *Candide* or *Gulliver's Travels*, the reader imaginatively shares the central character's experience while at the same time remaining outside it. In the last four chapters, Yossarian suddenly sees the pattern, rejects the official bribe and Catch-22, takes action for the first time instead of avoiding it.

The related method is also a conventional one: the abrupt reversal of the reader's expectations. Repeated changes of scale and value force the reader of *Gulliver's Travels* to question his preconceived ideas about human beings and their attitudes, and a similar intense reversal lies at the basis of *Catch-22*. Again and again we are briefly introduced to an incident that seems absurd, a fantasy. The chaplain, conducting a funeral, has a vision of a naked man up a tree, Major Major Major Major is only in when he is out, the American planes systematically bomb and strafe their own squadron. But in turn each incident proves to be sober fact: Yossarian is naked because he refuses to wear the uniform spattered with Snowden's blood; Major Major, who got his Christian names from parental spite and his rank from a computer, is simply avoiding contact with the men who frighten him; the bombing is the logical extension of Milo's capitalist enterprises for the contract carried 6 percent plus expenses. Others have demonstrated sufficiently the way in which absurdity is indeed a feature of contemporary life. As I write, the papers carry the story of six American soldiers who allege that they were forced to create from thin air heroic acts of imaginary combats so that a general in Vietnam could receive the Silver Star and the Distinguished Flying Cross before he left his division for a new assignment. (*Guardian*, 22 October 1970) This is only half the process, of course. The satirical corollary of "what seems absurd is real" is "what seems real is absurd." So it is that contemporary attitudes to war, sex, business, sport, medicine, psychiatry, religion are presented by Heller as shams and fantasies in a series of "logical" arguments. The educational system has produced Clevinger, who "knew everything about literature except how to enjoy it" (p. 70), Chief White Halfoat detests racial prejudice because "It's a ter-

---

* Page references are to the Dell edition, New York, 1962.

rible thing to treat a decent, loyal Indian like a nigger, kike, wop or spic" (p. 45), Major Major's father is a thrifty man who disapproves of any kind of government aid except for farming subsidies: "His specialty was alfalfa, and he made a good thing out of not growing any. The government paid him well for every bushel of alfalfa he did not grow. The more alfalfa he did not grow, the more money the government gave him, and he spent [61] every penny he didn't earn on new land to increase the amount of alfalfa he did not produce. . . . He invested in land wisely and soon was not growing more alfalfa than any other man in the county." (p. 85) General Peckem applies the concepts of business and Parkinson's Law to his army command. He welcomes Colonel Scheisskopf to his staff with delight: "An additional colonel on his staff meant that he could now begin agitating for two additional majors, four additional captains, sixteen additional lieutenants and untold quantities of additional enlisted men, typewriters, desks, filing cabinets, automobiles and other substantial equipment and supplies. . . ." (p. 327) The reader's initial instinct is to reject as absurd what his mind insists is only too like the truth. General Peckem's attitudes are typical of the central absurdity (or horror) which Heller seems to find in modern life: the treating of people as things. Lieutenant Scheisskopf dreams of winning the drill competition by sinking nickel pegs in each man's thighbone and attaching them to the wrists with copper wire; Colonel Korn orders the destruction of an undefended village without caring whether the road will be blocked but insisting on a good "bomb pattern" because General Peckem wants a good aerial photograph.

Heller also produces the same effect in a much more sustained and long-term way. For example, the early part of the book blandly tempts the reader to accept the values of most "big" war novels towards women, to see them essentially as objects of pleasure, to believe that it is somehow "natural" for men at war to spend their time with whores and to pursue anybody else who is willing: the maid in or out of her lime green panties, and Dori Duz who does. General Dreedle voices the authoritarian American attitude that a woman's rôle is to be as provocative as possible but that it's wrong if any man takes action as a result of it. He gloats over the nurse in her skin-tight uniform, whose wriggling drives Colonel Moodus crazy: "The first time I catch him putting a hand on her or any other woman I'll bust the horny bastard right down to private and put him on K.P. for a year." (p. 222) Luciana sleeps with Yossarian, but says she cannot marry because "No one wants a girl who is not a virgin." (p. 163) The absurdity of man's two irreconcilable views of woman, urging her to be promiscuous before marriage and virtuous after it, is dramatized in the scene when Nately, having pursued his whore for months, persuades her to marry him. Immediately he wants her to put on clothes before the other soldiers see her naked and to give up hustling because suddenly "It just isn't right for a nice girl like you to go looking for other men to sleep with." (p. 367) Her grief after his death and her desire for vengeance demand yet another reassessment of our attitudes.

A close examination of Heller's particular satiric effects shows that [62] four simple devices are repeatedly used, and that each of these turns on a sudden reversal. In addition, each is employed frequently in the early sections of the book for general humorous effects, and only then is it used on major satiric targets.

The first of these is the simple substitution of a single word, phrase or idea which runs contrary to the sense the reader expects, sometimes standing logic on its head to produce a new kind of truth. The opening pages contain many of these statements: "Yossarian had stopped playing chess with him because the games were so interesting they were foolish," "The Texan turned out to be good-natured, generous and likeable. In three days no one could stand him," "He was a self-made man who owed his lack of success to nobody," "Doc Daneeka was Yossarian's friend and would do just about nothing in his power to help him," "Dunbar loved shooting skeet because he hated every minute of it and time passed so slowly." Having established this simple convention, Heller then unleashes it on attitudes to war and the sanity/madness alternation: "McWatt was the craziest combat man of them all probably, because he was perfectly sane and still did not mind the war" (p. 60), a theme on which a whole series of logical variations are played (Stubbs says of Yossarian, "That crazy bastard may be the only sane one left," p. 114).

The second, related technique is that of deflating, questioning or reversing a familiar cliché, when an accepted, conventional attitude suddenly has the rug whipped from underneath it. In a sense the whole book is an attack on the cliché view of American life, which Yossarian sums up in the opening section as "The hot dog, the Brooklyn Dodgers, Mom's apple pie." (p. 9) Again Heller prepares the reader with simple comic examples in the early pages:

It was truly a splendid structure, and Yossarian throbbed with a mighty sense of accomplishment each time he gazed at it and reflected that none of the work that had gone into it was his. (p. 19)

Colonel Cathcart had courage and never hesitated to volunteer his men for any target available. (p. 57)

It was the face of a man of hardened integrity who could no more consciously violate the moral principles on which his virtue rested than he could transform himself into a despicable toad. One of these moral principles was that it was never a sin to charge as much as the traffic would bear. (p. 66)

However, later in the novel this undermining technique is used devastatingly to examine and reject current concepts of war and national pride in the discussion between Nately and the old man in Chapter XXIII, of free capitalist democracy in the activities of M & M Enterprises, of [63] the stereotyped responses of doctors, chaplains and—of course—officers.

The third of these effects is Heller's use of a deliberate conflict between tone and subject. The opening chapter describes in the coolest, unemotional terms both the soldier in white (liquid flowing into him from one jar and out of him into another, after which the two were switched over) and the dying colonel ("The colonel was in Communications, and he was kept busy day and night transmitting glutinous messages from the interior into square pads of gauze which he sealed meticulously and delivered to a covered white pail. . . ."). We recognize the same urbane handling of the outrageous, the same use of language somehow out-of-key with the realities involved in Heller's account of the bombing: "He had landed another contract with the Germans, this time to bomb his own outfit. Milo's planes separated in a well-coordinated attack and bombed the fuel stocks and the ordnance dump, the repair hangars and the B-25 bombers. . . . His crews spared the landing strip and the mess halls so that they could land safely when their work was done and enjoy a hot snack before retiring." (p. 264) Here phrases like "when their work was done"—the flat term for the deadly reality—are of the same kind as Swift's [in A Modest Proposal], "A child will make two dishes." There is the incident where McWatt buzzes the beach in his customary fashion, and his propeller slices a bather in half, leaving his legs standing, but spraying the rest of him over the beach. "Kid Sampson had rained all over." After the precision of the horror Heller uses a double shift of style to give edge to the conclusion:

McWatt lifted a wing and banked gracefully around into his turn . . .
turned again, dipped his wings once in salute, decided oh, well, what the hell, and flew into a mountain.
Colonel Cathcart was so upset by the deaths of Kid Sampson and McWatt that he raised the missions to sixty-five. (p. 349)

The final device is the reduction of meaningless choices to their simplest terms. The organization men of Catch-22 all like clear divisions (so when Yossarian shifts the line on the map, Bologna goes unbombed and General Peckem wins a medal). For them the world is neatly divided into friend and foe, officer and enlisted man, sane and crazy. So the men in the medical tent rush all those with temperatures *over* 102 to hospital, paint the gums and toes of those with temperatures *under* 102 with gentian violet, and get worried when the temperature is *exactly* 102. Yossarian knows how to cope with them. He puzzles the doctors with a pain in his liver that is just short of jaundice: "If it became jaundice they could treat it. If it didn't become jaundice and went away they could discharge him. But this just being short of jaundice all the time confused them." (p. 7) One of the favorite [64] devices of authority is shown as the generous offering of a choice that gives no option. Headquarters are alarmed at what might happen in a discussion group, but Colonel Korn has the situation under control. "Under Colonel Korn's rule, the only people permitted to ask questions were those who never did. Soon the only people attending were those who never asked questions, and the sessions were discontinued altogether, since Clevinger, the corporal and Colonel Korn agreed that it was neither possible nor necessary to educate people who never questioned anything." (p. 36) Here the simplification of a fairly stock official attitude makes us realize its absurdity —it is like Captain Black's loyalty crusade: "And this whole program is voluntary, Milo—don't forget that. The men don't *have* to sign Piltchard and Wren's loyalty oath if they don't want to. But we need you to starve them to death if they don't." (p. 118) Major Major is clearly a Communist because he doesn't sign the loyalty oath; he can't be allowed to sign it because that would defeat the purpose of the crusade. This is, of course, the trick that gives the novel its title. Anyone who is crazy will have to fly no more missions, but for this to happen he has to *ask* the doctor to ground him. *If* he asks the doctor to ground him, he can't really be mad, because he has enough sense to try to avoid combat duty—so he can't be grounded. This meaningless choice is Catch-22 itself.

Even this sketchy survey of methods and targets may have indicated that war itself plays a relatively small part in the satire. Indeed, in the narrative, warfare is deliberately kept off-stage and permitted to break through only for particular effects. Heller has set the book on an off-shore island, he has made his characters airmen, precisely to increase the sense of withdrawal, to "depersonalize" the combat. *Catch-22* is scarcely more a satire on war than *Animal Farm* is "about" agriculture. The service base on the island of Pianosa serves the novelist as a manageable microcosm of society, in which war conditions simply intensify the incongruities and absurdities of civilian life. Those who demand to know whether Heller opposed resistance to Hitler are refusing to read the book on its own terms. *Catch-22* is not a documentary, its real divisions are not national ones, but between manipulators and killers on the one hand and sufferers on the other, or even between the two tendencies in individuals. The war casts an apocalyptic shadow over the book, but Heller recognizes—in a phrase from *Slaughterhouse 5* that catches just his tone—that "even if wars didn't keep coming like glaciers, there would still be plain old death." (p. 3) This is the overriding theme. *Catch-22* is a book possessed by the thought of death: people are shot down in flames, riddled with bullets, sliced apart by propellers, thrown out of windows; they fly into mountains or other planes, they die in hospital, in the streets, suffocated by a cat in bed. [65] Yossarian is haunted by dreams of violent death, of people "plummeting like dead weights out of hotel windows with a *whoosh!*, accelerating at the rate of sixteen feet per second per second to land with a hideous *plop!* on the sidewalk and die disgustingly there in public like an alpaca sack full of hairy strawberry ice cream, bleeding, pink toes awry." (p. 171) The childish sound effects, the cool scientific formula, the down-to-earth images of sacks and ice cream somehow increase the horror. Perhaps the key word is "disgustingly": death is consistently presented as an affront, a joke in bad taste, and one that is omnipresent. Only three of the forty-two chapters, I think, do not contain references to death or to people dead or dying; the death-roll of those we meet in the novel has risen alarmingly by the last page. When Danby thinks it would be pleasant to live as a vegetable Yossarian offers him the choice of good vegetables, sliced for a salad, or bad ones, rotted down for fertilizer.

At a superficial level it is possible to treat this as being an element in the anti-war argument. Yossarian sees the issue clearly: "his only mission each time he went up was to come down alive" (p. 30), "The enemy . . . is anybody who's going to get you killed, no matter *which* side he's on" (p. 127), "let somebody else get killed." (p. 107) When people ask him what would happen if *everybody* felt that way, he retorts, "Then I'd certainly be a damned fool to feel any other way." (p. 107) When they assure him that the Germans aren't shooting at him alone but at everybody, he replies, "And what difference does that make?" The old man is another who cuts through the flabby clichés; he counters Nately's "Anything worth living for is worth dying for" with "And anything worth dying for is certainly worth living for." (p. 253)

Again this exploits a series of ironic reversals, especially alternating sanity and madness. From Yossarian's point of view, those in command are mad because they are trying to get him killed; from their point of view he is the one who is crazy. He thinks: "Everywhere he looked was a nut, and it was all a sensible young gentleman like himself could do to maintain his perspective amid so much madness." (p. 21) He believes that his pilot, Mc-Watt, "was the craziest combat man of them all . . . because he was perfectly sane and still did not mind the war." (p. 61) Most of the others refer to Yossarian in turn as "that crazy bastard!" because he won't fly to Bologna (though Doctor Stubbs does admit "That crazy bastard may be the only sane one left," p. 114). This madness/sanity alternation reaches its climax in the scene where the psychiatrist decides that Yossarian is out of his mind because he can't adjust to the idea of war (whereas Yossarian himself insists that this is a sign of sanity) : [66]

"You're immature. You've been unable to adjust to the idea of war."
"Yes, sir."

"You have a morbid aversion to dying. You probably resent the fact that you're at war and might get your head blown off any second."

"I more than resent it, sir. I'm absolutely incensed."

"You have deep-seated survival anxieties. . . . You know, it wouldn't surprise me if you're a manic-depressive!" (p. 312)

But when Yossarian imagines that this is going to keep him out of combat, the doctor disillusions him—

"Now you can take me off combat duty and send me home. They're not going to send a crazy man out to be killed, are they?"

"Who else will go?" (p. 314)

But at a more profound level, death is used not simply to demonstrate the follies of war, but even more pessimistically to question the whole point of human existence. When Yossarian thinks of great lists of fatal diseases, of the germs lurking in water, of the surgeon's knife, he is astounded at how long he has lasted. "Each day he faced was another dangerous mission against mortality. And he had been surviving them for twenty-eight years." (p. 180) The doctors have the same idea. Doctor Daneeka does nothing, because *any*thing might be dangerous. Doctor Stubbs reflects: "I used to get a big kick out of saving people's lives. Now I wonder what the hell's the point, since they all have to die anyway." (p. 113) The doctors in hospital turn on Yossarian when he says he isn't dying, and retort: "Of course you're dying. We're all dying. Where the devil else do you think you're heading?" (p. 187) Dunbar says to Clevinger: " 'Do you know how long a year takes when it's going away? . . . This long.' He snapped his fingers. 'A second ago you were stepping into college with your lungs full of fresh air. Today you're an old man. . . . You're inches away from . . . death every time you go on a mission. How much older can you be at your age?' " (p. 39) There is nothing new in the questioning of human purpose and significance in the light of passing time and inevitable death, but it is vividly done and appropriate to the major themes of the book, dealing as it does with men who deal out death and risk it in return. Yossarian tries to remember in bed at night all the people he has known who are now dead. "The number of dead people just seemed to increase. And the Germans were still fighting. Death was irreversible, he suspected, and he began to think he was going to lose." (p. 355) The central discussion about purpose is the one he has in Chapter XVIII, with Lieutenant Scheisskopf's wife, who is as much an atheist as he is, but thinks one shouldn't be cynical on Thanksgiving Day. As they exchange her reasons for optimism with his for pessimism ("Be glad you're even [67] alive." "Be *furious* you're going to die."), Yossarian concentrates increasingly on the *injustice* of God who includes pain, disease, and death in his scheme of Creation. The book as a whole uses death and sickness to question the idea of justice or purpose in the universe. The warrant officer with malaria as a result of fornication says: "Just for once I'd like to see all these things sort of straightened out, with each person getting exactly what he deserves. It might give me some confidence in this universe." (p. 175) At the human level men in positions of power use that power for arbitrary, selfish aims: the concept of Justice doesn't exist for them either. According to the colonel who is Chairman of the Action Board, "Justice is a knee in the gut" (p. 82); Major Danby's answer to a plea of innocence is that "they can get all the witnesses they need" (p. 452); General Dreedle can't believe that there is any limitation on his power: "You mean I can't shoot anyone I want to?" (p. 228) And meanwhile people accept the state of things because of fear, because of convention, because Major Danby says, "Look, fellows, we've got to have some confidence in the people above us who issue our orders. They know what they're doing." (p. 336), and because of Catch-22: "Catch-22 says you've always got to do what your commanding officer tells you to." (p. 60) When the old woman complains that the military police broke up the house and drove out the girls, she says that their authority was Catch-22, which "says they have a right to do anything we can't stop them from doing." Yossarian asks if they showed her their authority.

"They don't have to show us Catch-22," the old woman answered. "The law says they don't have to."
"What law says they don't have to?"
"Catch-22." (p. 416)

Catch-22 is the self-perpetuating, self-supporting system. It nearly wins Yossarian with the temptation to do what he has spent the book trying to do: he can save his life, go back home as a hero, if only he will *accept* the system: "Like us. Join us. Be our pal. Say nice things about us here and back in the States. Become one of the boys. Now, that isn't asking too much, is it?" (p. 436) It is surely on Yossarian's refusal of this offer that the book turns.

The conclusion of *Catch-22* seems to me persistently misunderstood because of the desire to force this book into a pattern. The argument seems to be that "The Eternal City" is out of key with the prevailing mood of black comedy so it must be a mistake; this is an anti-war book, so if Yossarian claims to have earned his medal that must be a damaging retraction; the structure is chaotic, episodic, and formless so there can't be any progress and the ending must be seen as without significance. [68] I believe, on the contrary, that the final chapters show a development on which understanding of the whole book depends.

Yossarian has been essentially the observer, consistently refraining from action, declining to take part or to be involved. The end of the book shows his realization that abstention is still tacit support of the system. He has been looking around him throughout the book to see who is responsible for suffering and injustice. Now he understands: "Getting stabbed by that bitch was the best thing that ever happened to me." (p. 457) The scene in Rome is admittedly over-written, but it shows Heller's final rehandling of the implications of the "fun," sex and violence of earlier chapters in such moments as Aarfy's unpunished raping and wanton killing of Michaela. Yossarian's experience in a ruined Rome full of hungry children, beaten women, wounded soldiers, maltreated animals is given the specific, rather obvious, gloss: "He knew how Christ must have felt as he walked through the world, like a psychiatrist through a ward full of nuts." (p. 424) He tries to think of all the suffering and injustice in the world, for the first time shows a real concern for someone other than himself (his feelings for the 12-year-old virgin graphically contrasted with Milo's), and realizes that it is not just "them" who are to blame, that *he* is responsible, that he is part of the corrupt, diseased system. Despite what he has said about the universality of death, his sense of outrage, of being threatened, *is* increased when he is aware that a particular individual is seeking to kill him. Nevertheless he accepts the responsibility; the girl is "on his conscience":

. . . she and everyone younger had every right to blame him and everyone
older for every unnatural tragedy that befell them; just as she, even in her
grief, was to blame for every man-made misery that landed on her kid sister
and on all other children behind her. Someone had to do something, sometime.
Every victim was a culprit, every culprit a victim, and somebody had to stand
up sometime to try to break the lousy chain of inherited habit that was
imperiling them all. (p. 414)

In a contemporary satire of this kind it is hardly possible to express the positives in terms of yet another ideal. The expression of pious ideals for crooked undertakings has been throughout the book one of the chief devices of the Catch-22 system. Milo urged Yossarian that "he was jeopardizing his traditional rights of freedom and independence by daring to exercise them" (p. 414), Danby that he should "think only of the welfare of your country and the dignity of man." (p. 435) The ideals are tarnished by the generals, politicians and businessmen who utter them to preserve their own power. Yossarian reflects: "Between me and every ideal I always find Scheisskopfs, Peckems, Korns and Cathcarts. And that sort of changes the ideal." (p. 454) [69]

Consequently it is hardly surprising that the "message" of *Catch-22* is not reducible to another ideal. However, even while Yossarian is proclaiming, apparently as he has done throughout the book, "From now on I'm thinking only of me" (p. 455), we are aware that this cannot be the whole truth, or else what prevents him from cynically being shipped home as a hero? The acceptance of responsibility must be taken as real. When Danby urges him to take the offer, saying "It's a way to save yourself," Yossarian retorts "It's a way to lose myself, Danby. You ought to know that." It is surely not far-fetched to hear echoes of "whosoever will save his life shall lose it; and whosoever will lose his life for my sake shall find it." (Matthew, 16, 25.) Yossarian demands justice and logic of a society where they no longer exist; he declines to "adjust" or to practice what the Chaplain calls "the handy technique of protective rationalization." "Someone had to do something sometime" is not the most elegant of positive statements, desertion from the forces not the most heroic of conclusions. Nevertheless on the evidence of the characters shown in the action of the book itself we must admit the power of the final reversal: "I'm not running *away* from my responsibilities. I'm running *to* them. . . . You know who the escapists are . . . ? Not me and Orr." (p. 461) [70]

Donald Monk
An Experiment in Therapy
A Study of "Catch-22"

A world in the toils of demented logic: a world in such a war as makes idealism or blind animal heroism equal anomalies: this is the stage on which is set the action of Joseph Heller's *Catch-22*. It is very much to the point that the Fighting 256 Squadron's enemy should be, not the *Luftwaffe* (withdrawn from the Italian campaign, and with it the temptation to view aerial war as the duelling of heroes), but the flak alone. The characters of the novel fight their battle against statistics: against the flak, claiming its victims with the grim impersonality of Russian roulette, and against fatigue, deadening the will to survive the odds. When there is co-present with this law of diminishing returns a correspondingly spurious law

SOURCE: *The London Review*, No. 2 (Autumn 1967), pp. 12–19. Reprinted by permission of the author and publisher. The author has slightly revised his essay for this book.

of increased demand, patriotism and its pressure for more missions, then the enemy cannot be identified by the color of his uniform, and becomes in fact the system mobilizing the world to make war. We do see a real world, the world of combat, but this "system" is the truest reality within it, explaining the fatal logic enmeshing Yossarian and his friends: where the "enemy" is the recognized pressure (the chain of command which orders the missions), where Yossarian's friends (as the "system" annihilates them) become themselves the presence of death, and where the escape of a pass to Rome (with its open submission to a dog-eat-dog morality) is only into a mirror-world which reflects and distorts the world of combat. It is a scene where hope, the dream of return home, is the last refinement of the torture; so that Hungry Joe sleeps better when on combat status, because this at least makes a certainty. Snowden's death is as shocking to us as it is to Yossarian—the cold wash of panic, Snowden's gaping flesh, the spilled remnants of tomatoes for breakfast—but the greatest horror is our sense of war as a machine.

The graphic horrors of the orthodox war novel, of *The Thin Red Line* or *The Naked and the Dead*, are only Heller's initial impetus; his major concern is with seeing how the condition of war comes to be justified, and showing how his hero finds his way back to life. War is seen as a state of insanity that like some nightmarish charade continues to go through the motions of sanity. Catch-22 itself, the *Section 8* of military regulations, acknowledges the right of man to protect his own life and the sanity of so desiring, but is so formulated that the sole proof of insanity is to get one-self killed. It is a stipulation absurdly reasonable, self-enclosingly perfect for a world directed to its own [12] destruction. It is the *reductio ad absurdum* of the mechanics of war, and non-conformity seems to lead direct to court-martial. Yossarian is the hero because of his isolated recognition of these facts, and the novel's action is complete when he knows how to break with the pattern. But for the larger part of the novel he is in the position of Alice in *Through the Looking-Glass*, an intelligent and unwilling participant in a game conceived by rules alien to his mind, but here hostile to his very existence. Like anyone in a similar situation he finds it hard to believe he alone can be sane and he finds salvation only when he begins to act on this unlikely assumption, rather than assert it in his usual half-humorous frenzy.

For this concentration of action and hallucination, Heller has developed a style stripped to essentials for the sake of rapidity. Its simplicity is that of the vernacular, but although similarly based on an elementary syntax with a minimum of clause subordination or modification, is at a far remove from Hemingway's "pebble in the brook" limpidity. One's dominant impression of Heller's prose is one of breathlessness, of successive paroxysms of forward-bursting energy, which are promptly jarred back on themselves

in bathos and cliché when the irrefrangible perimeter of the Catch-22
syndrome is again reached. A fair example is found in the description of
the aristocratic women of the apartment in Rome:

They were both superb creatures with pulpy, bright, pointed tongues and
mouths like round warm plums, a little sweet and sticky, a little rotten. They
had class; Yossarian was not sure what class was, but he knew that they had
it and he did not, and that they knew it, too. He could picture, as he walked,
the kind of underclothing they wore against their svelte feminine parts,
filmy, smooth, clinging garments of deepest black or of opalescent pastel
radiance with flowering lace borders, fragrant with the tantalizing fumes of
pampered flesh and scented bath salts rising in a germinating cloud from
their blue-white breasts. He wished again that he was where Aarfy was,
making obscene, brutal, cheerful love with a juicy drunken tart who didn't
give a tinker's dam about him and would never think of him again. (p. 160)*

Besides the syntax, based in the simplest conjunctions, the insistence on
sensation also resembles Hemingway. But the rising incidence of, and
tenuousness of, the adjectives which present this is different in conception
from anything in Hemingway, both in the swashbuckling and only half-
feigned literariness of "opalescent," "pampered" and "tantalizing" and in
the torque implicit in the self-mocking eroticism towards hallucination.
Yossarian is always eager to dream away from reality; seeing through
clothing, and vicariously enjoying what he mistakenly pictures his friend
Aarfy is engaged in. [13] With firecracker brilliance we progress incon-
gruously from one kind of expectation to its sudden reversal—from the
"rottenness" proving "class," to Yossarian's response at once to enjoy and
desecrate this, and then to sheer lust in a bathetic turn away from all suggestions of "class"—capturing man's inability to distinguish between the
real and the hallucinatory under extreme conditions of stress. Energy
gathers, is pushed back on itself, lunges again forward—the sinewy movement of a centipede over broken ground. What might deadeningly have
been mere cynicism is perpetually galvanized into humor, a Buster Keaton
mixture of deadpan and fantastic acrobatics. Major Major's father is
described:

On long winter evenings he remained indoors and did not mend harness, and
he sprang out of bed at the crack of noon every day just to make certain
that the chores would not be done. (p. 85)

and the crude energy of the actions stays with us, in defiance of the con-

---

* References are to the Dell edition (1962).

taining negatives, collapsing into the bathos of "crack of noon" with an explosive force.

In larger matters of technique, also, Heller seems an exploiter of the immediate more than a conscious craftsman. Frequent as the time-shifts are, they remind us rather of the erratic turns of *Tristram Shandy* than the modern self-conscious order of Conrad and Ford Madox Ford. But one extensively used technique, at the very base of Heller's wit, does seem to have been erected into an overall organizational principle. Consider one of the grotesque pseudo-epigrams, this one of General Dreedle's:

he believed that the young men who took orders from him should be willing to give up their lives for the ideals, aspirations and idiosyncracies of the old men he took orders from. (p. 222)

The humor derives from the parallelism of the "young men-old men" fixed in the pattern of command, pivoting on the one-sided sacrifice covered by the euphemistic "give up their lives." It has a neatness correlative to the ghoulishness of the system, ironically pointed by the insight which aligns "idiosyncracies" with "ideals." This humor comes from uncovering the relationship between "things-as-they-are" and "things-as-society-disguises-them." Imagine the terms involved in this ironic disparity blown up or enlarged into independent actions, the episodes which constitute the action of the novel, and what might be termed "sur-real montage" reveals itself as the basic technique within the structure of *Catch-22*. By this, what in real life would have been latent motivation or hidden prejudice is treated as if it too were an open reality. Consequently the fantastic and the real exist side by side, and with equal authority. Here is the effect on a larger scale, seen in a discussion between Cathcart and the chaplain:

The chaplain felt his face flush. "I'm sorry, sir. I just assumed you would want the enlisted men to be present, since they would be going along on the same mission." [14]

"Well, I don't. They've got a God and a chaplain of their own, haven't they?"

"No, sir."

"What are you talking about? You mean they pray to the same God we do?"

"Yes, Sir."

"And He *listens?*"

"I think so, sir."

. . .

"Oh, don't get me wrong, Chaplain. It isn't that I think the enlisted men are dirty, common and inferior. It's just that we don't have enough room.

Frankly, though, I'd just as soon the officers and enlisted men didn't fraternize in the briefing room. They see enough of each other during the mission, it seems to me. Some of my very best friends are enlisted men, you understand, but that's about as close as I care to let them come. Honestly now, Chaplain, you wouldn't want your sister to marry an enlisted man, would you?" (p. 199)

There are elements of realism—chiefly the psychological clash of the chaplain's diffident scrupulousness with Cathcart's hypocrisy within a rigid command system—but the effect is one of fantasy. What Heller has done, penetrating the superficial morality implicit in such jargon as "enlisted men," "fraternize," and "very best friends," is to show the actual thought-processes of prejudice as they would appear in direct speech. Less than conscious attitudes break out to assume their rightful priority alongside the noble clichés which would, in practice, mask them. This process leads to such hilarious *malentendus* as Yossarian's explanation to the psychiatrist that his dream of an orgy is really a "fish-dream." Here it is the Freudian ease of transference of all symptoms to a sexual drive that is the butt of the humour; Heller, like all satirists, takes great pleasure in shooting down over-readily accepted theories. Such rapid oscillation between dream and reality may not be original to Heller (it has obvious similarities to the fantasies of Henry Miller), but the consistency with which such juxta-positioning appears reveals it for the first time as a possible organizational principle for the building of a novel.

The sharp breaks and lifts of the reality-illusion juxtaposition, then, are contained by a narrative flow characterized by an ease and variety which might almost be thought of as "Augustan" if it bore more signs of good taste. But taste is not the greatest of virtues. Much more to the point are energy and vividness of delineation, virtues of Heller's he has in common with Charles Dickens. The characters of this vanishing exodus are often as memorably drawn as in Dickens, and with parallel intimations of having been created according to some theory of humors verging on caricature; and near-caricature always associates itself with a tendency to allegory. The Dreedle–Peckem–Scheisskopf line of succession is named with a Dickensian sense of onomatopoeia, but [15] also manifests a moral pattern-ing of the deterioration, as the wheels of war begin to turn, from (1) idealism through (2) opportunism down to (3) blind regimentation. Im-mediately subordinate to these we have the novel's equivalent to the Othello–Iago symbiosis, Cathcart and Korn: distinct but interdependent, the combination of ambition and indecision in the first matches itself to the empirical readiness always to exploit of the other. Lower still in the echelon of command we find such portraits as Major ——— de Coverley (a phantom of American frontiersman patriotism), Captain Black (a sadist straight out of silent melodrama), and ex-P.F.C. Wintergreen (an incarnation of the "grapevine," popular opinion). Embattled against these forces, which are as sinister as those unidentified which are trying, as Yossarian knows, to kill him, are the thinning ranks of his friends. These mainly represent the misled and the afflicted: Nately and Clevinger dying for their complementary idealisms, McWatt flying his plane with the unthinking bravado of a bronco-buster, and the combat-weary Hungry Joe in the last stages of neurasthenic disintegration. Also in the ranks of those fated to die we find the supercilious confidence of Appleby and Havermeyer, crack pilot and bombardier, whose confidence too in the end is to be shattered against the "elliptical precision" of Catch-22. It is a motley collection of monsters and dreamers, each shaped to his niche in the plot, each, one suspects, an overdeveloped expression of one facet of American Man.

That this galaxy of characters should be presented in a series of vignettes, so that at first the action seems much more episodic than it in fact is, contributes strongly to the effect of allegory. But unless we make Catch-22 some kind of pattern for the futility of all human endeavor, the novel overall is not conceived in terms of allegory. Some portions of the novel, it is true, such as the repeated appearance of Major —— de Coverley in the van at each liberated city, like some stone-hewn eagle of victory, are such manifest violations of reality that the term "allegorical" cannot be avoided, much as this term implies today creation at second-degree intensity. Nor can we see the picture of Major Major's father, "the God-fearing . . . individualist who held that federal aid to anyone but farmers was creeping socialism" (p. 85), and whose favorite doctrine is that "the Lord gave us good farmers two strong hands so that we could take as much as we could grab with both of them" (p. 86), as anything other than a perhaps overfamiliar indictment of the Calvinism implicit in the founding of the Republic, under the local conditions of the New Deal in the midwest. Other aspects of American society, such as Daneeka's doctor's dedication to money or Chief White Halfoat's illustration of racial prejudice in racial minorities, can indeed be singled out, but one doubts that there is some key yet to be found to an inclusive design. Allegorical anecdotes weave in and out of the pattern of fantasy, seemingly at random. An exception to this law of sporadicity would seem to be the saga of Milo Minderbinder, whose activities, in all detailed complexity, are reserved for revelation at crucial points in the action, such as Snowden's death and Yossarian's two refusals to serve. Milo, with his ingenious and endless juggling with marketing commodities [16] (an inflationary spiral is shown complete in his transactions over the Egyptian cotton crop), is, obviously enough, capitalist free-enterprise run amok. It would also seem that Heller suggests it is precisely this kind of profit-motive which permits the moral viciousness of a Catch-22. The well-intentioned amorality it conceals is pointed to when Milo, who had hitherto shown himself pathetically dependent on the goodwill of Yossarian (in this context, the American Public), does, when it becomes expedient, sell him down the river to Cathcart and Korn. And it is in this, the most naked allegory, we see most clearly the marks of strain. The aspirin which has to be given Snowden as he dies, because of Milo's appropriations, and the hiring out of the group for a German bombing mission, show us where the morality pattern, however accurately diagnosed, fails as art because *idea* totally dominates any credible reality. Another part of the novel that shows strain—the motiveless vendetta of Nately's whore against Yossarian—evidences the same flaw. Here the *idea* of transference of guilt by association is allowed an unnatural priority over something live and intrinsic to the action.

But by and large, considering the tightrope he walks, Heller makes few mistakes of this nature. In the main *Catch-22* sustains itself on its chosen ground, between the absurd we know to have been real (Cathcart's demand that the chaplain pray for tighter bomb-patterns is a manifest parody of General Patton's request for divine intervention during the Battle of the Bulge), and the absurd as it must have shaped itself to minds overstrained by combat, such as Yossarian's hallucinated expectation for Clevinger's plane to reappear from the cloud where it had been lost.

Superficially a chaotic novel, *Catch-22* in each of its parts—character, episodic allegory, and complex tracing of the power structure of command —shows us either microcosms of, or links in, a world gone mad, where the chief symptom of insanity is the system created to organize and perpetuate its insane condition. The only option for Yossarian, where the only reward for sanity is death, is like another American hero before him to make his own separate peace. But the false notes, the sticky sentiment of *A Farewell to Arms*, the rhetoric of Faulkner's *A Fable*, are superfluous in this indictment where the "system" makes motivation—love or hate, courage or cowardice, loyalty or sycophancy—in the end meaningless. *Catch-22*, however, though it disdains the innocent worldliness of Fitzgerald's Twenties or the idylls of Michigan childhood, does not deny the American Dream. The hero makes his exit in the direction of life, liberty and the pursuit of happiness. And the Dream, pursued by one man, himself a fugitive, is so much the more acceptable. There is a tough-mindedness about Heller's refusal to subside into melancholia, the habitual despondence in the modern reaction to the facts of the human condition.

Recall any one bizarre incident and this is sure to bring in its train a dozen equally vivid, all mingling laughter and pathos. At first the proliferated blind-alleys created by military logic [17] to maintain itself seems only the senseless grinding of pack-ice—but in the end Yossarian is catapulted free. Just when it seems the hero, to save his neck, will have to come to terms with the men and system responsible for the annihilation of his friends, the message is seen, the scales fall from his eyes. No doubt at this juncture Heller strains too hard to justify completely Yossarian's actions: the *Walpurgisnacht* of his AWOL wander through Rome, the recapitulation in gross detail of Snowden's death, and the Machiavellianism of Korn are excessive, since our need to see Yossarian freed is already acute. But the manner in which the message is brought home is perfectly acceptable. Orr, disquietingly not given a chapter of his own, a stray piece for much of the puzzle, is the message-bearer. Earlier, Yossarian had been misled into feeling only compassion for him:

Orr was an eccentric midget, a freakish, likable dwarf with a smutty mind and a thousand valuable skills that would keep him in a low income group all his life. (p. 321)

Add to this Orr's dedication to a single cause, self-preservation, and we have Heller's definition of *Homo Naturalis*. Keeping in mind the necessity of survival, polishing his apparently misplaced practical skills, Orr does in fact learn how to survive. There being no point in learning to fly "well," in view of the statistics of attrition, he looks for the flak, learns how to be shot down without danger, and practices for the final glorious improbability of his sea-voyage to Sweden in a dinghy. He is the Or in *Either/Or* and in "adapt or die." He devotes himself to survival, protecting himself from discovery by the crab-apples in his cheeks, and only when it is almost too late does Yossarian penetrate his disguise, and decide to learn survival also. Orr's escape, stimulating Yossarian to ignore the dangers implicit in opting out from the "system," is presented throughout in paradox and so reaches in the novel something of the order of a religious truth, identical in conception and execution to the parables of *The New Testament*.

And it is precisely here that we come against the greatest difficulty in seeing the meaning of *Catch-22*. What are the truths presented by the conclusions of the novel? Orr survives the real dangers of war, a real ditching, but *fantastically* navigates to Sweden. Yossarian makes his exit jumping out of the way of a knife-stroke *fantastically* directed at him out of the delusions of Nately's whore. It is not enough to complete a neat equation and simply say that, since the weapons of the "system" verge always on the fantastic, fire must be fought with fire. We must, I believe, stay much closer to psychological realities. Under conditions of extreme stress, the mind escapes reality and constructs for itself a fantasy world: but this condition is usually diagnosed as outside of sanity, and psychiatry devotes itself to removing the delusions and having the patient look facts in the face once again. Heller seems explicitly to deny the moral claims of the world of facts. War is a fact, the horrors of war are [18] facts; and while no one would deny war to be an act of insanity, it is hard to believe it has been banished from our society. So, given the fact and its undeniable horror, Heller constructs for his readers the therapy of the novel. A sublimation into fantasy is the necessary end of the novel: we find consolation in the ending of Catch-22 because, as Browne said of religious belief, it is impossible. Its very impossibility is the guarantee of its efficacy. Heller is no doubt an empiricist himself, and the final fact-facing becomes that some facts are too terrible to be faced: hence, the absurd transcendence of reality as Orr sails his rubber dinghy, sipping tea, to the world of neutrality. [19]

ON THE ABSURD

Vance Ramsey
From Here to Absurdity:
Heller's" Catch-22"

Catch-22, published in 1961, was greeted by extremely mixed reviews. Re-actions ranged all the way from frank adulation to contemptuous dis-missal. Nelson Algren said of it, "To compare Catch-22 favorably with The Good Soldier Schweik would be an injustice, because this novel is not merely the best American novel to come out of World War II; it is the best American novel that has come out of anywhere in years." [1] Julian Mitchell, writing in Spectator, called it "a book of enormous richness and art, of deep thought and brilliant writing." [2] On the other side are those like Whitney Balliett in his review in The New Yorker:

Heller uses nonsense, satire, non sequiturs, slapstick, and farce. He wallows in his own laughter and finally drowns in it. What remains is a debris of sour

---

[1] Nelson Algren, "The Catch," Nation, 193 (November 4, 1961), 358.
[2] Julian Mitchell, "Under Mad Gods," Spectator (London), 208 (June 15, 1962), 801.

SOURCE: Thomas B. Whitbread, ed., Seven Contemporary Authors: Essays on Cozzens, Miller, West, Golding, Heller, Albee, and Powers (Austin: University of Texas Press, 1968), pp. 99–118. Reprinted by permission of the author and publisher.

221

jokes, stage anger, dirty words, synthetic looniness, and the sort of antic behavior the children fall into when they know they are losing our attention.[3]

If this kind of criticism is too negligent and easy, presuming to register the author's state of mind as he produces his work, a more serious criticism ot the novel and one which suggests several points for consideration is made by R. G. Stern in *The New York Times Book Review*:

Catch-22 has much passion, comic and fervent, but it gasps for want of craft and sensibility. . . . Joseph Heller is like a brilliant painter who decides to throw all the ideas in his sketchbooks onto one canvas, relying on their charm and shock to compensate for the lack of design. . . . The [99] book is an emotional hodge-podge; no mood is sustained long enough to register for more than a chapter.[4]

While this indictment is overstated, especially the last statement, and while it misses certain unifying elements in the novel, it does point to strengths and weaknesses in the book. Even the book's most fervid admirers are forced to admit that a judicious pruning might have helped; and all but the most superficial of the book's detractors admit at least flashes of comic brilliance in the author's style.

The title, *Catch-22*, refers to that rider which seems to be attached to every code of the rights of men and which gives those in authority the power to revoke those rights at will. It has many clauses in the novel, the most memorable being that recorded in a conversation between Yossarian and the squadron medical officer, Doc Daneeka, concerning Yossarian's tentmate Orr, who they both agree is crazy and should be grounded.

All he had to do was ask; and as soon as he did, he would no longer be crazy and would have to fly more missions. Orr would be crazy to fly more missions and sane if he didn't, but if he was sane he had to fly them. If he flew them he was crazy and didn't have to; but if he didn't want to he was sane and had to. Yossarian was moved very deeply by the absolute simplicity of this clause of Catch-22 and let out a respectful whistle.
"That's some catch, that Catch-22," he observed.
"It's the best there is," Doc Daneeka agreed.[5]

For Yossarian it is a closed system leading only to his death, and every seeming exit is blocked as he makes for it. Since the colonel seems pre-

---

[3] Whitney Balliett, *New Yorker*, 37 (December 9, 1961), 247.
[4] R. G. Stern, *New York Times Book Review* (October 22, 1961), p. 50.
[5] Joseph Heller, *Catch-22* (New York: Simon & Schuster, 1961; repr. New York: Dell, 1962), p. 47. Further references are to the latter edition.

pared to raise the required number of bombing missions indefinitely, he doesn't see any escape from annihilation. He goes to the mail clerk who seems to be running everything, ex-P.F.C. Wintergreen. [100]

"What would they do to me," he asked in confidential tones, "if I refused to fly them?"
"We'd probably shoot you," ex-P.F.C. Wintergreen replied.
"*We?*" Yossarian cried in surprise. "What do you mean, *we?* Since when are you on their side?"
"If you're going to be shot, whose side do you expect me to be on?" (p. 60)

Courage, loyalty, all the standard wartime virtues give way to the need to survive in the face of imminent annihilation.

The answer of Dunbar, Yossarian's friend, to the imminence of death is to cultivate boredom by doing such things as striking up conversations with patriotic Texans. The years are slipping away from him, he tells Clevinger, whose idealism rings hollow in this atmosphere, and he is being carried too quickly toward his death. He is an old man already, because on every mission he is only inches away from death.

"Well, maybe it's true," Clevinger conceded unwillingly in a subdued tone. "Maybe a long life does have to be filled with many irrational conditions if it's to seem long. But in that event, who wants one?"
"I do," Dunbar told him.
"Why?" Clevinger asked.
"What else is there?" (p. 40)

Part of the dilemma is here. Life may be seen as irrational and even absurd, but beyond it looms an almost palpable nothingness, a void beyond life which is as much the experience of modern man, as expressed by Hemingway's *nada*, as is the unreason within life: "What did he fear? It was not fear or dread. It was a nothing that he knew too well. It was all a nothing and man was nothing too. . . . Some lived in it and never felt it but he knew it all was nada y pues nada y nada y pues nada." [6] Certainly this nothing is very real to [101] Yossarian. In the beginning of the novel other people exist for him primarily as they threaten his existence, are necessary to his survival, or as he puzzles over their estrangement from themselves in their absorption with principles which in the face of nothingness are simply without meaning.

---

[6] Ernest Hemingway, "A Clean, Well-Lighted Place," *The Snows of Kilimanjaro and Other Stories* (New York: Charles Scribner's Sons, 1927; repr. New York: Charles Scribner's Sons, 1961), p. 32.

The question of madness and sanity is central to the book's technique. The apparent sanity of some of the characters and the apparent insanity of others is revealed time and again as only apparent. Our first remembrance of *Catch-22* is probably of the many vivid characters throughout the novel. Many of the most vivid of these seem grotesques and madmen. Dunbar, for example, seeks out and cultivates boredom to "make the time go slow." Orr as a boy walked around with crab apples in his cheeks, or, as he says, " 'When I couldn't get crab apples . . . I used horse chestnuts. Horse chestnuts are about the same size as crab apples and actually have a better shape, although the shape doesn't matter a bit' " (p. 23). And the maddest of all the book's characters seems to be the hero, Captain John Yossarian.

Yossarian first appears malingering in a hospital, moodily censoring all the modifiers in the letters of enlisted men and signing the censor's name "Washington Irving," or, for variety, "Irving Washington." Crazy, it seems; but this madness of his begins to assume a different aspect when set beside the activities of the sane people around him. Clevinger, for example, knows that Yossarian is crazy and tells him so.

"They're trying to kill me," Yossarian told him calmly.
"No one's trying to kill you," Clevinger cried.
"Then why are they shooting at me?" Yossarian asked.
"They're shooting at *everyone*," Clevinger answered. "They're trying to kill everyone."
"And what difference does that make?"
Clevinger was already on the way, half out of his chair with emotion, his eyes moist and his lips quivering and pale. As always occurred when he quarreled over principles in which he believed passionately, he would [102] end up gasping furiously and blinking back bitter tears of conviction. There were many principles in which Clevinger believed passionately. He was crazy. (p. 17)

The satire entwined in the farce, the painful twinge in even the most humorous parts of the book, is revealed in such a passage. In such a situation the examination of traditionally assumed values becomes literally a matter of life or death. Yossarian least of all could be content to be just a portion of a faceless *everyone*, to die or not as chance wills. He is, the book says elsewhere, willing to be the victim of anything but circumstance.

In the face of the threats to his existence Yossarian has only one overriding principle—to stay alive—and to that end he malingers in a hospital, sabotages his plane, puts soap in the squadron's food, alters a combat map, and even at one time toys with the idea of murdering his commanding officer. He is, in short, the kind of character that the term "*antihero*" should have been reserved for. Many who are given this title are simply "*nonheroes*"—weak, ineffectual little men, little more than anguished consciousnesses. Yossarian, however, is aggressively, even belligerently, antiheroic, and in his antiheroism is a direct challenge to the values and ideals which the world claims to hold.

This challenge to these values and ideals is given telling expression in an exchange between Nately—like Clevinger a young man of high ideals— and a cynical old Italian. Nately is the kind of romantic figure who might have been the hero of the novel if it had been of the more traditional type of war novels. Like Prewitt in *From Here to Eternity*, for example, he is totally committed to his ideals; like Prewitt he is in love with a prostitute; and like Prewitt he is accidentally killed. But he is far from being the hero of this novel. The hero of this novel is Yossarian, and although Yossarian may be in constant danger of becoming a victim, he will never be a *pathetic* victim. The cynical old Italian indicates in an exchange with Nately just what is wrong with the younger man's outlook. [103]

"They are going to kill you if you don't watch out, and I can see now that you are not going to watch out. Why don't you use some sense and try to be more like me? You might live to be a hundred and seven, too."

"Because it's better to die on one's feet than live on one's knees," Nately retorted with triumphant and lofty conviction. "I guess you've heard that saying before."

"Yes, I certainly have," mused the treacherous old man, smiling again. "But I'm afraid you have it backward. It is better to *live* on one's feet than die on one's knees. *That* is the way the saying goes." (pp. 253–254)

There is a lucidity in this which reveals in the lofty pretensions of the sane and principled young men in the novel who are so unaware of the threat to their existence the very depth of absurdity. Indeed, integral to *Catch-22* is the notion of the absurd. This is true not only of the thematic implications of the novel but is central to its technique. A partial definition of the absurd by Camus is relevant to one aspect of the theme of the novel: "This discomfort in the face of man's own inhumanity, this incalculable tumble before the image of what we are, this 'nausea,' as a writer of today calls it, is also the absurd." [7]

Both in content and technique, *Catch-22* has affinities with the theatre of the absurd. We may see the affinity of the novel to the technique of absurd drama in the following description by Martin Esslin: "The means by which the dramatists of the Absurd express their critique . . . of our disintegrating society are based on suddenly confronting their audiences

---

[7] Albert Camus, *The Myth of Sisyphus and Other Essays*, trans. Justin O'Brien (New York: Vintage Books, 1955), p. 11.

with a grotesquely heightened and distorted picture of a world that has gone mad." [8] Esslin adds,

As the incomprehensibility of the motives and the often unexplained and mysterious nature of the Characters' actions in the Theatre of the [104] Absurd effectively prevent identification, such theatre is a comic theatre in spite of the fact that its subject matter is somber, violent and bitter. That is why the Theatre of the Absurd transcends the categories of comedy and tragedy and combines laughter with horror.[9]

This combination of laughter with horror occurs throughout *Catch-22* and has caused it to be placed with other works in recent fiction called "black humor."

The technique of "black humor" seems to have evolved in response to the needs of an age whose sensibilities have been largely blunted. As a technique, the humor serves to lower the reader's defenses so that the full force of the horror may be felt. One flaw in the usual novel out of World War II is that the piling up of horror upon horror finally makes the reader immune. In an age which has made a daily companion of horror (so that indifference has become a mode of survival), some change of technique is needed from the naturalistic accumulation of detail, which is designed to tell on the reader by its sheer weight and which is characteristic of most recent war novels; some new way is required to reach the reader once again and involve him.

Despite the presence of other novels in the list of works called "black humor," the term has not been explored well enough to shed much light on any particular work placed on the list. The detractors of *Catch-22* have usually regarded it as a disorderly mixture of comedy, satire, farce, and invective; the book's admirers, on the other hand, have stressed the basic seriousness and purpose beneath the apparently disorganized and purpose- less surface. Julian Mitchell, an admirer, called it "a surrealist *Iliad*, with a lunatic High Command instead of gods, and a coward for a hero" and went on to label it "one of the finest examples of the genre in which many of the best modern novels are written, that of the anguished farce (or, literally, the horror-comic)." [10] This is perceptive, and it indicates [105] what is lacking in a reading of the humor as simply jokes which go sour. The *Catch-22* joke is not even very funny the first time, and in fact, as we soon learn, it is no joke.

In the longest and in many ways the most perceptive review of the novel,

---

[8] Martin Esslin, *The Theatre of the Absurd* (New York: Anchor Books, 1961), p. 300.
[9] *Ibid.*, p. 301.
[10] Mitchell, "Under Mad Gods," p. 801. [See pp. 19–20 of this book.—Eds.]

Robert Brustein called the novel "a picaresque epic," and, however unfamiliar such a combination may seem, we may begin a description of the
book by holding to these two descriptions of it as an "anguished farce" and
a "picaresque epic." The first term will account for the reaction to the book
on the one hand as slapstick and on the other as intensely serious, while
the second term—"picaresque epic"—can help to make clearer a structure
which is *not* formless but which is also not in the Jamesian "well-made
novel" tradition.

Perhaps it was Evelyn Waugh who began the development of what
Mitchell calls the "anguished farce." In *Vile Bodies* the final image of the
General and a prostitute named Chastity engaged in sex in a staff car while
the sounds of battle commence around them has in it this combination
of comedy and horror. So have the novels of Nathanael West. Certainly
the two trials in *Catch-22* recall both Kafka and West.

> "Everything's going to be all right, Chaplain," the major said encouragingly.
> "You've got nothing to be afraid of if you're not guilty. What are you so
> afraid of? You're not guilty, are you?"
> "Sure he's guilty," said the colonel. "Guilty as hell."
> "Guilty of what?" implored the chaplain, feeling more and more bewildered
> and not knowing which of the men to appeal to for mercy. The third officer
> wore no insignia and lurked in silence off to the side. "What did I do?"
> "That's just what we're going to find out," answered the colonel. . . .
> (p. 389)

The specific tradition of the absurd not only operates on the social level,
pillorying the cruel idiocies of society, as in Waugh's early novels, but, as
Esslin says, faces [106]

> up to a deeper layer of absurdity—the absurdity of the human condition
> itself in a world where the decline of religious belief has deprived man of
> certainties. When it is no longer possible to accept simple and complete
> systems of values and revelations of divine purpose, life must be faced in
> its ultimate stark reality.[11]

As *Catch-22* begins, Yossarian has already faced the stark reality of his approaching death and nothingness, though at this point the reader is aware
only of the result—a man almost beside himself at the thought of death.
The event which has brought him the message of his own mortality is the
death of Snowden, a gunner in Yossarian's plane. Yossarian spent the better part of a flight home trying to minister to the dying gunner, only to find

---

[11] Esslin, *The Theatre of the Absurd*, p. 292.

that the wound he was treating was not the fatal one; the fatal wound—
mortality itself—was not subject to first aid. Mortality returns like a theme
in music, each time with variations of meaning, but each time essentially
the same. When questions are asked for at a briefing session, Yossarian asks
the question which is always with him:

"Where are the Snowdens of yesteryear?"
"I'm afraid I don't understand."
"*Où sont les Neigedens d'antan?*" Yossarian said to make it easier for him.
"*Parlez en anglais,* for Christ's sake," said the corporal, "*Je ne parle pas
français.*"
"Neither do I," answered Yossarian, who was ready to pursue him through
all the words in the world to wring the knowledge from him if he could. (p. 36)

Yossarian not only lives on the edge of the void as the others do, but
lives in constant knowledge of that void. The void has become "eloquent"
for him as Camus says in *The Myth of Sisyphus*:

In certain situations, replying "nothing" when asked what one is thinking
about may be pretense in a man. Those who are loved are well aware of this.
But if that reply is sincere, if it symbolizes that odd state of soul [107]
in which the void becomes eloquent, in which the chain of daily gestures is
broken, in which the heart vainly seeks the link that will connect it again,
then it is as it were the first sign of absurdity.[12]

Once the thing has been done it seems inevitable: where else to find the
very quintessence of the absurd other than in a modern military establishment in the middle of a modern war? This is what every ex-military man
misses in so many novels to come out of World War II and the Korean
War—that sense of grotesqueness of the situation, the irrationality and
inadequacy of the means for survival, and in general a feeling of mingled
terror and unreality. In short, the elements requisite to literature of the
absurd.

In literature of the absurd the apparently ordered surface of reality is
torn away to reveal the chaos and unreason beneath. Paradox, therefore, is
the very essence of the technique of literature of the absurd. Traditional
reason is revealed as unreason because it supposes an ordered, rational
world. Sanity in the traditional sense is really insanity; that is, if sanity is
the ability to come to terms with reality, then it is insane to act as if the
world is coherent and rational. Loyalty to traditional institutions can be dis-

---

[12] Camus, *The Myth of Sisyphus*, p. 10.

loyalty to oneself simply because the institutions may threaten the people they are ostensibly designed to serve.

Part of the difference between *Catch-22* and the usual war novel lies in this insistent world-view of a nothingness which threatens to invade even the selves of these men. A naturalistic novel, after all, keeps the integrity of the self, however that self may be buffeted about and even destroyed. In the world of *Catch-22*, however, the void is not only a constant presence; it also threatens to invade the self and it has its ally in a system which would make of these men anonymous and expendable cogs in a war machine so devoted to the purposes of men like Colonel Cathcart and General Peckem as to make the objective of winning the war almost an afterthought.

Throughout the book men are "disappeared," a chillingly apt [108] term. Dunbar, Clevinger, Major Major—in one way or another all seem to die or disappear. The terms of life or death, existence or nonexistence are irrational and arbitrary. Mudd, a man who was to have lived in Yossarian's tent but who was killed before he reported for duty, is alive administratively because to admit his death would be sloppy bookkeeping. Doc Daneeka, on the other hand, is administratively dead and spends the rest of his time forlornly trying to assert his existence. The faceless anonymity of the system is expressed in the career of this little man, throughout much of the book an eager accomplice of the system and one who has called the war a "godsend," only to spend the rest of his time trying to get those still within the system to recognize his existence. He finally loses his last link with a world in which he can exist when his wife moves, leaving no forwarding address after receiving a form letter of condolence: "Dear Mrs., Mr., Miss, or Mr. and Mrs. Daneeka: Words cannot express the deep personal grief I experienced when your husband, son, father or brother was killed, wounded or reported missing in action" (p. 354).

The ultimate in faceless inhumanity is achieved in the figure of the soldier in white:

> The soldier in white was constructed entirely of gauze, plaster and a
> thermometer, and the thermometer was merely an adornment left balanced
> in the empty dark hole in the bandages over his mouth early each morning
> and late each afternoon by Nurse Cramer and Nurse Duckett right up to
> the afternoon Nurse Cramer read the thermometer and discovered he was
> dead. (p. 171)

The other patients take offense against him, "rebelling against his presence as a ghastly imposition and resenting him malevolently for the nauseating truth of which he was a bright reminder" (p. 172). The soldier in white is not only a reminder of the imminence of death; he is also a con-

stant reminder to the men of their status within the system. The nurses
have two jars, one to drip liquid into the soldier in white and the other to
catch the liquid. At the end of [109] the process, the two jars are reversed.
" 'Why can't they hook the two jars up to each other and eliminate the
middleman?' the artillery captain with whom Yossarian had stopped playing chess inquired. 'What the hell do they need him for?' " (p. 174). The
reappearance of the soldier in white later is too much for Dunbar, who goes
berserk.

> "It's the same one!" Dunbar shouted at him emphatically in a voice rising
> clearly above the raucous commotion. "Don't you understand? It's the
> same one."
> "The same one!" Yossarian heard himself echo, quivering with a deep and
> ominous excitement that he could not control, and shoved his way after
> Dunbar toward the bed of the soldier in white. . . .
> It was indeed the same man. He had lost a few inches and added some
> weight, but Yossarian remembered him instantly by the two stiff arms and
> the two stiff, thick, useless legs drawn upward into the air almost perpendicu-
> larly by the taut ropes and the long lead weights suspended from pulleys
> over him and by the frayed black hole in the bandages over his mouth. . . .
> "There's no one inside!" Dunbar yelled at him unexpectedly. (p. 374)

Whether because Dunbar has guessed some secret of the system or because
he is simply inconvenient, he is immediately "disappeared." Throughout
the book, humor is mingled with a horror that at times, as in this image of
men being "disappeared," is reminiscent of 1984.

Such then is the atmosphere of Catch-22. There is a danger that in thus
insisting on the seriousness underlying the humor, the humor of the book
may be slighted. Almost no one, however, is prepared to deny the existence
of this humor and even to accept it, at least at times, as being of a very
high quality. The greater danger is to fall into the trap of too easily dismissing the novel as a hodge-podge of comic scenes by a novelist who is
unable to maintain the comedy. The comic is an integral element in the
novel, as it is in much literature of the absurd, but, also like other absurd
literature, it is present in a merging of the often ridiculous with the always
desperate. [110]

The larger structure of the novel is episodic, with a succession of scenes
following and sometimes interrupting each other like a jumbled series of
playlets. At first glance these successive scenes seem related only in that
they take place somewhere within the purview of the hero, John Yossarian.
Gradually, however, they reveal the same pervasive atmosphere of fear,
anxiety, and what Sartre has called the nausea of existence, all in something
like an asylum for the criminally insane. As this atmosphere begins to be-

come apparent the movement of the book becomes clearer. These apparently only tangentially related scenes have their relevance to the spiritual development of the book's hero.

At the beginning Yossarian has become fully aware of himself by becoming aware of the threat to himself; this awareness causes him to struggle violently to detach himself in order to survive. The moment of his beginning the attempt to detach himself has been the moment of his experience of Snowden's death; and his initial expression of it is to refuse to wear his uniform, the symbol of his involvement in a system which threatens to destroy him. The next response is to flee into the hospital. There is death in the hospital also, but at least in the hospital are those who can be called on for help, not because they are humane but because that is their function in the system; and death in the hospital is at least clean.

. . . outside the hospital the war was still going on. Men went mad and were rewarded with medals. All over the world, boys on every side of the bomb line were laying down their lives for what they had been told was their country, and no one seemed to mind, least of all the boys who were laying down their young lives. There was no end in sight. (p. 16)

Awareness of self such as Yossarian's is dangerous to the system and makes him hated and feared by those who serve the system with most enthusiasm. The ideal warrior now is not a heroic individual in the ancient mold, but someone unaware and consequently not quite human. Havermeyer, for example, according to Colonel [111] Cathcart, is "the best damned bombardier we've got" (p. 30). He seems absolutely unaware of the threat of death (until his sudden awareness near the end of the book); he is also a man who spends his evenings shooting field mice with dumdummed bullets.

Not only are many of the victims of the system unaware, the system itself seems to be solely in the hands of those who exist as little more than creatures of their need to succeed within the terms of the system. When Lieutenant Colonel Korn offers his immoral deal to Yossarian, he tells him,

"And there you have the crux of the situation. Colonel Cathcart wants to be a general and I want to be a colonel, and that's why we have to send you home."

"Why does he want to be a general?"

"Why? For the same reason that I want to be a colonel. What else have we got to do? Everyone teaches us to aspire to higher things. A general is higher than a colonel, and a colonel is higher than a lieutenant colonel. So we're aspiring." (p. 435)

One version and perversion of the American dream is thus presented starkly. Aspiration within the system with no examination of ends has become an end in itself; it has become a substitute for meaningful life. Colonel Cathcart and Colonel Korn exist only in their attempts to use an irrational system for their own irrational ends. It is no accident that the most irrational of them all, Scheisskopf, finally is put in charge. Modern evil exists in these men not in any overpowering, demonic guise, but in the guise of Horatio Alger dutifully climbing to success over the bleeding forms of his fellows.

Dutiful obedience is presented throughout the book as the height of madness. Clevinger is not merely a dutiful but a passionate supporter of the system. And he is a dope. Appleby is an all-American boy who wins at all games like Tom Stover at Yale and who dutifully reports Yossarian's attempt to malinger by catching malaria. He is only presented as sane when he comes to Yossarian after the latter has refused to fly any more and tells him, "I hope you do get away with it" (p. 409). [112]

Perhaps the most frightening character of all is Aarfy, who is so committed to clichés that he seems to have no substance at all. In his playful moods Aarfy likes to come into the nose of the plane and jab Yossarian as he wildly directs the pilot away from flak.

"I said get *out of here!*" Yossarian shouted and broke into tears. He began punching Aarfy in the body with both hands as hard as he could. "Get *away* from me! *Get away!*"

Punching Aarfy was like sinking his fists into a limp sack of inflated rubber. There was no resistance, no response at all from the soft, insensitive mass. . . .

Yossarian was dumbfounded by his state of rapturous contentment. Aarfy was like an eerie ogre in a dream, incapable of being bruised or evaded, and Yossarian dreaded him for a complex of reasons he was too petrified to untangle. (pp. 153–154)

Aarfy is a climber who works on Nately because Nately's father is rich and may give him a job; he divides all women into good ones and bad ones, and dates only the ones whose fathers can help him; he is prepared at the end to give perjured testimony against Yossarian at the request of Colonel Cathcart. In short, he is not only devoted to the same kind of success as the Cathcarts and Peckems, but his commitment is so complete as to make him inhuman.

Paradoxically (in terms of an older literary tradition) disengagement in this novel is not immoral but moral. The literature of social criticism of the thirties, for example, insisted that one finds himself only in social involvement. In *Catch-22* such involvement is the way to lose oneself, as the case of Appleby and others shows. It is as Yossarian disengages himself that he finds himself.

This is apparently what Brustein means when he calls the book a "picaresque epic." Yossarian is a picaro in that he is at odds with the role which society would thrust upon him, but by the end of the novel he is more than just a picaro, at least by intention. He has become what R. W. B. Lewis calls a "picaresque saint": ". . . in what seems to me the most fully developed portraits of the contemporary hero, he is apt to share not only the miseries of [113] humanity, but its gravest weaknesses, too, and even in its sins. He is not only a saint, as the novelists have been describing him. He is a picaresque saint." [13]

The structure of *Catch-22*, broadly, derives from Yossarian's struggle to detach himself in order to survive to a realization, convincing or not, that his detaching himself has a larger meaning. The process of disengaging himself from the institutions which threaten to victimize him leads to his total moral engagement with others. He accepts his guilt (as Camus says that each man must) in the form of being the target of Nately's whore, and he refuses the sure but immoral survival offered by Korn and Cathcart in favor of a much less certain but at least morally acceptable survival on his own terms. He chooses, as the old man says, to live on his feet rather than to die—or live—on his knees. The episodes concerning Orr have foreshadowed this change; the persuasiveness of the change is another question.

The disjunctive, episodic nature of the novel's structure is a real challenge to the artist's ability to make an organic whole, and Heller does not always succeed, particularly in the episodes involving Milo Minderbinder, the budding tycoon. That Heller is able on the whole to succeed in making these elements a unified whole, that he is able even to hold the reader through an initially bewildering series of wild scenes is due in no small part to his gift for constructing vital, memorable characters. Chief White Halfoat, who is determined to die of pneumonia, Hungry Joe, who is at peace only in combat and who finally dies in his sleep, suffocated by the same cat with which he had his most memorable battles, Major ———— de Coverley, ex-P.F.C. Wintergreen—the book overflows with characters who come to life in a sentence or two. Part of the meaning of the book, in fact, is in their enduring individuality in the grip of a system which threatens that individuality and their very existence.

The abrupt shifts in time and event are also not flaws of the book; [114] rather they are central to its technique. These are not really flashbacks, because they are not related either to a character's specific remembrance nor are they often explicitly related to the situation which they interrupt. One of the functions of these abrupt time-shifts, like Heller's use of paradox,

---

[13] R. W. B. Lewis, *The Picaresque Saint* (New York: J. B. Lippincott, 1958), p. 32.

is to wrench the characters out of the traditionally ordered, time-bound context of the novel. Events exist primarily not in any cause-and-effect or chronological relation to one another but simultaneously. This does not mean that time has been escaped in the novel; on the contrary, it has become more personal and hence more crucial. Because of the nearness of the book's characters to death, time is literally running out on them. Clock time is related to the notion of a measured, ordered eternity. For Yossarian, however, there is no God and therefore no eternity; there is only the space until his death and everything conspires to shorten this space.

This suggests why the last part of the novel is unconvincing. Despite the fact that the episodes of Orr are designed to foreshadow the change which takes place in Yossarian in the last part, the change is less than convincing. Like Yossarian, Orr seems to be crazy, but unlike Yossarian he has method in his madness. Orr is Yossarian's tentmate, who keeps telling two apparently pointless stories. One story is about his practice as a boy of keeping crab apples or, when he couldn't get crab apples, horse chestnuts in his cheeks. The other story is a reminder to Yossarian of the time when Orr stood laughing while an Italian prostitute hit him over the head with her shoe. As the two apparently most insane men in the outfit, the men have a fellow feeling which causes Yossarian to feel that Orr is trying to tell him something.

. . . Yossarian was willing to give Orr the benefit of the doubt because Orr was from the wilderness outside New York City and knew so much more about wild-life than Yossarian did, and because Orr, unlike Yossarian's mother, father, sister, brother, aunt, uncle, in-law, teacher, spiritual leader, legislator, neighbor and newspaper, had never lied to him about anything crucial. (p. 47) [115]

When he hears that Orr has made it to Sweden, Yossarian understands what Orr has been trying to tell him. The crab apples were to give him a look of apple-cheeked innocence, which is the only defense in a world where everything and everyone threatens. But the speeches of the characters are clues to the unnatural quality of the style of the last part of the book. The chaplain exclaims, " 'It's a miracle of human perseverance, I tell you. And that's just what I'm going to do from now on! I'm going to persevere. Yes, I'm going to persevere' " (p. 459). Even Yossarian's speech is changed: " 'Oh, why didn't I listen to him? Why wouldn't I have some faith?' " (p. 459).

Both the event of Orr's escape to Sweden and the meaning of it, then, have been amply foreshadowed throughout much of the novel. But the meaning of Orr's escape doesn't seem to fit with Yossarian's decision in the last of the book. When the chaplain asks Yossarian why the girl was hitting Orr with her shoe, he answers, " 'Because he was paying her to, that's why! But she wouldn't hit him hard enough, so he had to row to Sweden' " (p. 460). The message seems straightforward enough: in a world where he is constantly threatened with annihilation, a man must use enormous cleverness and resourcefulness to survive. This seems in keeping with Yossarian's growing feeling from the beginning; Orr's message is simply that survival is indeed possible. But somehow Yossarian's final decision is supposed to go beyond this doctrine of survival to a doctrine of social involvement. The last four or five chapters are devoted to this change, and indicative of the difficulty which the author apparently had in making this change convincing. Both atmosphere and technique change.

The book has two major flaws. In the first place, some of the material does not fit in. The picaresque structure allows a great deal of latitude, but the *atmosphere* must be consistent. In the midst of matters as momentous as life and death, such episodes as that of the Great Loyalty Oath Crusade seem excrescences. This is a voice from the postwar as is the inordinate space given to the enterprises of [116] Milo Minderbinder, including his strafing of his own men on commission from the enemy. The second flaw is greater. In keeping with the nature of the picaresque novel as standing outside society and making mostly negative comments upon it, the picaresque novelist often has difficulty in ending his novel, especially on a positive note. The last four chapters of the novel have a discursive quality not found in most of the other parts of the novel. The long philosophical argument between Yossarian and the ex-college professor is out of keeping with the technique of the rest of the book, in which actions and situations speak for themselves. In short, the book loses its dramatic quality.

This loss of the dramatic quality at the end of the novel points to an even deeper problem, the change in Yossarian. The first part of his story, his reaction to death and his need to disengage himself from all that threatens him, is made poignantly convincing; the last stage of his development, the decision that there is something greater than survival, is not so convincing. Yossarian's morality in saying 'no' to the forces which threaten to take him over is supposed to become a morality of social involvement; he is to go to Sweden to try to do something about all of the horrors he has seen in his last night in Rome.

It is possible to intellectualize this result: if Yossarian were to accept the deal offered him in order to survive, he might still lose his self to the system. We might even accept the point that Yossarian's whole career has been pointing toward this moment of total rebellion, of total refusal—the act of complete disengagement which is desertion. The flaw is that the end is not artistically convincing. In his all-absorbing involvement in the threat to his own existence, Yossarian has been so little aware of the threat to others that the sudden change to an awareness of them and dedication to trying to help them does not have the same force.

This is a familiar difficulty for several of the strains of literature represented in *Catch-22*. The comic writer whose comedy has been critical and biting often has the difficulty of restoring order to a context [117] which has been thoroughly disordered for comic effect. The absurdist writer has constant difficulty, having shown the logic of alienation and estrangement from life, in trying to restore a meaningful link to that life. The picaro who so determinedly disengages himself from society and the human institutions which strive to restrict him can only with difficulty become engaged again with his kind without at the same time becoming engaged with the institutions of his kind.

This difficulty of the ending of *Catch-22* is not fatal to the success of the novel; far from it. At the present time there is little literature of the absurd, black humor, or any other classification into which this novel might seem to fall which supplies a convincing, viable solution to the essentially negative treatment which it gives to modern life. The convincing positive elements in the novel are connected with the first three quarters, in which characters live and live vitally in the teeth of almost insuperable odds for death and anonymity. The discursive elements near the end, while eloquent, miss the success of the earlier dramatic portions because they belie an implicit theme of the novel: that which argues about and abstracts from each character betrays what is uniquely his own—his individuality— and is allied to the threat of facelessness and annihilation which he must constantly confront and oppose. In traditional literature, the ideal is juxtaposed to the real in order to demonstrate the falling away of the real from the ideal. In the paradox of absurd literature, the real and the ideal are radically incompatible; hence the ideal is largely irrelevant and even destructive. Yossarian's strength is not only that he consciously and resolutely *is*, but that he constantly rejects attempts to make him over in terms of any ideal. He is a compelling creation and probably the shape of many heroes to come. As a man in the novel says of him,

"That crazy bastard may be the only sane one left!" (p. 114) [118]

Norman Podhoretz
The Best Catch There Is

Not long ago, in an article in *Commentary*, Philip Roth complained that the world we live in "is a kind of embarrassment to one's own meager imagination" as a novelist. "The actuality," Roth went on to say, "is continually outdoing our talents, and the culture tosses up figures almost daily that are the envy of any novelist. Who, for example, could have invented Charles Van Doren? Roy Cohn and David Schine? Sherman Adams and Bernard Goldfine? Dwight David Eisenhower?" Anyone who follows the daily newspapers or watches television with some regularity will understand what Roth is getting at. We do often seem to be inhabiting a gigantic insane asylum, a world that, as Roth puts it, alternately stupefies, sickens, and infuriates. No wonder the American writer has so much difficulty "in trying to understand, and then describe, and then make *credible* much of the American reality."

I think Roth's observation goes far toward explaining why Joseph Heller's *Catch-22* has provoked more enthusiasm than any [228] first novel in years. Though ostensibly about an air force squadron in the Second World War, *Catch-22* is actually one of the bravest and most nearly successful attempts we have yet had to describe and make credible the incredible reality of American life in the middle of the 20th century. To describe and make credible; not, however, to *understand*: the secret of Mr. Heller's success lies precisely in his discovery that any effort to understand the incredible is bound to frustrate the attempt to describe it for what it really is. The way to portray insanity, in other words, is to show what insanity looks like, not to explain how it came about.

To be sure, Mr. Heller is a very good writer, with an exceptionally rich talent for comedy (both high and low) and a vitality of spirit that is nothing short of libidinal in its force. But I doubt whether even those virtues would have been enough to produce *Catch-22*; what was needed was the heroic power to resist all the temptations to understanding (or, if you like, sympathy) that must have arisen during the eight years it took to write this novel. I use the word "heroic" here without irony, for I can imagine that Mr. Heller was continually plagued by the fear that if he did not bow more

---

SOURCE: Norman Podhoretz, *Doings and Undoings* (New York: Farrar, Straus & Giroux, Inc., 1964), pp. 228–235. Copyright © 1962, 1964 by Norman Podhoretz. Reprinted by permission of the publisher.

deeply in the direction of simple plausibility, no one would find his story credible, and his characters and the fantastic situations he was putting them through would be understood as comic exaggerations rather than as descriptions of what the world actually does look like to a rational man. Who could have invented Charles Van Doren or Dwight David Eisenhower? Not, surely, a conventional painter of portraits, perhaps not even a great conventional painter of portraits. But Dickens could have invented them—only in this case he would not have been caricaturing (if in fact he was ever caricaturing); he would have been performing an act of photography. So too with Mr. Heller, whose gift for caricature has made it possible for him to achieve a very credible description indeed of the incredible reality around us.

The hero of *Catch-22* is a bombardier named Yossarian who is [229] convinced that everyone is trying to kill him. This idea makes various people angry, especially his friend Clevinger. Clevinger is a man who believes passionately in many principles and who is also a great patriot.

"No one's trying to kill you," Clevinger cried.
"Then why are they shooting at me?" Yossarian asked.
"They're shooting at *everyone*," Clevinger answered. "They're trying to kill everyone."
"And what difference does that make?"

Clevinger is certain that Yossarian is crazy. Yossarian, for his part, has not the slightest doubt that Clevinger is crazy. In fact, everyone is crazy who thinks that any sense can be made out of getting killed. When Yossarian is told that people are dying for their country, he retorts that as far as he can see the only reason he has to fly more combat missions is that his commanding officer, Colonel Cathcart, wants to become a general. Colonel Cathcart is therefore his enemy. So is the German gunner shooting at him while he drops his bombs. So is the nurse in the hospital who doesn't like him, and so are countless others (including bus drivers all over the world) who want to do him in. He is in constant peril of his life. All men are, but no one seems to realize it as keenly as Yossarian and some of his friends—Dunbar, for example, who cultivates boredom because boredom makes time go slowly and therefore lengthens his life. Everywhere, Yossarian reflects in contemplating the war, "men went mad and were rewarded with flying medals. Boys on every side of the bomb line were laying down their lives for what they had been told was their country, and no one seemed to mind, least of all the boys who were laying down their young lives." But Yossarian minds. He minds so powerfully that he can think of nothing else. After gorging himself on a marvelous meal one day, he wonders awhile if it isn't [230] perhaps "all worth it." But not for long. The very next sentence reads:

"But then he burped and remembered that they were trying to kill him, and he sprinted out of the mess hall wildly and ran looking for Doc Daneeka to have himself taken off combat duty and sent home."

Yossarian may mind about getting killed to the point of madness himself, but there is no question that we are meant to take his paranoia not as a disease but as a sensible response to real dangers. Colonel Cathcart, who keeps upping the number of combat missions the men in his command are required to fly before being sent home, is—just as Yossarian says—an idiot who cares only about becoming a general. General Dreedle and General Peckem and Colonel Cargill and Colonel Korn are all idiotic too, always engaged in ridiculous jurisdictional disputes and petty personal rivalries which are usually settled by the mail clerk at headquarters, ex-P.F.C. Wintergreen, through the simple expedient of forwarding one general's communications through channels and dropping the other's (whose prose Wintergreen considers too prolix) into the waste basket. There is also Milo Minderbinder, the mess officer, running a huge syndicate called M & M Enterprises in which the Germans too have a share (Milo even accepts a contract from the Germans to bomb his own outfit). Meanwhile, Yossarian has to go on bombing people he doesn't know, and men on the ground go on firing flak at Yossarian, whom *they* don't know. It is all very strange and bewildering.

The whole system is governed by Catch-22, which permits the authorities to do anything they please while pretending to a respect for the rights of the individual. Catch-22 contains many clauses. The most impressive we learn about early in the book, when the flight surgeon Doc Daneeka explains to Yossarian why he cannot ground a crazy man, despite the fact that the rules require him to ground anyone who is crazy. The catch is that the crazy man must ask to be grounded, but as soon as he asks he [231] can no longer be considered crazy, since "a concern for one's own safety in the face of dangers that are real and immediate is the process of a rational mind." Yossarian is "moved very deeply by the absolute simplicity of this clause of Catch-22." So is Doc Daneeka, whose terror of death (and of being shipped to the Pacific where so many dread diseases can be contracted) is almost as great as Yossarian's and whose attitude toward the world is correspondingly similar: "Oh I'm not complaining. I know there's a war on. I know a lot of people are going to suffer for us to have to win. But why must I be one of them?"

What is the war in *Catch-22* all about? The only explanation anyone ever seems able to offer is that men are dying for their country and that it is a noble thing to give your life for your country. This idea Mr. Heller takes considerable pleasure in ridiculing. What does Colonel Cathcart's desire to become a general have to do with anyone's country? And what is a country anyway? "A country is a piece of land surrounded on all sides by

boundaries, usually unnatural," an ancient Italian who has learned the
arts of survival tells the nineteen-year-old Lieutenant Nately. "There are
now fifty or sixty countries fighting in this war. Surely so many countries
can't *all* be worth dying for." Nately is shocked by such cynicism and tries
to argue, but the old man shakes his head wearily. "They are going to kill
you if you don't watch out, and I can see now that you are not going to
watch out." (This prophecy later comes true.) And in answer to Nately's
declaration that "it's better to die on one's feet than to live on one's knees,"
the old man tells him that the saying makes more sense if it is turned
around to read, "It is better to *live* on one's feet than die on one's knees."

The interesting thing is that there is scarcely a mention until the end of
the novel of Nazism or fascism as an explanation of why the war may be
worth fighting; if there were, Mr. Heller's point of view would have had a
far greater degree of resistance to [232] contend with than he actually allows
it to encounter throughout most of the book. That he is aware of this
problem is obvious from a dialogue between Yossarian and Major Danby
(a "gentle, moral, middle-aged idealist") that takes place in the closing
pages. Danby reminds Yossarian that the Cathcarts and the Peckems are
not the whole story. "This is not World War One. You must never forget
that we're at war with aggressors who would not let either one of us live
if they won." Yossarian is provoked by this unanswerable argument into
taking back everything he has previously stood for:

I know that. . . . Christ, Danby, . . . I've flown seventy goddam combat
missions. Don't talk to me about fighting to save my country. I've been
fighting all along to save my country. Now I'm going to fight a little to save
myself. The country's not in danger anymore, but I am. . . . The Germans
will be beaten in a few months. And Japan will be beaten a few months after
that. If I were to give up my life now, it wouldn't be for my country. It
would be for Cathcart and Korn. . . . From now on I'm thinking only of me.

This statement comes as a surprise: one had supposed that Yossarian had
been thinking only of himself all throughout the novel. If we take what
this new Yossarian says seriously, then the whole novel is trivialized, for
what we had all along thought to be a remorselessly uncompromising picture of the world written from the point of view of the idea that survival is
the overriding value and that all else is pretense, lying, cant, and hypocrisy,
now becomes nothing more than the story of a mismanaged outfit and an
attack on the people who (as Yossarian puts it with a rhetoric not his own)
always cash in "on every decent impulse and every human tragedy." No,
the truth is that Mr. Heller is simply not prepared to go all the way with
the idea that lies at the basis of his novel and that is the main tool he has
used in making an incredible reality seem credible. He is simply not pre-

pared to say [233] that World War II was a fraud, having nothing whatever to do with ideals or values. I don't blame him for not being prepared to say that; it would not be a true thing to say. Yet for the purposes of this novel, it would have been better if he *were* prepared to say it, for in shrinking from the final ruthless implication of the premise on which *Catch-22* is built—the idea that nothing on earth is worth dying for—he weakens the shock of the whole book.

Are we then to conclude that Mr. Heller doesn't really mean what *Catch-22* so unmistakably seems to be communicating for most of its first four hundred pages? I think we must, for if he really meant it, it would not have been possible for him to end the book as he does, with Yossarian heroically refusing to seek his own advantage through cooperating with the Cathcarts and the Korns. (The ancient Italian who lectures Nately and who really does believe that survival is the only thing that counts would most certainly have accepted the opportunity that Yossarian turns down.) Nor, for that matter, would Mr. Heller have been capable of the gusto and exuberance which is *Catch-22*'s most attractive quality: the morality of survival is more likely to breed a quiet and weary irony than the kind of joyful energy that explodes all over the pages of this book.

Perhaps without quite knowing it, Mr. Heller has given us in Yossarian another brilliant example of a figure who first appeared in J. P. Donleavy's *The Ginger Man* a few years ago: the youthful idealist living in a world so insane that he can find nothing to which his idealism might genuinely attach itself, and who therefore devotes all his energies to exposing the pretenses of everything that claims to be worthy of his aspirations and his loyalty. He hungers desperately for something that might be worth laying down his life for, but since nothing is available and since he is above all an honest man, he tells himself that he has in effect chosen to live only for his own survival and that he had better not kid himself about it. But of course he *is* kidding himself—he is [234] not capable of the ruthlessness and opportunistic cunning it takes to live such a life. Now that he has learned that preserving his honor means more to him than saving his skin, the only way out is to run off somewhere, to extricate himself from the insane and murderous world that has somehow grown up around him. And so Yossarian bolts and will try to make it to Sweden. Only—I find myself wanting to ask Mr. Heller—what will Yossarian come upon there, in that peacefully neutral place, that is worth dying for? After all, a life devoted to preserving the "self" is not so very different from a life devoted merely to staying alive, and you have just told us that Yossarian needs something bigger to attach his spirit to. So you see, there are more clauses in Catch-22 than even you knew about. [235]

John W. Hunt
Comic Escape and
Anti-Vision:

Joseph Heller's "Catch-22"

The initial response to *Catch-22*, when it was first published in 1961, tells us a great deal about the degree to which the [91] notion of the absurd was accepted as an adequate analysis of experience. It may be unfair to hold reviewers for our national weeklies closely to their hastily written words, but it is significant that few of them felt it necessary to hedge. Most of the reactions were extreme, with little middle ground. Because the novel was too complex in technique for the quick look and short appraisal, some, such as Richard G. Stern, found it "an emotional hodgepodge," lacking in design and gasping "for want of craft and sensibility."[1] Stern refused to call the book a novel at all, while Whitney Balliett in *The New Yorker* would not even call it a book.[2] It was also too subtle in theme for the reader who is content only with clear and ultimate solutions. Robert Brustein and a few others saw this, but most, such as the anonymous reviewer of *Daedalus*,[3] could not see beyond the caricatures, the stale jokes, and the *non sequiturs* to the purpose for which they were being used. Many reacted with what can only be called outrage, almost as if the mixture of tragic and comic elements violated some sacred purity of form the presence of which is one of our most cherished guarantees that art will not bring us too close to life. In a sense Heller got from these readers the response he was looking for: the realization, as their laughter subsided, that what they were laughing at was their own absurd world.

The story itself has a classically comic structure. The focus is upon John Yossarian, a bombardier stationed on the fictitious Mediterranean island of Pianosa during the Second World War. Yossarian opposes his society

---

[1] *The New York Times Book Review*, October 22, 1961, p. 50.

[2] December 9, 1961, p. 248.

[3] Winter, 1963, pp. 155–65. [For the Brustein review, see pp. 6–11 of this book; for the *Daedalus* review, see pp. 27–39.—Eds.]

SOURCE: Nathan A. Scott, Jr., ed., *Adversity and Grace: Studies in Recent American Literature* (Chicago: University of Chicago Press, 1968), pp. 91–98. Copyright © 1968 by The University of Chicago and reprinted by permission.

and seeks ways of escape. The novel's action arises from his various attempts to overcome the obstacles standing between him and the kind of new world he would like to live in. Obstacles are everywhere; everyone and everything is out to murder him. "The enemy," he says, "is anybody who's going to get you killed, no matter *which* side he's on." [4] Besides the Germans who [92] shoot at him, and his colonel who keeps increasing the number of missions the men must fly, there are other enemies; the whole universe, in fact, is designed for murder, down to the very cells of one's own body, each one of which is "a potential traitor and foe" (p. 177), because it can contract a fatal disease. The novel's denouement comes with Yossarian's decision to answer his dilemma rather than solve it, to withdraw from his society, that is, rather than to try to live within it. His decision is possible because of a turn in the plot in which he discovers that his tentmate Orr—representative to him of the simple-minded good people of this world—has successfully escaped to Sweden. The character of reality in Sweden is left vague; we know it only as a place without war and more desirable than Pianosa. We are told that the war is almost over, so that Yossarian's decision to desert becomes, in context, a refusal to participate in a society which he can no longer help and which, if he stays, will only kill him. When he learns of Orr's escape, his decision to make a separate peace is confirmed, and, taking Nately's whore's kid sister with him, he bids his own farewell to arms with hope in his heart.

Within this comic framework, the story could be told in many ways. Heller has chosen to write what Henry James called a "novel of saturation," and to include at face value elements of fantasy in both description and incident which appear initially not only to undercut the narrator's reliability but also to make the whole performance lacking in seriousness. All the tricks in the comedian's bag are used, especially unincremental repetition and immediate reversal. In the early chapters characters are only glimpsed, the world is wide and busy and complex, and scenes shift quickly before the reader's feelings become committed or his beliefs threatened. As the narrative wears on, however, a number of sober matters are being attended to within the comic framework. The first two-thirds of the story provides no clear present tense, but toward the end one becomes aware that the novel's clocks [93] have been the number of missions the men are forced to fly and the deaths of Yossarian's friends. As the missions are performed and as the men die, so the novel moves.

Carefully timed disclosures of the motivations accounting for crucial incidents and the slow release of information as the chronology of the

---

[4] Joseph Heller, *Catch-22* (New York: Dell, 1962), p. 127. Subsequent references in *Catch-22* appear in parentheses following the quotation.

novel's incidents comes into focus make it apparent that a deeply bitter vision is in control, a rational vision outraged at the world's lack of rationality. "Where are the Snowdens of yesteryear?" (p. 35), for example, a question initially funny simply as a pun since we know nothing of Snowden, becomes, with later knowledge, horrible. Yossarian's whole attitude toward the war and society, we learn near the end of the book, had come to him as he helplessly watched his dying comrade Snowden while on the mission to Avignon. "Man was matter. . . . The spirit gone, man is garbage. That was Snowden's secret. Ripeness was all" (p. 450). In such a world values are inverted, and to set them right Yossarian insists that the good guys are the cowards and other men of principle, while the bad guys are the patriots and other opportunists. One by one Yossarian's friends meet death—by accident, or disease, or suicide, if not in battle. "They've got all my pals" (p. 445), he discovers as the war nears its end. Some, like Clevinger, disappear quite accountably, while others, like Dunbar, disappear because of mysterious forces; Doc Daneeka, still quite alive, is declared officially dead, while Mudd, killed on his first mission before checking into the squadron, is not acknowledged ever to have existed at all. Thus when the denouement comes, the inversion of values, the confusion of perceptions, the triumph of chaos and brutality make Yossarian's otherwise cowardly flight an admirable withdrawal, a deliberate choice not simply to survive but to act morally by refusing a world that is immoral. It is flight from the inhumanity of a situation where people are always "cashing in on every decent impulse and every human tragedy" (p. 455). He knows that to desert the squadron he must, in a sense, flee the whole world and that he will "always be alone," "in danger of betrayal" (p. 460), an outrider of the law. But the law, the rule of social order, is [94] exactly what Yossarian is refusing, for the law is the rule of discontinuity, the rule of Catch-22.

The key to the novel's vision is in the title reference to Catch-22, the phrase used for the pandemic paradox of evil. Catch-22 is the catch by which an otherwise coherent and rational world is rendered absurd; it is an elliptical inner logic defeating all perception: "How can he see he's got flies in his eyes if he's got flies in his eyes?" This flippant formulation of the paradox, Yossarian feels, makes "as much sense as anything else" (p. 47), simply because the principle of Catch-22 means that ultimately all sense is frustrated. The contradictions enhancing the rule of stupidity and blindness and cruelty are shown to be operative in the military realm in the authority of expediency by which the commanding officer can set aside all demands of decency and justice. They are operative in the economic realm in the glowing success of Milo Minderbinder's international cartel which can contract for both bombing and defending the same target. The irrationality and brutality of the social order are highlighted when the meaning of Aarfy's boast, "I never paid for it in my life" (pp. 246, 427), becomes clear. M.P.'s burst into the officers' apartment in Rome, arrest Yossarian for not having a pass, and apologize for the intrusion to Aarfy, who has just raped and murdered the maid. And so on. Catch-22 is the principle that anyone has a right to do anything he can get away with doing.

On this premise Heller bases his whole novel. Because absurdity underlies every dramatic incident, the narrative abounds in false syllogisms, *non sequiturs*, paradoxes, and contradictions which Heller fully exploits for their comic possibilities. Subtly the novel builds to a symbolically potent climax. In "The Eternal City," a chapter much in debt to Joyce's "Ulysses in Nighttown," the story's considerable laughter turns to Dantesque groans of agony, as the bizarre, violent scene treated earlier with farce is given the metaphysical weight of an apocalyptic vision from Dostoyevsky or Kafka: "The tops of the sheer buildings slanted in weird, [95] surrealistic perspective, and the street seemed tilted" (p. 421). At the sight of an urchin on the streets of Rome,

. . . Yossarian was moved by such intense pity for his poverty that he wanted to smash his pale, sad, sickly face with his fist and knock him out of existence. . . . He made Yossarian think of cripples and of cold and hungry men and women, and of all the dumb, passive, devout mothers with catatonic eyes nursing infants outdoors that same night with chilled animal udders bared insensibly to that same raw rain. Cows. Almost on cue, a nursing mother padded past holding an infant in black rags. . . . What a lousy earth! He wondered how many people were destitute that same night . . . how many husbands were drunk and wives socked, and how many children were bullied, abused or abandoned. . . . How many suicides would take place that same night, how many people would go insane? How many honest men were liars, brave men cowards, loyal men traitors, how many sainted men were corrupt, how many people in positions of trust had sold their souls. . . . The night was filled with horrors, and he thought he knew how Christ must have felt as he walked through the world, like a psychiatrist through a ward full of nuts, like a victim through a prison full of thieves. What a welcome sight a leper must have been! At the next corner a man was beating a small boy brutally in the midst of an immobile crowd of adult spectators. . . . Mobs with clubs were in control everywhere (pp. 421–26).

So powerful is Yossarian's exposure to undisguised evil that the reader begins to feel as Tappman the chaplain felt when trying to find the human touch in a world governed by Catch-22: "So many monstrous events were occurring that he was no longer positive which events *were* monstrous and which *were* really taking place" (p. 287). Something of this is also felt by

Yossarian, who concludes, with surprising philosophical cogency about the ontological status of evil, that Catch-22 is a legal fiction: [96]

Catch-22 did not exist, he was positive of that, but it made no difference. What did matter was that everyone thought it existed, and that was much worse, for there was no object or text to ridicule or refute, to accuse, criticize, attack, amend, hate, revile, spit at, rip to shreds, trample upon or burn up (p. 418).

In fact, man himself—Mudd, Doc Daneeka, the soldier in white—is almost a legal fiction in this book. Since existential man bears the scars of the threat of non-being, it is appropriate for Heller to use the language of paradox to describe his condition.

Yossarian is no hero, not in the social sense, for he decides for self and against society. In context this is a decision for sanity as opposed to absurdity, for reason as opposed to chaos. Catch-22 defeats rational connections: *he* will make them; it disallows responsibility: *he* will be responsible. His is a decision to survive, because he judges both himself and life to be worth saving: "I've been fighting all along to save my country. Now I'm going to fight a little to save myself. The country's not in danger any more, but I am" (p. 455).

Heller's success in keeping the comic structure while projecting a bitter vision about the whole human enterprise is not a pure one. In order to qualify Yossarian for the comic role he must keep his background vague, leave his character undeveloped, and rest the burden of Yossarian's appeal upon his sense of the future. Ambiguity is also necessary about the new society into which Yossarian is to go, for if Catch-22 is a metaphysical principle of inbuilt chaos, certainly it obtains in Sweden as well as in Pianosa. Consequently there remains some confusion about just who the enemy is, about whether the obstacles which stand in the way of the comic hero are only social or also metaphysical. But of the quality of reality obtaining in this society—Pianosa, *our* world—there is no doubt: it is irrational, disconnected, incongruous; it provides no basis for moral action: it is, withal, absurd.

Elements of fantasy, therefore, are not incongruous. The fantastic becomes the norm. Heller joins here a long tradition [97] of those who have written of the fantastic, but only with his contemporaries—Bellow, Malamud, Styron, Durrell, Beckett, Golding—does he share the distinctively modern way of treating it. In his book we do not feel, as we do in Edgar Allan Poe, for example, even where Poe's narrative seems methodical and dispassionate, that the events before us are really to be looked upon as special, rare, fantastic. Rather, the novel's atmosphere is such that what is taking place is *of course* what we all know to be true of our humdrum experience. It is the non-absurd world which strikes us as special and fantastic. By use of the comic structure, qualified in some of the ways I have indicated, Heller is able to take the surprise out of absurdity. With absurdity established as a premise rather than a conclusion, Heller can probe its moral implications as adroitly as a Camus or a Sartre and yet react with a completely different temperament; he can, with Kafka, employ the surrealistic archetypes of nightmare and yet avoid Kafka's malaise; and he is able to express a concern for the seriousness of evil that is very close to Dostoyevsky's, without ending in the utter philosophical skepticism which is sometimes Dostoyevsky's final position. [98]

Nelvin Vos
The Angel, the Beast, and the Machine

The thin line between pretense and actuality is often the place where laughter is heard. If the clown wears an ugly mask, we laugh uproariously with him about his pretense. If a man is really ugly, we may still laugh, but it is a laugh of bitterness at him. And thus, when a man for a moment forgets that he is a man, and nothing less and nothing more, we respond with laughter, for, by contrast, he is again telling us who we are.

He who pretends to be angelic or god-like is laughable; the pompous, pedantic, and pretentious clergyman who falls on a banana peel is a mere man.

He who pretends to be an animal is also laughable; the man who poses as a grizzly bear or a huge elephant is really only Daddy.

And he who pretends to be a machine is laughable; as Bergson said, "We laugh every time a person gives the impression of being a thing."

The first two options have been exploited for laughter throughout history, but not until the nineteenth century with its impersonalized view of man and society did the conflict of man and machine become a source of [53] dramatic possibility. The tension between freedom and bondage has now become the focus. The protagonist desires to be free from all the caughtness of his existence: from Hardy's Immanent Will, from Kafka's

SOURCE: Nelvin Vos, *For God's Sake Laugh!* (Richmond, Va.: John Knox Press, 1967), pp. 53–58. Copyright © 1967 by M. E. Bratcher. Reprinted by permission of the publisher.

world of desperate castles and grotesque trials, and from Ionesco's and Beckett's deity which is absent yet manipulates the movements of man's destiny. If a man actually becomes mechanically rigid and utterly conforming, he has lost his humanity. Tragedy occurs when Mr. Zero of Rice's *Adding Machine* is condemned to be the machine's slave and when Willy Loman blindly follows the American dream of success. But we laugh at Professor Higgins in *My Fair Lady* because while he is scornfully referring to Eliza as a mere thing, he himself is behaving as a mechanical monster.

At what do we laugh then in the mid-twentieth century? We respond to the improbable Dr. Strangelove, to the macabre feats of James Bond, to the grotesque fantasies of Kopit's *Oh Dad, Poor Dad, Mamma's hung you in the closet and I'm feelin' so sad,* and to the bitter buffoonery in Albee's *Sandbox.* In each of these literary visions, man is threatened with becoming an object, and his attempts to escape make us laugh. Our discovery of this insight provokes us to laugh, but the laughter is frequently a nervous giggle, or self-conscious twitter, and sometimes the laughter dies in our throats. For what we are laughing at is not light and frivolous, but dire and distressing, such as death and the bomb. Thus the predominant laughter we are hearing among ourselves can only be called black laughter.

Eugéne Ionesco's description of *l'humour noir* (to "link pleasantry with the atrocious, buffoonery with [54] distress, and gravity with derision") catches a grab bag of such contemporary novelists as Pynchon, Donleavy, Nabokov, Barth, Southern, Purdy, and Friedman. They generally share the same targets. The best of them hold some things too sacred to be smeared with hypocrisy. So they mock, and delight in salting the sores of every hypersensitive subject of contemporary mores and morals: sex, religion, death, Mom, war, and the bomb. And no book has caught more forcefully the contemporary imagination that sees the preposterous as the normal than Joseph Heller's *Catch-22.*

The opening pages of the World War II novel set the tone. In his hospital bed, Yossarian, the bombardier, is surrounded by "three brisk and serious men with efficient mouths and inefficient eyes":

"Still no movement?" the full colonel demanded.
The doctors exchanged a look when he shook his head.
"Give him another pill."

Both the seeming gravity of the malady and its remedy prepare us for a world which can perhaps be made most vivid by presenting a montage of this comic *danse macabre:*

"Everybody is crazy but us" (p. 14).

Men went mad and were rewarded with medals (p. 16).

"We're all in this business of illusion together" (p. 188).

Some men are born mediocre, some men achieve mediocrity, and some men have mediocrity thrust upon them. With Major Major it had been all three (p. 85).

Major Major is thus similar to all of the other [55] characters whose names give titles to the chapters of the book; each of them represents the notion of a war hero turned completely upside down. The bombing pilots have fears, the officers accept bribes, the Chaplain doubts God, and ingenious Milo, a caricature of the successful American businessman, does business both with the Allies and with their enemies. All have only one aim: to survive, to persevere, to resist being made into a thing, a number.

But the only law of probability which governed the lives of all, whether soldiers or prostitutes, was Catch-22, an ordinance which was always able to catch all the contradictory possibilities of any victim:

There was only one catch and that was Catch-22, which specified that a concern for one's own safety in the face of dangers that were real and immediate was the process of a rational mind. Orr was crazy and could be grounded. All he had to do was ask; and as soon as he did, he would no longer be crazy and would have to fly more missions. Orr would be crazy to fly more missions and sane if he didn't, but if he was sane he had to fly them. If he flew them he was crazy and didn't have to; but if he didn't want to he was sane and had to (p. 47).

It was Catch-22 which permitted the destruction of the house of the prostitutes, and it was Catch-22 itself which indicated that the destroyers need not show the prostitutes the law. Yossarian finally insists that

Catch-22 did not exist, he was positive of that, but it made no difference. What did matter was that everyone thought it existed, and that was much worse, for there was no object or text to ridicule or refute, to accuse, [56] criticize, attack, amend, hate, revile, spit at, rip to shreds, trample upon or burn up (p. 418).

Thus the very caprice of Catch-22 puts all of the characters in its bondage, and becomes at the same time a powerful symbol of Yossarian's real enemy, nothing less than the whole, mad, mucked-up system. Nothing, and therefore everything, makes coherent logical sense. The bombardier's response is to laugh at this world so highly organized and institutionalized that it manifests itself only in anarchy and chaos. And we are laughing with him at the incommensurate absurdities as he, at the end of the novel (like Huck Finn and all other comic heroes), "takes off" into the unknown. He is free at last. Ambivalently happy endings are conceded to Huck and to Yossarian because they would learn nothing from tragic ones. They have at least escaped being made into things.

Heller is thus one of "those clowns of conscience," as Bruce Jay Friedman calls them, who turn somersaults, stand the world on its head, and perform intricate antics in order to arouse the surprise-proof public. The line is thin, say the purveyors of black laughter, between fantasy and reality—a world in which a conflict of a half-million men is not called a war, in which the federal government swings into action about a murder of a woman because her "civil rights have been violated," and in which our lives are lived underneath the mushroom cloud. Such a clown of black laughter wishes to jolt, to shock, to rupture our consciences, to expose the complacency by ridicule and mockery. His approach is often critical, for he, like many modern men, is distinguished by self-consciousness. He is both conscious and afraid—[57] afraid that he will be, or appear to be, less than conscious. The conscious man laughs primarily as a critic; his laugh, as Leonard Pronko suggests, is "the laugh of awareness." And the artist succeeds in alerting his audience to awareness by jarring their certainties, distracting them, muddling them, so that time and time again they must review their own reactions to the incongruities they are beholding. [58]

Josh Greenfeld
22 Was Funnier than 14

At a Wednesday briefing a few months ago—one of those "deep background" sessions —a brigadier general said with a smile:

"Well I'm happy to say that the Army's casualties finally caught up with the Marines last week."

There was a gasp. A civilian United States mission officer, sitting next to the general, turned and said incredulously: "You don't mean you're *happy*."

The general was adamant. "Well the Army should be doing their job too," he said.

Jim Pringle, the bureau chief of Reuters, turned to me and whispered: "My God, this is straight out of *Catch-22*."

BERNARD WEINRAUB, from a story describing a *Times* reporter's life in Vietnam

SOURCE: *The New York Times Book Review*, March 3, 1968, pp. 1, 49–51, 53. Copyright © 1968 by The New York Times Company. Reprinted by permission of the publisher.

Some novels appear ahead of their time, others come out at just the right time, but only a very few seem to belong to any, or all, time. It would appear from the prevalence of such stories as the above that Catch-22, by Joseph Heller, is making a strong bid to transcend its own time. A recent revisit to the heady island of Pianosa has impressed on me, as I admit I suspected it might, how much more germane—and more darkly hilarious—the novel seems today than it did when it was published in October, 1961. Yet I was also struck by the extent to which either it or I have aged.

In case you've forgotten, or never knew, Catch-22 is the story of Yossarian, the Assyrian World War II bombardier with the Armenian name, a Jewish Talmudic mind, an all-American heart, and the irresolution of the most famous Dane. Yossarian "has decided to live forever or die in the attempt and his only mission each time he went up was to come down alive."

Yossarian always views the war with himself at the center of the big picture in a zoom-lens close-up. But though he desperately wants out, he always comes up against the unremitting logical non-reason of military bureaucracy: anyone who is crazy must be grounded; anyone who is willing to fly combat missions must be crazy; ergo, anyone who flies should be grounded. But, in order to be grounded it is required that one request grounding; no one crazy enough to fly missions would ask; and if one should, "there's a catch . . . Catch-22. Anyone who wants to get out of combat duty isn't really crazy." Ergo, no exit, except by way of the casualty lists.

There seems no denying that though Heller's macabre farce was written about a rarefied part of the raging war of the forties during the silent fifties, it has all but become the chapbook of the sixties. Over two-million copies of Catch-22 have been sold in its Dell paperback edition, approximately another half-million copies are in print, and the release of the motion-picture version scheduled for next year will mean, according to paperback-publishing formula, the sale of another three-quarters of a million to a million copies. The hard-cover edition published by Simon & Schuster sold over 35,000 copies originally and continues to sell at the rate of one to two thousand copies a year. Add on the substantial sales figures of the book's prestigious Modern Library and high-priced Delta paperback editions and it can be estimated that before too long Catch-22 will have sold some three-and-a-half million copies—not bad for a first (and so far the author's only) novel that started rather slowly, with spasmodic sales and mixed reviews.

Since the history of Catch-22, like all success stories, is a unique one; and since it also launched not one but three notable publishing careers—an author's, an agent's and an editor's—it is perhaps worth delving into before considering the book itself.

In 1953, when Heller began writing the novel, he was a 30-year-old curly-haired post-bar mitzvah Puck from the Coney Island section of Brooklyn who had been a navigator in the Air Force during the war. He had sold some short stories to the *Atlantic, Esquire* and *Cosmopolitan* in the late forties and then stopped writing and had gone off to teach college English from 1950 to 1952. In 1955, his agent, Candida Donadio, an Italian lady from Brooklyn who looks a little like a Late-Show Kay Francis, placed a chapter in *New World Writing* as one of her first acts of agentry. Two years after that, in the summer of 1957, Robert Gottlieb, a Woody-Allenish, 26-year-old editorial hand at Simon & Schuster who up to then had been entrusted with the guidance of but one book, read 75 pages of the manuscript, entitled *Catch-18*, and reported to his superiors: "This is a wonderful, funny, thoughtful book about life in the army." In February of 1958 he saw more and enthusiastically signed it up.

As *Catch-18* the "crazy book" was completed and scheduled for publication in the fall of 1961, but it ran into another catch—actually another 18. Leon Uris's *Mila 18* was announced by a rival publisher; to avoid a confusion of titles somebody had to give. And since Uris was a somebody and Heller a nobody, the somebody who gave was the nobody. So after incubating seven years as *Catch-18* the book was retitled by Heller *Catch-14*. Gottlieb, however, found himself restless and unhappy with the title; after much mulling, head-scratching and chin-rubbing he made what he regards to this day as his major editorial contribution [1] to the work: "I suggested the title be changed to *Catch-22*. I thought 22 was a funnier number than 14." In the spring of 1961 Gottlieb happily announced in a note to his impatient author: "*Catch-22*, once '18' but a prey to inflation is now going to press."

For Gottlieb, who now says that "*Catch-22* was a once-in-a-lifetime experience," it earned him the reputation as "the man who edited *Catch-22*," which did not hinder his subsequent progress up the ladder at S & S, from where he was recently plucked to fill the position of editor-in-chief at the prestigious publishing house of Alfred A. Knopf. Along the way he has been responsible for overseeing Bruce J. Friedman's *Stern*, Wallace Markfield's *To an Early Grave*, Robert Crichton's *The Secret of Santa Vittoria*, and Chaim Potok's *The Chosen*, among other successes.

For Candida Donadio, who still rereads the book annually with a "constant sense of newness," *Catch-22* also was a singular experience. "It was what Bob [Gottlieb] and I have come to call a 'loved-one book'—the kind of book that can flop so easily but you love so [49] much that you want to do everything possible to protect it." For her, too, its publication marked the early point in a career that has seen her become one of the more sought-after agents in the business. She now serves as den mother to most American-Jewish novelists (Bellow, Friedman, Malamud, Markfield and Roth) but also handles Mario Puzo and John Cheever just to show she's ecumenical.

The enthusiasm that Gottlieb and Miss Donadio had for *Catch-22*—and its author (Gottlieb: "Joe is shy, brusque, loyal and brilliant.")—was communicated throughout Simon & Schuster. The firm's advertising manager, Nina Bourne (who will accompany Gottlieb to Knopf) helped develop a hard promotional sell for the book that is to this day considered a classic campaign by students of both publishing and advertising.

First they garnered pre-publication quotes galore to arm themselves against the possible slings of reviewers. Then, after pub date—and the appearance of a decidedly mixed batch of reviews (this Review ran a piece that dismissed the novel "for want of craft and sensibility")—they began, and continued for over a year, to run lively ads containing enthusiastic quotes, progress reports to past and future readers, and even a happy birthday notice. Slowly, by word of mouth and print of ad, the book began to move. Though it never reached the best-seller lists, by the time the paperback edition appeared, in the fall of 1962, it had sold 35,000 copies, a figure which would be the envy of almost any novelist, let alone a first one. By the fall of 1962, *Catch-22* had completely caught on: nearly a million copies were sold within the first few months of its appearance in paper.

After that, according to Heller, whose silver-lined hair now makes him look like a pre-Clairol Jewish Duke Snider, and who affects the well-tailored conservative suiting of a customer's man, "Sales leveled off. Until two years ago. Suddenly paperback sales shot up again." This sudden surge may mark the book's emergence from transient popularity to the position of a popular classic, if a classic can be defined as a book written in one age that speaks to another. Heller thinks so. Actually, he attributes the acceleration to three reasons, which he checks off on his fingers as efficiently as a broker explaining the potentialities of a growth stock:

"First, it's a great book. I've come to accept the verdict of the majority.

"Second, a whole new generation [50] of readers is being introduced to it, the generation that was 11 or 12 when it first came out.

"Third, and most important: Vietnam. Because that was the war I had in mind; a war fought without military provocation, a war in which the real enemy is no longer the other side but someone allegedly on your side. The ridiculous war I felt lurking in the future when I wrote the book. So *Catch-22* certainly has more meaning in regard to Vietnam than World War II."

Heller is unquestionably right that the world of Pianosa is closer to Da Nang than Sardinia, but I don't think the novel is as contemporary as it seems. Rereading *Catch-22* it struck me that its origins and ambience lie in between the forties and the sixties—in the decade when Heller conceived and wrote it. For if the fifties can be characterized as the age of acquiescence, when whispered demurral amounted to near-heroic protest in the face of Senator McCarthy's assault on the left (strange to recall that Joseph Welch and Edward R. Murrow were our heroes), then *Catch-22* belongs more to that decade than to the present one, when active protest has reemerged in such relatively extreme forms as draft resistance and military desertion.

For while the theme of *Catch-22* is a variation of what Norman Mailer has called "exquisite totalitarianism" as it applies to the military, its implementation—though it is at once as intricately complicated and precise as a medieval tapestry, as slapstick as a Keystone Kops chase, as fast-moving as a cinema verité film—remains curiously static. The characters are almost all caricatures, in an arrested state, at least up to the point of death, when they seem to dress for the occasion by assuming flesh. And Yossarian himself—the novel's central character and spine—though he appears to be Heller's attempt to create a cosmopolitan "everyman," is really more like a plain nobody. For he essentially lacks bedrock character—hard and individual substance; actions rub against his character rather than his character being the hard cutting edge that delineates actions.

In fact, by identifying with Yossarian the would-be rebel can remain the would-be rebel. Caught up in motion—and emotion—as he glides along the establishment tracks, he can avoid coming to grips with the implications of the movements and actions of the real rebel who has character enough to make his own tracks. With Yossarian's obedience, his commitment [51] to and unwillingness to confront the organization that is out to destroy him (for instance, he cannot lend his sanction to a buddy's proposal to assassinate the C.O.), his personal and nonideological opposition to war, he best represents a case-study example of the kind of liberal mentality—or sentimentality—that must proceed to great neurotic lengths of mental gymnastics before being able to step off the curb and take one self-committing baby step into the street.

That is why, I think, the ending of *Catch-22*—when Yossarian finally decides to desert—seems flat and unconvincing. It is the result of a repetition of process rather than an expression of character, giving the reader, at least in retrospect, the disappointing sensation of having observed a great deal of warm-up exercise just to witness the lifting of a five-pound barbell.

That Yossarian learns the hard way what a more substantial character might have started out knowing was, I should in fairness point out, a great argument for the book when it came out, and it can be used as even a greater argument today. It is, in fact, Heller's argument. But I still cannot help believing that to structure an anti-war novel upon a base implicitly requiring one to view war as a learning process or a game is a mistake, for it is to fall into the trap that leads to the glamorization of war itself. The tendency to do so was a hangover from World War II that many of us suffered in the fifties (a hangover which helped to put one of the war's heroes in the White House), but there are hopeful signs that it is passé in the sixties. What diverts the reader of *Catch-22* from the conclusion that it is really a fifties cop-out is, of course, Heller's marvelous technical ability to create suspense by playfully promising significant jigsaw pieces to complete puzzles that—like Yossarian's character—do not really exist. And while Heller's blackly humorous ability may also be a fossil of the forlorn fifties—when cool humor in the face of despair was the style—it is still astonishingly effective, possibly the best example of its kind. I mean that I found the antic humor of *Catch-22* still robustly fresh, still side-splittingly funny. I know of no book written in the last twenty years that continues to make me laugh out loud so much. So if I must conclude that it is not a great book —whatever that means—and not as bold, far-out and venturesome as it pretends to be, I still think it is a major work. [53]

Jean Kennard
Joseph Heller: At War with Absurdity

Catch-22 is much more than an anti-war novel. Heller's vision of the horrifying absurdity of service life in World War II is, as the constant references in the novel to its wider implications indicate, merely an illustration of the absurdity of the human condition itself. *Catch-22* reflects a view of the world which is basically that of Jean Paul Sartre and the early Albert Camus. The world has no meaning but is simply there; man is a creature who seeks meaning. The relationship between man and his world is therefore absurd; human action having no intrinsic value is ultimately futile; human beings have no innate characteristics. Reason and language, man's tools for discovering the meaning of his existence and describing his world, are useless. When a man discovers these facts about his condition he has an experience of the absurd, an experience which Sartre calls "nausea." But there are innumerable contemporary novels which are fundamentally Existentialist. What is interesting about *Catch-22* is that the experimental

SOURCE: *Mosaic*, Vol. 4, No. 3 (Spring 1971), pp. 75–87. Reprinted by permission of the Editors of *Mosaic*, a Journal for the Comparative Study of Literature.

techniques Heller [75] employs have a direct relation to Existentialist ideas; they are an attempt to "dramatize" his view of the human condition rather than merely describe it.

The treatment of the soldier with convulsions which Yossarian witnesses in Rome is a heightened example of many futile actions which take place throughout the novel. A group of observers lifts the soldier from the street to the hood of a car and then, because they can think of nothing else to do, back onto the street again. The pointless repetition is characteristic of almost everyone's work in the service. Major Major, for example, is involved in signing a useless proliferation of documents. Ex-P.F.C. Wintergreen digs holes in Colorado and recognizes that this is not a bad assignment in wartime. "Since holes were in no great demand, he could dig them and fill them up at a leisurely pace, and he was seldom overworked." [1] It is, as he points out, "a matter of duty . . . and we each have our own to perform. My duty is to keep digging these holes" (p. 108).

But for whom or what is one to perform this duty? The question of authority is central to the novel. God certainly no longer runs the organization, though He lingers on in certain distorted images some characters still have of Him. Colonel Cathcart wishes to use Him when it is convenient, when prayers before missions, for example, might help him get his name into *The Saturday Evening Post*, a project which he only gives up when he discovers that the enlisted men do not have a God and a chaplain of their own and would have to be included in the prayers. Mrs. Scheisskopf is too modern a woman to believe in God, but is distraught when Yossarian suggests that God might be evil and malicious. The God she does not believe in "is a good God, a just God, a merciful God" (p. 185). To Yossarian "He's playing. Or else He's forgotten all about us" (p. 184). Even the chaplain is beginning to lose faith in the "wisdom and justice of an immortal, omnipotent, omniscient, humane, universal, anthropomorphic, English-speaking, Anglo-Saxon, pro-American God" (p. 293). As Dunbar repeats from time to time throughout the novel, "God is dead" (pp. 129 and 130).

Duty is now owed to such vague abstractions as patriotism and free enterprise, which have become exactly the tyrannous absolute values that Camus talks of in *L'Homme révolté*. The old man in the brothel in Rome exposes patriotism as illogical: "Surely so many countries can't all be worth dying for" (p. 253). Capitalism and free enterprise lead Milo to bomb his own unit and he excuses his action with the old slogan that what is good for money-making interests is good for the country. "Incentive" and "pri-

---

[1] Joseph Heller, *Catch-22* (New York: Dell, 1962), p. 108. All subsequent page references are to this edition.

vate industry" are "goods" and their evil results cannot change anyone's attitude towards them.

Such assertive values as patriotism, then, are merely words, words which have become divorced from meaning. Heller's awareness of the separation of word and idea, which Sartre talks of, is apparent in several places in the novel. General Peckem who "laid great, fastidious stress on small matters of taste and style" (p. 328), has lost all sense of what words *mean* and writes his directives in a manner which combines impeccable grammar and trite adjectives. Language no longer communicates but serves to confuse things [76] further. When Yossarian makes a game of censoring letters, declaring one day "death to all modifiers," the next declaring a "war on articles" and finally blacking out everything except "a," "an," and "the," he finds that it creates "more dramatic interlinear tensions . . . and in just about every case . . . a message far more universal" (p. 8). Unable to obtain any sensible answer to his questions from the corporal in charge of the education session, Yossarian declares himself "ready to pursue him through all the words in the world to wring the knowledge from him" (p. 36).

In the world of the novel the authoritative values which determine the rules of behavior are man-made. But it would be false to suggest that they are the creation of any specific men, for example, of superior officers trying to trap underlings, as Yossarian so often imagines in the early part of the novel. " 'Maybe they should give him three votes,' said Yossarian. 'Who's they?' Dunbar demanded suspiciously" (p. 15). It is this indefinable "they" who organize this world, and everyone is trapped in the organization, everyone is caught by Catch-22. Catch-22 is, of course, Heller's illustration of the irrational nature of the world. Any attempt to argue logically and reasonably ends in a paradox; one reaches that point where thought reaches its confines, which Camus talks of. The most frequent example of Catch-22 is the argument over the relation between being "crazy" and flying more missions. Yossarian asks whether Orr can be grounded if he is "crazy" and the doctor replies:

"He has to be crazy to keep flying combat missions after all the close calls he's had. Sure, I can ground Orr. But first he has to ask me to."

"That's all he has to do to be grounded?"

"That's all. Let him ask me."

"And then you can ground him?" Yossarian asked.

"No. Then I can't ground him."

"You mean there's a catch?"

"Sure there's a catch," Doc Daneeka replied. "Catch-22. Anyone who wants to get out of combat duty isn't really crazy."

. . . Yossarian saw it clearly in all its spinning reasonableness. There was an elliptical precision about its perfect pairs of parts that was graceful and shocking, like good modern art (pp. 46–47).

Further examples of Catch-22 occur over the rules for asking questions in the education session and during Yossarian's visit to ex-P.F.C. Wintergreen.

Catch-22 is composed of rules which apparently operate to make it impossible for a man to find a reasonable escape from them. They do not exactly contradict each other, but are continually inadequate to the occasion and always disregard the individual human life. They are intended to impose order upon chaos, but life so exceeds these rules that they only serve in the end to create more chaos. One of the clearest examples of this is the firemen who leave the blaze they are attempting to control at the hospital in order to obey the rule that they must always be on the field when the planes land. Another is the case of Doc Daneeka who is declared dead and treated as such, because his name was on the flight log of a plane that crashed, although he was never in the plane and is, as everyone knows, still alive.

Since the rules do not work, anything may happen. There is no reasonable justice. Yossarian, on leave in Rome without a pass, discovers that Aarfy [77] has raped and murdered a servant girl. Yossarian expects the police to come and arrest Aarfy and in time they do arrive, only to apologize to Aarfy for interrupting him and to arrest Yossarian for being in Rome without a pass.

In a world where philosophical ideas, traditional morality and reason itself are apparently useless, all man has to hold on to is his own physical body. The value which Heller supports throughout the novel is that of human existence, the individual human life. "Clevinger was dead. That was the basic flaw in his philosophy" (p. 107), and the secret which Snowden reveals to Yossarian is that "man is matter" (p. 450). Dunbar, questioned about his habit of cultivating boredom to increase his life span by making time pass more slowly, replies that, even if such a life is not very enjoyable, "what else is there?" (p. 40). There is no talk of love or even of close friendship in the book; the pleasures of life are purely physical—food, liquor, sex—just as the only real horror is physical pain and ultimately death. "In an absurd universe," writes Frederick Karl, "the individual has the right to seek survival . . . one's own substance is infinitely more precious than any cause." [2]

The view of the world in *Catch-22*, then, is the same view as that pre-

---

[2] Frederick R. Karl, "Joseph Heller's *Catch-22*: Only Fools Walk in Darkness," *Contemporary American Novelists*, p. 136 [and pp. 159–165 in this volume].

sented by Sartre and Camus, and the aware individual in this world comes to very much the same realizations about it as do Roquentin and Mathieu in Sartre's novels. He realizes that there is no ultimate reason for doing one thing rather than another: Captain Flume is told by Chief White Halfoat that one night he is going to slit his throat. He "turned to ice; his eyes flung open wide, staring directly up into Chief White Halfoat's, glinting drunkenly only inches away. 'Why?' Captain Flume managed to croak finally. 'Why not?' was Chief White Halfoat's answer" (p. 58).

The aware individual realizes, too, that there is "no way of really knowing anything" (p. 274). The chaplain sees or thinks he sees a naked man in a tree and finds it impossible to decide whether he actually saw him or whether it was an hallucination. Colonel Cathcart becomes involved in the same complex maze of possible interpretations when he attempts to evaluate other people's attitudes to him, and at the end of the novel we learn that there are always two widely divergent official reports for every event that takes place.

When everything is questionable, it is a small step to questioning one's own identity and Heller gives several illustrations of the effect of this problem on his characters. Yossarian proves with admirable logic that the second soldier in white is the first one, because all his identifiable characteristics, bandages and tubes, are the same. The colonels in the brothel in Rome find they have no identity without their uniforms: " 'We'll never be able to convince anyone we're superior without our uniforms' " (p. 364). When he enters kindergarten, Major Major discovers he is not Caleb Major, "as he had always been led to believe, but instead was some total stranger named Major Major Major about whom he knew absolutely nothing and about whom nobody else had ever heard before" (p. 87). Names, uniforms, marks of identification are all a man has in Heller's world to assure him of his own identity.

Yossarian and the chaplain, probably the two most aware characters in [78] the novel, both have experiences of the absurd very similar to those of Roquentin in Sartre's La Nausée. The chaplain experiences "terrifying, sudden moments when objects, concepts and even people that the chaplain had lived with all his life inexplicably took on an unfamiliar and irregular aspect that he had never seen before and made them seem totally strange" (pp. 209–210). Yossarian's experiences also have the effect of alienating him from his environment, but are less concerned with the strangeness of objects than with their profusion and gratuitousness. The first takes place when he is walking in the woods:

Along the ground suddenly, on both sides of the path, he saw dozens of new mushrooms the rain had spawned poking their nodular fingers up through the clammy earth like lifeless stalks of flesh, sprouting in such necrotic profusion everywhere he looked that they seemed to be proliferating right before his eyes. There were thousands of them swarming as far back into the underbrush as he could see, and they appeared to swell in size and multiply in number as he spied them (p. 147).

In spite of all the aspects of this passage which link it to the specific situation of Catch-22—the suggestion of Yossarian's numerous dead friends, for example, and the rapid increase in their numbers—it would not be out of place in La Nausée. Yossarian's second experience of the absurd is caused by a burst of flak hitting his plane:

Wind whistling up through the jagged gash in the floor kept the myriad bits of paper circulating like alabaster particles in a paperweight and contributed to a sensation of lacquered, waterlogged unreality. Everything seemed strange, so tawdry and grotesque (p. 154).

Heller, like Sartre and Camus, is not however totally pessimistic. Valid action is possible for the individual; there is even the suggestion of a sane universe which Sweden may represent. The hope of Sweden is perhaps a false note in the novel, but it is important to remember that it is only a possibility, a state of mind rather than a real place. Although Orr has, at least reportedly, reached Sweden, ironically by pretending to be "crazy," Yossarian at the end of the novel does not really expect to get further than Rome.

In a discussion of the techniques which Heller has employed to convey his view of the world it would be easy to ignore the obvious. Catch-22 is a very funny book. It would be easy to ignore this because, in spite of the laughter it evokes, the overall impression is as much of horror as of humor. The laughter evoked is not of the kind that unites us warmly in sympathy with the human race as we enjoy its foibles, but rather that which serves to alienate us by exposing the bitter ironies of existence. Nevertheless I believe that humor is a way of understanding the techniques of the novel. Laughter, as Bergson suggests, is caused by incongruity, by a frustrating of our expectations of a certain result, and it is a failure to fulfill certain of the reader's expectations which is the link underlying the so-called absurd techniques of the novel.

What is the basis of these expectations? When we discover that Milo has become mayor or civic leader of almost every town in Europe and North [79] Africa, we are amused because that is impossible. We do not expect that to happen to anyone in life. It is not life-like, not realistic. But when the reader is confronted with the juxtaposition in one sentence of references to several unrelated events about which he so far knows nothing, we cannot say that it is not like life. Actually it is; we often overhear conversations which are meaningless to us because we do not understand to whom or to what they refer. Yet we are surprised to find it in a novel. In this instance, obviously, it is our expectations about the nature of the novel, not about life, which are not being fulfilled. This is, I think, the key to defining the absurd techniques. In some way each of them plays against and frustrates the reader's expectations of a novel, the illusions, one could say, that he has about the nature of the novel.

In an essay called "Sur quelques notions perimées" Robbe-Grillet has pointed out the extent to which the modern reader's view of the novel is still based upon a definition of the realistic nineteenth-century novel in spite of experiments in form by writers like Joyce and Kafka. He feels that this view is perpetuated by critical terminology; that we are so accustomed to discussions of "character," "atmosphere," "form" and "narrative ability," that we fail to recognize that it represents an idea about the novel and not the "nature" of the novel.[3] He believes that a novel is for most readers a story and that the judgment made on the book will consist chiefly of an appreciation of its plot, its gradual development, its equilibrium.[4] It is obvious that the narrative technique of *Catch-22* does not fulfill the expectation of the reader for a continuous line of action in which one episode is related to the next, at the very least chronologically, and in which events are life-size and probable. Situations which are initially familiar enough to the reader may be gradually exaggerated to the point of absurdity. Oil was always discovered wherever Chief White Halfoat's family pitched their tents, Halfoat explains, and the oil companies began sending out representatives to follow the family. Suddenly the whole action becomes incredible:

"Soon whole drilling crews were following us around with all their equipment just to get the jump on each other. Companies began to merge just so that they could cut down on the number of people they had to assign to us. But the crowd in back of us kept growing. We never got a good night's sleep. When we stopped, they stopped. When we moved, they moved. . . . They began to follow us around from in front. They would try to guess where we were going to stop next and would begin drilling before we even got there, so we couldn't even stop. As soon as we'd begin to unroll our blankets, they would kick us off" (p. 45).

Captain Black's "Glorious Loyalty Oath Crusade" gets out of hand in a similar way when he makes everyone sign "two loyalty oaths, then three, then four" and introduces "the pledge of allegiance and after that 'The

---

[3] Alain Robbe-Grillet, *For a New Novel*, trans. Richard Howard (New York: 1965), p. 25.
[4] *Ibid.*, p. 31.

Star-Spangled Banner,' one chorus, two choruses, three choruses, four choruses" (p. 117), as do Dobbs' plans to murder Colonel Cathcart which end in his planning to [80] murder almost everyone. Many of the descriptions of exaggerated action concern Milo, whose activities become increasingly complex as the novel progresses.

The futility of all human action is suggested by Heller in the number of times events or conversations are repeated so that the reader, like Yossarian, eventually has the feeling that he has "been through this exact conversation before" (p. 455). The dialogue which concludes with the realization that "crazy" men can be grounded, but only "crazy" men will fly occurs numerous times, as does the pattern of Yossarian's conversations with the chaplain in which comments are punctuated continually by the phrases " 'that's bad' " or " 'that's good' " (p. 12). Colonel Cathcart's comment to Major Major when he tells him that he is the new squadron commander is similarly repeated. There are two trial scenes in the novel, one concerning Clevinger and the other the chaplain, and each follows the same pattern and comes to the same conclusion: "Clevinger was guilty, of course, or he would not have been accused, and since the only way to prove it was to find him guilty, it was their patriotic duty to do so" (p. 82).

The same sense of the futility of human endeavor is conveyed by circular actions like the episode of Hungry Joe and Huple's cat. Hungry Joe dreams that Huple's cat is sleeping on his face, suffocating him, and when he wakes up Huple's cat is sleeping on his face. Yossarian organizes a fight between Joe and the cat, but the cat flees and Joe is declared the winner, goes to bed victorious and dreams that Huple's cat is sleeping on his face, suffocating him.

The narrative technique serves to confuse the reader about time and to destroy any certainty he may have about what has taken place, thus creating in him the same doubts about reality that Yossarian experiences and that Sartre and Camus speak of. Heller employs three basic methods of disrupting the expected chronological flow of the action. The first is a simple one. He often makes a statement about an event which has taken place and deliberately omits the clarification which the statement requires. Therefore many of the major events in the novel are referred to two or three times, sometimes in increasing detail, before the full account is given. There are two references to Milo's bombing his own squadron before we are given the details; two to his ability to buy eggs at seven cents and sell them at a profit at five cents. The first reference to Snowden comes in the question Yossarian asks in the education session and we learn simply that he was killed over Avignon. Half of the scene in which Snowden dies is described some twenty pages later, and it is almost two hundred pages before that scene is picked up again and continued until Yossarian sees Snowden. In the next reference we learn that Yossarian treated Snowden for the wrong wound and then finally, almost at the end of the novel, we are given the whole account. Occasionally the initial statement may be about an apparently impossible event, like the casual reference to the "dead man in Yossarian's tent" who "was simply not easy to live with" (p. 22). It is a hundred pages before we discover that this really refers to the possessions of a man who has been killed in action.

The second device creates confusion in the mind of the reader by presenting him with two apparently contradictory statements about the same event before providing a clarification. For example, Doc Daneeka tells Yossarian that he was drafted just when his business was beginning to show a profit [81] and later says "fortunately just when things were blackest the war broke out" (p. 41). Finally the explanation is given: "Fifty grand a year I was knocking down. . . . And look what happened. Just when I was all set to really start stashing it away, they had to manufacture fascism and start a war horrible enough to affect even me" (p. 52). The war initially improved his business, but being drafted prevented his profiting from it. A similar effect is created by the apparently absurd coincidence of Major Major and Yossarian independently signing Washington Irving's name to official papers, until it is revealed that Major Major obtained the idea by hearing about Yossarian's activities from a C.I.D. man.

The third method is an extension of the second: contradictory accounts are given of an event and no solution is provided. The reader is left uncertain of the truth and in some instances asked to believe the incredible. The C.I.D. man is supposed to have caught a cold from the fighter captain who, we are told, did not have a cold; Milo claims that he did not direct the anti-aircraft fire upon his own planes, then that he did. Chief White Halfoat's incredible story about his family being moved every time oil is discovered is called a lie by Yossarian, but Halfoat is transferred to Pianosa from Colorado at the first mention of oil.

As well as confusing the reader about the time or exact nature of the events in the novel, Heller also frequently shocks him by adopting attitudes to objects or situations opposite to the expected ones. By introducing these unexpected attitudes in a very casual way, he not only challenges the traditional value system but suggests through his tone that nothing unusual is being said, thus doubling the shock effect. Nately, we are told, "had a bad start. He came from a good family" (p. 13), and "did not hate his mother and father, even though they had been very good to him" (p. 255). Yossarian is sorry to hear that he and the chaplain have a mutual friend, because "it seemed there was a basis to their conversation after all" (p. 12). The Texan is "good-natured, generous and likable. In three days no-one could stand him" (p. 10).

The disparity between tone and subject matter is exploited by Heller most successfully in his treatment of horrific situations, particularly those involving death or human suffering. Lieutenant Scheisskopf, anxious to have his men march in perfect formation in parades, wishes to nail "the twelve men in each rank to a long two-by-four beam of seasoned oak to keep them in line," but:

The plan was not feasible, for making a ninety-degree turn would have been impossible without nickel-alloy swivels inserted in the small of every man's back, and Lieutenant Scheisskopf was not sanguine at all about obtaining that many nickel-alloy swivels from Quartermaster or enlisting the co-operation of the surgeons at the hospital (p. 75).

Heller's methods of characterization, like his narrative techniques and his use of tone, depend upon a frustration of the reader's expectations. Robbe-Grillet claims that the idea that the novelist has to create characters is another obsolete notion. He explains that according to the traditional view a character has to have a proper name, parents, heredity, profession and a personality [82] which permits the reader to judge him, love him or hate him.[5] None of the great contemporary novels, Robbe-Grillet claims, corresponds to the norm of criticism on the question of character. Beckett, he points out, changes his hero's name and shape in the course of the same narrative; K of Kafka's *The Castle* is content with an initial, has no possessions, family or face, and probably is not even a land-surveyor.[6]

There are two possible ways, then, of failing to fulfill a reader's expectations about character in a novel: one is to change the character's identity, provide multiple personalities for the same name, or one name for various figures, and thus disturb the reader's whole conception of identity, as do John Barth and Samuel Beckett; the other is to provide caricatures, figures who are no more than puppets and in whom the reader is not expected to believe. Heller occasionally appears to experiment with the first method, as, for example, in the scene where Yossarian pretends to be a dying officer whose parents fail to recognize him, or where Yossarian and Dunbar discover they can change identities by changing hospital beds. But although in these scenes the characters experience doubts about their identities, the reader is always quite clear about the identity of the character and no real confusion is created.

Most of the characters in *Catch-22* are, however, caricatures, cardboard figures who are distinguished for the reader by their particular obsessions. Each lives with an illusory view of the world which isolates him and makes the results of his actions very different from his expectations. Each is, in his way, the unaware individual who, as Camus illustrates in *Le Mythe de*

---

[5] Robbe-Grillet, p. 32.
[6] *Ibid.*, p. 28.

Sisyphe, believes that he can operate in the world as he imagines it and that his actions will achieve their purpose. So Hungry Joe devotes his life to taking pictures which never come out, Scheisskopf to conducting parades, Major Major to avoiding everyone. General Peckem, continually writing memoranda recommending that his Special Services Division be placed in control over the combat forces, finds that by the time he has succeeded he has been "promoted" to head of combat forces and someone else is now his superior. Colonel Cathcart, anxious for promotion to General, institutes a variety of plans to make himself popular with his superiors, but each of them leaves him less popular than before.

Most of these characters are introduced to us in deceptively explanatory paragraphs which appear to sum up their personalities in a few adjectives, but which really provide the reader with irreconcilably opposite traits. Colonel Cathcart, for example, was a "slick, successful, slipshod, unhappy man of thirty-six who lumbered when he walked and wanted to be a general. He was dashing and dejected, poised and chagrined" (p. 191). Gradually the characters become increasingly absurd as the personality traits of each are seen to be one, an obsession. It is believable that one of Milo's moral principles was that "it was never a sin to charge as much as the traffic could bear" (p. 66), but by the time his activities have taken over Europe and North Africa in one vast syndicate and he has bombed his own men, he has become little more than a personification of greed. Scheisskopf's enjoyment of parades may be initially credible but his childish delight in calling off [83] parades that have never been scheduled is not. These characters may have names, parents, heredity, professions and faces, but we cannot very long sustain the illusion that they are "real" human beings.

The most important device a novelist has to suggest an irrational world is, of course, the treatment of reason itself. Reasoning, in *Catch-22,* invariably ends up in some variation of Catch-22; apparent logic is used to destroy sense. The reader is led into following an argument which progresses logically, but which arrives at an absurd conclusion. Clevinger is on trial for attempting to disrupt Scheisskopf's parade:

"In sixty days you'll be fighting Billy Petrolle," the colonel with the big fat mustache roared. "And you think it's a big fat joke."

"I don't think it's a joke, sir," Clevinger replied.

"Don't interrupt."

"Yes, sir."

"And say, 'sir,' when you do," ordered Major Metcalf.

"Yes, sir."

"Weren't you just ordered not to interrupt?" Major Metcalf inquired coldly.

"But I didn't interrupt, sir," Clevinger protested.

"No. And you didn't say 'sir' either. Add that to the charges against him,"

Major Metcalf directed the corporal who could take shorthand. "Failure to say 'sir' to superior officers when not interrupting them" (p. 77).

A similar conversation takes place between Yossarian and Luciana, who will not marry Yossarian because he is "crazy" and knows he is "crazy" because he wants to marry her.

Individual sentences in the novel may appear to be absurd when they are in fact completely logical: "I didn't know there were any other Captain Yossarians. As far as I know, I'm the only Captain Yossarian I know, but that's only as far as I know" (p. 13). In other instances the structure and tone of sentences suggest meaning where in fact there is none: "He had decided to live for ever or die in the attempt" (p. 30). " 'You're American officers. The officers of no other army in the world can make that statement. Think about it," (p. 28), says Colonel Cargill to his men.

Sentence structure is used throughout *Catch-22* to add to the reader's confusion about characters and events and contributes to the impression of an irrational world. The novel is full of complex sentences in which the individual clauses and phrases are not related to each other or are related at a tangent: "McWatt wore fleecy bedroom slippers with his red pajamas and slept between freshly pressed colored bed-sheets like the one Milo had retrieved half of for him from the grinning thief with the sweet tooth in exchange for none of the pitted dates Milo had borrowed from Yossarian" (p. 61). As the sentence progresses each new clause or phrase does not clarify what has gone before but adds new complications: "Immediately next door to Yossarian was Havermeyer, who liked peanut brittle and lived all by himself in the two man tent in which he shot tiny field mice every night with huge bullets from the .45 he had stolen from the dead man in Yossarian's tent" (p. 18).

A statement is often qualified by a negative clause which gives the appearance [84] of clarifying but, of course, adds nothing. For example, Nately "had gone every free day to work on the officers' club that Yossarian had not helped to build" (p. 18), and "on the other side of Havermeyer stood the tent McWatt no longer shared with Clevinger, who had still not returned when Yossarian came out of the hospital" (p. 18). Heller's favorite stylistic device is the use of double or triple negatives in one sentence. This gives that effect of language constantly trying, but always just failing, to describe or define, which the reader is aware of throughout the novel. "And if that wasn't funny," we are told, "there were lots of things that weren't even funnier" (p. 17). "But Yossarian couldn't be happy, even though the Texan didn't want him to be" (p. 16). And Major Major's father has learned that "the more alfalfa he did not grow, the more money the government gave him, and he spent every penny he didn't earn on new land to increase the amount of alfalfa he did not produce" (p. 85).

Frederick Karl describes Yossarian as "the man who acts in good faith to use Sartre's often-repeated phrase," and claims that all Yossarian "can hope to know is that he is superior to any universal force (man-made or otherwise), and all he can hope to recognize is that the universal or collective force can never comprehend the individual." [7] He goes on to call Yossarian's final decision "a moral act of responsibility," "reflective, conscious and indeed free," while the other characters are not free, he considers, because they are unaware.[8] This is all true; it is obvious that Yossarian is a man of whom Sartre would approve, but it does not go far enough. Certainly awareness is a prerequisite to the right action as Heller sees it. It is proved useless to be simply good like the chaplain or merely innocent like Nately, unable to detach himself from his father's values. And certainly Yossarian acts in freedom, but in the name of what? I do not think that it is only in the name of his own individual life, although this is his starting point. What most critics have overlooked is that Yossarian changes, is the one character who learns from his experience in the novel.

At the beginning of *Catch-22* Yossarian attempts to exercise his reason to escape from the situation he is in. "Everywhere he looked was a nut, and it was all a sensible young gentleman like himself could do to maintain his perspective against so much madness" (p. 21). He soon learns, however, that everyone considers everyone else "a nut" and that when he attempts to argue logically against flying more missions he comes up against Catch-22. He realizes that to use reason in the face of the irrational is futile and that the way out of Catch-22 is simply to rebel, in Camus' sense, to take a stand, to say "no." He refuses to fly any more missions. This is, of course, the way the problems of Catch-22 have been solved earlier in the novel: the young officers solve the problem of the "dead man" in Yossarian's tent simply by throwing out his possessions; Major —— de Coverley solves the "great loyalty oath" Catch, which is preventing the men from getting their meals, simply by saying " 'Give everybody eat' " (p. 120).

Until the final episode in the book, Yossarian is the great supporter of individual right. He explains to Clevinger that someone is trying to kill him [85] and answers Clevinger's explanation that they are shooting at everyone with " 'What difference does that make?' " (p. 17). When he complains that someone is trying to poison him, the conversation follows the same pattern. "That men would die was a matter of necessity; which men would die, though, was a matter of circumstance and Yossarian was willing to be a victim of anything but circumstance" (p. 69). Yossarian indeed realizes, as Karl suggests, "that one must not be asked to give his life unless everybody is willing to give his," [9] but by the end of the novel he has come to realize the logical extension of this concept, that, if what

---

[7] Karl, p. 137.
[8] *Ibid.*, pp. 137–138.
[9] *Ibid.*, p. 136.

is true for one must be applied to all, then one cannot attempt to save one's own life at the expense of others. One cannot give tacit acceptance to other people's deaths, without giving everyone the same right over oneself.

This is surely the significance of the episode in which Nately's whore tries to stab Yossarian and its relevance to his change of mind. Yossarian is given the chance to save his own life if he lies about Colonels Cathcart and Korn to their superior officers. He will, in accepting the offer, probably act as an incentive to his fellow officers to fly more missions in which many of them may be killed. He is given a chance, in Camus' terms, to join forces with the pestilences. After accepting the offer he is stabbed by Nately's whore and realizes perhaps that by joining those who are willing to kill, he has given everyone the right to kill him. If one rebels, one must rebel in the name of a value which transcends oneself, human life is the value for which Yossarian rebels and runs off to Rome, but it is not merely his own individual existence.

This point is stressed by Heller in Yossarian's declaration that he is going to try and save the kid sister of Nately's whore, is going to perform an unselfish act. If we look back at the novel in the light of what Yossarian's decision reveals, we can see that Heller has presented us with a series of character studies of selfish men and has shown how their actions for their own gain have involved death for others. They are all like Major Major's father, "a long-limbed farmer, a God-fearing, freedom-loving, rugged individualist who held that federal aid to anyone but farmers was creeping socialism" (p. 85). Milo, another "rugged individualist," bombs his own men; Colonel Cathcart, aiming at impressing the generals to obtain promotion, keeps raising the number of missions his men must fly. To claim as Karl does, that these characters "are not really evil in any sinister way" but just "men on the make" [10] is inaccurate. The "man on the make" is evil to Heller, since he gains at the expense of others and asks them to do what he is not willing to do himself.

The last ten pages or so of the novel may be sentimentally handled, as critics have suggested, but they present the key to a full understanding of what Heller is saying. In an irrational and gratuitous world the aware individual has to rebel, but his rebellion must be a free act and in the name of a value which can be applied to all men and does not limit their freedom.

The style of *Catch-22*, like the narrative technique, the tone and the methods of characterization, serves to frustrate the reader's expectations. Each of the techniques I have discussed depends for its effect upon a preconception of the reader that a novel tells a story, is peopled with recognizably [86] human beings and is written in a style which justifies Ian

---

[10] *Ibid.*, p. 137.

Watt's claim that "the function of language is much more largely referential in the novel than in other literary forms." [11] In spite of the nineteenth-century novelist's frequent side comments to his audience and in spite of early twentieth-century experiments in form, Watt is surely correct when he says: "Formal realism, in fact, is the narrative embodiment of a premise . . . which is implicit in the novel form in general: the premise, or primary convention, that the novel is a full and authentic report of human experience." [12] The reader expects to be drawn into the world of a novel, then, but *Catch-22*, while initially providing him with familiar human situations, ends by rejecting him. The novel itself becomes an object which provides the reader with the experience of the absurd, just as the trees provide it for Roquentin in Sartre's *La Nausée*. After attempting to relate his preconceptions about novels, his "illusions" about the form, to this novel, the reader is finally stripped of them. *Catch-22* simultaneously shows man's illusory view of the world, employs techniques to suggest the irrational nature of the world and is itself an object against which the truth of its statements may be tested. [87]

---

[11] Ian Watt, *The Rise of the Novel* (Berkeley: 1964), p. 30.
[12] *Ibid.*, p. 32.

Handwritten planning chart (watermarked "TWO INTERVIEWS AND A REMINISCENCE")

OFFICER / ENLISTED MEN	MAJOR DANBY / MAJOR —ING	COLONEL KORN / COLONEL CATHCART	GENERAL PECKEM / GENERAL DREEDLE	ITALIANS	NURSE / OTHER
MAJOR MAJOR LOOKS LIKE HENRY FONDA	CATHCART A HARVARD GRAD WHO WITH A CIGARETTE HOLDER			
WINTERGREEN ADVISES YOSSARIAN TO DO HIS DUTY	PROMOTED BY AN IBM MACHINE				SCHEISSKOPF HAS A YEN FOR YOSSARIAN
	TRAINED AT CADET SCHOOL AS A PILOT	BECOMES A FULL COLONEL AT AGE 36. LONGS TO BE A GENERAL	DREEDLE HAS TAKEN HIS SON-IN-LAW, COLONEL MOODUS, INTO THE BUSINESS		
	FINDS TRUE HAPPINESS AS A COMBAT PILOT, WHERE HE FINALLY FITS IN.	ARRIVES AS THE NEW GROUP COMMANDER AND RAISES MISSIONS TO 30			
		REPRIMANDS YOSSARIAN, THEN DECIDES TO PRO- MOTE HIM AND GIVE HIM A MEDAL			
	MAJOR MAJOR IS APPOINTED SQD. COMMANDER WHEN PREDECESSOR IS KILLED OVER PERUGIA	DISAPPROVES OF BLACK'S LOYALTY OATH CAMPAIGN BUT AFRAID TO INTERVENE			
	AS SQD COMMANDER HE IS OSTRACIZED AND ACCUSED AND MADE THE VICTIM OF BLACK'S LOYALTY OATH CRUSADE			NATELY'S WHORE SITS NAKED IN A ROOM FULL OF ENLISTED MEN WHO IGNORE HER	
WINTERGREEN REFUSES TO HELP AND LECTURES YOSSARIAN ON HIS DUTY TO BE KILLED	AFTER HE IS BEATEN UP ON THE BASKETBALL COURT, HE TURNS HIMSELF INTO A RECLUSE AND SEES NOBODY	KORN CLOSES THE MEDICAL TENTS WHILE THE MEN ARE WAITING TO FLY TO BOLOGNA	PECKEM RECEIVES A MEDAL AND RECOMMENDING THAT BOMBING ACTIVITIES BE PLACED UNDER HIS OWN SPECIAL SERVICE COMMAND	THE OLD MAN IN THE WHORE HOUSE	
WINTERGREEN'S OWN DUTY, AS HE SEES IT, IS TO MAKE A PROFIT ON HIS BLACK MARKET OPERATIONS			PECKEM IS SMOOTH POLI-		
SNOWDEN IS SHOT THROUGH THE MIDDLE AND DIES	DANBY MOANS WHILE CONDUCTING BRIEFING	KORN FOR		NATELY'S WHORE LIKES CAPTAIN BLACK AND GIVES HIM SOME OF THE MONEY NATELY PAYS HER	
			AWARDS MEDALS AND SIDES WITH YOSSARIAN WHEN CATHCART OFFERS TO PUNISH HIM		
SNOWDEN HAS ALREADY BEEN KILLED WINTERGREEN, AS MAIL CLERK, IS NOW INFLUENTIAL	MAJOR MAJOR VISITED BY CID MAN AND REFUSES TO SIGN PAPERS WASHINGTON IRVING	CATHCART HAS RAISED MISSIONS FROM 25 TO 50	DREEDLE AND PECKEM ARE FEUDING AND VYING FOR POWER	NATELY'S WHORE IS BORED WITH HIM AND PAYS HIM LITTLE	YOSSARIAN IS WITH A DUCKIE
		CATHCART STRIVES TO IMPRESS BOTH GENERALS FAVORABLY	NEITHER GENERAL TAKES ENOUGH NOTICE OF CATHCART TO INTERVENE EITHER WAY		
	MAJOR MAJOR VISITED BY SECOND CID MAN AND PUTS HIM ON THE TRAIL OF THE				

'The Realist'
An Impolite Interview With Joseph Heller

Q. *Has* Catch-22 *been banned anywhere?*

A. No.

Q. *Are you disappointed?*

A. Not anymore. I'm really delighted because it seems to have offended nobody on the grounds of morality or ideology. Those people it has offended, it has offended on the basis of literary value. But I'm almost surprised to find that the acceptance of the book covers such a broad political spectrum and sociological spectrum as well.

This pleases me first because it pleases my ego, but next because I put an optimistic interpretation on it: I think there is close to a common reservoir of discontent among people who might disagree with each other and not realize that their basic disagreements might stem from the same recognition of a need for correction in certain areas.

I learned from Murray Kempton's column also—and this to my surprise—that it's quite an orthodox book in terms of its morality. He referred to its being almost medieval in its moral orthodoxy, which had not occurred to me. But of course as soon as I read his column, I realized he was correct. I suppose just about everybody accepts certain principles of morality. The differences appear in testing certain institutions against those basic principles.

There is a tradition of taboo against submitting to examination many of our ideological beliefs, religious beliefs; many things that become a matter of traditional behavior, or habit, acquire status where they seem to be exempt from examination. Or even to suggest that they do be examined becomes a form of heresy.

Now the book might be surprising in that respect, but—with the exception of a certain appreciation for lechery, which you wouldn't find among the basic virtues; you might find it among the deadly sins— I don't think

SOURCE: *The Realist*, Vol. 39 (November 1962), pp. 18–31. Reprinted by permission of the publisher and Mr. Heller.

there's any principle of morality advocated in the book with which most intelligent—even *in*decent—people will disagree.

Q. *Well, when I was reading it, I first did a double take when Yossarian is censoring the letters, and my sympathy immediately fell to the people who were getting these letters.*

A. Really? Well, that hadn't occurred to me. They probably have the same status as the victims during a Shakespeare play. When critics deal in terms of classical tragedy—when they interpret Shakespearean tragedy—they see this as an examination of crime, the tragic flaw, and the retribution as representing a certain system of justice; but they ignore, let's say in *Macbeth*, all those children of—was it Macduff or Malcolm?—his wife is killed, his children are killed, and Banquo is slaughtered. All the peripheral characters seem to be exempt from the working-out of this moral principle.

I suppose it had not occurred to me that these people getting these letters would be perplexed by them. I'm not particularly disturbed by that.

Q. *Maybe I'm hypersensitive. . . . Getting back to what you said about people not being offended, isn't this type of satire by its very nature subversive—in the James Thurber sense of the word—to the establishment?*

A. Oh, I think anything *critical* is subversive by nature in the sense that it does seek to change or reform something that exists by attacking it. I think the impetus toward progress of any kind has always been a sort of discontent with what existed, and an effort to undermine what is existing, whether it's barbaric or not barbaric.

So, in the sense that the book is aware of certain faults or shortcomings —as much, I think, in the make-up of the individuals' characters as in the make-up of a society—in that sense, it is a very critical book, certainly. But it doesn't necessarily follow from that, that people would take exception to it.

Q. *What about the people who are criticized?*

A. I've met nobody yet who did not identify with my sympathetic characters. And among the people who did identify were a few of the prototypes of some of the more reprehensible characters in the book. I think anybody today feels, for example, that he is at the mercy of superiors—who don't know his job as well as he does, who don't know their own jobs as well as *he* knows their jobs and who, he feels, hamstring him or limit him in the execution of his duty.

Q. *And this includes superiors?*

A. Oh, yes—this includes his superiors as well. It occurred to me at a certain point that even General Walker, at the height of his troubles, could very easily have identified with one of my sympathetic officers, because he himself was being the victim of the Pentagon and the politicians in Washington who were jeopardizing everything, say, good—and preventing *him* from existing and performing work at the height of his capabilities.

Q. *Have you gotten any unofficial reactions to the book from Air Force personnel?*

A. I have gotten no official reaction. I've gotten fan letters from people in the service—at least two, I believe, from officers, one of whom is with the Air Force Academy, but he was writing to express his approval of the book as literature rather than expressing any sympathy with the ideas.

I think another reason I have not heard any objections is that most people *are* treating it as a *novel* and judging it in those terms, as a work of fiction rather than as an essay or as a propaganda tract. It's not *intended* to be a sociological treatise on anything, although it—the substance of the fiction—is almost an encyclopedia of the current mental atmosphere.

It is certainly a novel of *comment;* there are comments about the loyalty oath, about the free enterprise system, about civil rights, about bureaucracy, about patriotism—but these are the ingredients out of which to create a fictional narrative.

In writing the book I was more concerned with producing a *novel* that would be as contemporary as possible. I don't mean contemporaneous with World War II; it is contemporary with the period I was writing in. I was more concerned with producing a work of fiction—of literary art, if you will—than of converting anybody or arousing controversy. I'm really afraid of getting involved in controversy.

Q. *Are you serious?*

A. Oh, yes—I'm a terrible coward. I'm just like Yossarian, you know. It's the easiest thing to fight—I learned that in the war—it *takes* a certain amount of courage to go to war, but not very much, not as much as to refuse to go to war. I think that's the danger that the world faces today; war might be the easiest solution to problems, and one country or the other might rely on war as a solution, not because it's dictated, but simply because it's a way out of frustration.

Q. *I can't accept your implication, a minute ago, that involvement in controversy is necessarily a barometer of bravery—because I love controversy, but I'm a coward, too.*

A. No, I didn't mean that. I don't love controversy—I don't like *personal* controversy.

Q. *No, no, I don't mean personal controversy, I mean controversy of ideas—*

A. Oh, yes, that's fine—but when I have a complaint against a department store, I try to avoid making it in person, I try to avoid using the phone—I'd much rather put it on paper and avoid all danger of any personal combat.

Q. *Your book received some fanatically favorable reviews, but there was one stern critic who said: "If* Catch-22 *were intended as a commentary novel, [the] sideswiping of character and action might be taken care of by thematic control. It fails here because half its incidents are farcical and fantastic. The book is an emotional hodge-podge; no mood is sustained long enough to register for more than a chapter." Now I don't want to put you in the silly position of saying, "But I don't sideswipe character and action"—*

A. Well, I *do* sideswipe character and action. I think that's one of the approaches to the book that gives it what effect it has. I tried to avoid, first of all, the conventional structure of the novel; I tried to give it a structure that would reflect and complement the content of the book itself, and the content of the book really derives from our present atmosphere, which is one of chaos, of disorganization, of absurdity, of cruelty, of brutality, of insensitivity, but at the same time one in which people, even the worst people, I think are basically good, are motivated by humane impulses.

And I tried to emphasize this by the structure, much the same way that many of your modern artists have resorted to a type of painting as being most suitable to the emotions they want to express, to the visions they have; and your very good contemporary composers are using dissonances and irregular tempos and harmonics to get this same feeling.

I did consciously try to use a form of what might be called dramatic counterpoint, so that certain characters suffer tragedies, and they're dismissed almost flippantly—a line or two might describe something terrible happening to a character, whereas whole pages might be concentrated on something of *subordinate* dramatic value.

And by doing that, I tried to do two things. One was to emphasize the sense of loss, or the sense of sorrow, connected with it; and also to capture this thing in experience which permits us to survive the loss of people who are dear to us, so that nobody's suffering lingers with us very long.

People die and are forgotten. People are abused and are forgotten. People suffer, people are exploited, *right now;* we don't dwell upon them 24 hours a day. Somehow they get lost in the swirl of things of much less importance to us and to them and to the human condition.

So in that case I don't quarrel with the review; there was a definite technique, at the beginning of the book particularly, of treating people and incidents almost in terms of glimpses, and then showing as we progress that these things do have a meaning and they do come together.

Q. *That same reviewer also said: "As satire* Catch-22 *makes too many formal concessions to the standard novels of our day"*—

A. I don't know what he means. I don't know whether his standards of satire should be accepted. There are formal concessions to the standard novel, certainly. You can't write a novel on piano. So as soon as you begin using words, then you begin making concessions to the form.

Catch-22 is not to my mind a far-out novel; it is not to my mind a formless novel. If anything, it was constructed almost meticulously, and with a meticulous concern to give the appearance of a formless novel. Now that's much different, in much the same way as with Joyce's *Ulysses*, which is possibly one of the most confusing novels when you first approach it, and yet there's a structure and tension in virtually every word.

Incidentally, it's turning out to be a very easy novel to read, because among the letters I get are *many* from people in high school and freshmen in college. I have a collection of letters that could be called love letters— from people of all three sexes, probably, and of all ages, and they're just rhapsodic in their enthusiasm.

I've yet to receive one letter that criticizes, but that may be that when people don't like a book they just don't write letters about it. What I do get is a kind of "God bless you" approach, or maybe a "This might save the world" feeling.

One thing I'm certain of, all these letters—and there must be about three or four hundred by now—I'm sure that the writers of each of these letters would like each other enormously if they met. People that I have met as a result of these letters—if they're in New York and I have seen them— there's almost an instantaneous rapport.

I think that comes from the fact that I express so much of my own views in the novel, and my own personality, with the result that anybody who responds to the book is going to respond to me. We meet, and almost immediately we're conversing like old friends.

· · · · ·

Q. *I was talking to Ralph J. Gleason, and he was wondering how you feel about certain other writers' approaches to the insanity of our time. I'll name them one at a time. Louis-Ferdinand Céline?*

A. Céline's book, *Journey to the End of Night*, was one of those which gave me a direct inspiration for the form and tone of *Catch-22*.

Q. *Nelson Algren?*

A. *The Man With the Golden Arm*, which I had read earlier, became an almost unconscious influence in the form of this type of open hero.

Q. *Ken Kesey?*

A. I haven't read *One Flew Over the Cuckoo's Nest* yet—his book came out after mine—but I bought it a few weeks ago.

Q. *Terry Southern?*

A. I read *The Magic Christian* very quickly, and there were parts of it I liked enormously, and parts that just eluded me. I'm not a very good reader. I had not read his book before I wrote *Catch-22*, but I think those people Southern influenced through his book might very well have influenced me.

Q. *Richard Condon?*

A. I read *The Manchurian Candidate* and I read *The Oldest Confession.* When I read the review of *The Manchurian Candidate*, I was in about the middle of *Catch-22*, and I had a feeling, well, here's a guy who's writing the same book *I* am; I'd better read this quickly because he might have already written it.

And then I read it, and I think there's a great deal of similarity, first of all in the concern, or the use of political and social materials—or products of the political and social conflicts—as the basis for his book, and there's a great similarity in the attitude toward them, so that they are at once serious and at the same time it's almost like watching a kind of burlesque and also a kind of everyman show on stage.

There's a definite feeling of kinship with him, but I don't think they're the same kind of novel. Mine is, I suppose, an optimistic novel with a great deal of pessimism in it—there's a very heavy sense of the tragic—particularly toward the end, where I almost consciously sought to re-create the feeling of Dostoevsky's dark passages, and I have one or two allusions to chapters in Dostoevsky.

Q. *In relation to the humorous aspect of the book, I want to ask you about the use of exaggeration as a vehicle for satire; do you think you may have exaggerated too much beyond the possibilities of reality?*

A. Well, I *tried* to exaggerate in almost every case, gradually, to a point beyond reality—that was a deliberate intention, to do it so gradually that the unreality becomes *more* credible than the realistic, normal, day-to-day behavior of these characters.

Certainly, there are things in there which could not—well, there's one thing that could not . . . well, everything could *possibly* happen; nothing in there is supernatural—but it defies probability. But so much of what we *do*—without even thinking about it—so much of what is *done* in our day-to-day existence defies probability if we stop to examine it.

And this is the effect I wanted to achieve. Now, I was hoping to do this, and with many people I succeeded, to make these characters seem more real in terms of their eccentricities carried to absurdity.

Q. *You started to say that there was one thing in particular in the book that defies probability.*

A. That's a scene which to many people is the high spot of the book and to other people it's the point at which their credulity was strained. And that is the incident—incident is an incongruous word for it—in which Milo bombs his own squadron and escapes without punishment.

I would say that more critics who praised the book singled this out as a triumph, with special appreciation, than any other single incident. On the other hand, most people in conversation, in discussing it, say that this was the one thing that they found hard to believe.

Now, I sincerely think that this is an impossibility; this is the one thing that could not happen—literally. I don't think that in time of war a man could get up and actually drop bombs deliberately on his own people and then escape without punishment, even in our society.

I think people in every country commit *actions* which would cause infinitely more *damage* to the national strength, to the national survival, to their fellow citizens; even commit actions which result in more deaths, physical deaths, as well—and be *lionized* for it; be made into heroes for it. But I don't think the actual *act* of killing would be allowed to escape punishment with everybody's approval.

Q. *There are other things which I think go beyond the area of possibility. The soldier in white, for example, who is nourished by continuously being fed his own waste products intravenously—*

A. No, he's not—well, yes he is, I suppose—that had not occurred to me. Of course, if you assume that there's a human being inside the bandages, then he could not be kept alive by his own waste products; that's a scientific impossibility. But if you begin to question, as I do, whether there *is* a human being inside, then it becomes a matter of economy just to keep using the same fluid to put back inside him.

But he is handled almost always as a kind of gruesome symbol of many things. In one instance, he is discussed as a middle-man. If you look at man—remove the conscience, remove the sensibility—well, if you look at his position in the nature of things, in one sense he can be no more than a middle-man: he takes matter, he absorbs it, he excretes it or uses it up, and this is a natural process in which he is just one tiny phase of the whole cycle.

As an animal, man is a vegetable. And that was the point of using the soldier in white that way.

No, he could not happen, I suppose, unless there *was* some gigantic conspiracy—it's almost supernatural—in which the reasons defy explanation; they decide to put this form swathed in bandages in the hospital and put nothing inside.

Q. *Did you ever read* Johnny Got His Gun—*which was about a basket case—by Dalton Trumbo?*

A. Oh, sure. The thing that I liked best about *Johnny Got His Gun* was that the *Daily News* wrote an editorial recommending it and praising it. It came out when the *News* was in its isolationist phase; anti-Roosevelt phase.

Q. *I understand* The Daily Worker *was serializing it at the time, and they suddenly stopped right in the middle without a word of explanation when the peace pact between Stalin and Hitler was signed. . . . There were a couple of other areas in your book of probability versus possibility. Like eating chocolate-covered cotton—*

A. Oh, it's not impossible that a man would try to market cotton covered with chocolate. It is impossible, I suppose, that they can eat it. And nobody does eat it in the book. In fact, when Milo gives it to Yossarian, Yossarian tastes it, then spits it out and says, "You can't give it to people, they'll get sick." So this is not done; in the book people do *not* eat chocolate-covered cotton, but there is a man trying to *market* it. Now, I think the corollaries of *that.* . . .

Q. *What about the loyalty oath scene, where they have to pledge allegiance hundreds of times and sing* The Star-Spangled Banner *all over the place—*

A. Again, that is not a physical impossibility. You know, in the first outline of this book, when it was first conceived—in my mind; it was never down on paper—there were going to be a number of deliberate anachronisms, very *conspicuous* anachronisms—there are anachronisms in now that are deliberate—there were going to be a number of supernatural things taking place, without any explanation for them, so that the impossible—the physically impossible—would be worked in with the possible, and be recognizable.

And then, I forget the motive, I decided nothing in this book would be something that's physically impossible.

Consequently, even in the latter half of the book, where you have this whore with the knife coming up in all kinds of disguises, the effect I give is that she's moving from place to place with the speed of light, because the scale there is changed to give you fast action; but it's always two hours or three hours that go by, so that he pushes the girl out of the plane in Rome, then flies back to the airfield, and you get the impression that she's waiting there, she's beat him there, and she stabs him, but if you look, he spends a few hours running to find Hungry Joe, the pilot, to fly him back.

So the explanation would be: in that time, she could've hopped a plane somehow and gotten there. In the first writing, she was going to pop up with a speed that would've been impossible. And then I decided, let's keep consistent about this.

Now there are, I suppose, things which don't even occur to me, like the soldier in white. But it's not physically impossible that somebody, for reasons of their own, would take this zombie—which is what he's supposed to be: a zombie, really, or nothing; and I don't know if there's much difference, let's say, between the human animal that lacks sensibility, and nothing but matter—but it is not physically impossible, it's *improbable*, that an organization would exist to perpetrate this kind of trick.

If any government wanted to, for reasons of their own, get some kind of wire-structured *papier maché* and cover it with bandages and pass it off as a man who's been seriously wounded in the war—I'm saying they *could* do it; that's what I mean by its not being physically impossible.

Q. *All right, what about the family visiting the hospital and failing to recognize that Yossarian isn't their son?*

A. Well, the only one who accepts him as the son almost instantly is the mother.

Q. *Of all people. . . .*

A. Well, it's easier for mothers to accept strangers—I've noticed that about women and men—women seem to be much fonder of other people's children than of their own, and men don't care; the only children men care for are their own.

In that scene, it makes no difference to the mother; she says, "What difference does that make?" The sailor says, "He's not Giuseppe, he's Yossarian." And I forget what the father does. In that unforgettable chapter, I forget what happens.

Again, it is improbable—certainly, it is improbable—but, again, it is not *impossible* that this conversation should take place. It's an unusual reaction, but not an impossible one.

Q. *In retrospect, are there any important changes you would make in the book?*

A. I can't think of any. I would not change Milo bombing his squadron because, on one level, this book is an allegory—not on a level, but there are *passages* where it becomes allegoric; there are other passages where it becomes realism—and I think that, allegorically, that is a consistent action and a most logical action.

It's no more improbable than other things Milo has done out of the goodness of his heart. What is improbable is not that a man should *do* this and find a *rationale* for doing it—Milo is very good at finding that— but what's improbable is that any society would permit it to go unpunished.

Q. *Some of the stuff that does go unpunished in real life makes it seem almost possible after all—*

A. Well, it is possible, for example, in this country, and in Russia, in England—it is possible for individuals to be murdered, put to death, without any legal sanction for it, and for the people who did it to be known and to escape punishment. That is conceivable. In fact, it's almost a daily occurrence here.

But Milo's action transcends this. It's a time of war, and he bombs indiscriminately, and it's an act of *physical* violence. It is conceivable to me that somebody might manufacture a food product or a drug product that would *poison* people, and the punishment for this would be slight; there would be extenuations if not justifications.

I don't think it's probable that this same person could indiscriminately run through New York, let's say, firing a machine gun, and escape without punishment.

It depends to a large extent, *always*, on whom your victims *are*. Or who *you* are. And in this case it was just an attack on his own society; it's the society, or the members of it, that are being attacked almost without discrimination. That couldn't—it's just inconceivable that it *would*—go unpunished.

I suppose if I re-read the book—each time I do read it, I find I'm angling for something; I'll read a chapter and I'll say, "Maybe I can make this into a recording," or "Maybe this would go well at Upstairs at the Downstairs [a New York night club]" and the next thing you know, I'm scheming commercially—but I think one thing I would probably do would be to cut.

And what I would cut would probably be language rather than incident. I did cut enormously. Bob Gottlieb, my editor, and a very tactful man as well, made only two suggestions, really. Let me say also that at the time I handed this book in, it was 800 typewritten pages, and his first reaction was that it's the most upsetting book he's ever read, and it's a splendid, splendid book, and he would publish it just as is.

I said to him, "Well, if you have any suggestions. . . ." And he said, "Well, of course, we'll talk about it. . . ." It was down to about 600–625 typewritten pages when it was finally submitted. And that's an enormous amount of cutting. He never said *cut*, but on the basis of his suggestions, I went back and made my own corrections.

With this suggestion in mind, I cut something like a third of the first

200 pages—about 60 pages—without cutting a single incident; it was all in terms of language or dialogue.

Even in its final version, one of the general criticisms against the book is that it's too long and that it does tend to be repetitious. Other people take this repetitious quality—they don't use that word—if they *don't* like the book, it's repetitious; if they *like* it, it has a recurring and cyclical structure, like the theme in a Beethoven symphony.

Q. *Now—this being quite unusual—your sympathetic central character is an atheist; was there any reaction to this, say by members of the clergy?*

A. None whatsoever. One of the nicest and earliest letters I got was from a member of the clergy on the faculty of Notre Dame. This flabbergasted me. I remember I was in the office at *McCall's* [Heller wrote the promotional copy for that magazine] when I got the envelope from Notre Dame, and it was addressed to me at Simon & Schuster, which meant it was in reference to the book. A chill went through me—the same kind of chill I got when I received this letter from the Air Force Academy—you know: *here it comes* . . . until I knew what was inside . . . and then I was amazed and delighted.

Then I realized that my amazement comes from my own naïveté about other people. I've been very naïve about the Republican mind, because a few friends I have who are Republicans embraced this book immediately; I thought it was a liberal book, and they said "No, it's not a liberal book, it's anti-everything."

And I was very naïve about the mind of the intellectual Catholic or the intellectual religious leader—a friend who was educated at Marquette told me about the Jesuit Catholic as opposed to many of the superstitions and practices and narrowmindedness of other Catholics. The book got a good review in *Jubilee*, which is a Catholic publication, and a fairly good review in the University of Scranton, which, I think, reads for the Index and classifies books.

But Yossarian is the kind of atheist—I'm not sure he's an atheist—

Q. *Well, I'm taking his word for it—*

A. Does he say he's an atheist?

Q. *Sure.*

A. When?

Q. *When he's talking to Scheisskopf's wife on Thanksgiving.*

A. Oh, he had that argument over God. He says to her, "I thought you didn't believe in God." And she says, "I don't believe in God as much as you don't, but the God I don't believe in is a humane God." So I suppose that is a giveaway, . . . but I don't conceive of Yossarian as an atheist any more than I conceive of the chaplain as necessarily believing in God.

I see Yossarian as having no positive attitude on the subject, and I see the chaplain as having no definite attitude on the subject. I would prefer to think of Yossarian as an atheist when pushed for an answer, but also as someone who regards any discussion of it as having no relation to the problems of the moment.

I don't think he's un-Christian in his feelings if we take the term Christain to mean what it ought to mean.

Q. *Why did you have an Assyrian as the central character?*

A. Because I was looking for two things. I got the idea, frankly, from James Joyce's placing Bloom in Dublin. I wanted somebody who would seem to be *out*side the culture in every way—ethnically as well as others.

Now, because America is a melting pot, there are huge concentrations of just about every other kind of nationality. I didn't want to give him a Jewish name, I didn't want to give him an Irish name, I didn't want to symbolize the white Protestant—but somebody who was almost a *new* man, and I made him Assyrian (but what I was ignorant of, for one thing, his name is not Assyrian; I've since been told it's Armenian).

But I wanted to get an extinct culture, somebody who could not be identified either geographically, or culturally, or sociologically—somebody as a person who has a capability of ultimately divorcing himself completely from all emotional and psychological ties.

Q. *There was some speculation by a couple of my friends that you got the idea from William Saroyan's "Twenty Thousand Assyrians."*

A. It was from that story that I first learned the Assyrians were extinct, or almost extinct. But my purpose in doing so was to get an outsider, a man who was *intrinsically* an outsider, who had the capability of being a complete outsider. It's very hard for a person really to shake off all his roots.

I like to think that I am not Jewish, but certain tastes for foods, certain odors, associations. . . .

Q. *If you like Chinese food, too, that doesn't make you Chinese.*

A. No, not the same way. I don't like Chinese food. And I don't like *Jewish* food. I think Jewish food is worse than Chinese food. But there's a consciousness. Even if I could forget it, other people won't let me forget it completely. And I imagine this is true of everybody. I have certain friends from the South who are always self-conscious.

That's the big myth about this country, by the way—the melting pot. It isn't. They never melted. I think everybody in this country has a minority complex. Even the majority—they're guilty about being the majority.

Yossarian will be able even to be outside his own family tradition. You know, his family is never mentioned—I *think* it's never mentioned—brothers, sisters, father, mother. I forget now whether I refer to his grandmother and aunt, or other children's on the block. But he has no family. I'm not sure where he came from.

His background—you don't know whether he went to college or not— you assume he did because he gets in certain discussions and conversations which would presuppose a degree of education. I wanted to be vague in those areas, but the name would be the same, without making it one of these Restoration names, where the name itself suggests a word.

Q. *My biggest shock in the book was to find out that Yossarian's first name was John.*

A. I thought that was funny to mention just once. That it should be a name like John. There were certain instances in there where I just could not avoid putting something in because it made me laugh. I think, too, that he should have a first name, so that he doesn't become completely a symbol. I wanted to give him some orientation.

You know, he's not a perfect hero. There are certain things he does of which I don't approve. He has certain flaws in relationship to women, for example. Now, to an extent, it's joyous and robust, but it's not *nice*—it's not really gracious on his part—never to think of this girl by her name, but always as Nately's whore.

And there are other instances, in which he reacts—well, when he punches Nately in the nose, I think, is an indication of the extreme emotional state he's in, that he'd do this, but he himself is contrite immediately afterward.

I certainly didn't want him to become the ideal hero. He's human, and the temptation to sell out when he's offered and he agrees to do it—is another indication of that. And I think *John* just puts him right back where he belongs.

If he were English, I probably would have called him Charlie, because the word Charlie in England has certain associations; it's a synonym for *chump*. A John is the name that call girls use to identify customers, so it's so typically *nebbish*, you know?

Q. *Just for the benefit of people not in the know, what's the translation of Lieutenant Scheisskopf's name?*

A. Shithead.

Q. *Thank you.*

A. Yeah, but who's not in the know?

Q. *I wasn't in the know; somebody had to tell me.*

A. *I* didn't know; I had to ask my secretary. When I got to him, and I had to give him a name, I decided I'd want to call him the German translation of shithead, and my secretary's roommate then was a Fulbright scholar from Germany, so I wrote down, "Find out. . . ."

But there again, that let me use an inside joke which pleased me very much, and possibly which other people didn't notice. At one point in dialogue, someone says, "I wonder what that Shithead is up to"—with a capital S there. I have a number of things like that which I like to think are only mine; it gives me an edge on the world. But one by one, I give them away.

Q. *All right, how about the background of the chaplain being an Anabaptist?*

A. There again, the explanation is similar to the one that accounts for Yossarian's name. I am not that well informed about religion, but I assume that Anabaptists are either extinct or not very militant. I was looking, again, for a religion that would sound familiar and yet would not have associations with any of our established religions.

So, the chaplain, by virtue of being associated with this kind of faith, could then be capable of certain acts, certain thoughts, and sympathies. They'd be a little more plausible, rather than anybody associated with a religion with which we're familiar, because people who think in stereotypes —well, people *are* stereotypes to begin with—and you don't want a rabbi or a Baptist minister, or a Catholic priest acting too far outside the stereotype or the circumference of behavior which *other* people think limits his action. They may not exist, but people have conceptions of how other people's professions act.

This gives the chaplain a certain amount of latitude of reaction and response in actions. Also, I didn't want him to be either sympathetic or non-sympathetic to any of these groups. He's really a religious man, but he's a nondenominational minister.

Q. *Jacques in* Candide *was an Anabaptist—*

A. I didn't know that. I've never read *Candide.*

Q. *That's funny, because some people I know have thought all along that this was one of your private jokes.*

A. I'll tell you, I got this letter from an English instructor who wanted to do a paper on *Catch-22*, and he asked me a whole load of questions, with a certain intent to know the symbolic value, and I replied as honestly as I could. He was right, I had not thought of it, that one of the prevailing ideas was one of withdrawal. It had not occurred to me. I know I have characters disappear, and I have characters who disappear by dying, and I have Yossarian disappear at the end. I had not seen this pattern that extensively. So I learned something from him.

But then he got to miracle ingredient Z-247, which is mentioned at the beginning, as Yossarian is boasting, "I'm Pepsodent, I'm Tarzan, I'm miracle ingredient Z-247. . . ." He looked that up and found it's an element called Einsteinium, named after Einstein.

And then, toward the end, in that chapter, "The Eternal City," Einstein becomes the universal hero when Yossarian, just brooding, subtracted all the people who were suffering and all the people afflicted, and you might be left with Albert Einstein and an old violinist somewhere.

Now he had linked these two up!

Q. *You mean the secret ingredient and this reference to Einstein?*

A. Yes. He said he can't believe that's just accidental. That I picked this ingredient Einsteinium because of Albert Einstein.

Q. *And it was pure coincidence?*

A. Yes, I didn't know this. I just picked Z-247 right out of the blue.

. . . . .

Q. *In the process of writing* Catch-22, *did you ever change your mind about how you were going to end it?*

A. No. The ending was written long before the middle was written. I suppose right after I sold the book, I was riding on the subway one day, and I actually wrote the words to the ending—this was perhaps four years before the book was finished—and I didn't change it once.

I couldn't see any alternative ending. It had a certain amount of integrity, not merely with the action of the book—that could've permitted anything —but with the moral viewpoint of the book; the heavy suffusion of moral content which is in there, it seemed to me, required a resolution of *choice* rather than of accident.

Q. *But you know what people will say—and this is one of the things I meant before when I asked about people who might've found the book objectionable—Yossarian deserts at the end. Now this is what people always say about pacifists and conscientious objectors: If this is the moral, then everybody should desert, and we would've lost the war.*

A. I thought I had gone beyond that point by a discussion preceding his act of running. The last chapter or two is almost in the nature of disputation, in which all the possibilities are discussed and resolved. The answer to that one—that if everybody deserts—then he would be a damn fool *not* to.

When he says, "I'm tired, I have to think of myself, my country is safe now," he's told, "Well, suppose everyone felt that way," and he says, "Well, I'd be a damn fool to feel differently."

I also tried to make it very evident that the war was just about over.

Q. *Would it have made any difference if the war weren't over?*

A. Oh, certainly. I mean if this book had been set two or three years earlier, before the beachhead, then it would be a completely different book.

Q. *Suppose he had flown that many missions, and it was still the middle of the war?*

A. Well, if the book were written then—if he had that many missions and the other conditions were the same, that he were being asked to fly more purely to help a superior officer achieve a promotion—then I would've had him desert, because the replacements are waiting there, as they are at the end of the book; there are replacements ready. So there would not have been any great loss as far as the military effort were concerned.

But if you postulate *this* situation: It's right after Pearl Harbor, and we *don't* have enough planes, and we *don't* have enough men, and Hitler *is* in a dominant and threatening position, then it would be a completely different situation.

I regard this essentially as a peacetime book. What distresses me very much is that the ethic that is often dictated by a wartime emergency has a certain justification when the wartime emergency *exists*, but when this thing is carried *over* into areas of peace—when the military, for example, retains its enormous influence on affairs in a peacetime situation, and where the same demands are made upon the individual in the cause of national interest; the line that I like very much is when Milo tells Yossarian that he's jeopardizing his traditional freedoms by exercising them—when this wartime emergency ideology is transplanted to peacetime, then you have this kind of lag which leads not only to absurd situations, but to very tragic situations.

I worked over certain lines very carefully. On that loyalty oath crusade, I don't remember the actual words, but a sentence is used to the effect that the combat men soon found themselves at the mercy of the administrators appointed to serve *them*. You have this inversion.

Now this is the kind of thing that happens very easily. There's no question that policemen are public servants, but they're *not* in a position of servitude in relation to the people that they're supposed to serve.

There's a kind of blindness which did carry over to peacetime. I recognize the difference that if a house is on fire you grab something and run out and you leave the door open; if the house is not on fire then it should be locked up.

The stimulus for certain action justifies an action. If the stimulus is not there and the action exists anyway, then you've got a right to examine why you're doing it.

Q. *In the end, Yossarian deserts in order to find sanity in Sweden—*

A. But he's not going to get there, he knows that.

Q. *He's not?*

A. Oh, no. I mean he's told, "You'll never get there." And he says, "I know, but I'll try."

Q. *People aren't sure of this, just as they're not sure whether Franny is pregnant or not—*

A. They're not sure because they're hopeful he'll get there, I suppose. For one thing, he's choosing the wrong way. You could get there by rowing the way Orr did, but he's going to Rome, and he's told two or three times, "You'll never make it." Or, "You can't get there from here." But he says, "Well, at least I'll try."

There's also implicit—well, it's not implicit if people miss it—that this is an act of opposition or an act of protest. It's the only way left that he *can* protest without cutting his own head off. And he doesn't choose to do that; he's not a martyr. But the very act of *doing* what he does will stir up things, will stir up a certain amount of talk and dissension, will embarrass his superior officers. I don't think Sweden is paradise.

Q. *That's what my question was going to be. Whether or not Yossarian gets there, do you think Sweden doesn't have Catch-22?*

A. Oh, I don't know. Sweden was important to me as a *goal*, or an objective, a kind of Nirvana. It's important, if you're in a situation which is imperfect to an extent where it's uncomfortable or painful, that you have some *objective* to move toward in order to change that situation.

Now, in Yossarian's situation—his environment, his society, the world; and it's not just America, it's the world itself—the monolithic society closes off every conventional area of protest or corrective action, and the only choice that's left to him is one of ignoble acceptance in which he can profit and live very comfortably—but nevertheless ignoble—or *flight*, a renunciation of that condition, of that society, that set of circumstances.

The only way he can renounce it without going to jail is by deserting it, trying to keep going until they capture him. I like to think of him as a kind of spirit on the loose. You know, he is the only hope left at the end of the book. Had he accepted that choice. . . .

Q. *Is he the only hope? What about the chaplain and Major Danby?*

A. Well, until Yossarian makes that decision, he is the only hope. Major

Danby and the chaplain are sort of inspired by him. But, remember, a consequence of his accepting the compromise that's offered him—the rest of the men will then continue to fly more missions without protesting.

Now all the way through, there is this theme about the bulk of the men either being *indifferent* to what's happening to them, or not *knowing* what's happening to them. It occurs in their acceptance of Milo. Even in Yossarian's acceptance of Milo. Yossarian is actually fond of Milo, and I am too, as an individual. There's a certain purity of purpose about him. Even about his hypocrisy. It's not nearly as malignant as other characters in the book. Although he does the most damage.

There's that situation when Yossarian is kidding Milo about the time the mess sergeant poisoned the men: put laundry soap in the sweet potatoes to prove that the men don't know what's good for them. They all came down with this epidemic of diarrhea. And Milo said, "I guess that showed him how wrong he was." And Yossarian said, "No, on the contrary, it showed him how right he was. The men lapped it up and clamored for more." They *knew* they'd been poisoned, though they didn't know how, or why, and they really didn't care.

Now Yossarian doesn't care—this does not motivate him—this business of selling out the other people. At this point he has become estranged from them, as individuals. But one of the consequences of his accepting the medal would be that everybody *else* would continue to fly more missions without protest.

And yet there is also this hint of dissatisfaction, because while he's ostracized in the daytime, at night different people keep popping up and asking him the same question, "How are you doing?" But in the daytime they won't associate themselves with him. Even Appleby, who has been the perfect model of a very good combat man, begins to have misgivings toward the end and pops up out of the darkness to tell him that they're going to offer you this deal, and he's beginning to become disillusioned with the concept of following orders because they're orders.

Q. *Let me just read this little clipping to you—it sounds as if it's right out of your book:*

STOCKHOLM, NOV. 6 [AP]—Security arrangements within the Swedish armed forces are under scrutiny following the recent disappearance of 24,000 secret documents from the offices of the Comptroller General of the Armed Forces, it was disclosed today.

The documents were gone for nine days before a civilian truck driver returned them, saying he had picked them by mistake.

The documents contained full information on Swedish ammunition supplies, estimated ammunition needs in case of mobilization and locations of Swedish munition dumps.

Security police said the truck driver, employed by an electronic firm, had orders to pick up eight boxes of electronics equipment at the Comptroller General's office.

A. It's not out of *Catch-22*; I like to think that *Catch-22* is right out of circumstances like *that*. Things like this are inevitable. I think if you want to start clipping paragraphs from newspapers, you'll find that organization today, any organized effort, must contain the germ of continuing disorganization.

The most effective business enterprise, I should think, is a single proprietorship, where one man goes into business for himself and has to hire nobody. The next best possibly is two men as partners; they work harder —there must be some kind of mathematical ratio, particularly when it involves government, I think, because government is so *huge*.

And that includes the Army, for example. You're dealing with millions of people, and there are certain personality- or mental-types that are attracted to that kind of work, either because they can't get a job anywhere else, or because they like doing that.

I cannot imagine anybody who's really ambitious, anybody with any real talent, anybody of any real intelligence, choosing to place himself within a large organization, where he functions in relationship to dozens or hundreds of other people, because every contact is an impairment of his efficiency.

And the kind of person who would stamp documents or classify documents is a kind of person that would not normally be expected to excel in the matter of efficiency or in the matter of making astute judgments, value-judgments.

Q. *But you know that intelligent people do go into large organizations; the trend is more and more toward that—*

A. I'm speaking mainly of government. I would say no, that there are certain types of intelligence that do well in business; I think that to succeed in business—and this is based on limited observations, but personal observations—to really get to the higher echelon of a large company requires at least one special kind of intelligence, and requires a great deal of energy and hard work and ambition.

At the same time, the company, the organization that these people manage, is *incredible*. I mean, nothing in my book—nothing in the wildest satire—goes beyond it. The inter-office rivalries; the mistakes in communications; the difficulties of finding people to promote who can do a job well—the amount of waste in the life of any corporation, at the least the ones I've been with, is just extraordinary.

Now, on the other hand, it's hard to find anybody you'd classify as an intellectual as being associated with a business. To me, and I think to most people who have a high degree of intelligence, creative intelligence, business is boring after a certain point. There really are no new challenges.

The kind of choice becomes between showing the gross profit 4 million dollars one year, how do we boost it to 4½ million the next year, how do we keep it from slipping back—and after a while you really don't give a damn.

And I begin to wonder whether the people involved *really care* about it as a profit thing. I think they care about it in terms of (1) their own security and (2) their own ego-fulfillment. It becomes a personal challenge rather than distributing more gaskets.

I don't think they really care about the stockholders—the widow who is dependent on increased dividends—it's just even like a beaver building a dam. A beaver builds a dam—I don't know why a beaver wants a dam, by the way, but I have a feeling that it may not even *need* the dam—it builds a dam because it's a *beaver*. And a person trained to one occupation, even when he gets to the top, he continues doing accountancy because he's an *accountant*.

Q. *I have a few real-life items in mind which, I think, say more about what Catch-22 is than any definition possibly could, and I'd like to get whatever reactions they evoke in you. Item: The Department of Welfare has finally revised a long-standing rule so that now, when a public assistance case is closed because of the death of the person who had been receiving the public assistance, it's no longer necessary that the deceased person be notified by mail that he won't get any further public assistance.*

A. It does not surprise me at all. That's like that educational session in the beginning of the book, with the rule Colonel Korn employs: to cut off these embarrassing questions; the only ones who would be allowed to ask questions were those who never did.

But it does not surprise me. There is a law of life: People in need of help have the least chance of getting it. Here again, we can almost establish a mathematical relationship. The chance of a person getting help is in inverse proportion to the extent of his need.

And this is true of mental cases; this is true in social work; it's certainly true in business; it's true of people who want credit; it's true of friendship.

Now, that happens with Major Major too. I hate to keep referring to my book—I *love* to keep referring to my book—there's a line about Major Major: Because he needed a friend so desperately he never found one.

I think it's certainly true of mental cases. A person who's in out-and-out need, who's on the verge of suicide, who *is* paranoic on the strength of it, is going to get no help from anybody; a mild neurotic will be encouraged to see a psychiatrist, his friends will want to help him and indulge him, but when the need becomes critical, then—if I might quote an old philosopher—goodbye, Charlie.

Q. *Do you think that, in the film version of* Catch-22, *Major Major should be played by Henry Fonda or by an actor who looks like Henry Fonda?*

A. Assuming that that's left in the movie version, then I would say an actor who either *looks* a little like Henry Fonda or who looks nothing at *all* like Henry Fonda.

But, you know, I must have 40 to 60 characters in this book; there's so much, just physically, that won't be able to go into a picture. And you start thinking, what are those things that are most valuable, which you want to keep? One of the first things you have to put in the nonpriority category are those things which are funny and nothing else.

And what are most valuable? Well, the things of continuity, the theme of insanity accepted without any eye-blinking, the feeling of frustration— of impotence, actually—a succession of scenes where the characters just can't *do* anything, physical or mental.

This chapter that comes earlier, that people don't talk about as much as I thought they would, which impresses me enormously every time I think of it—it's a scene in the nose of the plane, where Yossarian is there with Aarfy, the navigator, and he tries to tell him to go out to the back of the plane, and Aarfy smiles—because he's not afraid of the flak, and he does not hear what Yossarian is saying.

And Yossarian—mounting frustration—between guiding the pilot out, turning around and being poked in the ribs by Aarfy, and hitting the ceiling because he thinks he's dying, and then finally he's slamming Aarfy with all his might, and Aarfy keeps *smiling*—it's like hitting a sofa pillow. And he bursts into tears in utter frustration; the whole thing has become so unreal to him. Well, there's a sense of inability to get across something so simple in a time of danger.

The truth is so simple and so evident. Later on, he's bleeding, he's wounded, and Aarfy is there again. And you have almost the same scene repeated. He thinks he's been hit in the testicles—he hollers, "I lost my balls!"—he's sitting in a puddle of blood, and Aarfy doesn't hear him, and doesn't understand. And Yossarian says, "I'm dying and nobody knows."

The truth—the dangers—are so obvious and so simple, yet he can't make himself understood. That is something I'd want to keep in the picture version. I want to keep this sense of injustice—the element of the tribe— the judges waiting to judge, having this tremendous amount of power of force behind them.

Ken Barnard
Interview with
Joseph Heller

Husky, tanned and good-natured, Joseph Heller hunched over a luncheon plate of gefilte fish he had just spooned from a jar.

Far from the flak sent up by his wildly satirical novel, *Catch-22*, and the movie made from it, he sat in his Fire Island cottage attired in walking shorts. Around his neck was a long string of love beads made by his 18-year-old daughter, Erica.

"She told me that after about three days, I'd get used to them," he said. "This is the third day and, you know, she's right."

Erica and her brother Teddy, 13, were spending a few days with their mother, Shirley, shopping in Manhattan, so Heller was taking advantage of the quiet to work on a second novel. Unlike *Catch-22*, it is not a war novel, but it deals with a corporate executive who, not unlike Yossarian in *Catch*, worries about how his life is to end. The first draft is on long, yellow legal pads, in longhand.

The Hellers will have been married for 25 years come next October, and says he: "Neither one of us has ever had a divorce. We're beginning to think there's something wrong with us."

While Lucy, Heller's beagle, joined me in listening attentively, the author talked about the movie, in which Alan Arkin portrays the desperately unhappy bombardier, Yossarian, and the book he started in 1953, *Catch-18*.

"*Catch-18?*"

Right. That was the title under which he wrote the book. As he recalls it, "The first chapter was published in 1955 in *New World Writing No. 7*. It used to be a quarterly anthology that published parts of books people were working on. When the book was done, they were ready to set type as *Catch-18*.

"Then one day when I was working for *McCall's* (in the promotion department), I got a frantic call from my editor who said: 'Come over here. Something terrible has happened.'

"The something terrible was they had just read in *Publisher's Weekly*

SOURCE: *Detroit News*, September 13, 1970, pp. 19, 24, 27–28, 30, and 65. Reprinted by permission of the publisher.

that a few weeks before *Catch-18* was to come out, Leon Uris was publishing a novel called *Mila 18*. Leon Uris was then very well known because he had done *Exodus*. They felt it would have been disastrous to have two books coming out with the number 18 in the title. If people had to make a choice, they would choose his rather than mine.

"So we spent about two weeks of great, great depression and soulsearching trying to come up with [19] another title. We actually deluded ourselves, three adults—me, my editor and the woman in charge of promotion—that there was no substitute for 18. It had to be 18. We were too rational; we were behaving like lunatics. We had to find an explanation for the feeling, and I found the explanation. It was that it's the only number that begins with a vowel, and *Catch* ends with a consonant. And that's why no other number sounds like it. And they accepted that!

"Then we found another exception. 'Eleven' begins with a vowel, but we couldn't use 11 because it has an extra syllable, and there was a movie out then called *Ocean's 11*.

"For two weeks I was going through *Bartlett's Quotations* looking for ideas. Then my editor called up and said, 'I've got it; I think I've got it. Don't say no too quickly. I want you to think about it.' So I said, 'Well, what is it?' and he said: '*Catch-22*.' I said, 'Yeahhh, that's it.'

"He and I liked the fact that the number 22 has a relevance to the novel because so many things do repeat themselves. The soldier in white comes back a second time, the dying soldier sees everything twice, and the chaplain thinks that everything that happens has happened once before. For that reason the two 2's struck me as being very appropriate to the novel."

So *Catch-22* was published in 1961 and the following year Columbia Pictures paid Heller a total of $125,000 for the movie rights, which were eventually conveyed to Paramount, under whose banner the movie directed by Mike Nichols is now playing.

When the novel first appeared it was panned by *The New York Times*, which later contritely featured a cover story on Heller in its Sunday book review. *Catch-22* never did sell enough copies in a single week to make the *Times'* best-seller list, though it did rack up sales of 32,000 copies in the first year before the paperback appeared and became an instantaneous best seller.

Heller's most recent statement from his publisher shows that into the early part of last year there have been purchased [24] 575,000 copies of the paperback edition. The sales will undoubtedly be stimulated further by the movie.

Heller still grimaces when he remembers the review of his book run by *The New Yorker* magazine. "Oh boy! I mean, *The New Yorker* attacked me and the book. They were real nasty."

People are always asking Heller, who flew 60 missions as a World War II bombardier, why he waited until 1953 to begin the novel about the hapless Yossarian and his zany bombers.

His reply: "I started the book when I was ready. There's a line in Samuel Beckett's *Endgame* when he asks his parents, 'Why did you have me?' and the father replies, 'We didn't know it would be you.' I didn't have *Catch-22* to write until I began writing it. It's not as though I postponed writing that particular novel until 1953 when I had the idea and began it. I don't think I could have written or even conceived it right after the war.

"What *Catch-22* is more about than World War II is the Korean War and the Cold War. The elements that inspired the ideas came to me from the civilian situation in this country in the 1950's when we did have such things as loyalty oaths to say when we were at war in Korea and Mac-Arthur did seem to be wanting to provoke a war against China, when Dulles was taking us to the brink of war against Russia every other week and it seemed inevitable that we were going to plunge right into another major war.

"Until that time we were in a process of restoring ourselves. The same factionalism, the same antagonism, the mortal enmity that exists between groups today in this country existed then as well. But to me it was a new phenomenon. I chose the war (World War II) as a setting because it seemed to me we were at war. Certainly that was the start of the civil rights movement, for example. There were whites who wanted to kill every black. I remember those really disgustingly terrifying photographs of little children going to school in Clinton, Ky., and New Orleans—little black kids going into kindergarten and those white monsters with clubs—the women snarling and cursing and their faces contorted by such hatred.

"Then there was the same type of antagonism developing between (Senator) Joseph McCarthy—and Nixon and his committee—and people who, well, it then was called the Communist conspiracy. Teachers and Quakers were being fired. There was a kind of war going on between groups.

"I see *Catch-22* as not about World War II. It certainly does not reflect my attitude toward that war. For everybody after Pearl Harbor, it was a war we wanted to fight—a war we knew had to be won. It doesn't reflect my emotions of combat, which were different from Yossarian's. An important point in the book is that the war in Europe is drawing to a close as the danger to Yossarian from his own superiors intensifies. He was able to say in the end of the book that the war against Germany is just about over and the country's not in danger any more, but he is. It's essentially a conflict between people—American officers and their own government. They are the antagonists of *Catch-22*—much more so than the Germans and Hitler, who are scarcely mentioned.

"The combat men found themselves at the mercy of the people who are employed to serve them, the administrators. In order to get their flak suits they have to sing the Star-Spangled Banner twice; in order to get the maps they have to recite the Pledge of Allegiance; and they suddenly find themselves enslaved by those officials whose original function was to be of service to them.

"I think we've had such a situation continuing since the end of World War II, and the novel applies even more today."

Heller believed he was distorting ridiculous systems of logic that an entrenched officialdom can hatch. The symbolic novel he thought he was writing has been transformed by ensuing events into a realistic novel. A propos of the development, he summons a wry smile as he asks: "Remember reading in the papers about this general and the master sergeants who were investigated for watering PX (post exchange) booze and sending money into Switzerland?" The smile [27] becomes a hearty laugh as he adds: "To me the funniest part is that they took back their medals!"

For 15 years after the war it was impossible to persuade Heller to get aboard an airplane. He still thinks you have "to be nuts or have a potential for being nuts to become a pilot."

He flew more than 20 missions before he saw a plane shot down with men bailing out. "Till then it was a lark. Even when the missions were dangerous, I was too stupid to realize it. It was like a movie to me."

It was his 37th mission—his second to Avignon—which is described in the book and movie and left him looking forward passionately to becoming an ex-flier. During it, the co-pilot went "a little berserk" and grabbed the controls away from the pilot. Heller was in the nose of the bomber and did not know what had happened. For a while he felt they had lost a wing and were going straight down. He had just seen an engine blow up on the aircraft ahead of his ship with a wing falling off, the plane going down and no parachutes coming out.

"Then suddenly after we dropped our bombs," he says, "our plane started to go straight down and I was pinned to the top of the cabin. The co-pilot had thought we were climbing too steeply and would stall. He grabbed the controls to shove us back down. We went down and I thought I was dying.

"Then the plane straightened out and flew through flak and my earphones were pulled out. I didn't know my headset was out. You know, when you press the button to talk, you hear a click, but I pressed it and heard nothing, so I thought I was already dead.

"For a while the rest of the crew couldn't hear me, and when I did plug in I heard this guy—the co-pilot—hysterical on the intercom yelling, 'The bombardier doesn't answer. Help him! Help him! Go help the bombardier.' And I said, 'I'm the bombardier; I'm OK,' and he said, 'Go help the gunner.' He was shot through the leg and that's in the book and movie. But I added to it and had him shot in the middle."

Heller made a promise to himself that if he survived the war he would stay off airplanes. For years he was true to his word. Then he spent 24 hours on a train from Miami to New York—"and that's when I changed my mind: I decided I'd rather be dead."

Being especially facile with humor, dialog and chase scenes, Heller has hired out for script work on such movies as *Sex and the Single Girl, Casino Royale,* and *Dingus Magee.*

But unless he needs the money, he's not looking for movie assignments: "I would rather spend my effort on something I value and has a greater possibility of endurance. You can say much more in a novel than you can in a movie. But I'm very good at rewriting movies. I can do them like lightning because I'm good at dialog and humor, and I can characterize quickly."

He admits that he suffers through the construction of expository passages in his novels, always looking forward to when he can break into dialog.

He has no desire to do an entire screenplay. It would take as much work as turning out a novel—"and yet it's not autonomous. Movies are made with a popular audience in mind, whereas in a novel I can write for my own audience and myself. I can't write unless I give it everything I've got. When I was writing advertising presentations, which I was doing when I was writing *Catch-22,* the reason I was good at it was that I put as much imagination into those slide shows as I was putting in the evenings into *Catch-22.*"

Heller kept his distance from the filming of his novel. A formal invitation was extended to him, but he regarded that as a courtesy, deciding that he wasn't really wanted. He didn't care to go to the movie locale in Mexico since he thought he would be in the way and might make people nervous.

"Also, I've been on the set when movies were being made and it's the dullest procedure in the world," he says. "If you're not involved in working on that thing, it's monotony. And it would be irresponsible for me to be raising questions or setting goals if I'm not the one who has to achieve them. I had only one conversation with Mike [28] Nichols and (scenarist) Buck Henry. They had me read a script—I think it was the script before the final—and wanted my opinions. I gave a few.

"I told them what I liked about it and a few things that would give me concern if I had to make the movie. Nichols was intelligent enough to ignore a couple of my suggestions. One or two things I thought would not work worked beautifully in the film. This was another good reason why he was smart to keep me away."

After he saw the movie, alone with his wife and daughter and Nichols in a screening room, he took the director aside and told him he was overwhelmed, that it was "maybe the best picture I ever saw, which was honestly the way I felt about it—and he was relieved.

"The opening was so hypnotic that by the time the titles were finished, I forgot it was a movie about a book I had written and I was just waiting to see what would happen."

He regards the picture version not as an adaptation, but rather a translation. In Heller's view, most adaptations of books and plays don't work: "They don't make particularly good movies. One reason is that they stick too closely to the architecture of what is essentially a literary work. I think what Nichols did was exploit the visual potential of the cameras, and there are many setups that seem to me to be almost museum paintings."

Heller says he is "delighted beyond words" that Nichols didn't go for easy laughs or yaks. As Heller puts it, "*Catch-22* is anything but a comedy. It's almost heartbreaking." Before the screening, he feared that the movie might be frivolous or irrelevant.

Heller and his wife were in agreement on the scene that had the greatest emotional tug for them. It takes place in an Italian brothel that the American military police have raided. A lonely old woman remains, answering Yossarian's questions, and when he wants to know what authority the MP's had for the raid, she tells him they cited the maniacal regulation that is the book's title—or, as she [30] phrases it solemnly, "Catch-a-22."

The old man seen earlier who thought he could accommodate to any situation is gone, dead, and she sits there confused. Says Heller: "She does it all almost without changing expression and a tone of resignation.

"She's sitting there smoking a cigarette—I don't think she even looks at the camera. She's not crying; she's not upset. There's just such a philosophical weariness in what she's saying—that everything's been smashed and there's no way to stop it. You've seen that room only once before and it's been filled with people. They didn't focus on a sex scene even then. You see girls in the background and guys hanging around, and now it's empty, a kind of cathedral-like room. That's a scene with a sense of despair and futility."

Two scenes he thought could never be rendered on the screen. One shows blackmarketeer Milo Minderbinder, played by Jon Voight, having his own base bombed in a deal with the Germans. Heller was worried about its inclusion because in the novel it's allegorical, not literal. He felt people wouldn't believe it on screen, but now rates it a "most effective" scene.

His second misgiving concerned a sequence for which he admits having "a genuine distaste" in the script. Had he been consultant or writer, he would have argued against it: "Yet on the screen it's a completely visual thing. You see, without knowing what Nichols had in mind for each scene, my comments could have been irrelevant."

He's referring to the interlude showing servicemen waiting in line at a brothel in Rome. Heller recalled its impact: "You see these men standing in line and it's a long line; it seems endless in memory. This is one of the haunting qualities about the movie. Memory creates things and distorts what was thought. I've seen it twice and it's still one scene I think they shot in slow motion even though I know it hasn't been.

"Those guys are standing in line and not moving—most of them American soldiers, a few sailors—and the line just winds and turns the corner, and there's the girl at the desk who's selling them admission to the whorehouse. I got a feeling from it that they've been there since the world began and they'll be there till it ends."

The title of the novel he's trying to wrap up this summer is *Something Happened*. Very different from *Catch-22*, it's set in a New York corporation and deals with a man in his 40's who's not getting on as well as he'd like with his children or his wife.

As the author describes it: "He's got a very good job and he doesn't like that any more either and wonders what he's to do with the end of his life, if anything, and knows inwardly that he's not going to do anything about it. The title is ironic because actually nothing happens. His biggest concern—if you want a plot line, and you're going to think it's facetious, but it's true—is whether or not he's going to be allowed to make a three-minute speech at the company convention."

Heller, who's 47 ("I know I look 22, but I'm really 47"), numbers very few performers among his friends. Exceptions include Alan Arkin, Richard Benjamin and wife, Paula Prentiss, and Eli Wallach. He thinks that maybe his candor and sense of humor may be upsetting when he's talking to actors.

"Performers live lives of anxiety," he says. "If they don't know now what they're going to be acting in when they're finished with what they're doing, they get feelings of being unloved and unwanted. I've seen this even with the biggest Hollywood stars. They get panicky when there's nothing ahead of them."

In his heart he knows that *Catch-22* is an excellent movie, but he has to wait a while for most of his reward from it. He's due to receive 2½ percent of the profits. But the picture, with interest charges, cost about $16 million to make. Add on advertising, promotion and other expenses, and it may have to take in as much as $30 million before profit can be counted.

Glancing down at the manuscript of *Something Happened*, he went on, "I hope the film will be so successful for me that I won't have to finish this novel." Then a big laugh emphasized his fervent wish: "I may never have to work again!" [65]

Clayton L. Balch
Yossarian to Cathcart and Return:
A Personal Cross-Country

Preflight

Catch-22 first flashed across my awareness in 1962 as I spun a supermarket paperback book rack. A B-25 suddenly flew by backward and my aircraft recognition circuit activated: "*B-25—combat—1944—flak—seventy missions—Corsica.* Being still half in love with my programmed soul, I was gratified that the circuit tested operationally OK."

"Ah," I thought, scanning the book, "a reminiscence of World War II flying, and one in which I had participated! No doubt a romantic (sexual), patriotic (blood and guts), potboiler." So I read it. I think that my initial reaction was one of puzzled amusement. I suppose that I had wanted the romantic-patriotic. Instead, I seemed to be drawn into an intellectual exercise because of the convolutions of the plot, which was punctuated with hilarious anecdotes. It was years before I realized that *Catch-22* was really a profound philosophical confrontation and that my laughter had long since turned hollow and died.

But in 1962, I was as diverted by the superficiality of Heller's humor as I had been diverted by my own shallow perceptions of the actual events of 1944–45 in Corsica. I believed that any horror or nightmare associated with that earlier time existed, surely, only in the crazed mind of Yossarian, who obviously had "had it"—the World War II phrase for combat fatigue. I therefore set all that aside and found great reward in comparing my own reminiscences of people and events.

Journey

It was, of course, Corsica and not Pianosa. And, although the 340th Bomb Group had been bombed, it was by the Germans and not by Milo's com-

SOURCE: This essay was written especially for this book.

mercial fleet. But that was nit-picking: I had a store of characters and happenings of my own.

The central facts of life then were the daily mission and the number of anti-aircraft guns defending the target and the amount of flak those guns would produce. Like all good bird hunters, the German gunners always led you, and, given a steady target for more than twenty seconds, they would hit you. Thus, in the three or four minutes over the target, the lead bombardier who could carry his formation through a pattern of evasive action that varied enough to outwit the German gunners, yet find twenty seconds to devote to a straight and level bomb run at precisely the correct time and place—that lead bombardier was both artist and hero. Make no mistake about it; we were good. Tight formations of six B-25's would careen all over the sky, then suddenly seem to pause quietly while bomb bay doors snapped open and twenty-four 1,000-pound bombs fell simultaneously away. At the lurch of bomb release confirmed by the bombardier's cry of "Bombs away," the evasive careen began again until the formation was out of range of the anti-aircraft fire. We did this daily, and we regularly hit railroad bridges that were thirty feet long and two tracks wide. But for ten minutes, you lived in a world of 88- and 105-millimeter flak. It would burst in front of you and you would fly through it. Depending, therefore, upon the accuracy and luck operative on both sides, you might observe it blossoming lazily and quietly ahead, or, closer, hear its loud pop and see the angry bees shoot out toward you from the suddenly disturbed core. Or, perhaps, you might never see or hear *the* one.

The good news on my first mission was that the legendary Major Iron-Ass Grow would fly that day. Major Iron-Ass Grow had earlier completed a tour of fifty missions, but, finding the States unstimulating, had returned for a second tour. The sobriquet "Iron-Ass" had been bestowed on him by a grateful 310th Bomb Group because the presence of Iron-Ass on a mission in some way neutralized the flak. If Iron-Ass flew, the toughest target became a milk run. Presumably, the Germans stood in similar awe of the courage and greatness of Iron-Ass. We imagined the gun crews at rigid Teutonic attention as our formations swept majestically over the target. Months later when I had flown my last mission and was on my way home (no second tour for me!), Major Iron-Ass Grow still strode through the squadron area with his magnificent jaw line poised always at the proper angle of attack. What a memorable image!

Or, consider our Flight Surgeon, Doc Anderson, who, we understood, had been a big-time OB-Gyn man in Chicago. Doc dispensed his APC's and his Atabrine efficiently, but he concentrated his attention on the pregnant local peasants. Doc delivered babies at every opportunity, and his ability to cope with the "blue baby" phenomenon caused the natives to name him "The Wizard of Maison Blanche." To ease his own tensions,

Doc would illuminate us laymen around the bar with juicy clinical details such as the technique for manually scooping out afterbirth. Doc would cackle gleefully at the rapid departure of the weak-stomached.

Or, the names escape me now, our singer-navigator who every night at the bar was persuaded by an old lieutenant colonel to warble "Embraceable You" *a cappella*. Great tears would roll down the old (age twenty-eight) lieutenant colonel's cheeks.

Or A. K. Adams, portions of whose autonomic nervous system concluded an early separate peace. AK's bowels no longer functioned automatically. On, say, Monday, AK would head for Doc Anderson's office. "Where to, AK?" we would ask. "To get unplugged," AK would mutter. For two or three days AK went nowhere without a roll of toilet paper tucked under his arm. On Thursday, we would chorus, "Where to, AK?" "To get plugged," AK would retort weakly.

Then there was the pet monkey brought back from Cairo by two "old-timers." (Old-timer: one who had joined the Group when the tour was fifty missions. It was now seventy.) The pet monkey soon became a full-fledged aircrew member with the slightly hysterical old-timers. I was flying their wing at the time—a ringside seat to observe the antics of the monkey! First he would be in the cockpit with the pilots, then in the nose with the bombardier. Occasionally he would pop up in the tail turret. One day over the target, the old-timers' bomb bay doors opened and their bombs fell out with the monkey firmly astride the top bomb! In that instant I comprehended what a "look of wild surmise" really was.

There were other funny pet stories. As the winter of 1944-45 set in, a pet cat took to crawling into the dying ashes of his master's fireplace. One cold day the innocent master, returning from a mission, tossed a can of 100-octane gasoline into the fireplace in the customary quick warmup manner. The squawling ball of fire that rose from the ashes, flew through the door, and disappeared into the cypress forest caused a near heart attack in the master and near hysterics for the rest of us. Funny. Almost as funny as the monkey.

I try to explain the distorted humor on two counts. Basically, we were only kids. We were absolutely convinced, for example, that no one over the age of twenty-one could possibly do what we were doing. A conspicuous exception was our tail gunner, James Mason Madison, of Virginia (a direct descendant), who spoke from the lofty plateau of his twenty-eight-year-old maturity. Not so much in arrogance as in innocence, I would argue irrelevancies with him. He would finally crinkle his eyes at me with tolerant amusement and apply the perfect squelch: "You right, lieutenant! You got the rank in this crowd."

As for the day-to-day living, I don't think that any of us really expected to survive. Seventy missions simply loomed as an insurmountable obstacle.

Old-timers like Dick Gimmie always referred to their fiftieth through seventieth missions as "borrowed time." Joe Althouse came in from the flight line one afternoon, spread his hands, looked somewhere into the distance, and announced that he was dead. Joe had accidentally dropped a plane load of fragmentation bombs on the ramp while preflighting his bombing system. When the frags didn't explode, Joe concluded, I suppose, that he had now borrowed so much time that he was too deep in debt to death to survive further.

Superstitions and rituals abounded. Having started it, I was expected by my crew to pronounce a benediction after each mission while we were waiting for the truck. I would say, "Sixty-five more (or forty-four more, or twenty-seven more, or one more) like that one and I'm gonna quit!" Or, I recall, I never bought more than one postage stamp at a time.

We outdid Heller's story of Orr's gas generator. We built a hot shower building! Picture the medieval town of Ghisonaccia, tame jackasses roaming the dusty streets in search of their owners, who had been moved out so that we would have billets, and rising in its midst, a huge rectangular metal and brick structure dedicated to piping hot water over tender pink American bodies. It was a veritable cathedral of cleanliness! The structure was months abuilding. Imagine the complexities: water supply, water pressure, a boiler, pipes, drains. But finally, late in February, we were able to come together to commune and hymn in an Americo-Christian Hot Shower! And what a monstrous blunder it turned out to be! Clean, we could now smell everything else; we became weak and susceptible to viruses. The only gain was the mental strength and serenity which settle over the freshly scrubbed and disinfected Wasp.

We didn't have nurses; the hospital was elsewhere. But we did have a Red Cross girl. Well, we didn't, the Group Commander did. She had been going with one of the lead bombardiers, but eventually she succumbed to the obvious superiorities that colonels possess over captains, even if the captain is an artist-hero. I was pleased, last year, to meet this same lead bombardier deep in the Pentagon, and was gratified to observe that he, like Yossarian, had survived both the Red Cross girl and the Group Commander.

Ah, as *Playboy* would put it, The Girls of Rome! To us latent adults accustomed mainly to the Great American Virgin, the girls of Rome were magnificent. Never mind that they were prostitutes. The mere fact that ladies' shoes cost $35 led us easily into the magnanimous concept that a day or two with us allowed these fallen to acquire the necessities of life. Besides, this was corrupt and evil Europe. Perhaps some of our superior morality would rub off as further military aid and assistance. One night as I was removing my blouse in Rosa's dismal room, she pointed to my newly won Air Medal ribbon. "What did you get thees for?" "Oh," I replied, "for bombing the little northern town of Casale Monferrato." By amazing coincidence, Casale Monferrato was Rosa's home town! I struggled mightily with my Italian phrase book to explain to Rosa that what we bombed was the railroad bridge on the *edge* of town, but relations with Rosa were never really the same after that.

Like Yossarian, I received my DFC on a sun-baked parade ground, but unlike Yossarian, I was conservatively clad in a Class-A uniform. My DFC was presented by Lieutenant General Ira C. Eaker, then commander of Mediterranean Army Air Forces. There was no further incident. However, in 1965 I was assigned to fly General Eaker, now retired and pursuing a journalistic career, from Dayton to Denver. "General," I cried, somewhere over Iowa, "You pinned my DFC on me in Corsica in 1944!" Observing me with appropriate caution, the General replied, "I see you made it."

Surprisingly, most of us did make it. My seventieth and last combat mission had a romantic element to it. Our Bomb Wing was moving from Corsica to Italy as we pushed the German Army back into the Fatherland. For maximum efficiency, the airplanes would take off from the old bases in Corsica, fly a mission, and then land at the new bases in Italy. So, as simple folk will, we celebrated our last night in Corsica with a farewell party. At the height of the revelry, someone started a fire in the air-raid shelter behind one of the billets. Soon we were all adding miscellaneous combustibles to the blaze: old ammunition which brought a fine Fourth-of-July flavor to this foreign land, broken tree branches, 100-octane gasoline, perhaps an old bed or dresser. We were surely Boy Scouts around a campfire. At some point, I noticed that the number of spectators was increasing. The new ones were the original inhabitants (We called them *gooks*, mind you!), and they were coming home. Ringed in the firelight, they seemed to be almost like hunted animals drawn in fascination to the hunter's fire, forest creatures lured to the forest fire. Despite the heat, something cold blew through my heart. And that part of my heart, when I allow it, is still cold and black.

Debriefing

And that, I think, is what Heller's vision became to me: he saw early what we were really doing, or perhaps more charitably, what was being done to us. At the time, we, like Yossarian, were interested only in survival, but unlike Yossarian, we would survive by adapting to the system, not by fleeing from it when our consciences could take no more. In the film version of *Catch-22*, which I am drawn to again and again, I am most struck when the B-25's taxi by for the early morning takeoff. Those faceless and identical young men in the cockpits! I keep searching for myself.

I wish that I could say that I saw it on the first reading of *Catch-22*;

however, Heller had laid a series of depth charges in my path. And, as I witnessed the madness of the Southeast Asia involvement unfold, and as I participated in it myself, I now looked through Yossarian's eyes. I saw the Dreedles and the Cathcarts and the Natelys and the Orrs, and worst of all horrors, I could see the Cathcart and the Dreedle in me.

I cut my teeth on pulp magazine adventures of World War I. In World War II, I saw, of course, that *Flying Aces* spoke of a simpler chivalric code. Now we had created a clean and surgical war of formation patterns and secret Norden bombsights for the purpose of controlling irrational people like Hitler, and, by extension, Nature herself. What innocence! We thought that we were directing and enjoying the services of an amenable servant-giant, but, of course, it was only the genie's little toe we saw. The rest of him lay waiting to burst, all but out of control from the first, from the sands of Alamogordo.

At the peak of Milo's bombing raid upon his own Group, even Cathcart tries to stop him, but Milo, unruffled and secure in his motives, calmly orders one plane back to get a shed it had missed and another to strafe because its bombs were all dropped. "*Strafe?*" Alvin Brown [the pilot] was shocked.

"We have no choice," Milo informed him resignedly. "It's in the contract."

"Oh, okay, then," Alvin Brown acquiesced. "In that case I'll strafe."

There is now forever in my mind a hard straight line that begins in that scene, passes through the Vietnam experience, and shoots out into the impending chaos of exploitation, waste, overpopulation, pollution, and death. We have never been bereft of prophets—seers such as Heller. Some listen, but as always, too many do not hear; there's no profit in prophets.

	Event	Description	McWatt / Dunbar	Nately
	MISSIONS RAISED TO 55	1. Yossarian goes to Daneeka again with the idea of being noted crazy, but is turned down. He now has 48 missions. 2. Goes to Wintergreen for help and is turned down, missions are raised to 55 while he is away.		
	Yossarian keeps FLYING	Goes to Major Major for help but is turned away. He tackles Major Major in a ditch in order to see him. He now has 51 missions.		
	MISSIONS RAISED TO 60	1. Yossarian tries Doc Daneeka again to no avail. He still has 51 missions when missions are raised to 60. 2. Yossarian protects the chaplain when the colonel tries to throw him out		
	YOSSARIAN WOUNDED	He is wounded in the leg on a milk run when Aarfy gets lost and leads the planes over flak.	McWatt is the pilot and administers first aid	Nate... copilot... Miss...
	YOSSARIAN IN THE HOSPITAL	1. Yossarian gooses Nurse Duckett and a love affair starts between them. 2. Refuses again to join Dobbs in the plot to murder the colonel because he's sure he will be sent home. 3. A psychiatrist finds him insane, but he is returned to combat and a different man is sent home in his place.	Dunbar goes into the hospital just to keep Yossarian company.	
	ORR LOST IN COMBAT	Yossarian continues flying missions when colonel volunteers for Bologna again. Yossarian goes to Dobbs and agrees to the murder plot.		
	BETWEEN ORR AND KID SAMPSON	1. Yossarian is distressed by the assignment to destroy a whole village in order to create a road block. 2. Yossarian is ready to kill McWatt when McWatt buzzes with Yossarian in the plane	McWatt buzzes Yossarian. Dunbar turns surly and starts to crack up	
	KID SAMPSON KILLED / McWATT commits SUICIDE	Yossarian is on the beach with Nurse Duckett when McWatt's plane cuts Kid Sampson in...	McWatt lets the others bail out, then ... into a mountain	
	NATELY GETS HIS GIRL	1. In Rome he alone for Luciana and is ready to fall in love with Nurse Duckett. He is lonely and does not know what to do with himself. 2. He helps Nately rescue his girl... higher rank	Dunbar goes along to help Nately	Nate... rescue girl... her sleep
	YOSSARIAN BREAKS NATELY'S NOSE	After Milo's Thanksgiving ... is awakened in terror by ... so angry he grabs the man who fired the gun ... tries to restrain that ... so savagely that ...	Dunbar ... asleep in the hospital and is disappeared	Nate... friend to ... as ... of w...
	70 MISSIONS FINISHED / NATELY KILLED	... Yossarian ... refer to ... overseas ... to Milo		Nately in ... crash ... La S...
	YOSSARIAN REFUSES to FLY MISSIONS	... Rome ... a rest ... whore about his ... him. He escapes		
	GOES AWOL TO "The ETERNAL CITY"	... back to Rome to find ... kid sister. He is ... being in Rome without a pass ... turned		
	ACCEPTS KORN'S DEAL. Is stabbed	Yossarian accepts the chance to become "one of the boys" in return for being allowed to go home a hero		
	In the hospital HE REPUDIATES THE DEAL	Yossarian cannot go along with the deal even though it will mean his life will be saved. Does not know what he will do		
	YOSSARIAN RUNS AWAY joyously when he learns Orr is safe	Heads for Rome to try to save Nately's kid sister, and then for Sweden but does not expect to get there. HAS 71 MISSIONS		

Love,
Dad

Second Lieutenant Edward J. Nately III was really a good kid. He was a slender, shy, rather handsome young man with fine brown hair, delicate cheekbones, large, intent eyes and a sharp pain in the small of his back when he woke up alone on a couch in the parlor of a whorehouse in Rome one morning and began wondering who and where he was and how in the world he had ever got there. He had no real difficulty remembering *who* he was. He was Second Lieutenant Edward J. Nately III, a bomber pilot in Italy in World War Two, and he would be 20 years old in January, if he lived.

Nately had always been a good kid from a Philadelphia family that was even better. He was always pleasant, considerate, trustworthy, loyal, helpful, friendly, courteous, kind, obedient, cheerful, not always so thrifty or wise but invariably brave, clean and reverent. He was without envy, malice, anger, hatred or resentment, which puzzled his good friend Yossarian and kept him aware of how eccentric and naïve Nately really was and how much in need of protection by Yossarian against the wicked ways of the world.

Why, Nately had actually enjoyed his childhood—and was not even ashamed to admit it! Nately *liked* all his brothers and sisters and always

SOURCE: *Playboy*, December 1969, pp. 181–182, 348. Reprinted by permission of the author.

had, and he did not mind going home for vacations and furloughs. He got on well with his uncles and his aunts and with all his first, second and third cousins, whom, of course, he numbered by the dozens, with all the friends of the family and with just about everyone else he ever met, except, possibly, the incredibly and unashamedly depraved old man who was always in the whorehouse when Nately and Yossarian arrived and seemed to have spent his entire life living comfortably and happily there. Nately was well bred, well groomed, well mannered and well off. He was, in fact, immensely wealthy, but no one in his squadron on the island of Pianosa held his good nature or his good family background against him.

Nately had been taught by both parents all through childhood, pre-adolescence and adolescence to shun and disdain "climbers," "pushers," "*nouveaux*" and "parvenus," but he had never been able to, since no climbers, pushers, *nouveaux* or parvenus had ever been allowed near any of the family homes in Philadelphia, Fifth Avenue, Palm Beach, Bar Harbor, Southampton, Mayfair and Belgravia, the 16th *arrondissement*, the north of France, the south of France and all of the good Greek islands. To the best of his knowledge, the guest lists at all these places had always been composed exclusively of ladies and gentlemen and children of faultless dress and manners and great dignity and aplomb. There were always many bankers, brokers, judges, ambassadors and former ambassadors among them, many sportsmen, cabinet officials, fortune hunters and dividend-collecting widows, divorcees, orphans and spinsters. There were no labor leaders among them and no laborers, and there were never any self-made men. There was one unmarried social worker, who toiled among the under-privileged for fun, and several retired generals and admirals who were dedicating the remaining years of their lives to preserving the American Constitution by destroying it and perpetuating the American way of life by bringing it to an end.

The only one in the entire group who worked hard was Nately's mother; but since she did not work hard at anything constructive, her reputation remained good. Nately's mother worked very hard at opening and closing the family homes in Philadelphia, Fifth Avenue, Palm Beach, Bar Harbor, Southampton, Mayfair and Belgravia, the 16th *arrondissement*, the north of France, the south of France and all of the good Greek islands, and at safeguarding the family traditions, of which she had appointed herself austere custodian.

"You must never forget who and what you are"; Nately's mother had begun drumming it into Nately's head about Natelys long before Nately had any idea what a Nately was. "You are not a Guggenheim, who mined copper for a living, nor a Vanderbilt, whose [181] fortune is descended from a common tugboat captain, nor an Armour, whose ancestors peddled putrefying meat to the gallant Union Army during the heroic War between the States, nor a Harriman, who made his money playing with choo-choo trains. Our family," she always declared with pride, "does *nothing* for our money."

"What your mater means, my boy," interjected his father with the genial, rococo wit Nately found so impressive, "is that people who make new fortunes are not nearly as good as the families who've lost old ones. Ha, ha, ha! Isn't that good, my dear?"

"I wish you would mind your own business when I'm talking to the boy," Nately's mother replied sharply to Nately's father.

"Yes, my dear."

Nately's mother was a stiff-necked, straight-backed, autocratic descendant of the old New England Thorntons. The family tree of the New England Thorntons, as she often remarked, extended back far past the Mayflower, almost to Adam himself. It was a matter of historical record that the Thorntons were lineal descendants of the union of John Alden, a climber, to Priscilla Mullins, a pusher. The genealogy of the Natelys was no less impressive, since one of Nately's father's forebears had distinguished himself conspicuously at the battle of Bosworth Field, on the losing side.

"Mother, what is a regano?" Nately inquired innocently one day while on holiday from Andover after an illicit tour through the Italian section of Philadelphia, before reporting to his home for duty. "Is it anything like a Nately?"

"Oregano," replied his mother with matriarchal distaste, "is a revolting vice indulged in by untitled foreigners in Italy. Don't ever mention it again."

Nately's father chuckled superiorly when Nately's mother had gone. "You mustn't take everything your mother says too literally, son," he advised with a wink. "Your mother is a remarkable woman, as you probably know, but when she deals with such matters as oregano, she's usually full of shit. Now, I've eaten oregano many times, if you know what I mean, and I expect that you will, too, before you marry and settle down. The important thing to remember about eating oregano is never to do it with a girl from your own social station. Do it with salesgirls and waitresses, if you can, or with any of our maids, except Lili, of course, who, as you may have noticed, is something of a favorite of mine. I'm not sending you to women of lower social station out of snobbishness, but simply because they're so much better at it than the daughters and wives of our friends. Nurses and schoolteachers enjoy excellent reputations in this respect. Not a word about this to your mother, of course."

Nately's father overflowed with sanguine advice of that kind. He was a dapper, affable man of great polish and experience whom everybody but Nately's mother respected. Nately was proud of his father's wisdom and sophistication; and the eloquent, brilliant letters he received when away at school were treasured compensation for those bleak and painful separations from his parents. Nately's father, on the other hand, welcomed these separations from his son with ceremonious zeal, for they gave him opportunity to fashion the graceful, aesthetic, metaphysical letters in which he took such epicurean satisfaction.

Dear Son (he wrote when Nately was away at Andover):
   Don't be the first person by whom new things are tried and don't be the last one to set old ones aside. If our family were ever to adopt for itself a brief motto, I would want it to be precisely those words, and not merely because I wrote them myself. (Ha, ha, ha!) I would select them for the wisdom they contain. They urge restraint, and restraint is the quintessence of dignity and taste. It is incumbent upon you as a Nately that dignity and taste are always what you show.
   Today you are at Andover. Tomorrow you will be elsewhere. There will be times in later life when you will find yourself with people who attended Exeter, Choate, Hotchkiss, Groton and other institutions of like ilk. These people will address you as equals and speak to you familiarly, as though you share with them a common fund of experience. Do not be deceived. Andover is Andover, and Exeter is not, and neither are any of the others anything that they are not.
   Throughout life, you must always choose your friends as discriminately as you choose your clothing, and you must bear in mind constantly that all that glitters is not gold.

                                                                Love, Dad

   Nately had hoarded these letters from his father loyally and was often tempted to fling their elevated contents into the jaded face of the hedonistic old man who seemed to be in charge of the whorehouse in Rome, in lordly refutation of his pernicious, unkempt immorality and as a triumphant illustration of what a cultivated, charming, intelligent and distinguished man of character such as his father was really like. What restrained Nately was a confused and intimidating suspicion that the old man would succeed in degrading his father with the same noxious and convincing trickery with which he had succeeded in degrading everything else Nately deemed holy. Nately had a large number of his father's letters to save. Following Andover, he had moved, of course, to Harvard, and his father had proved equal to the occasion.

Dear Son (his father wrote):
   Don't be the first person by whom new things are tried and don't be the last person to set the old things aside. This pregnant couplet came to me right out of the blue only a few moments ago, while I was out on

the patio listening to your mother and a Mozart clarinet concerto and spreading Crosse & Blackwell marmalade on my Melba toast, and I am interrupting my breakfast to communicate it to you while it is still fresh in my mind. Write it down on your brain, inscribe it on your heart, engrave it for all time on your memory centers, for the advice it contains is as sound as any I have ever told you.

Today you are at Harvard, the oldest educational institution in the United States of America, and I am not certain if you are as properly impressed with your situation as you should be. Harvard is more than just a good school; Harvard is also a good place at which to get an education, should you decide that you do want an education. Columbia University, New York University and the City College of New York in the city of New York are other good places at which to get an education, but they are not good schools. Universities such as Princeton, Yale, Dartmouth and bungalows in the Amherst-Williams complex are, of course, neither good schools nor good places at which to get an education and are never to be compared with Harvard. I hope that you are being as choosy in your choice of acquaintances there as you know your mother and I would like you to be.

Love, Dad

P.S. Avoid associating familiarly with Roman Catholics, colored people and Jews, regardless of how accomplished, rich or influential their parents may be, although Chinese, Japanese, Spaniards of royal blood and Moslems of foreign nationality are perfectly all right.
P.P.S. Are you getting much oregano up there? (Ha, ha, ha!)

Nately sampled oregano dutifully his freshman year with a salesgirl, a waitress, a nurse and a schoolteacher, and with three girls in Scranton, Pennsylvania, on two separate occasions, but his appetite for the spice was not hoggish and exposure did not immunize him against falling so unrealistically in love the first moment he laid eyes on the dense, sluggish, yawning, ill-kempt whore lounging stark-naked in a room full of enlisted men ignoring her. Apart from these [182] several formal and rather unexciting excursions into sexuality, Nately's first year at Harvard was empty and dull. He made few close friends, restricted, as he was, to associating only with wealthy Episcopalian and Church of England graduates of Andover whose ancestors had either descended lineally from the union of John Alden with Priscilla Mullins or been conspicuous at Bosworth Field, on the losing side. He spent many solitary hours fondling the expensive vellum bindings of the five books sent to him by his father as the indispensable basis of a sound personal library: *Forges and Furnaces of Pennsylvania; The Catalog of the Porcellian Club of Harvard University, 1941; Burke's*

Genealogical and Heraldic History of the Peerage, Baronetage and Knightage; *Lord Chesterfield's Letters Written to His Son*; and the Francis Palgrave *Golden Treasury* of English verse. The pages themselves did not hold his interest, but the bindings were fascinating. He was often lonely and nagged by vague, incipient longings. He contemplated his sophomore year at Harvard without enthusiasm, without joy. Fortunately, the War broke out in time to save him.

Dear Son (his father wrote, after Nately had volunteered for the Air Corps, to escape being drafted into the Infantry):

You are now embarked upon the highest calling that Providence ever bestows upon man, the privilege to fight for his country. Play up, play up and play the game! I have every confidence that you will not fail your country, your family and yourself in the execution of your most noble responsibility, which is to play up, play up and play the game—and to come out ahead.

The news at home is all good. The market is buoyant and the cost-plus-six-percent type of contract now in vogue is the most salutary invention since the international cartel and provides us with an excellent buffer against the excess-profits tax and the outrageous personal income tax. I have it on excellent authority that Russia cannot possibly hold out for more than a week or two and that after communism has been destroyed, Hitler, Roosevelt, Mussolini, Churchill, Mahatma Gandhi and the Emperor of Japan will make peace and operate the world forever on a sound businesslike basis. However, it remains to be seen whether the wish is just being father to the thought. (Ha, ha, ha!)

My spirit is soaring and my optimism knows no bounds. Hitler has provided precisely the right stimulus needed to restore the American economy to that splendid condition of good health it was enjoying on that glorious Thursday just before Black Friday. War, as you undoubtedly appreciate, presents civilization with a great opportunity and a great challenge. It is in time of war that great fortunes are often made. It is between wars that economic conditions tend to deteriorate. If mankind can just discover some means of increasing the duration of wars and decreasing the intervals between wars, we will have found a permanent solution to this most fundamental of all human ills, the business cycle.

What better advice can a devoted parent give you in this grave period of national crisis than to oppose government interference with all the vigor at your command and to fight to the death to preserve free enterprise—provided, of course, that the enterprise in question is one in which you own a considerable number of shares. (Ha, ha, ha!)

Above all this, to your own self be true. Never be a borrower or a lender of money: Never borrow money at more than two percent and never lend money at less than nine percent.

Love, Dad

P.S. Your mother and I will not go to Cannes this year.

There had been no caviling in the family over Nately's course once war was declared; it was simply taken for granted that he would continue the splendid family tradition of military service that dated all the way back to the battle of Bosworth Field, on the losing side, particularly since Nately's father had it from the most reliable sources in Washington that Russia could not possibly hold out for more than two or three more weeks and that the War would come to an end before Nately could be sent overseas.

It was Nately's mother and Nately's eldest sister's idea that he become an aviation cadet, since Air Corps officers wore no wires in their dress caps and since he would be sheltered in an elaborate training program while the Russians were defeated and the War was brought to a satisfactory end. Furthermore, as a cadet and an officer, he would associate only with gentlemen and frequent only the best places.

As it turned out, there was a catch. In fact, there was a series of catches, and instead of associating only with gentlemen in only the best places, Nately found himself regularly in a whorehouse in Rome, associating with such people as Yossarian and the satanic and depraved mocking old man and, even worse, sadly and hopelessly in love with an indifferent prostitute there who paid no attention to him and always went off to bed without him, because he stayed up late arguing with the evil old man.

Nately was not quite certain how it had all come about, and neither was his father, who was always so certain about everything else. Nately was struck again and again by the stark contrast the seedy, disreputable old man there made with his own father, whose recurring allusions in his letters to oregano and rhapsodic exclamations about war and business were starting to become intensely disturbing. Nately often was tempted to blot these offending lines out of the letters he saved, but was afraid to; and each time he returned to the whorehouse, he wished earnestly that the sinful and corrupt old man there would put on a clean shirt and tie and act like a cultured gentleman, so that Nately would not have to feel such burning and confusing anger each time he looked at him and was reminded of his father.

Dear Son (wrote his father):

Well, those blasted Communists failed to capitulate as I expected them to, and now you are overseas in combat as an airplane pilot and in danger of being killed.

We have instructed you always to comport yourself with honor and taste and never to be guilty of anything degrading. Death, like hard work, is degrading, and I urge you to do everything possible to remain alive. Resist the temptation to cover yourself with glory, for that would be vanity. Bear in mind that it is one thing to fight for your country and quite another thing to die for it. It is absolutely imperative in this time of national peril that, in the immortal words of Rudyard Kipling, you keep your head while others about you are losing theirs. (Ha, ha, ha! Get it?) In peace, nothing so becomes a man as modest stillness and humility. But, as Shakespeare said, when the blast of war blows loose, then it is time for discretion to be the better part of valor. In short, the times cry out for dignity, balance, caution and restraint.

It is probable that within a few years after we have won, someone like Henry L. Mencken will point out that the number of Americans who suffered from this War were far outnumbered by those who profited by it. We should not like a member of our family to draw attention to himself for being among those relative few who did not profit. I pray daily for your safe return. Could you not feign a liver ailment or something similar and be sent home?

Love, Dad

P.S. How I envy you your youth, your opportunity and all that sweet Italian pussy! I wish I were with you. (Ha, ha, ha!)

The letter was returned to him, stamped KILLED IN ACTION. [348]

'Catch-22'
Revisited

Where the airfield stood, there is nothing. The planes are gone, the tents are gone. It's almost as though there had never been an American air base here on the eastern shore of Corsica. It's almost, in fact, as though there had never been a war. [45]

Bastia, the largest city in Corsica, was empty, hot and still when we arrived. It was almost one o'clock, and the people in Corsica, like those in Italy,

SOURCE: *Holiday*, Vol. 41 (April 1967), pp. 45–60, 120, 141–142, 145. Reprinted by permission of the author.

duck for cover at lunchtime and do not emerge until very late in the afternoon, when the harsh and suffocating summer heat has begun to abate. The hotel in Île Rousse, on the other side of the island, had sent a taxi for us. And driving the taxi was François, a sporty, jaunty, chunky, barrel-chested, agreeable ex-cop. He was in his forties, and he wore a white mesh sport shirt, neat slacks and new leather sandals.

There were two roads from Bastia to Île Rousse, a high road and a low road. "Take the low road," said my wife, who has a fear of dying.

"*D'accord*," François agreed, and began driving straight up. In a minute or two the city of Bastia lay directly below us.

"Is this the low road?" asked my wife.

It was the high road, François informed us. He had decided, for our own good, that we should take the scenic high road to Île Rousse and then, if we still insisted, the low road coming back. François was indeed an agreeable person; he agreed to everything we proposed and then did what he thought best.

I had remembered from my military service that there were mountains in Corsica, but I had never appreciated how many there were or how high they rose. For the record, there is one peak 9,000 feet high and eight more than 8,000. It was one of these 8,000-foot mountains we were now crossing. The higher we drove, the more the land began to resemble the American West. We soon saw cactus growing beside the road, and then eagles wheeling in the sky—down below us!

After about two hours we had crossed the island and came to the other coast, still riding high above it. We drove southward now, passing, on a small beach, some German pillboxes no one had bothered to remove. Soon we saw Île Rousse resting in a haze below us between the mountains and the shore. The road descended slowly. We continued through the town and out to the hotel, which stood almost at the end of a narrow spit.

My main purpose in coming to Corsica again was to visit the site of our air base, to tramp the ground where our tents had stood and see what changes had occurred to the airstrip on which our planes had taken off and landed so many times. This was not in Île Rousse but back on the other side of the island, about fifty miles south of Bastia. I had come to Île Rousse now because it's a summer resort, and because the Air Force had a rest camp there during the war. I was disappointed in what I found now. The Napoléon Bonaparte, the large luxury hotel that had accommodated the officers, was not open. The hotel in which enlisted men had stayed was dilapidated. There was not, of course, any of the wartime noise, energy and excitement. With the exception of Rome and Naples, almost all the towns and cities I was to visit that were associated with my war experiences brought me the same disappointment. They no longer had any genuine connection with the war, but it was only through the war that I was acquainted with them.

We went swimming that afternoon. A jukebox at the beach played records by Bob Dylan, the Beatles, the Rolling Stones and Nancy Sinatra. At the tables were a number of teen-age girls and boys, good-looking and ultra cool, down for the season from Nice, Marseilles and even Paris. They were inert and blasé, determinedly paying no more attention to us than they did to each other.

That evening I was taken to dinner by a man who had been an important public official in Île Rousse for eighteen years and would be one still if he had not grown weary of the honor. We drove down the coast several miles to the village of Algajola, where we had dinner in a small new hotel perched on a hill overlooking the water. He introduced me to an old man who had worked at the Hotel Napoléon Bonaparte as a bartender when it was an American rest camp. The old man had nothing unpredictable to offer in the way of recollections. There was much liquor and few women, except for occasions when Army nurses were brought in for dances from other parts of Corsica.

More interesting than the rest camp was my host himself, [46] a stout, generous, dark-complexioned man in his fifties who had been in his youth an authentic *bon vivant*. He had gone to school in Paris and had planned to spend the rest of his life there in pleasure and idleness. Then, in a short period, he had lost his father, uncles and grandfather, and it was necessary for him to return to Corsica to take charge of the family's business affairs. He had lived in Corsica ever since. He really loved Corsica, he told me without conviction, although he missed the opera, the ballet, the theater, literature, good food and wine, and the chance to talk about these things with others who enjoyed them as much as he did. He smiled frequently as he spoke, but his geniality was clouded with a tremendous regret. He had a grown son who was supposed to return for us with the car at ten o'clock. He would arrive here on time, I was assured. And precisely at ten his son appeared. [48]

"He is always on time," my host remarked sorrowfully as we rose to go. "He does not even have enough imagination to come late once in a while." Here, in a small village in Corsica, I had found Ethan Frome, for this was truly a tale of blasted hopes and wasted years that he had related.

Early the next day we headed back across the island in search of the old air base. François made us listen as he sounded the horn of the car. It was a Klaxon. He had installed it for the journey back over the low road, so that we all might be more at ease. Each time we whizzed into a blind curve, I instructed François, "*Sonnez le Klaxon*," and he was delighted to oblige.

The low road from Île Rousse was very high for part of the way. But the land soon leveled out, and we found ourselves whizzing along comfortably on flat ground. Jokingly, I remarked to François that I might bring him back with me to New York, [49] where I knew he would excel in the Manhattan traffic. François pounced so readily on this chance at the big time that I had to discourage him quickly. A New York taxi driver, I told him, works for other people, makes little money and *n'est pas content, jamais content*, and only someone very rich, like Alan Arkin, could afford his own car and chauffeur. While François was still pondering this information solemnly, the fan belt snapped, and a wild clatter sounded from the front of the car. François eased the car softly to a stop at the side of the road, in back of a small truck already parked there. Two men lifted grease-stained faces from beneath the truck's open hood and looked at us questioningly. It turned out that we had been forced to come to a stop, purely by chance, directly in front of the only garage in miles.

In minutes we were ready to proceed. François, while asking directions to the old American air base, chanced to mention that I was one of the officers who had been stationed there. Both mechanics turned to me with huge grins, and one of them called for his wife to come out of the house to see me. To François this reaction was electrifying; it had not occurred to him that he was driving a potential dignitary whose presence could enlarge his own importance. Chest out, the cop in authority again, he pushed his way between me and this welcoming crowd of three, keeping them back as he screened their questions. After a minute he declared abruptly, to us as well as to them, that it was necessary for us to go. They waved after us as we went driving away.

I was unable to spy anything more familiar than the Mediterranean. Instead of the ageless landmarks I recalled, I saw Fire Island cottages that I *know* had not been there during the war. We did, however, find the crossroad to Cervione, another mountain village to which we used to drive in a jeep every now and then for a glass of wine in a cool, darkened bar. The bar was still there. It was larger now and much brighter. Coca-Cola was advertised, and a refrigerated case offered *gelati alemagne*, German ice cream, direct from Leghorn, in Italy. The several patrons inside were a generation or two younger than the silent, brown, old men in work clothes I remembered. These wore summer sport shirts and wash-and-wear trousers.

François entered first and announced to all in the room that he had brought them an American officer who had been stationed at the airfield below and had returned for a visit after so many years because he loved Corsica and loved the people of Cervione. The response was tumultuous. Ice cream and cold soda appeared for my wife and children; beer, wine and other flavorful alcoholic drinks appeared for me. I was, it turned out, the only American from the air base who had ever returned, which helped account for the exuberant celebration. My wife asked through the noise whether we could have lunch in Cervione. A meal was ordered by tele-

phone, and we walked to the restaurant ten minutes later, following François who swaggered ahead with such inflated self-importance that I was
certain he had exaggerated enormously the part I had played in beating
Hitler and vanquishing Japan.

The only restaurant in Cervione was on the second floor of the only
hotel, and it seemed to be part of the living quarters of the family who ran
it. A large table had been made ready for us in the center. Food began ar-
riving the moment we sat down, and some of the things looked pretty
strange.

"Don't drink the water," my wife warned the children, who ignored her,
since they were thirsty, and no other suitable beverage was available.

"Don't drink the water," François said to me, and popped open a bottle
of wine.

My wife and children got by on cooked ham, bread and cheese. I ate
everything set before me and asked for more. The main dish was a slice of
what seemed like pan-broiled veal, which was probably goat, since kid is a
specialty of the island.

Back at the bar we had coffee, and then a strange and unexpected ceremony took place. The entire room fell silent while a shy, soft-spoken young
man stepped toward us hesitantly and begged permission to give us a
cadeau, a gift, a large, beautiful earthenware vase from the small pottery
shop from which he gained his livelihood. It was touching, sobering; I was
sorry I had nothing with which to reciprocate. [51] After Cervione, the
airfield, when we finally found it, was a great disappointment. A lighthouse
that had served as a landmark for returning planes left no doubt we had
the right place, but there was nothing there now but reeds and wild bushes.
And standing among them in the blazing sunlight was no more meaningful, and no less eccentric, than standing reverently in a Canarsie lot. I felt
neither glad nor sorry I had come; I felt only foolish that I was there.

"Is this what we came to see?" grumbled my son.

"The airfield was right here," I explained. "The bombers used to come
back from Italy and France and land right out that way."

"I'm thirsty," said my daughter.

"It's hot," said my wife.

"I want to go back," said my son.

"We aren't going back to Île Rousse," I said. "We're spending the night
in Bastia."

"I mean back to New York!" he exclaimed angrily. "I'm not interested
in your stupid airfield. The only airfield I want to see is John F. Kennedy."

"Be nice to Daddy," my daughter said to him, with a malicious twinkle.
"He's trying to recapture his youth."

I gave my daughter a warning scowl and looked about again, searching
for a propeller, a wing, an airplane wheel, for some dramatic marker to

set this neglected stretch of wasteland apart from all the others along the shore. I saw none; and it would have made no difference if I had. I was a man in search of a war, and I had come to the wrong place. My war was over and gone, and even my ten-year-old son was smart enough to realize that. What the grouchy kid didn't realize, though, was that *his* military service was still ahead; and I could have clasped him in my arms to protect him as he stood there, hanging half outside the car with his look of sour irritation.

"Can't we go?" he pleaded.

"Sure, let's go," I said, and told François to take us straight to Bastia.

François shot away down the road like a rocket and screeched to a stop at the first bar he came to. He had, he mumbled quickly, to go see his aunt, and he bounded outside the car before we could protest. He was back in thirty seconds, licking his upper lip and looking greatly refreshed. He stopped three more times at bars on the way in, to see his mother-in-law, his best friend and his old police captain, returning with a larger smile and a livelier step from each brief visit.

François was whistling, and we were limp with exhaustion, by the time we arrived in the city, where the heat was unbearable. Add humidity to Hell, and you have the climate of Bastia in early July.

François and I went to the nearest bar for a farewell drink. He was jaunty and confident again. "New York?" he asked hopefully.

I shook my head. He shrugged philosophically and lifted his glass in a toast.

"*Tchin-tchin,*" he said, and insisted on paying for the drinks.

The first time I came to Corsica was in May, 1944, when I joined the bomb group as a combat replacement. After four days I was assigned to my first mission, as a wing bombardier. The target was the railroad bridge at Poggibonsi.

Poor little Poggibonsi. Its only crime was that it happened to lie outside Florence along one of the few passageways running south through the Apennine Mountains to Rome, which was still held by the Germans. And because of this small circumstance, I had been brought all the way across the ocean to help kill its railroad bridge.

The mission to Poggibonsi was described to us in the briefing room as a milk run—that is, a mission on which we were not likely to encounter flak or enemy planes. I was not pleased to hear this. I wanted action, not security. I wanted a sky full of dogfights, daredevils and billowing parachutes. I was twenty-one years old. I was dumb. I tried [53] to console myself with the hope that someone, somewhere along the way, would have the good grace to open fire at us. No one did.

As a wing bombardier, my job was to keep my eyes on the first plane in our formation, which contained the lead bombardier. When I saw his bomb-bay doors open, I was to open mine. The instant I saw his bombs begin to fall, I would press a button to release my own. It was as simple as that—or should have been.

I guess I got bored. Since there was no flak at Poggibonsi, the lead bombardier opened his bomb-bay doors early and took a long, steady approach. A lot of time seemed to pass. I looked down to see how far we were from the target. When I looked back up, the bombs from the other planes were already falling. I froze with alarm for another second or two. Then I squeezed my button. I closed the bomb-bay doors and bent forward to see where the bombs would strike, pleading silently for the laws of gravitational acceleration to relax just enough to allow my bombs to catch up with the others.

The bombs from the other planes fell in an accurate, concentrated pattern that blasted a wide hole in the bridge. The bombs from my plane blasted a hole in the mountains several miles beyond.

It was my naïve hope that no one would notice my misdemeanor; but in the truck taking us from the planes a guy in a parachute harness demanded:

"Who was the bombardier in the number two plane?"

"I was," I answered sheepishly.

"You dropped late," he told me, as though it could have escaped my attention. "But we hit the bridge."

Yeah, I thought, but *I* hit the mountain.

A few days after I returned to Italy from Corsica with my family, we rode through Poggibonsi on our way south to Siena to see an event there called the Palio. The railroad bridge at Poggibonsi has been repaired and is now better than ever. The hole in the mountains is still there.

As soon as we checked in at our busy hotel in Siena, a flushed, animated woman in charge smiled and said, "Watch out for pickpockets! They'll steal your money, your checks, your jewelry and your cameras! Last year we had three guests who were robbed!"

She uttered this last statistic in a triumphant whoop, as though in rivalry with another hotel that could boast only two victims. The woman cradled an infant in her arms, her grandchild; her daughter, a tall, taciturn girl in her twenties, worked at a small tabulating machine. Our own children, in one of those miraculous flashes of intuition, decided not to attend the Palio but to remain at the hotel.

Something like 40,000 people packed their way into the standing-room section of the public square to watch the climax of this traditional competition between the city's seventeen *contrade*, or wards. Soon many began collapsing from heat exhaustion and were carried beneath the stands by running teams of first-aid workers. Then, up behind the last row of seats in our section, there appeared without warning a big, fat, bellowing, intoxicated, 200-pound goose with crumbs in his mouth and a frog in his throat. He was not really a goose but an obese and obnoxious drunk who wore the green and white colors of his own *contrada*, which was, I believe, that of the goose or duck or some other bird. He had bullied his way past the ticket taker to this higher vantage point, from which to cheer his *contrada* as it paraded past and to spray hoarse obscenities at the others. Immediately in back of us, and immediately in front of him, was a row of high-school girls from North Carolina, touring Europe under the protection of a slender young American gentleman who soon began to look as though he wished he were somewhere else. One of the girls complained steadily to him in her Southern accent.

"How do you say policeman in Italian? I want you to call that policeman, do you hear? That Italian is spitting on me every time he yells something. And he smells. I don't want that smelly Italian standing up here behind me."

With us at the Palio were Professor Frederick Karl, the Conrad authority from City College in New York, and his beautiful wife, the Countess D'Orestiglio, who is an Italian from Caserta. [55] The countess, who has a blistering temper, was ready to speak out imperiously, but could not decide to whom. She found both principals in this situation equally offensive. Before she could say anything, the horse race started, and a great roar went up from the crowd that closed off conversation.

We did not see who won, and we did not particularly care. But the outcome apparently made a very big difference to other people, for as soon as the race was over three men seized one of the losing jockeys and began to punch him severely. Suddenly fistfights were breaking out all over, and thousands of shouting people were charging wildly in every direction. Here was the atmosphere of a riot, and none of us in the reserved seats dared descend. As we sat aghast, as exposed and helpless on our benches as stuffed dolls in a carnival gallery, a quick shriek sounded behind me, and then I was struck by a massive weight.

It was the drunken goose, who had decided to join his comrades below by the most direct route. He had simply lunged forward through the row of girls, almost knocking the nearest ones over, and tumbled down on us. With instinctive revulsion, Professor Karl and I rolled him away onto the people in the row ahead of us, who spilled him farther down, on the people below them. In this fashion our drunken goose finally landed sprawling at the bottom. He staggered to his feet with clenched fists, looking for a moment as though he would charge into us, but then allowed himself to be swept along by the torrents of people.

Somehow, after ten or twenty minutes, all the fighting resolved itself into a collective revelry in which people from different *contrade* embraced each other, joined in song and pushed ahead to take part in a procession through the city behind the victorious horse. The sense of danger faded. In a little while we went down and moved toward the exit, passing pasty-faced people lying on stretchers and an occasional Peeping Tom staring up solemnly at the legs of women who were still in the stands. Once outside, we kept near the walls of the buildings, clutching our money, jewelry and cameras, and returned to the hotel, where our two bored and rested children told us they wanted to return to Florence that same night, and where the woman in charge was exclaiming rapturously about the race and the three men who had beaten up a jockey.

While my wife went upstairs to pack, I drew the woman aside to talk to her about the war. Tell me about it, I asked; you were here. No, she wasn't. She was in Bologna during the war, which was even better; she was at the railroad station there with her little girl the day American bombers came to destroy it in a saturation attack. She ran from the station and took shelter on the ground somewhere beside a low wall. When the attack was over and she returned to the station, she could not find it. She could not distinguish the rubble of the railroad station from the rubble of the other buildings that had stood nearby. Only then did she grow frightened. And the thought that terrified her—she remembered this still—was that now she would miss her train, for she did not know when it would leave, or from where.

But all that was so far in the past. There was her little girl, now grown up, tall and taciturn at the adding machine, and the woman would much sooner talk about the Palio or about Siena, which at the request of the Pope had been spared by both sides during the war—for Siena is the birthplace of Saint Catherine, patron saint of Italy. So the Germans made their stand a bit farther north, at Poggibonsi, which was almost completely leveled.

Poor Poggibonsi. During those first few weeks we flew missions to rail and highway bridges at Perugia, Arezzo, Orvieto, Cortona, Tivoli and Ferrara. Most of us had never heard of any of these places. We were very young, and few of us had been to college. For the most part, the missions were short—about three hours—and relatively safe. It was not until June 3, for example, that our squadron lost a plane, on a mission to Ferrara. It was not until August 3, over Avignon, in France, that I finally saw a plane shot down in flames, and it was not until August 15, again over Avignon, that a gunner in my plane was wounded and a copilot went a little berserk at the controls and I came to the startling realization—*Good God! They're trying to kill me, too!* And after that it wasn't much fun.

When we weren't flying missions, we went swimming or played baseball or basketball. The food was good—better, in fact, than most of us had ever [56] eaten before—and we were getting a lot of money for a bunch of kids twenty-one years old. Like good soldiers everywhere, we did as we were told.

Had we been given an orphanage to destroy (we weren't), our only question would have been, "How much flak?" In vehicles borrowed from the motor pool we would drive to Cervione for a glass of wine or to Bastia to kill an afternoon or evening. It was, for a while, a pretty good life. We had rest camps at Capri and Île Rousse. And soon we had Rome.

On June 4, 1944, the first American soldiers entered Rome. And no more than half a step behind them, I think, must have come our own squadron's resourceful executive officer, for we received both important news flashes simultaneously: the Allies had taken Rome, and our squadron had leased two large apartments there, one with five rooms for the officers and one with about fifteen rooms for the enlisted men. Both were staffed with maids, and the enlisted men, who brought their food rations with them, had women to cook their meals.

Within less than a week friends were returning with fantastic tales of pleasure in a big, exciting city that had girls, cabarets, food, drinking, entertainment and dancing. When my turn came to go, I found that every delicious story was true. I don't think the Colosseum was there then, because no one ever mentioned it.

Rome was a functioning city when the Germans moved out and the Allies moved in. People had jobs and homes, and there were shops, restaurants, buses, even movie theaters. Conditions, of course, were far from prosperous; food, cigarettes and candy were in short supply, and so was money. Clothing was scarce, although most girls succeeded in keeping their dresses looking pretty. Electric power was rationed, limiting elevator service, and there was a curfew that drove Italian families off the street—men, women, children and tenors—just as they were beginning to enjoy the cool Roman evenings.

Then, as now, the busiest part was the area of the Via Veneto. What surprised me very strongly was that Rome today is pretty much the same as it was then. The biggest difference was that in the summer of 1944 the people in uniform were mainly American and the civilians all Italian, while now the people in uniform were Italian and the civilians mainly American. The ambience there was one of pleasure, and it still is. This was vastly different from Naples, where it was impossible to avoid squalor, poverty and human misery, about which we could do nothing except give a little money. In this respect, Naples too is unchanged.

On the Via Veneto today the same buildings stand and still serve pretty much the same purpose. The American Red Cross building, at which we would meet for breakfast and shoeshines, was in the Bernini-Bristol Hotel, at the bottom of the Via Veneto; American rest camps were established in the Eden, the Ambasciatori and, I think, the Majestic. The Hotel Quirinale on Via Nazionale was taken over by New Zealanders, and a man at the desk still neatly preserves a letter of praise he received from their commander. The men who now work in the motor pool at the American embassy are the same men who worked as civilian chauffeurs for the American military command then, and they are eager to relate their war experiences as automobile drivers during the liberation. They could not agree on the location of the Allied Officers Club, a huge nightclub and dance hall whose name, I think, was Broadway Bill's. For the war itself, one must go outside the center of the city, to the Fosse Ardeatine, where more than 300 Italian hostages were massacred by German soldiers.

During the war we came from Corsica by plane and stayed five or six days each time. Often we would take short walks during the day in search of curiosities and new experiences. One time on a narrow street, a sultry, dark-eyed girl beckoned seductively to me and a buddy from behind a beaded curtain covering the entrance to a store. We followed her inside and got haircuts. Another time we were seized by a rather beefy and aggressive young man, who pushed and pulled us off the sidewalk into his shop, where he swiftly drew caricatures of our heads on printed cartoon torsos. He asked our names and titled the pictures *Hollywood Joe I* and *Hollywood Joe II.* Then he took our money, and then he threw us out. The name of the place was the Funny Face Shop, and the name of the artist was Federico Fellini. He has made better pictures since. [59]

Only once in all the times I came there as a soldier did I attempt any serious sight-seeing; then I found myself on a bus with gray-haired majors and with Army nurses who were all at least twenty years older. The stop at the catacombs was only the second on the schedule, but by the time we moved inside, I knew I'd already had enough. As the rest of the group continued deeper into the darkness, I eased myself secretly back toward the entrance and was never heard from again.

Today, of course, it's a different matter in Rome, for the great presence there, I think, is Michelangelo. He complained a lot, but he knew what he was doing. His *Moses* is breathtaking, particularly if you can see it before the groups of guided tourists come swarming up and the people in charge give the same apocryphal explanations of the horns on the head and the narrow scar in the marble of the leg. The story about the latter is that Michelangelo, overwhelmed by the lifelike quality of his statue, hurled his ax at it and cried, "Speak! Why won't you speak?"

The story isn't true. I have seen that statue, and I know that if Michelangelo ever hurled an ax at it, Moses would have picked up the ax and hurled it right back.

With the ceiling of the Sistine Chapel, however, I have recurring trouble. The gigantic fresco has been called the greatest work ever undertaken by a single artist. No summer tourist will ever be able to tell, for no summer tourist will ever be able to see it, his view obstructed by hundreds of others around him. The lines outside are as long as at Radio City Music

Hall, and the price of admission is high. Once inside, you walk a mile to get there. And once you arrive, you find yourself in a milling crush of people who raise a deafening babble. Women faint and are stretched out to recover on the benches along the side. Attendants shout at you to keep quiet or keep moving. Jehovah stretches a hand out to Adam and pokes his finger into the head of the Korean in front of you. If you do look up, you soon discover it's a pain in the neck. The ideal way to study the ceiling would be to lie down in the center of the floor. Even then the distance is probably too great for much sense to be made of that swirling maelstrom above. E. M. Forster defined a work of art as being greater than the sum of its parts: I suspect that just the reverse may be true of the Sistine ceiling, that it is much greater in its details than in total.

However, Michelangelo's fresco of the Last Judgment, on a wall in the same chapel, is another matter entirely. The wall is forty-four feet wide and forty-eight feet high, and the painting is the most powerful I know. It is the best motion picture ever made. There is perpetual movement in its violent rising and falling, and perpetual drama in its agony and wrath. To be with Michelangelo's *Last Judgment* is to be with Oedipus and King Lear. I want that wall. I would like to have enough money and time someday to fly to Rome just to look at it whenever I felt a yearning to. I know it would always be worth the trip. Better still, I would like to put that wall in my own apartment, where it would always be just a few steps away. But my landlord won't let me.

After Rome was captured by my squadron executive officer, the fighting rapidly moved northward. By the middle of June French forces captured Leghorn, where broken blocks of stone from the battle still lie near the docks and will probably remain forever. On August 13 the Americans were in Florence. Before the Germans evacuated the city and moved up into the mountains beyond, they blew up the bridges across the Arno River; they hesitated about the Ponte Vecchio and then blew the approaches instead, leaving the old bridge standing. The damage at both ends of the Ponte Vecchio has been restored with buildings of stone and design similar to those around them, and only a searching eye can detect that the destruction of the war ever touched there.

Perugia, Arezzo, Orvieto, Siena and Poggibonsi were all on our side of the action now. Pisa was captured on September 2, and the Germans pulled back along the flat coastal land to take positions in the mountains past Carrara. This was the Gothic Line now, extending clear across the country to the Adriatic; they were able to hold it all [60] through the winter and far into the following spring. It was not until the middle of April that the Allies were able to push through to Bologna, and by then the war in Europe was all but over.

Rome, Siena and Florence had all been given over by the Germans in fairly good condition. In the tiny village of Saint Anna, high up in the mountains, past the marble quarries of Carrara, some 700 inhabitants, the entire population, were massacred by the German army in reprisal for the killing of two soldiers. When the deadline came and the town did not produce the guilty partisans, every house was set on fire, and the people were gunned down as they fled into the streets. One can only wonder why people so indifferent to the lives of other human beings would be so sparing of their cities. Perhaps it's because they expected to come back.

Every spring now they do come back, as German tourists thirsting for the sun. Unmarried girls, I have heard, descend in great, aggressive crowds on Rimini and other spots along the Adriatic shore in a determined quest for sunburns, sex and sleep, in that order. On the western coast, where we stayed for several weeks on a fourteen-mile stretch of sand beach known as the Versilian Riviera, menus, signs, notices and price lists are printed in four languages—Italian, English, French and German. This area includes [120] Viareggio, Camaiore, Pietrasanta, Forte dei Marmi. There was no doubt in June that German families were the main visiting group. By the beginning of July, they had all but vanished. Every year, we were told, they come early and depart before July. The Tuscans, who dislike the Germans with well-guarded propriety, sometimes hint that the Germans leave so soon because the high season starts and rates go up. I suspect there is something more. By July Italy turns hot; there is warm weather closer to home.

The Hotel Byron in Forte dei Marmi is an inexpensive jewel of a family hotel. The rooms are comfortable, the food is meticulously prepared, and the setting is beautiful; but more delightful than any of these are the owner, the manager, the concierge and the entire staff of maids and waiters, who are all exquisitely sweet, polite, accommodating and sympathetic. They would fall to brooding if I snapped at my daughter or my son looked unhappy. A brief compliment to any one member of the staff was enough to bring us grateful smiles from all the rest. This was true in almost every restaurant and hotel in Italy. In Italy a word of praise, particularly for an endeavor of personal service, goes a very long way toward creating happiness.

The owner of the hotel had served in Africa with the Italian army and could tell me nothing from his own experience about the war in Italy. I did not tell anyone at the hotel about mine, for we had flown many missions to targets in this area. We bombed the bridges at Viareggio at least once, those at Pietrasanta at least four times.

I was soon very curious to visit Pietrasanta because of a strange war memorial near the road bridge there. The bridge was new and smooth and spanned a shallow river no wider than a city street, which helped explain why it had been bombed so frequently—it was so easy to repair. The war memorial was a bombed-out house that the people of Pietrasanta had decided to leave standing as an eternal reminder of the German occupation. I almost smiled at the incongruity, for the building stood so close to the bridge that it must certainly have been destroyed by bombs from American planes. On the new bridge was a memorial of another kind, which I found more moving—a small tablet for a girl named Rosa who had been killed there by an automobile not long before.

One day my wife thought she recognized Henry Moore, the famous English sculptor, having lunch at the hotel. The manager confirmed it. It was indeed Henry Moore. He owned property in Forte dei Marmi and had many acquaintances around Viareggio and Pietrasanta. Shortly after that we met Stanley Bleifeld, a sculptor from Weston, Connecticut, and his wife. That made two sculptors we had come upon here in a short period of time, and [141] Bleifeld told us about others—Jacques Lipchitz, who owns a spectacular mountain villa on the way to Lucca, and Bruno Lucchesi, who sells, it is said with envy, everything he produces, and many more sculptors who come to this part of Italy every summer to work and play. They work in bronze, which is cast in Pietrasanta in the foundry of Luigi Tommasi, who thinks they are crazy.

He thinks they are crazy because of the work they do and the money they pay him to have it finished. Tommasi is a smiling, handsome man of about forty in blue Bermuda shorts and dust. His basic source of income is religious objects and, I suppose, leaning towers of Pisa—good, durable items of established appeal. But he is happy to set this work aside every summer when his artists arrive. Neither he nor his workers can convince themselves that the clay models they receive are deliberate; he has, however, given up trying to correct the errors he sees, for he has found in the past that such good intentions have not been appreciated. His foundry is a striking treasure house of works in various stages of progress. As we walked through, Bleifeld could not restrain himself from flicking out nervously with his thumbnail at a piece of residue on a casting of one of his own works, while a young laborer regarded him coolly. In the yard stood a tall and swarming statue by Lipchitz, a fecund and suggestive work of overpowering force and beauty that will soon stand before a building in California.

Florence is the nearest large city to Forte dei Marmi, and we went there often to revisit the masterpieces of Michelangelo and Botticelli and to buy earrings for my daughter. Florence is the best city in the world in which to have nothing to do, for it offers so much that *is* worth doing. Except to my son; he had nothing to do but review all the uncomfortable places he had visited. One evening in Florence we all went to the race track to watch the trotters. Children are admitted, and many play politely on the grass in back of the grandstand or sit on the benches with their parents and watch the horses run. The minimum bet is small. The race track is a family affair, social and safe. My son picked four straight winners and came out eight dollars ahead. The next day he no longer wanted to go home. He wanted to go back to the race track. There were no races that night, so I took him to the opera instead. After that he wanted to go home.

Soon he was a step nearer, for we were leaving Italy by train, on our way to Avignon. We arrived in a debilitating heat wave that settled for days over all of southern Europe. My family had never heard of Avignon before from anyone but me, just as most of us in Corsica had never heard of Avignon before the day we were sent there to bomb the bridge spanning the River Rhône. One exception was a lead navigator from New England who had been a history teacher before the war and was overjoyed in combat whenever he found himself in proximity to places that had figured importantly in his studies. As our planes drew abreast of Orange and started to turn south to the target, he announced on the intercom:

"On our right is the city of Orange, ancestral home of the kings of Holland and of William III, who ruled England from 1688 to 1702."

"And on our left," came back the disgusted voice of a worried radio gunner from Chicago, "is flak."

We had known from the beginning that the mission was likely to be dangerous, for three planes had been assigned to precede the main formations over the target, spilling out scraps of metallic paper through a back window in order to cloud the radar of the anti-aircraft guns. As a bombardier in one of those planes, I had nothing to do but hide under my flak helmet until the flak stopped coming at us and then look back at the other planes to see what was happening. One of them was on fire, heading downward in a gliding spiral that soon tightened into an uncontrolled spin. I finally saw some billowing parachutes. Three men got out. Three others didn't and were killed. One of those who parachuted was found and hidden by some people in Avignon and was eventually brought safely back through the lines by the French underground. On August 15, the day of the invasion of southern France, we flew to Avignon again. This time three planes went down, and no men got out. A gunner in my plane got a big wound in his thigh. I took care of him. I went to visit him in the hospital the next day. He looked fine. They had given him blood, and he was going to be all right. But I was in terrible shape; and I had twenty-three more missions to fly.

There was the war, in Avignon, not in Rome or Île Rousse or Poggibonsi or even Ferrara, when I was too new to be frightened; but now no one in Avignon wanted to talk about anything but the successful summer arts festival that was just ending. More people had come than ever before, and the elated officials in charge of this annual tourist promotion were already making plans for doing still better the following year.

Avignon subsists largely on tourism, I was told, and this surprised me, for the city is small. It is so small that the windows of our bedrooms, at the rear of the building, were right across a narrow street from what I took to be a saloon and what the people at the hotel hinted was a house of ill repute. A woman with a coarse, loud voice laughed and shouted and sang until four in the morning. When she finally shut up, a baker next door to her began chopping dough. The following day I asked to have our rooms changed, and the man at the desk understood and advised me not to visit the place across the street from the back of the hotel.

"It is a very bad place," he observed regretfully, as though he was wishing [142] to himself that it were a much better one. He transferred us to rooms in the front of the hotel, overlooking a lovely dining patio with an enormous tree in the center that shaded the tables and chairs.

A day later we were traveling by train again, my tour of battlefields over. It had brought me only to scenes of peace and to people untroubled by the threat of any new war. Oddly, it was in neutral little Switzerland, after I had given up and almost lost interest, that I finally found, unexpectedly, my war. It came to me right out of the blue, from a portly, amiable middle-aged Frenchman whom we met during our trip on one of those toylike Swiss trains that ply dependably over and through the mountains between Montreux and Interlaken.

He spoke no English and smoked cigarettes incessantly, and he stopped us at one station from making a wrong change of trains. He was going to Interlaken, too, to spend his vacation with a friend who owned a small chalet in a village nearby. That morning he had parted from his wife and son in Montreux; they had boarded the train to Milan to visit Italy, where his son wanted to go.

He volunteered this information about his family so freely that I did not hesitate to inquire when he would be rejoined by his wife.

Then it came, in French, in a choked and muffled torrent of words, the answer to the questions I hadn't asked. He began telling us about his son, and his large eyes turned shiny and filled with tears.

His only boy, adopted, had been wounded in the head in the war in Indochina and would never be able to take care of himself. He could go nowhere alone. He was only thirty-four years old now and had lain in a hospital for seven years. "It is bad," the man said, referring to the wound, the world, the weather, the present, the future. Then, for some reason, he said to me, "You will find out, you will find out." His voice shook. The tears were starting to roll out now through the corners of his eyes, and he was deeply embarrassed. The boy was too young, he concluded lamely, by way of apologizing to us for the emotion he was showing, to have been hurt so badly for the rest of his life.

With that, he turned away and walked to the other end of the car. My wife was silent. The children were subdued and curious.

"Why was he crying?" asked my boy.

"What did he say?" my daughter asked me.

What can you tell your children today that will not leave them frightened and sad?

"Nothing," I answered. [145]

			FIRST CHAPTER BEGINS HERE	9/4 - ALLIES ... PAST P...
				10/... SIGFRIED LI COLLAPSES. Ru... OCCUPIES Boul
	YOSSARIAN GOOSES NURSE DUCKETT			10/... ... APPROACH ...
	THEY BECOME LOVERS	ORR DITCHES AND IS GIVEN UP FOR LOST		
	SHE TRIES TO REFORM HIM			
	SHE IS ON TOP BEACH WITH HIM WHEN KID SAMPSON IS KILLED	KID SAMPSON CUT IN HALF McWATT FLIES INTO MOUNTAIN	DANEEKA, BY REFUSING TO INVOLVED IN ANYTHING BEING "DEAD" ALL TH...	
NATELY'S WHORE GETS A GOOD NIGHT'S SLEEP AND FALLS IN LOVE WITH HIM			AS SOON A... GIRL HE TURN... BOURGEOISE A... EVERYBODY	
NATELY'S WHORE IS FURIOUS WITH YOSSARIAN FOR HITTING HIM	WARNS YOSSARIAN THAT THEY ARE GOING TO DISAPPEAR DUNBAR	DUNBAR HE IS DISAPPEARED	NURSE DUCKETT HAS BEGUN TO TH... HER FUTURE. She WANTS A DOCTOR AND HAS DISASSOCIATE HERSELF ... WHOM SHE DO... ... AS A SUITABLE HUSBAND	12/16-1/20 ... BATTLE OF ...
		NATELY DOBBS KILL...	MILO AND CATHCART HAVE EACH FLOWN ... NO MORE THAN FIVE MISSIONS	3/7 - Remagen ... CAPTURED
NATELY'S WHORE TRIES TO STAB YOSSARIAN AND BEGINS HER CHASE AFTER HIM	NURSE DUCKETT IS EMBARRASSED BY YOSSARIAN STAND		NATELY'S WHORE BECOMES A SYMBOL OF HIS GUILT AND RESPONSIBILITY FOR NEVER INTERVENING IN THE INJUSTICES HE KNOWS EXIST EVERYWHERE	4/1 - Russians AUSTRIA 5/3 - BERLIN
KID SISTER IS ADRIFT IN ROME WITH NO ONE TO HELP HER		OLD MAN DIES OF OLD AGE MRS MURDERED AARFY 131		GERMANS SURRENDE IT...
NATELY'S WHORE STABS YOSSARIAN AS HE LEAVES THE OFFICE				
		HUNGRY JOE DIES IN HIS SLEEP	IN MAKING THE DECISION TO DESERT, YOSSARIAN ACCEPTS THE RESPONSIBILITY HE NOW KNOWS HE HAS TO THE OTHER MEN AS HE SAYS, HE IS NOT RUNNING AWAY FROM HIS RESPONSIBILITIES, BUT TO THEM	
NATELY'S WHORE IS RIGHT BEHIND YOSSARIAN WITH A KNIFE	NURSE DUCKETT HELPS HIM ESCAPE BECAUSE SHE IS EAGER TO BE RID OF HIM			

NOVEL INTO FILM

Anonymous

Some Are More Yossarian than Others

MC WATT'S VOICE* (*filtered, yelling*): Help him! Help him!

YOSSARIAN (*into mike, yelling*): Help who?

MC WATT'S VOICE (*filtered, yelling*): Help the bombardier!

YOSSARIAN (*into mike, yelling*): I'm the bombardier. I'm all right.

MC WATT'S VOICE (*filtered, yelling*): Then help him. Help *him!*

The chronicle of war is the Bible of irony. The original victim of that mistaken-identity crisis was a B-25 bombardier named Joseph Heller during a World War II raid over Avignon. He was a dozen feet from the pilot; yet they were separated by layers of chaos and terror. It was not Heller who was hurt—it was his gunner who was bleeding copiously into his flight suit. It was Heller's 37th mission. From that instant of agony he grew petrified of flight. When his war ended, he took a ship home; it was some 15 years later before the flyer entered another plane.

---

* In the novel, it is Dobbs' voice; see pp. 51, 231, and 446.—Eds.

SOURCE: *Time*, June 15, 1970, pp. 66–74. Copyright Time Inc., 1970. Reprinted by permission of the publisher.

The experience was too extravagant to be fiction and too real to be borne. Heller furnished the corpse with a vaudeville wardrobe, mixed in '50s America, and called his novel *Catch-22*. Black, mad and surreal, it told of a bombardier named Yossarian impaled on the insanity of war and struggling to escape. Undergraduates still see Yossarian as a lionly coward, the first of the hell-no-we-won't-go rebels who had to go anyway. To them, the book's final sentence limns the human condition as well as the hero's: "The knife came down, missing him by inches, and he took off."

Catch-22 smacked of Restoration comedy. The characters trapped with Yossarian in the 256th Squadron had arch names: Major Major, General Dreedle, Colonel Korn, Milo Minderbinder. The contents seemed to be a series of hyperbolic World War II anecdotes, but its author confesses: "I wrote it during the Korean War and aimed it for the one after that." The book was criticized as flatulent, self-indulgent and anachronistic—"Engine Charlie" Wilson's General Motors, thinly disguised, was one of its arch-villains. Moreover it followed Hilaire Belloc's irritating dictum: "First I tell them what I am going to tell them; then I tell them; and then I tell them what I told them."

Nearly 5,000,000 readers nevertheless found it one of the most original comic novels of their time. They found it so funny, in fact, that surely half of them ignored Heller's own warnings: that *Catch-22* is no more about the Army Air Corps than Kafka's *The Trial* was about Prague; that "the cold war is what I was truly talking about, not the World War"; and that the second biggest character in the novel is death.

From Neurosis to Hysteria

The biggest, of course, is Yossarian. Like most larger-than-death heroes, he is everyman. Still, some men are more Yossarian than others. Mike Nichols knows. And Alan Arkin knows. And Mike Nichols knows that Alan Arkin knows. "It was the only part I've ever worked on which didn't demand a conception," says Arkin, "because there isn't much difference between me and Yossarian." Viewing Arkin in the film of *Catch-22* is like watching Lew Alcindor sink baskets or Bobby Fischer play chess. The man seems made for the role. Fear rides on his back like a schizoid chimp. His voice climbs from neurosis to hysteria—and winds back down again, without missing a moan. On Yossarian's tortured face is a look of applied sanity that befits only saints and madmen. He walks through a closed system to which everyone but the dreamer has a key.

Arkin's complex, triumphant performance is due in part to good genes— he looks more like Yossarian than he does like Arkin. In part it is due to a virtuoso player entering his richest period. But in the main it is due to the quirky talent of Director Mike Nichols, whose previous successes have been wrung largely from the bland and facile. It is as if Neil Simon were to turn out *Endgame* or Peter Sellers to turn into Falstaff.

The film is far from whole. Occasionally, it moves too slowly. Despite its determined timelessness, it suffers from inescapable time lag. The feudal state of the Army has the aspect of ancient history; bombing in World War II was like bombing in no other war before or since. When the novel was published in 1961, its nonviolent stance was courageous and almost lonely. But antiwar films have become faddish lately, and *Catch-22* runs the risk, philosophically, of falling into line behind *M*A*S*H* and *How I Won the War*.

Comedy, of all things, is the film's weakest component. As an adapter, Buck Henry has supplied a terse, sufficient script; it is as a comic actor that he is wanting. In the part of Colonel Korn, he violates the first rule of humor: if what you're doing is funny, you don't have to be funny doing it. Playing outpatients of *Dr. Strangelove*, he and his Tweedledummy Colonel Cathcart (Martin Balsam) [66] italicize every punch line. Even their faces are overstatements. As General Dreedle, Orson Welles sweeps past like Macy's Thanksgiving Day Parade, all plastic and gas. Dreedle need only have GREED lettered across his middle to complete the cartoon.

But Nichols was not making *Super-M*A*S*H*. From the beginning, he was aware that laughter in *Catch-22* was, in the Freudian sense, a cry for help. It is the book's cold rage that he has nurtured. In the jokes that matter, the film is as hard as a diamond, cold to the touch and brilliant to the eye. To Nichols, *Catch-22* is "about dying"; to Arkin, it is "about selfishness"; to audiences, it will be a memorable horror comedy of war, with the accent on horror.

With psychiatric insight, Nichols has constructed *Catch-22* like a spiral staircase set with mirrors. Yossarian ascends by dols, units of pain, glimpsing pieces of himself until he comes to a landing of understanding. It is 1944, Mussolini has collapsed, and Allied victory is inevitable. But for the bombardment group, there is no surcease. Colonel Cathcart compulsively keeps raising the number of missions required before an airman can be rotated Stateside.

Like a carnivore among vegetarians, Cathcart careers through the defenseless. The Chaplain (Anthony Perkins) is chewed out for not writing inspirational sermons that will gain the unit a spread in the *Saturday Evening Post*. The flyers are ordered to raid civilian towns so that they can concentrate on producing nice tight bomb patterns in the aerial photographs. Most horrible of all, Milo Minderbinder (Jon Voight) is encouraged in his murderous wartime profiteering.

Yossarian moves numbly through it all, reminiscent of the Steinberg drawing in which a rabbit peers out of a human face. He begs Doc Daneeka (Jack Gilford) to ground him as being insane with fear. But the flight surgeon dutifully recites the Air Force manual's imaginary Catch No. 22: Naturally, anyone who wants to get out of combat isn't really crazy. So supernaturally, anyone who says he is too crazy to keep flying is too sane to stop. On such circular reasoning rests the plot, the dialogue, and indeed the film's essence.

Repulsive and Instructive

The dominant image is the circle. Catch-22 is as cyclic as the Soldier in White, a mummy-like form completely encased in bandages. At one end, a bottle feeds fluid into the region of some upper vein. At the other, a pipe conducts the fluid out of the kidney region and into another bottle. At a given signal, preoccupied nurses exchange the bottles, and the cycle begins anew.

Fully loaded, the bombers take flight, make their lethal gyres and return empty. Under Nichols' direction, the camera makes air as palpable as blood. In one long-lensed indelible shot, the sluggish bodies of the B-25s rise impossibly close to one another, great vulnerable chunks of aluminum shaking as they fight for altitude. Could the war truly have been fought in those preposterous crates? It could; it was. And the unused faces of the flyers, Orr, Nately, Aardvaark, could they ever have been so young? They were; they are. Catch-22's insights penetrate the elliptical dialogue to show that wars are too often a children's crusade, fought by boys not old enough to vote or, sometimes, to think.

Yossarian's mind circles five times to that instant in which McWatt [Dobbs in the novel] calls out, "Help him!" Each time Yossarian's arc of memory lengthens as he bends to aid the mortally wounded Snowden— until at last he sees the man's flesh torn away and his insides pour out. It is at once the film's most repulsive and instructive moment. From that time Yossarian cannot accept the escape bargain his superiors finally offer him: "All you have to do is like us." He cannot betray his fellow victims of what Norman Mailer called "exquisite totalitarianism." It is then that the rabbit must run or perish.

Most of the film has the quality of dislocation. It is lit like a Wyeth painting and informed with the lunatic logic of Magritte. Only twice does it grow didactic. In an Italian whorehouse, 19-year-old Nately (Art Garfunkel) confronts a 107-year-old pimp. The scene is photographed narrative, almost word-for-word from the book's symbolic and simplistic confrontation: weary but supposedly immortal Italy v. vigorous but naive and supposedly doomed America. When the boy accuses the ancient of shameless opportunism, the centenarian defends himself with the ultimate weapon: age. "I'll be 20 in January," answers Nately. There is no answer to the old man's Parthian shot: "If you live."

As the film progresses, Minderbinder descends from mess-hall hustler to full-time racketeer. In a crude and overdrawn caricature, the loutish blond fly-boy suddenly becomes a Hitlerian symbol who bombs American bases in a deal with the Germans and sells stocks in the war because it is good business. Here Nichols—like Heller—cannot let [67] hell enough alone, and Engine Charlie's oft-quoted G.M. dictum is paraphrased: "What's good enough for M & M Enterprises is good for the country." But not for the movie.

Nichols had made his villains brobdingnagian. In lesser hands, the morality farce could have been substandard anti-Establishmentarianism: capital is evil; war is inhuman; people are groovy. There is something to be said for George C. Scott's appraisal of Yossarian's actions: "What the hell good does it do to take your clothes off, climb a tree and refuse to come down? What kind of rebellion is that?"

Waugh Parties in a Dirigible

Yet, because of the director's persistent focus, it all makes the kind of perfect nonsense that finally is the concomitant of wisdom. Like *Through the Looking-Glass*, *Catch-22* overturns commonplaces and makes them fresh. Its optimism is despairing; its doubt is born of faith. "When Yossarian runs away in the end," says Heller, "I never said that he would get all the way. I wrote: 'The knife came down, missing him by inches, and he took off.' But he tries, he changes. That's the best that can be said for any of us." It is the best that can be said of Nichols, who with this major film has discernibly altered not only his career but himself.

"*Catch-22* has made me feel differently about what I lay on the line and what I do with my money too," Nichols says. "There are suddenly so many urgent things that we must do for one another to make sure that we continue to live on this earth. The kind of *après-moi-le-déluge* parties and lifestyle that goes with them seem more and more distasteful. The accounts of such rounds are beginning to sound like Evelyn Waugh parties in a dirigible during a war."

That general critique could be written in the margin of Nichols' autobiography. If he is indeed breaking camp, his move is Yossarianic in its scope. Nichols was the original enthusiast of urbane Waughfare. In the '60s he compiled an unbroken string of Broadway smashes. He was a certified Beautiful Person, intimate of Lenny and Jackie, chum of Gloria Steinem, an original backer of Arthur, the slipped discothèque. Twice married, once divorced, once separated, he was the most eligible married male in Manhattan. His upper West Side triplex was decorated by Billy Baldwin. His Rolls waited obediently at the curb while he visited his fellow greats. His corporation was acquired by AVCO Embassy Pictures Corp. for $4,-

500,000. And yet, and yet, at that palmy time—was it only the day before yesterday?—there was a reason offered for Mike's acidulous tongue and his lofty penthouse picture of society. It was the standard one, heavily merchandised by paperback Freudians: an unhappy childhood.

With Nichols, the reason was real. An émigré from Hitler Germany, Michael Igor Peschkowsky arrived in the U.S. in 1939. The seven-year-old could speak but two sentences in his new tongue: "I do not speak English" and "Please do not kiss me." Forbearance is difficult for a little boy; there are people who will kiss a child no matter what he pleads. Mike learned how to offer a cheek and withdraw a psyche. He was a great sponge of a boy who decided to absorb the world.

One month after his arrival, Mike's accent fell away like hand-me-down overalls. His father, a doctor, died when the boy was twelve. There was hardly any cash; the brilliant, aggressive student subsisted on scholarships and formed a lasting grudge against the unfeeling. To this day he remembers learning in terms of combat. "In grammar school you fight for your life and try not to get the crap beat out of you after school," he recalls. "In high school you figure things are frozen forever in a certain pattern; there are a couple of guys you can beat up and a lot who can beat you up, and there are a few girls who'll go out with you and some more that won't, and that's the way the rest of life will be. Then you get to college, and things seem to be a little more open." A little, but not enough. Faced with this anatomy of melancholy, he opted for heavy anesthetic. He slept 16 and 18 hours a day.

Rinse Out, Please

In 1949, at the University of Chicago, like many another converted introvert, he woke up to performing. Wit is far more often a shield than a lance; Mike set up a complex of defenses that made him the fastest tongue in the Midwest. The second fastest was a hostile chick named Elaine May. It was love at first fight. "Elaine held me like an autistic child," Nichols remembers. The child bride he had taken at 19 was cast off. Elaine became a surrogate, although, says Mike, "it was much too serious for marriage." And much too funny not to play it for audiences.

They began playing together in 1954, and by 1957 had improvised their way into national prominence as the mockingbirds of the American aviary. When they were around, no peacock, no eagle was secure. In their Broadway show, *An Evening with Mike Nichols and Elaine May*, they did scenes in the style of O'Neill, and Batman, Proust, Pirandello and Noel Coward. Each swatch of material had a shiny button—as when Nichols, playing an English dentist, leans over his beloved patient: "I knew even then that I loved you. There, I've said it. I do love you. Let's not talk about it for a moment. Rinse out, please."

Their rise was based on more than matched metabolism and high literacy. Their stagecraft was impeccable. Elaine had been a child actress; before Nichols & May were joined with an ampersand, he had taken classes with Lee Strasberg. The guru of the Actors Studio had helped Mike along financially simply because he was overwhelmed by the kid's "earnestness and directness."

Saint Subber's Stomach

Richard Burton remembers meeting Nichols and May backstage when he was starring in *Camelot*. "Elaine was too formidable . . . one of the most intelligent, beautiful and witty women I had ever met. I hoped I would never see her again." Mike was less formidable, more agreeable. The mustard-colored eyes glinted, but the face had an unlined, almost feminine softness. The voice was as warm and resonant as a cello. Burton, who knows role playing when he sees it, was at first unconvinced by the proffered friendship and admiration. But eventually he enrolled Nichols in the Richard Burton fan club; it was an attachment that would one day pay off handsomely for Nichols.

Making up the act was a mutual [68] idea; breaking it up in 1961 was Elaine's. Closing the Broadway show, the comedians split amicably—only to rejoin when Elaine wrote *A Matter of Position*, a comedy starring Mike as a manic market researcher depressively afraid that people would hate him. They did. They also hated the play, which folded in Philadelphia after 17 performances. "It was not a pleasant experience," admits Mike. "I behaved very badly toward Elaine." She abandoned performing for about six years. Mike, as he says, "might have been Dick Cavett today" except for Saint Subber's stomach. The producer owned a play by a TV comedy writer named Neil Simon. He remembered a funnyman who might just be able to direct. "Mike had misgivings and doubts," Saint Subber recalls. "He said, 'Why do you come to me?' I said, 'I chose you because I thought it out in my stomach. In the theater all you have are instincts.' "

Sharp Enough to Slice

Nichols remembers: "The first day of rehearsal, I knew, my God, this is *it!* It is as though you have one eye, and you're on a road and all of a sudden your eye lights up, and you look down and you know, 'I'm an engine!' " An engine that could. The play was called *Barefoot in the Park*.

What made it a smash hit, and far more than an expanded honey-

mooners skit, was the Nichols style: timing, vibrance and a slavish attention to detail. Nichols and failure became antonyms. *Barefoot* was followed
by *The Knack*, *Luv* and *The Odd Couple*. The director came to resemble
Somerset Maugham's *nouveau* novelist, Alroy Kear, who read that genius
was an infinite capacity for taking pains. "If that was all, he must have
told himself, he could be a genius like the rest."

Producer Alexander Cohen still remembers with awe when Nichols
called him one night to rage: "This theater is in total darkness!" One of
the 30 lamps on the balcony rail was flickering. Saint Subber's marrow
freezes when he remembers Nichols' insistence that *The Odd Couple* set
be repainted 24 hours before opening. When he cast *Barefoot*, Nichols
was even more demanding. "Mike insisted on getting a real telephone man
or a taxicab driver to play the telephone man," recalls Subber. "I thought:
this has to be a put-on. But I ended up getting a cab driver—and he is
now an actor: Herb Edleman."

Though audiences could no longer feel it, Nichols' tongue was still
sharp enough to slice. Richard Burton likes to retell the story of Walter
Matthau, "a frenetic soul, and he finally blew his stack at Nichols' *Odd
Couple* direction. 'You're emasculating me,' Walter cried. 'Give me back
my balls!' From out front, Mike called back: 'Props.' "

Mike was Burton's kind of boy. As the Liz-Dick *scandale* deepened
during the filming of *Cleopatra*, Burton recalls, "Ninety percent of our
friends avoided our eyes. Mike flew to Rome from New York to be with
us." Nichols stayed by Elizabeth's side when Burton went off to make
another film. Favors like that one remembers. In 1966, the Welshman
and his lady were signed for *Who's Afraid of Virginia Woolf?*, and Elizabeth insisted on Nichols as director. Virginia Woolf could have been a
mini-Cleopatra, but its below-the-belt punches intrigued critics and audiences. The second time out, with Dustin Hoffman and *The Graduate*,
he won it all: money, the Oscar, and freedom for his third film, *Catch-22*.

By then, his manipulation of actors had become a patented amalgam
of ad lib and calculation. "He makes you feel kind of like a kite," says
Hoffman. "He lets you go ahead, and you do your thing. And then when
you've finished he pulls you in by the string. But at least you've had the
enjoyment of the wind." To Richard Burton, "He conspires *with* you to
get the best from you." Buck Henry's appraisal is shrewder: "He tries to
make you think that what he's telling you is your own idea."

Mike's idea for *Catch-22* began at Heller's beginning, in Italy. Production Designer Richard Sylbert and Producer John Calley began hunting
for Heller's old base on the coast of Corsica. "We asked in our failing
Italian, 'Where is World War II?' " Sylbert says. Answer: nowhere. The
base had been wiped out by highways and refineries. It was not until they
flew over a mountain range dubbed "Goat's Teats" near Guaymas, Mex-

ico, that they found a place with what Sylbert called that "how-do-I-get-outta-here feeling." Nichols took one look and flipped.

Do You Think Natalie Wood?

He had decided that the main design of the film should be as circular as the dialogue: holes in walls, arches, bombs. There were other circles involved. *Catch-22* was a convergence of innumerable wheels. Jon Voight came to prominence playing opposite Dustin Hoffman in *Midnight Cowboy*, a job Hoffman would not have landed had he not been in Nichols' *The Graduate*, an assignment Hoffman won because of his excellence in the play *Eh?* directed by Arkin. After playing Yossarian, Arkin was to direct *Little Murders*, by Jules Feiffer, who has written Nichols' next project, *Carnal Knowledge*.

To onlookers, journalists and occasional tourists, the interrelationships on the set seemed to be a piece-by-piece reassemblage of a New York cocktail party in the Mexican boondocks. Nichols played chess, anagrams and his famous-name games: "What did Cary Grant? Do you think Natalie Wood?" There were sexual boffs: When Nichols wanted to record a special sound from Nurse Duckett, he had Arkin grab Paula Prentiss' thigh. Nichols, unnoticed, stood behind her and lunged for her breasts. "Mike was very happy with my hoot," says Prentiss. "Then I was so overcome I had to go into a corner and be let alone. Whenever someone touches me I'm in love with him for about eight hours."

John Wayne came down, got snubbed [73] and drunk. Nichols danced down an airplane runway with Candice Bergen, who had come to take pictures and write an article. Bob Newhart, the paranoid Major Major, replayed his stand-up routines. Perkins restaged his staircase scene from *Psycho*. And underneath, it was one of the tensest, most grueling areas since Anzio beach.

"Mike has a funny blind eye when he works," says Buck Henry. "He thinks everybody is always having a grand time. Everything may look rosy with a group of actors playing dirty-word games in the shade, but inside the command post the subtext is going on: an actor is on the verge of being fired; the lighting director isn't speaking to the director; someone's trying to negotiate with Orson Welles in Spain from the only phone on the base, which went through three Mexican cities on party lines."

Nichols decided that Stacy Keach, cast as Cathcart, was "too young and light for the part." The actor was spirited away at dawn. Keach, who distrusted the parochial atmosphere, now identifies Nichols with the psychotically ambitious Cathcart. "Psychologically," he says, "I saw him in that position. In fact, I think he should have played the role."

Taking My Life Tonight

Orson Welles arrived and began his lecture series: to Nichols on direction, to Film Editor Sam O'Steen on cutting, to actors on acting. But he consistently blew his lines and ended by being led through his readings by Nichols. When a B-25 roared over the compound and 18,000 sticks of dynamite ripped into buildings, huts and shacks, an actor forgot his lines. It was at times like this that Nichols would whisper to Buck Henry not quite facetiously: "You carry on; I'm taking my life tonight." The costs kept rising. The end result totaled some $15 million—much of it invisible on-screen. It will have to gross $37.5 million before it turns a profit.

Even beyond Mexico, there remained a residue of despair. After four months of shooting in Guaymas, two months in Rome and a month in Los Angeles, Nichols confessed that he was "pregnant with a dead child." In everything he had previously accomplished, there had been an accretion of finicky brush strokes that became a character or a landscape. With *Catch-22*, there was a stripping away. He pared easy gags from the script. He erased nearly 300 extras because the picture "was beginning to look like *Twelve O'Clock High*." Sylbert was instructed to strip the sets bare; a whorehouse became a room, a bed a radiator. On the set, characters were dropped. In the cutting room, during eight months of editing, speeches were shaved. There was no musical score.

One afternoon, after three months in the dark, cluttered editing room, Nichols called to Calley: "Hey! I want you to come and look. I think I love it."

In its finished form, the movie contains several stylistic allusions to other film makers. *Catch-22*'s degenerate Roman tour is frankly Fellini. The airborne scenes have obvious overtones of Kubrick—indeed, Nichols bowed to his film-making friend by repeating a brief and thunderous musical theme from *2001*. *Catch*'s galvanic jumps in time owe much to Richard Lester. Still, the film has the force of a source—the kind of work that other film makers will soon be quoting.

To a degree, the film's premonitory quality is a result of externals. Says Henry: "Heller was writing about a man who finally decided to opt out and who, in the end, ends up in Sweden. That was a total absurdity when he wrote it in 1961, a really far-out kind of insanity. Well, it's come true." Not literally—the fictional fugitive of 1944 had paid his dues; it is too facile to see him merely as a Viet Nam dropout 25 years before his time. Calley regards the film as an extension of the 7 o'clock news: "Unfortunately," he says, "it seems that you can always count on the country to do things to keep a picture like this timely." Heller himself says, "When I saw the film I expected to be disappointed—after all, I had no part of it. But I saw what Mike had done. He didn't try to make it just an antiwar movie or an insane comedy. He caught its essence. He understood."

And All Ours

Apparently it is not all he understood. "You can't increase the size of your nature," Nichols says. "But you can be true to it." Gazing at the rear-view mirror, he confesses that a second look at *Virginia Woolf* "bored me. I hate the way it's photographed." *The Graduate?* "My eyes pass it as I look. It's like a blank place in my head."

As for the stage work back in the Broadway days, the harshest judgments come from a friend, Buck Henry, and an enemy, Scenarist William Goldman. Says Henry: "Mike is one of the most famous directors in the U.S., but he hasn't made one significant contribution to the theater. I think it's a fanatical waste of time, but he's crazy not to do Pinter. He should have done Joe Orton's farces. But Mike doesn't want to do anything badly. He takes a risk, but he takes a risk on things he knows he can do better than anyone else."

In his carping book *The Season*, Goldman (*Butch Cassidy and the Sundance Kid*) devoted a whole chapter to Nichols sardonically entitled "Culture Hero." Wrote Goldman: "Nichols' work is frivolous—charming, light and titanically inconsequential. . . . What Nichols is is brilliant. Brilliant and trivial and self-serving and frigid. And all ours."

Let's Begin

Until *Catch-22*, Nichols' demur would have been as hollow as his hits. Abruptly, he has supplied his own defense. The film, he claims, perhaps too extravagantly, has "helped me discover how I want to live—I'm going to get rid of myself in stages." In any case the film has apparently made him demand more of himself professionally. Says Nichols, "It's come clear that you have to make your own statement. I'm well aware of the separation between what you say and do. But it has to be begun, so all I'm really saying is, 'Let's begin.' "

The speech has the ring of a World War II bombardier who has chosen a difficult—and perhaps impossible—way home. Will anyone call the way trivial and self-serving and frigid? If so, the only reply can be: "The knife came down, missing him by inches, and he took off." [74]

Joseph Heller
On Translating
'Catch-22'
into a Movie

The huge problems of translating *Catch-22* to a movie: I suppose this can be discussed from several points of view. One can talk about making a movie from the point of view of the original studio, which was Columbia. Having purchased *Catch-22*, people at Columbia probably said, "Well, it never made the best-seller list, and we're stuck with it. Which one of you said we should buy it?"

One can deal with it from the point of view of the actor. From 1962 to 1965 each one had his own view of how the part should be played and was convinced that only he could do it well. I had letters from a couple of movie stars saying I wrote about them. Alan Arkin, at the time the book came out in 1961, was rehearsing for his first play *Enter Laughing* and did read the book before publication and expressed a wish and a kind of prayer that someday he would act in it.

One could deal with it from the point of view of director Mike Nichols, who said, "Okay, get me a good script," and then went off to direct four plays and *The Graduate*, and would check in from time to time with the screenwriter.

Or one could deal with it from the point of view of the screenwriter, Buck Henry, who probably said, "Oy, Veh! There is no plot in this book."

Or one could deal with this from the point of view of Paramount Pictures, which eventually produced it, and I can almost hear the outcry up there: "Fifteen million dollars! For what?! We thought this was going to be a cheap movie!"

Or one could approach it from the point of view of the author of the novel, who really was unconcerned with any of this from the beginning, and that's me; and that's what I'll talk about, my experiences with the movie version of *Catch-22*. This sounds kind of surprising to many people,

SOURCE: This selection is an abridgment of remarks made by Joseph Heller at the Poetry Center, Young Men's Hebrew Association, New York City, in December 1970. Reprinted by permission of the author. The editors wish to thank the Poetry Center for having made available a recording of Mr. Heller's talk.

and perhaps even corrupt, but I really didn't give a damn what happened to it, once I sold it to Columbia Pictures and the first check cleared.

I don't really think there are that many good movies made in the history of motion pictures for me to realistically expect that a good picture would be made from any book, including *Catch-22*. I had to do a commendable job of acting for the next four or five years because just about everybody else I met was desperately concerned that they not "spoil" my book, that they "do justice" to my book, and I would have to pretend that I was equally concerned, but I really wasn't. I did have the right by contract to do the first script; they did not have to use it, but they did have to pay me for doing the first script. So little concerned was I that very quickly in the process I waived that right, and wisely so. I didn't want to do a movie script of *Catch-22* because if I did work on it, I *would* have to be concerned with what came out, and I know that a scriptwriter has very little control, very little to contribute really, very little influence in determining the difference between what he has in mind when he writes the screenplay and what eventually emerges on the screen.

The novel was published in 1961. I guess the first inquiries about stage rights and movie rights came a few weeks before official publication and continued for a month or so afterward. There would be calls to my agent, asking, "Are the movie rights available?" and she would say, "Yes." Then they would say, "I'll get back to you, I'll get back to you," and never hear from them again.

David Merrick called me about adapting the novel to the theater. I was so much in awe of him that I scarcely listened to the terms he offered to acquire the stage rights, but in retrospect I realize they were extremely generous.

The book did not make *The New York Times* best-seller list. It was, I would think, successful as a first novel—sold about thirty or thirty-two thousand copies in the course of the first year—but that's not enough to make a best seller. The studio readers just didn't know what to make of the book, and if any of them did try to read it, they stopped by about page eight, ten, or twelve, but a few people really did want the book and did see it as a motion picture. I have a lawyer who is a kind of Svengali and a hypnotist, and he finally got two studios in a reluctant auction for it, but the scale was pretty low at the beginning. I had a pretty good job then as an advertising man, and although I didn't need money particularly, I wanted it desperately, because good as the job was, I hated it and wanted to be able to afford to quit it. Just as things were building up, the man doing negotiations for one of the companies dropped dead; so there was only one studio left, and that was Columbia, and Columbia did buy it.

What happened from then on was, I guess, a kind of realization—another one of those dreams come true that, when they do come true, disappoint you. I began to meet very famous people, actors from Hollywood who would call me up or arrange through mutual friends to meet me and then whisper in my ear that they were the only ones who should be in *Catch-22*. I remember the first of these. I got a phone call from a person I knew named Sam Shaw. He said, "Tony Quinn is in town; he's leaving for Yugoslavia tonight or tomorrow. He wants to talk to you about *Catch-22*; he's got to see you right away."

And I said, "Okay, where do we meet?"

And he said, "The Stage Delicatessen."

And I said, "What the hell is Anthony Quinn doing at the Stage Delicatessen, and why must we meet there?"

And he said, "You've got to come here because he is interviewing a secretary," which raised other questions that seemed pretty good. So I went to the Stage or Sixth Avenue Delicatessen, and I met Anthony Quinn, and he's somebody to meet. As soon as he hired the secretary, we sat down at one of those small tables. Luckily they didn't seat anybody next to us. We began talking about *Catch-22*, and he ran through every well-known actor explaining why each could not do the job—this one couldn't, that one couldn't, this one couldn't—and *his* only reservation was that perhaps he was too old to play Yossarian, and he said, "Do you think I'm too old?"

And I said, "No, of course not. You're just the guy I had in mind when I wrote it."

This was a reply I was to use perhaps twenty or thirty times in connection with actors ranging all the way from Wally Cox to Jack Lemmon, John Gielgud, and Zero Mostel. To whomever I found myself with who said, "Don't you think I'm right for the part," I would say, "Nobody else."

And I really believed it when I was saying it; that's the thing that troubled me in getting ready to talk to you tonight; I realized that I really believed it. I really believed that John Gielgud or Laurence Olivier could play Yossarian, with a few changes made. And I don't know whether it was because I genuinely felt that *Catch-22* as a novel was so adaptable that any good actor could play it, or whether I was corrupt, more corrupt than I understood myself to be.

Another reason Columbia didn't make the movie back in 1962 or 1963 was that it was the time of what I think of as the year of the "double war." It wasn't a war that I was involved in but it was a war that Columbia Pictures was involved in. They found themselves in the unfortunate position of producing two anti-war movies in one year, and the Pentagon doesn't like this. (Apparently each studio is allowed to produce one anti-war movie a year, but not two.) Columbia had financed Stanley Kubrick's *Dr. Strangelove*. An independent organization had financed a picture called *Fail-Safe*. When there were certain similarities between the two, a lawsuit began. They resolved the lawsuit by Columbia buying *Fail-Safe*. So they had *Fail-Safe* and *Dr. Strangelove* in the same year, and the Pentagon didn't like it. Each of the studios has a man in Washington who talks to the generals and admirals, and keeps them happy, and they didn't want to embark on another movie that they thought the Pentagon might not like. Then a stockholders' fight got in the way. All this time my reputation was suffering because the rumor was spreading that *Catch-22* was hard to adapt to the screen. And I was getting stigmatized. People in Hollywood and New York were saying, "That's Heller over there—his books don't make good screenplays." I stopped being invited to parties. Credit became tight at Brooks Brothers and Paul Stuart, and the rumor was going around that it was impossible to adapt *Catch-22* into a screenplay, whereas I knew that no effort was being made.

Richard Brooks had made two very successful pictures then, I think, for United Artists; one was *Elmer Gantry*, and one was, I think, *Cat on a Hot Tin Roof*. Richard Brooks said he would make movies for Columbia only if he could make two of his favorite works of literature. And those two were Joseph Conrad's *Lord Jim* and Joseph Heller's *Catch-22*. So he embarked on *Lord Jim*. Brooks is the kind of director who is very finicky about details, does everything himself. In between working on *Lord Jim* he would come to New York. I think I spent a solid week with him in New York having lunch with him, while he asked me questions about *Catch-22*. He wanted to understand it thoroughly, and I answered them, and he kept assuring me he wanted to be very faithful to the book, and I kept pleading with him not to make that his objective because there's a vast difference, which I understand and many Hollywood people don't, between a work of fiction and a motion picture; and if he really succeeded in being faithful to the novel, he would have a twelve-hour picture that everybody would find interminably dull and pretentious and verbose, and that would really not be a reflection of the book.

At any rate, Richard Brooks went off to make *Lord Jim*, and he spent between two and three years doing it and came back exhausted from very, very exotic places like Bangkok and London, and the movie came out and got very bad reviews, and he was so discouraged he told Columbia quite frankly that he didn't want to take on another tough movie. So now Columbia had it back, and nobody wanted to make it, nobody at Columbia, and along about this time Mike Nichols had begun to establish himself as a director. *Luv* was one of the things he had directed.

I went to see *Luv* (that's a play by Murray Schisgal in which Alan Arkin starred), and after seeing it, I did call up Mike Frankavitch—he was in charge of production for Columbia—to say that I thought he could do much worse than to consider Alan Arkin for the part and Mike Nichols for the director. There's another producer named Martin Ransohoff, who from the time *Catch-22* appeared, was taken by it and wanted to do the movie. He spoke to Mike Nichols. He said he'd like Mike to direct a movie for him. Nichols said he would only agree to do it if it were *Catch-22*. Ransohoff did buy the motion picture rights away from Columbia for a small amount more than Columbia paid for it.

I was out of touch with all of this, by the way, because, number one, I didn't care and, number two, there's no reason anybody should have kept me in touch. I don't have much sympathy with novelists who go on television and complain about the movies that are made from their books. I think in the course of selling a book or a play for a movie, he knows what he's doing. I'd never felt, for example, even when the movie was made that they had any obligation to remain faithful to the book or to me or to make a good movie. When Nichols eventually got around to contacting me about it, I was kind of embarrassed; I was hoping he wouldn't. But when he did, we met and spoke a couple of times about it. The first I knew that Nichols was involved was through an announcement that said Mike Nichols was going to direct *Catch-22* and Alan Arkin was going to play the part of Yossarian. Now this was at a time when only the people in New York knew who Alan Arkin was; he had not made *The Russians Are Coming*. Once the announcement was made, I began to receive congratulations. Then when the rumors got up to twenty or thirty million dollars (the movie didn't cost that much), somehow people think I'm getting it all. And I'm not disabusing them because I discovered what I'd always known, that if people think you're rich, they'll do anything for you. You can get credit, and presents; it's the people who really need help who have trouble getting it.

About two years ago, my phone rang and my daughter answered it and said, "It's another one of your friends."

And I said, "Which friend?"

She said, "I don't know, but he's giving me false names."

And I said, "I don't have friends like that, you do."

And she said, "Well, he says he's Mike Nichols."

So I got on the phone and sure enough it's Mike Nichols, and it's the first contact I've had with him ever, and he's very polite and very charming, and he says that he feels it might be a good idea to consult the author *before* the picture is made, and would I meet with him, talk about it, and I said, "Sure," and he said, "O.K., I'll get back to you." And about fourteen months passed. I'm out at the beach; it's the summer, and the phone rings again, and it's Mike Nichols getting back to me. He apologized, and I said I hadn't been waiting, really. He explained that the reason he hadn't gotten back to me was because they wanted to get a script close to a final version before they showed it to me, and I kept saying, "You know, you don't have to show it to me. I just might make things a little complicated for you." But he said, "No, no; Buck Henry has been busy rewriting and the script is being mimeographed now. We're ready to meet, and would you come in to the city?"

I said, "Yeah," and he said, "Okay. I'll get back to you," and I said, "Sure, anytime."

And then fourteen more months passed, and then I did get a call asking would I read the script. He sent it over to my house, and I read it. I know this about movie scripts: on paper they all look terrible; they all sound terrible. As literature they're just very bare and sparse, and it's almost impossible to evaluate them in terms of quality. There was much in the script that I didn't like and much that I did. What I liked most of all was a structure that indicated an effort to include very tough scenes from the book in the movie, scenes that I myself would have eliminated automatically if I were doing the screenplay.

I read about half or three-quarters of the script and then Nichols and I met for dinner at a Chinese restaurant which he thinks is very good, and he had Buck Henry join us, which was extremely awkward because he wrote the script, and they wanted to know what I thought and I had never met Buck before. I empathized with him so strongly that I really didn't know what to say. He said, "Say what you want to," and Nichols said the same. It was never clear in my mind—and it still isn't clear—whether they were really interested in what I had to say or whether they just wanted my opinion of that Chinese restaurant. It was a courtesy.

In the course of that meal, they told me something that was very revealing to me, that the first draft of the movie script was 385 pages long. The novel is 440 pages. A typical two-hour movie script is about 120 pages. Now the very fact that the first script was 385 pages indicated to me that they had made an effort to include in the motion picture everything in the book that they themselves liked, and that was pretty much the whole book. A 385-page movie script, well, if you figure two hours for 120 pages, an hour for 60 pages, that's about a six-and-a-half or seven-hour movie—which they weren't going to make—so they went through a kind of painful process of eliminating scene after scene after scene, but even at 185 pages it was too long. Very generally I told them that I felt there was too much dialogue in it of a transitional nature. I expressed the other feeling that I thought in the first 70 pages or so there was lots of action and lots of comedy, but nothing seemed to be happening in the way of developing the story or Yossarian's character. Nichols was later to remember that comment and say he had the same feeling and was very much afraid that considerable cutting had to be done in the first 70 or 75 pages.

When we parted, Mike said, "Get up a list of specific suggestions, and we'll talk about them some more. And of course you'll be paid for it."

The way things happened, I had at that time the same agent that Nichols had. Nichols said, "We'll work out a deal for paying you, and I'll get back to you."

I went halfway through the script working up a list of changes and suggestions, and I never heard from him, and I realized that "I'll get back to you" means "I'll see you around." I let it go then. I never did send my comments in. Buck had spent as many hours working on this motion picture script, well possibly as many hours, as I had spent working on the novel—possibly three years of concern with the script—and it's kind of unfair and too easy for me to come in and find problems and make suggestions without providing solutions for them and leave them with this feeling that I hate what they're doing.

Then they went off to make the movie, and I had a kind of lukewarm invitation to come down, but I didn't because it wasn't Acapulco. If it had been Acapulco, I would have come down, but they were in some God-awful place. People did start to go crazy there by the way; some of you may have read the *Newsweek* story or the *Times* magazine story on it. Bob Newhart did go crazy one time. One week he *pretended* to go crazy, and it was a lot of laughs, but about two days later he really did freak out, and the others were sitting around laughing and applauding him before somebody came over to him and I think gave him an injection. And he was so sick of that place—this was in Guaymas, Mexico—that he arranged to have a taxi come down from Arizona, and the day he was through, his bags were packed. When Nichols said, "Okay, print it," Newhart got in the taxicab, and that taxicab drove him to Arizona from Mexico. He just couldn't stand it anymore.

The reason I didn't go down there is that I'd been on a set where a movie was being made, for one day, and I realized that if a person is not working he might just as well be on a torture rack if he has to hang around there. I think what Nichols did was this: every actor who had to work in Mexico was signed up for the full period. Now the full period I think was about four months, twelve or sixteen weeks of shooting. Almost everybody in Mexico was there for the full four months, and most of them had very few working days. Jack Gilford started one scene, and for some reason they stopped and Nichols said, "Okay, we'll finish it in a day or two." I think seven weeks went by and then Gilford mailed a letter to Nichols right from the movie set. It began, "Dear Mr. Nichols, you are in Mexico making a movie; I am in Mexico not making a movie. I have some acting experience and if you have a spot for me perhaps to finish a scene or so, I'd be happy to work for you."

The next day Nichols remembered, so he got Gilford and they did finish the scene.

Then John Wayne arrived and breezed into his hotel from his own plane, and these were all kids so nobody knew who he was; and he got drunk and broke a foot going out. Orson Welles came and intimidated them all. He is a legend and his very presence was one that just got everybody up tight. Even people on the movie who were not too happy working for Mike Nichols say that Nichols showed his true genius in handling Welles, who was in a position really to shatter everything.

Meanwhile the cost of the movie was going up. Nichols is a perfectionist. I have a feeling he makes a movie pretty much the way I write a novel, and that is I might write one page over four or five times, then probably decide the first way was best. Or I might write three handwritten pages over twelve different ways and then decide a paragraph will do. But I can't be convinced that only a paragraph will do until I've gone through those three pages and all the approaches to it. I think Nichols on this picture went through this same thing.

Finally, the movie was finished; everybody was let go; people came back from Mexico. Almost everybody in the movie was unhappy with his role, which to me was a kind of a tribute to Nichols. This fact is an indication he would not let any actor take over the picture or let any actor take over any of the scenes; he had his conception of the picture. He had an image of the movie, and that's pretty much what came on the screen. Even he could not get all he wanted. It's not the cast he would have chosen as his first choice. Many things he thought he had on film he discovered later he didn't have, but then there was no way of getting them on film.

When he went into the period of cutting the movie, he took a long, long time, and every once in a while I would see him or hear from him, and people would tell me that he was very much concerned about how I would react to the movie, which made me feel great because at bottom I suppose my own ego was affronted. How dare he think he could make a movie from my book without my help?

I was off in a small town in Ohio on a Friday night just before getting ready to speak when there was a phone call for me, and it was Mike Nichols, who said they had just screened it in Boston at two sneak previews the night before. He thought and Paramount thought the reaction was very good and if I wanted to see it he'd stay over that weekend to show it to me and any friends I cared to have. I said I'd like very much to see it, but I'd kind of like to see it alone. He was surprised; he said okay. And I went on a Sunday with my wife and my daughter, who was eighteen, and we saw it in one of these screening theaters that have about three hundred seats, and I sat alone and they sat alone and the movie unfolded and I found it kind of overpowering. When it was over, Nichols was kind of slipping away and I took him by the arm and pulled him aside and I said, "Well, as far as I'm concerned, it may be one of the best movies I've ever seen."

He was glad to hear that, and then he said, "Do you want a drink?" and

I said, "Let's go talk," and we went to The Russian Tea Room and I discussed it with him. Then he told me some of the things in the movie he didn't like but he had no choice but to use, and I told him the things I did like about it very much and that I was pleased with it.

There is one change that took a lot of adjusting to—I've seen the movie three times, and only by the third time could I get used to Mike Nichols' concept of Milo Minderbinder, which is one big change in characterization. The Milo in the book is much different from the Milo on the screen. But by the third time I saw it I could get used to Jon Voight playing Milo the way Mike Nichols directed him to. My wife and my daughter had the same reaction I did. Essentially, we found it a very grim and very powerful and very engrossing and disturbing movie. I was pleased that if some change in basic objective had to be striven for, that it be a heavy one, a pessimistic one, a melancholy one, rather than an easy one—which would have been sex and comedy, because to my mind, at least, *Catch-22* does resolve itself into a novel in which the last eighty to one hundred pages are very morbid and very frightening and almost hopeless and perhaps hopeless. There's a glimmer of what might or might not be hope at the end, and the same effect is carried through in the movie.

After the preview, Nichols went back to make a few slight changes in the film, mainly with the sound. The reaction in Boston was superb, by the way, and I was at Boston University last week and talking to students, many of whom were at the preview, and they said they went to see it hoping to hate it and came out being stunned. It's only in New York that I find people who dislike the movie very much, who criticize it very much. I've been to about six colleges this year since the movie has been shown, and most of the people I meet—I won't say all, but most of the students and faculty—think of it as a very exceptional motion picture. It's a kind of picture that people are going back to see more than once.

So the movie opened. Some of the reviews were ecstatic; some were attacks, on the movie, I'm glad to say. The book came through beautifully. I was kind of surprised to find so many reviewers throughout the country who think of *Catch-22* as a very good book. There weren't that many when it came out. The movie did very well at the box office the first six, eight, or ten weeks, depending on the city, and then it slackened off, and now it's doing better than expected in those cities where it has gone into what they call showcase theaters.

During the summer I got a call from Dell Publishing. This was, I guess, mid-August. Two people called me up, each not knowing the other was calling me and each to tell me he had just heard from the sales department that in a six-week period *Catch-22* had become the fastest selling book Dell had ever produced. They redesigned the cover for the motion picture. The book sold a million copies in six weeks, which is about what it sold in a full year when it came out as a paperback. As soon as they told me that, I stopped working on my new novel, and I won't have to do any more work on that for a year. I was very pleased by the sale; the Dell edition also made the paperback best-seller list, the only time *Catch-22* has been on the best-seller list. Although it made me very happy, it also amused me in a kind of sadistic way, because I know that of these million copies, almost all were bought by women on their way to the beauty parlor or in drug stores by people who had never heard of the book before and who wouldn't be able to get past page six or eight. It's nice to get money from these people who make millionaires out of Harold Robbins and Jacqueline Susann.

The way we stand today, the movie is out, and I had nothing to do with it, really nothing. People say, "Well, you wrote the book," but it doesn't mean anything. I mean, Nichols could choose or leave out anything he wanted to. It is pretty much his movie. But as I talk to you now, I'm kind of rich and famous and successful, but unchanged by success; I'm still as corruptible as I was the day I sold it to Columbia, and God willing, I'll remain that way. Thank you.

Questions and Answers*

Q. *You mentioned Jon Voight and Orson Welles; are there any other specific criticisms or praise you have for the film?*

A. I myself? In saying that I couldn't get used to Voight, it doesn't mean that I disapprove of Nichols' conception. Nichols' conception of Milo was different from mine. To say it's different is not saying that in a pejorative sense. I think, for example, that the way Milo goes out of the book, which is kind of vanishing, he just disappears to go smuggle tobacco, would not be as effective on the screen. I think Voight's last moment on the screen is tremendously effective, if you recall it. It's just to say the Voight characterization was different. I had no objection to Welles in the movie. I think that it could have been just as well played by Martin Balsam or somebody else, that Welles was wasted in the sense that he is a huge personality and should have had more.

Q. *Would you name some of the things you really liked and some of the things you didn't?*

A. I wasn't as reactive to the comedy in the movie as audiences were. I think there were moments on the screen where more could have been made out of the minute or two or three when the characters were talking

---

* In the following section, the questions asked of Mr. Heller have been summarized.—Eds.

and there was a kind of nonsense dialogue going on, which added nothing; it was just time filling. If you want a specific example, there is a scene when Alan Arkin is trying to make love to Paula Prentiss on the beach, and she is saying something, just talking nonsense: "I'm the only girl on the base and it's so difficult." In that moment, minute or minute and a half, I think that it would have been better to have gotten in what is in the book, that she herself is breaking off a love affair of some duration with him so that she too was rejecting him and it wasn't simply a kind of rape scene on the beach but an indication that he was losing something he wanted. And that would have given a little more meaning to a later scene, which I don't understand, where Arkin is swimming in the water toward the raft and she is on the raft naked. I think there were about two or three places where they tried to create a dialogue like *Catch-22* dialogue which didn't work, for me anyway; there was no need to have any dialogue at all in those places.

I missed one thing only from the book. I wished that they had put in the movie at least one of what I consider the interrogation scenes or inquisition scenes or trial scenes. There are three in the book. I know three fairly full ones. There were none in the movie. And yet I can't think of anything in the movie I would take out that would allow the five or six minutes that would be necessary to provide for that scene. To me one of the most, I guess *the* most effective, scene is the one of the Italian woman in the whorehouse with Yossarian when he comes back to the whorehouse and it's empty and she's sitting there smoking a cigarette, and she just answers, almost doesn't react. There's a kind of weary age-old resignation in her remarks. He is reacting to what she's saying with horror and surprise; then she says, "Catch-a-22." It's as though she realizes, as the old man did, that in the long view of history this is the way life is. And you know she's not happy about it, but why all the surprise? That remains I think for me the most powerful of the scenes. The gory scenes are gory, and they make an impact, but I don't think they're as meaningful as that particular scene.

Q. *How realistic are the details in* Catch-22?

A. I would say all the physical details, and almost all of what might be called the realistic details do come out of my own experiences as a bombardier in World War II. The organization of a mission, the targets—most of the missions that are in the book were missions that I did fly on. The structure of a B-25, the fact that there are no fighters in *Catch-22* (there were no German fighters when I was overseas), the organization of a squadron, the fact that there is an intelligence tent, there is a mess hall, there are enlisted men, there was a squadron commander, the flight surgeon—all of these as details come out of my experience. In many cases, actual people I know were starting points for the characters. The mission to Avignon, for example—and that's the one on which Snowden gets killed —corresponds perhaps ninety percent to what I did experience. I did have a co-pilot go berserk and grab the controls. The earphones did pull out. I did think I was dying for what seemed thirty minutes but was actually three-hundredths of a second. When I did plug my earphones in, there was a guy sobbing on the intercom, "Help the bombardier," but the gunner was only shot in the leg. The other part is something I did add to it.

I want to stress it's just the physical details. Yossarian's emotions, Yossarian's reaction to the war in the squadron were not those I experienced when I was overseas. *Catch-22* is not really about World War II. It was written during the Korean War and during the period when Senator Joe McCarthy was riding high in the Senate and when John Foster Dulles was bringing us to the brink of war with Russia about every other week. There are many other [laughter]. . . . Well, he was and he did boast about it. That's his phrase that he used in an interview in *Life* magazine. Now I think my tensions, my antagonisms, my concerns are those which are in *Catch-22*, along with, I suppose, an age-old preoccupation with mortality which runs all through the book. I very carefully set the moment of decision for Yossarian, his approach to the point of crisis, to coincide with the collapse of Germany as a military threat. Now none of that's in the movie, but in the novel I trace the course of the European war and Germany's collapse as a threat is all over at the time that Yossarian has to make his decision, and Yossarian is able to say near the end, "The country's not in danger anymore, but I am," and be speaking truthfully. And *Catch-22*'s pretty much about a quarrel, a conflict, a predicament I think we in this country have had ever since the end of World War II. That is, a conflict, a danger, not so much from foreign military force but from our own authorities and our own superiors. I felt that at the time that I wrote *Catch-22*. Nothing is said of Hitler in *Catch-22* although here and there is an opposition to Fascism, and I think that's almost self-evident. Nothing is said of Japan, but the conflicts and dangers do come from the superior officers who were either corrupt, indifferent, or stupid, or unconcerned with the human factors.

Q. *Do you know why the pictures on the wall in Major Major's office change?*

A. Concerning the movie, do I know why the pictures on the wall of Major Major's office would change? Usually you have to see the picture two or three times to realize that each time Major Major crosses in front of a photograph, the photograph changes. First it was Roosevelt, then it's Stalin (I forget), then it's Churchill. I would say that was an attempt at humor, whimsical humor, on the part of the people who made the movie. It's nothing I would have recommended doing, and if I were consulted I would say, "Don't do it." There's another place in the movie that Nichols told me his friends advised him to delete. I didn't see *2001*, but apparently it has a Richard Strauss theme in it—and when Yossarian's eyes fall on Luciana, that theme is played and the audiences, when I've seen it, do laugh. Now he was told by certain friends, "Don't do it—it's inside humor, and it's self-indulgence," and he told me this, that he weighed it and wrestled with it, and figured that he's allowed a certain amount of self-indulgence; so he left it in there. I laughed just because the music seemed to lend something to the moment; I didn't know it was in *2001*. I had a feeling that the thing with the photograph was of that nature as well—a kind of whim—that's it. There is a framework to the movie which doesn't exist in the book, and if somebody wants to go very deeply into literary criticism and interpretation, they would have to deal with this difference. In the movie, anything is permissible because it all can be explained in terms of an hallucination, a nightmare, by Yossarian, who is nearly dead and is reliving all this in terms of how events of the past cross his imagination, so none of it has to be literally true. That's in the movie and that can be explained, I suppose, in terms of Yossarian's consciousness, awareness of people like Churchill and Roosevelt, and the other one, Stalin. In the novel, everything that happens *really does happen*. Almost everything, except for a few things described as dreams. Now if one wanted to go into the method of interpretation, one can actually come up with two different meanings because of that fundamental difference, but I don't think anybody is going to go into it that deeply.

Q. *What do you think of people who say you must read the book, see the film, then read the book again in order to get it?*

A. People who have not read the book and seen the film tend to react more favorably to the film than people who had read the book first. And even mixed in with their reaction is a large degree of puzzlement. There are many loose ends in the film, but somehow those loose ends in themselves form a pattern of the inexplicable. If there were just one loose end in the film, one thing that was not tied up, then you might say it's an oversight, but there are five, six, or seven. Now the question was asked of me while I was waiting to come out here tonight, and it's been asked of me before, about how people can know who stabs Yossarian, if it's Nately's whore. Most people miss it who don't know the book. I bumped into Buck Henry a few weeks ago on Second Avenue, and we talked for an hour or two about it, and it was not the intention to leave that vague. Certain things just don't show up in certain scenes as planned, but by that time I had come around to the opinion that even if you thought that it was a GI, a strange GI who you never saw before, who took this big knife and sunk it into his side, it would not be inconsistent with what is happening in the movie with everything else that is attacking him or endangering him.

Q. *How do you think the film presents "Snowden's secret"?*

A. Well, the film doesn't work out Snowden's secret as Snowden's secret because that question isn't raised in the film. I think the film does work out the very slow death and the discovery of death in a most effective and dramatic way. The novel is literary; the film doesn't try to be literary. Most films that are adaptations of novels and plays don't succeed as films, and one reason they don't succeed is because they try to do little more than to photograph, in the case of a novel, to photograph a work that is mainly literary, to put literary values into visual terms. *Catch-22* as a movie doesn't do that; it's non-literary. So the phrase "Snowden's secret" is never evoked. Other things that are of a verbal nature are never introduced. People have asked me this question: "Was Henry Fonda ever thought of for Major Major?" Since nothing is said in the film about the resemblance of Major Major to Henry Fonda, there would be no point in putting Henry Fonda into the part. I think Nichols did what I would have advised him to do; that is, he took the novel and ceased considering it as a novel; kind of flattened it out into material and out of that material tried to arrange a motion picture which said partly what the novel said, mostly what the novel said; and mostly what he himself feels. Now I think, it's been intimated to me, that Nichols did want an Aryan for Milo Minderbinder. In terms of Nichols' own experiences with the Nazis, he wanted a Nazi, not an American middle-class executive, and that's why Voight was chosen and that's why he was developed that way. It is really Nichols' conception of a film taken from material in *Catch-22*, and I think it would have been an atrocious film if he'd tried any other thing.

Q. *How would you describe the structure of* Catch-22?

A. The structure of the book, and it's not entirely an original structure because I think William Faulkner does it in many of his works, is to tell a large narrative largely in terms of fragments and slow feeding of interrupted episodes. Things do happen twice in *Catch-22* or more than twice; things do repeat themselves. The time structure, chronological time, becomes immaterial. For example, Snowden has been wounded and dies before the time of the first chapter. The mission to Bologna has been flown before the first chapter. Milo has bombed his squadron before the time of the first chapter. Most of the events with which the book deals have already taken place. Chronological time is kind of meaningless in the novel itself; what seems to be operating is psychological time. Now I know *why* I wanted things to recur. There are two reasons. I'll tell you quite frankly that one of those reasons is that I felt intuitively the story could better be told that way rather than any other way. (I could have been wrong in that or right.) The second one is a theme that I wanted to give, a feeling of timelessness, that the same things will happen again unless something is done, and do happen again. The chaplain's sense of *déjà vu* which he has is not inaccurate because almost all the things he thinks he has experienced before have happened before, if not to him then we know they've happened. And when Yossarian makes that trip through Rome, called "The Eternal City," it's really a surrealistic scene told in realistic details. As he goes from one scene of cruelty and crime and brutality to another, a sense of guilt begins developing in himself—a feeling of responsibility—and he comes to understand why (I may have even used this sentence): although he has done nothing to cause Nately's death, he's done nothing to prevent it. When he's on that street and watching that man beat the little boy, and there's a crowd around him (this I know is in there), he wonders why nobody intervenes and then realizes he is there also and he is not intervening. What he does is that he doesn't stop the man but he runs away from that scene to the next one. And after the last one (I think it's an old woman who is being defrauded in some way by a younger woman), he turns away again into the darkness, but I have him do it with a growing sense of guilt—afraid that the woman would now start following him. I forgot your question, but things do happen recurringly.

Q. *Do you feel that you have been hurt by the success of* Catch-22?

A. No; I can only answer consciously; nobody can ever give explanations in terms of his own subconscious because by definition he doesn't know it. I don't feel that I am at all inhibited or restrained by *Catch-22* or the success of *Catch-22*. If the truth must be known, I don't really feel I wrote *Catch-22*. It's about seventeen or eighteen years ago that I got the idea for *Catch-22* and spent about five or six months outlining it, and then after I outlined it I began it. It's almost twenty years ago that that happened, about 1952 or 1953; it's a long time back. Consciously, I don't feel at all inhibited by it. I'm going along with the new novel [*Something Happened*]. A few people have read it, and they think it's very good; they think it's superb. It's a very hard novel to write; it'll be much harder to read. Even if it's a terrible novel, which it probably won't be, it'll sell a fantastic amount of copies when it comes out. But when I'm doing novels and when I'm working on the book, it's between me and the paper. I kind of forget the audience, and it's turning out to be eight or ten times longer than I expected it to be. It's really the only kind of work that I consider serious work. The play wasn't serious work. When I do polish a movie script, it's not serious work.

Q. *Do you like the ending of the film?*

A. The first time I saw it in the film I thought it was fine. It was kind of comical and humorous and with feeling. You saw the way the camera pulled back and you realized how far he had to go. Then I had a discussion with a very bright writer for a Los Angeles paper who saw it here and was very familiar with the book and he raised a point, and the point was that he found the ending a little ludicrous because it seemed impossible that Yossarian could get to Sweden in the boat. Then I remembered that in the novel Yossarian doesn't say that he's going to get to Sweden. In fact, two or three times Major Danby says, "You're never going to get there," and he says, "I know, but I can get to Rome if you keep your mouth shut." Then I mentioned to this guy that it would have been a good idea in the film if Yossarian had said, "Well, I think I can get to the mainland if you just keep quiet when I leave here." I think if you saw him in that boat, the tiny yellow raft, and you knew he had to get from this island to the Italian mainland, and make his way from there, you would believe that he had a good chance of making it. The way it ends with Sweden, I think you have a feeling that maybe there's no chance at all. But anyway, at least he's trying. I like the ending—I think it would have been a little more effective if you knew a little more convincingly that the struggle would continue to go on. The novel ends with the fact, I think it's implied or stated, that he'll get to Rome and from then on he's a fugitive. It would have been a good idea to have Nately's whore after him with a knife again, just to indicate that he was not getting out of danger too easily. A surprising number of reviewers and people who wrote letters just take it for granted that Yossarian escapes to Sweden in a boat. They got that impression from the movie. It's not the impression Nichols wanted to create, which is why he organized that scene with a close-up of Arkin paddling that raft and then the camera pulls back and shows him only about ten yards off shore with miles and miles and miles to go. So it was not Nichols' intention to indicate he's getting to Sweden.

Q. *Do you like the sense of humor in the film?*

A. I think there is a much smaller quantity of humor, a lower proportion of humor in the film than there is in the book. But I think underlying the book from the very first chapter—and I know this because I wrote it—there is an undercurrent of the morbid danger of war.

Q. *How would you rate the film adaptation of the novel?*

A. Look, I think it's a better book than a movie, if you're going to ask me that question. I would like to have seen this done (but it couldn't be done), that if this film were an Italian film by Fellini or Antonioni (and it came to this country with titles and we didn't have to use dialogue—all dialogue is bad in a film) I think every American critic who saw this film by Ingmar

Bergman (or whoever else) would have hailed it as an unprecedented film masterpiece. Everybody would. It's because so many of the people, the reviewers, know the book so well that comparisons, I suppose, are inevitable, but I don't think they're valid. I judge it as a film. I can't think of any film I've seen in years, any American film, that I would put on the same level. I can think of a few European films, but that has to do with my taste, and I know what I like in films and I know what I like in novels. But if it's going to be compared with the book, then it suffers in just this inevitable way: I can't think of any film ever adapted from any work of literature that I or other people feel has any quality to it that even approaches the original work of literature that was its source.

FILM REVIEWS AND CRITICISM

Jacob Brackman
Review of 'Catch-22'

There's always a catch. If you're crazy, they have to take you out of combat, but the catch is you have to *ask* them, and if you're trying to get out of combat then you can't be crazy. That's Catch-22. If you think about it hard, it can drive you crazy. Then maybe they'll let you out. No, because you'd have to ask them first, remember? That same catch, number 22, may also be a law according to which certain women can be summarily seized to become servicemen's whores, all profits to a syndicate so gigantic it makes deals with major powers, a syndicate controlled by a bland, personable Acting Mess Officer. But obviously that's nonsensical. Selling shares in devastation! Does war make men crazy? Do men make war because they are crazy to begin with? If you think about it hard, you can tumble into an unbalancing circularity. That's not exactly being crazy, but sometimes it's hard to know just where to draw the line. Like when there's war and you find yourself in the middle of it, even though the war is over. Like when what you destroy doesn't matter so long as you produce tight bombing patterns for the aerial photos. Why not ask your friends? The zombies,

SOURCE: First published in *Esquire*, Vol. 74 (September 1970), pp. 12, 14. Copyright © 1970 by Esquire, Inc. Reprinted by permission of Jacob Brackman, c/o International Famous Agency, and the publisher.

murderers and corpses. But if *Catch-22* had been directed by Brian Hutton or almost anybody out there, it would have wound up indistinguishable from *Kelly's Heroes*. Under Mike Nichols, this is true only about forty percent of the time.

The unsavory part of me that sat looking over *Catch-22* with an appraiser's eye kept commuting, it seemed, between two movies that had been intercut by some moon-struck studio editor. The one a dark, hysterical masterpiece, a Moby Dick of movies. The other a dumb, undergraduatey jackoff, a $15,000,000 Hasty Pudding Show. The one as if Lewis Carroll had redone *The Inferno*—to make you laugh and steal the sound of your laughter. I respected it; even, a few times, stood in awe of it. For minutes at a stretch. I'd feel I was undergoing something like a new *kind* of movie, and therefore one of historical eminence.

From the movie I admire, a few sequences: the refrain around which Yossarian's epic undulates: Y alone in a bleached-out frame, receiving radio instructions over earphones. Then ineptly reassuring Snowden, the wounded gunner: "You're going to be okay." Five times the scene returns, each time elaborated, like a repressed trauma floating back piecemeal from the edge of childhood memory. Next time, a spurting leg wound revealed. "Listen, kid, it's not bad. I'm gonna put a tourniquet on it." Later, when Snowden complains of the cold, Y sees the red blotch of his body wound. Finally he conjures, in a millisecond's image, the body ripped wide, spilling its innards. The plane careens. Snowden shivers. Arkin careens, a silly smile plastered across his face. "There, there," he keeps repeating.

A vision from his delirium: Y swimming toward Nurse Duckett on a raft. She strips and beckons playfully, her breasts slow-motion jouncing. Amazed, frantic with longing, he seems almost to rise like a porpoise from the water. He quickens his stroke. Exhausted, he begins to sink. Through the foregoing, the sound of wind and distant guns.

The airstrip brilliantly lit by searchlights, installations exploding along its perimeters. Minderbinder (lit, as usual, from down low) directing the air raid over loudspeakers, [12] from the control tower. The strafing begins. Y running, his pistol absurdly at the ready, reversing his direction, yelling for Nately, panic and incredulity doing battle in his eyes.

But spritzled all through this order of stuff is a bomber-load of fairly contemptible burlesque. The General's WAC (an early-Forties Betty Grable type) licks her lip and twenty-seven fly-boys fall all over each other offering her twenty-seven folding chairs. The General warns against further moaning; the Major moans (not over the WAC) and the General orders that he be taken out and shot. The Lieutenant Colonel screams, like a quarter-pint Bilko, at the frightened Chaplain.

The *Catch-22* I hold cheap features Martin Balsam as Colonel Cathcart, Buck Henry as Lieutenant Colonel Korn, Bob Newhart as Major Major,

Orson Welles as General Dreedle, Austin Pendleton as Colonel Moodus, and sometimes Jon Voight as Lieutenant Milo Minderbinder. (Minderbinder, a borderline case, seems to play a role in both movies.) Not that these performances are poor—just apparently conceived to suit a broad, inconsequential entertainment, like *Kelly's Heroes*. With Arkin trying to make the devil roar, these fellows second banana as if to a Westbury matinee.

Self-conscious, lap-over transitions zap us from one sequence into the next. For instance, the Colonels Balsam and Henry put their heads together, chortling over how General Dreedle would handle Y's malingering. One pipes up, "Kick 'im in the balls." Bam! cut to Nurse Duckett kicking Y in the balls as he fumbles for her buttons. Most of the transitions operate in just this dimension of cleverness. Yet often as not they're connecting moments of substance that elicit dense emotional responses; moments which can be laughed at, but don't *demand* to be laughed at. The cutesy cuts turn out to be most destructive in their trivializing, because the film's structure—a new . . . disjointed time-jumping spiraling swirlback—turns out to be the most harrowing thing about it. Second most harrowing: how, in the fearful dissociations of war, friendship is impossible. Friendship was the last redeeming myth.

Some of *Catch-22* is so impressive—startling, really—that I like to think Mike Nichols is finding his grown-up stride at last. I begin here to sense the man's complexity, to hear something of the cry beneath his facile send-ups, to anticipate large work from him. However, to account for all the choices which only serve to reintegrate his schizzy *Catch-22* back within the safe conventions of Service Comedy, I must imagine he still labors under the residual bad advice of old, flyweight buddies. Weight classification, a Norman Mailer metaphor, of course, reminds me that Mailer once (in a stroke of that colossal, brutish blindness we allow him, not always cheerfully) miscalled Salinger "the greatest mind ever to stay in prep school"—a title which, a number of us are coming to suspect, properly belongs to the lively Mr. Buck Henry, author.

Can I quit without avowing that *Catch-22* just shines on when Arkin's in the frame? His Yossarian is one of the all-time *full* movie characterizations. This Arkin is inexhaustibly original (he never reads a line the way anyone else might read it) and totally human (you always know him from somewhere). There's also a wonderful performance by the young actor who, in *Midnight Cowboy*, picked up Jon Voight on Forty-second Street and did the virtuoso four-minute turn through lust, nauseated guilt, and, as he finally reneged on the promised payment, terror. Here Bob Balaban plays a wry, mysterious pilot of sudden smiles—a child, like most of our fighting men—whose propensity for crashing into oceans may just be in dress rehearsal for a master escape.

He symbolizes for Yossarian the most urgent personal question about war, a question that stands at the precise center of *Catch-22* and, now, of several million young lives: How can it be escaped from? [14]

Grover Sales
Catch-$22

Mike Nichols' *Catch-22* is an epic disaster predetermined by the children's pop novel on which it is based. To explain what went wrong with the most fervently awaited film of a novel since *Gone With the Wind* entails a retrospective of the Joseph Heller prose to which Nichols found himself both committed and enchained.

For several months after its publication in 1961, the middling sales of *Catch-22* gave no indication of the runaway best seller to come. Slowly, "War and Peace" rave reviews cemented an unlikely confederation of *Time, The Nation,* Art Buchwald, Robert Brustein, Philip Toynbee, Walt Kelly, A. J. Liebling and the Associated Press. It became the most widely read American fiction of the Sixties, supplanting *Catcher in the Rye* as touchstone of the disaffiliated young who recognized in Heller's simplistic reworkings of Orwellian "double-think" the built-in contradictions of a technocratic officialdom riddled with madness. *Catch-22* lent its name to a generation that used the book's title as an all-embrasive epithet to ridicule the Establishment's contorted postures on Vietnam, pot, sex, race and the Chicago Convention. Its much-touted "black comedy" found slavish imitation in novel and film.

The pressures to read it were intimidating—one could as soon avoid Warhol, Bob Dylan, *Blow-up* or the zodiac—as were the persuasions to embrace it as *the* novel of the Second World War. The party line of the middle-aged youth cult decreed that unless we dug *Catch-22* we couldn't relate to our kids. One pop-rock columnist confided to half a million readers that "my world is divided between those who dig it and those who do not." And when Dwight Macdonald said *he* didn't dig it—poor old Macdonald, still quaintly fussing about standards while the under-30s were mischievously peeing on every standard within range—he was put down as a "radical square," though no one determined what manner of squares were Jules Feiffer and Nat Hentoff when *they* didn't dig it.

SOURCE: *San Francisco,* October 1970, pp. 9, 10, 13, 86–88. Reprinted by permission of the author.

Nelson Algren turned me on to *Catch-22* eight years ago with a rhapsodic notice in *The Nation*, hailing it as "the best American novel that has come out of anywhere in years." As I had long felt this way about his *A Walk on the Wild Side*—too much for the Establishment that buried it and too early for the counter-culture that might one day exhume it—Heller's first (and only) novel was nothing to be lightly kissed off. Therefore, it took a dozen entries and re-entries before I could feel secure in dismissing Yossarian & Crew midway in the arrival of Major Major Major Major, marveling that the creator of Dove Linkhorn and pimp Finerty should go asiatic over such a raggedy-ass outfit as this.

In preparation for seeing the film, I returned to the book last month, this time to completion. It was harder going than *Critique of Pure Reason* and as fully devoid of wit. As writing, as humor, as satire and as an anti-war statement, *Catch-22* seemed a grandiose, oversold fake unparalleled in American letters.

To picture war as the ultimate insanity of the Establishment, Heller attempted a different kind of combat novel, showing the Second World War not as it was, but how it might have become had official Air Force derangements been carried to grotesque extremes: To insure marching perfection, a parade-happy officer plans to "sink pegs of nickel alloy into each man's thigh bones and link them to the wrists by strands of copper wire with exactly three inches to play, but there wasn't time . . . and good copper wire was hard to come by in wartime."

"Catch-22," the contradiction-gag at the core of Heller's contrivance, says that a crazy airman must be grounded. But since "a concern for one's safety in the face of dangers that were real and immediate was the process of a rational mind," an airman who asked to be grounded could not be crazy. Like all else in the novel, this bit gets dialogued, diagrammed, explained, milked and resurrected like a conundrum hammered home to a classroom of mongoloids.

Buried within the repetitions and echolalia that compose the bulk of its 463 pages lies the kernel of a workable short story in Milo Minderbinder's black market finagling, were this nurtured by the hand of a craftsman. But every cluttered page bears proof that Joseph Heller cannot write. His "style" suggests the novice flipping through a thesaurus in random pursuit of fancied-up lingo: "cerulean water," "homiletic memoranda," "snickered with a slight mucid sibilance," "a noise that was stertorous," "Nurse Sue Ann Duckett's callipygous ass." Heller finds Eng. Comp. delight in "the bloozy, blowsy, bleary-eyed flozzy in the overloaded white brassiere."

From a cast of hundreds, not an individual can be found to surface, only pop-up mannikins, snide villains and fumbling idiots, interchangeable save for their asinine names. Adjective-stacking is Heller's means of building a character:

Colonel Korn was an untidy, disdainful man with an oily skin and deep, hard lines running almost straight down from his nose between his crepuscular (sic) jowls and his square, clefted chin.

General P. P. Peckem . . . was a handsome, pink-skinned man of fifty-three. His manner was always casual and relaxed, and his uniforms custom-made. He had silver-gray hair, slightly myopic eyes and thin, overhanging sensual lips.

Nowhere to be found is the terse, immemorial fixing of a character that signals the touch of a master, like Nathanael West's "Homer . . . had on loose blue linen slacks and a chocolate flannel jacket over a yellow polo shirt. Only a Negro could have worn it without looking ridiculous and no one was ever less a Negro than Homer."

Though some partisans insist the book is not funny, but "deadly serious," one must assume Heller hankered after some comic effect, for how else to explain the awesome stockpilings of bizarre names?

Colonel Cathcart liked Big Chief White Halfoat because Big Chief White Halfoat kept punching that lousy Colonel Moodus in the nose every time he got drunk and Colonel Moodus was around. He wished that Big Chief White Halfoat would begin punching Colonel Korn in his fat face, too.

Then there are those certified credentials from *Life* ("uproarious"), *Time* ("mad laughter"), James Jones ("should be roared over"), Walt Kelly ("a very funny man"), Morris West ("full of belly laughs"), *The New York Times* ("savagely funny"). Yet the book abounds with the belabored wheezes of Depression radio, early TV and Catskill cabaret—that stalwart vaudevillian corn we had thought irrevocably ploughed under by Mort Sahl and successors.

"Men," Colonel Cargill began in Yossarian's squadron, "you're American officers. The officers of no other army in the world can make that statement. Think about it." (The author thinks about it enough to repeat it verbatim in the next paragraph.) "Nately's mother . . . was a Daughter of the American Revolution. His father was a Son of a Bitch." "He had decided to live forever or die in the attempt." "We've got to turn that bastard Major Major out of his trailer—I'd like to turn his wife and kids out into the woods, too. But we can't. He has no wife and kids."

Lest I be accused of quoting Heller out of context, although it would be difficult to quote him any other way, there follows a generous dollop of the "Mr. Bones" minstrel dialogue that unavoidably shaped Buck Henry's script of the Nichols movie:

"When I was a kid," Orr replied, "I used to walk around all day with crab apples in my cheeks. One in each cheek."

Yossarian . . . braced himself suspiciously. A minute passed.

"Why?" he found himself forced to ask finally.

Orr tittered triumphantly. "Because they're better than horse chestnuts," he answered. . . . "When I couldn't get crab apples," Orr continued, "I used horse chestnuts. Horse chestnuts are about the same size as crab apples and actually have a better shape, although the shape doesn't matter a bit."

"Why did you walk around with crab apples in your cheeks?" Yossarian asked again. "That's what I asked."

"Because they've got a better shape than horse chestnuts," Orr answered. "I just told you that."

"Why," swore Yossarian at him approvingly, "you evil-eyed, mechanically-aptituded, disaffiliated son of a bitch, did you walk around with *anything* in your cheeks?"

"I didn't," Orr said, "walk around with *anything* in my cheeks. I walked around with crab apples in my cheeks. When I couldn't get crab apples I walked around with horse chestnuts. In my cheeks."

And there's more. The celebrated Heller *patois* lumbers along on these flabby retreads of old Abbott and Costello "Who's on first?" patter. The passage quoted is no longer and no sillier than others I could have chosen, and the reader should be reminded that such passages are numberless.

That such whooping juvenilia is embraced by a public susceptible to the satiric bite of Nabokov, Beckett, the Beatle films and Lenny Bruce begs some explanation. I can find no reasons for the ensnaring of Algren, Brustein or Liebling. Like Mailer's fondness for *I Am Curious (Yellow)*, I must write it off as an isolated lapse—the prerogative of unique minds. But what of *Catch-22*'s contagion among the alienated young and their swinging siblings, those Bobs & Carols & Teds & Alices frantically fending off the stigma of squaredom with *I Ching*, Hobbitt and Lichtenstein print? Lucky Heller, his book collided with that historical moment when the counter-culture grew from a cult to an army ready to unloose its total assault on the culture of the Elders. During its skinny-dip into every imaginable pond posted Off Limits, the rebels often came up with pearls—Allen Ginsberg, Herbert Marcuse, the Beatles, the discovery of Hesse, and the re-mining of our mother lode of folk and the blues. And with the pearls came handfuls of infantile crud—the home movies of Andy Warhol, *Zap Comics* and the demonstrable goofiness of astrology and tarot cards—to fling at the technology, the groves of academe and anything thought to be respectable taste. *Catch-22* was a heaven-sent gift, the first novel of the Second World War to view our involvement, not as an unavoidable crusade against Nazi Germany, but as a cynical caper fully equatable to the grotesque buffoonery of Korea and Vietnam. Legions of readers for whom the Third Reich was as remote as the Ottoman Empire believed *Catch-22* to be about Vietnam.

At the novel's end, the anti-hero Yossarian deserts to Sweden, viewing his enemy as "anybody who's going to get you killed no matter *which* side he's on, and that includes Colonel Cathcart," the C.O. who keeps upping the number of missions. True, I never knew a soldier whose murderous impulses weren't aroused more by some chickenshit captain bucking for major than by anonymous German snipers. Also true that manipulators like Milo got rich out of the war—but there's a catch, Catch-1.

"This is not World War I," Major Danby tells Yossarian. "You must never forget that we're at war with aggressors who would not let either of us live if they won." Right on, Danby. That's the catch, and it's the best there is. Lenny Bruce bowed to this simple truth with his throwaway line: "When I was in the war, that is, the *good* war, the war against Hitler." Had the Yossarians, Hungry Joes and Natelys never flown those missions, the Nazis might have won the war, and they came chillingly close. No Eldridge Cleaver, no Mario Savio, no Che, no Rolling Stones and no Bob Dylan whose parents would have made that gas oven walk with the rest of the Chosen People. That Heller found nothing to distinguish the American colonel who ordered Yossarian to fly from the Luftwaffe that tried to shoot him down, that he consistently made virtues of opportunism and mere survival in a world faced with such frightful alternatives amount to nothing less than moral obscenity.

Because Mike Nichols is a comic genius, if not yet a cinematic one, and Joseph Heller a Madison Avenue wiseacre, the movie outclasses the book that imprisons it. There are a few superb touches—the *leitmotif* of Snowden's death with its blinding overexposed yellows, and Yossarian's Kafkaesque wanderings through depraved midnight Rome. But soon after its perky start the film begins its doleful descent, slowly churning through Heller's labored hijinx. The episodes meant to be funny are relentlessly grim, while the weighty statements on War and Life evoke a boredom reminiscent of its sister-failure, *How I Won the War*. At the root of this ruination lies Nichols' fanatical devotion to the spirit of the novel which he caught with a fidelity that, ironically, has almost no parallel in the bedraggled annals of books-into-film. But Nichols couldn't have shaken free of Heller had he wanted to. Once he was handed the directorial plum every Frankenheimer lusted after, with a budget reputed to be $22 million and a cast that outdazzled *King of Kings*, he was committed to authenticity. He could slash away at Orr's crab apples. Nately's Whore's Kid Sister, Scheisskopf's parades and halve the hilarity of Heller's fans by cutting the Major Majors from four to two. But he was stuck with Yossarian, that astonishing dialogue and the moral-historical lie upon which the book is grounded.

Nichols did not always edit Heller wisely. He dashed through the best of the novel—Milo's cagey speculation in eggs and Zippo lighters—to squander interminable footage on Milo's bombing his own base to fulfill a German contract. He kept the bogus death of Doc Daneeka, the naked Yossarian at Snowden's funeral and General Dreedle's "take him out and shoot him," thus inheriting the most wanton improbables of the book. The natural absurdities, the real Catch-22s to be found in the Air Corps, were too rich to be enhanced by Heller's engrossments. I recall that through clerical error, a massive troop shipment equipped and long-johned for Arctic service wound up in Saudi Arabia. During their Russian roulette flights over the Himalayas, transports carried Kotex, ice cream, shrubbery for the lawns of Chiang's officials—and at one time a Steinway grand for Madame Chiang, which the pilot jettisoned over Mount Kanchenjunga, getting a sound never dreamed of by Karlheinz Stockhausen. One of the few plausible inspirations of the novel was Yossarian's "capture" of Bologna by the simple expedient of moving the red bomb line on the intelligence battle map; given the structure of Army disorganization, the resultant brouhaha was almost a logical certainty, yet Nichols left it out of the film.

The episodes that did not work for Heller don't work for Nichols simply because they stretch credulity. Had Yossarian appeared unclothed before General Dreedle and his nurse, he would have been strait-jacketed in the time required to holler "M.P.!" When Doc Daneeka sat down to chow, his messmates wouldn't assume him dead just because his name fraudulently appeared on the passenger log of a crashed aircraft. Conversely, the exchange between Nately and the cynical Paisano, weary bromide that it is, glows brighter in retrospect as the one genuinely credible dialogue in the film. Recall that the one false note in an otherwise glorious M*A*S*H, the dentist's Last Supper suicide, didn't work because it strained our belief, and it was still funnier than anything in Catch-22.

The comparison with M*A*S*H is inevitable, for if history smiled on Heller's timing of the novel, it cursed Nichols with an earlier release of M*A*S*H. With a modest budget, unknown director and, Elliott Gould aside, an almost anonymous cast, M*A*S*H blew Catch-22 right out of the air. The door at which Heller and Nichols so vainly pounded, swung so easily for Robert Altman and his marvelous crew: the lampoon of the military mind, "black humor," improvisational glee, the delight of sex, a casual zaniness, the pursuit of sanity in an insane set-up and, after M*A*S*H's own crafty fashion, the awfulness of combat. Nothing in Catch-22 could approach these likeable medics, hanging on to their civilian marbles, doing their necessary body repairs in the Korean War they knew was a shuck.

Since there are no characters in Catch-22, most of the stellar cast amble about in a Pirandello search for identity. Alan Arkin adds an expressive depth to the hysterical Yossarian, though I continue to find him a curiously unfulfilled and overrated performer. He exudes a tough Hebraic shrewdness, but rarely shakes off his little actor's tricks—the slack-jawed stammers and sidelong darting of eyes. Except for *Popi*, his best work, Arkin always seems either miscast or saddled with material that is beneath him. Orson Welles, resembling some outsized debauched toad, started to walk off with the film, but could only radiate discomfort over the simple-minded lines he was given. Anthony Perkins as the Chaplain gave the finest performance, rivaling his work in *Pretty Poison*. Jon Voight, who filmed this before his magnificent *Midnight Cowboy*, made a surprisingly listless Milo. Martin Balsam and Buck Henry seemed an aptly one-dimensional Cathcart and Korn, and the ingratiating talents of Jack Gilford were wasted on the insipid Doc Daneeka. Bob Newhart may be pardoned for the stark dreadfulness of his Major Major whose posturings represent Heller at his sleaziest. Paul Simon's partner Art Garfunkel ingenuously captured the angelic schnook that is Nately.

Because *Catch-22* is "against the war," we of the Unsilent Minority are stampeded into the arms of the film, as we were the book. Recently, a group of beseeching liberals asked me if I didn't find *Catch-22* more "effective" than *M*A*S*H* as an anti-war statement, an echo of the Thirties when the radical movement judged a work by how it served The Cause—or, often, how closely it followed the "party line." If we learned nothing else, the Thirties should have taught us that art and politics don't share the same criteria, as witness the wholesale vanishment, save Brecht, of agitprop literary saints, while the "reactionaries" Lawrence, Eliot and Pound seem to endure. We should further have learned that kitsch drives out Art: in the counter-culture supermarkets of both San Francisco and Marin you will not find a copy of *A Walk on the Wild Side* or Mailer's *Why Are We in Vietnam?*, while *Catch-22* is stacked to the ceiling.

Kitsch also corrupts great artists. For the unique energies of Mike Nichols to be funneled into the filming of this worthless book is a sad and deplorable waste. [88]

Mort Drucker
Stan Hart
Catch-All-22

SOURCE: *Mad*, No. 141 (March 1971), pp. 4–10. Copyright © E. C. Publications, Inc. Reprinted by permission.

Just **pretend** you're their **dying** son, Shmoessarian!

The **audience** won't know! If they **don't think** it's funny, then they'll think it was **supposed** to be funny! And if they think it **IS** funny! they'll never know it **wasn't** funny!

and this is supposed to be funny?!?

You mean . . .

Right! That's NICHOLS' "Catch-all—22"!

How come a very **minor** character like **you** seems to be in almost **every** scene?

I wrote the **screenplay**! I made **sure** that I was!

Boy, that's **chutzpah**!

Say one more **nasty** thing, and I'll **LET** him **shoot** you!

The script is **better** than the book! **Much** better! I **love** it! LOVE IT!!

All right, **planes**! Be careful not to hit our **warehouses**! Just men and hospitals!

Wily! You're INSANE!!

It's strictly a **commercial** arrangement, Shmoessarian!

I made a **deal** to get rid of those **parachutes** we've been stuck with! I **swapped** them for some bombs!

Okay, but did you **have** to arrange to have them **DELIVERED**?!

Bon giorno, Shmoessarian! Is-a my **Nutly** come-a soon?

No . . . they got him!

The **Germans**?!

No . . . the **Truant Officers**!!

Hey!

Hey, this is **terrific**!

Whoopie! I finally **got out** of that **screwy** picture!

What makes you **think** so?

Don't you see all those **disgusting**, **sordid** things going on in these Rome streets? I'm in a **FELLINI** movie!

Gordon Gow
Review of
'Catch-22'

A rambling novel has become a wayward film, frequently brilliant, sometimes leaden. I had the impression that Mike Nichols must have taken up a lot of slack in the editing phase, thereby making bits of the dialogue too cryptic, and occasionally changing gears with a judder which causes a few of the quieter passages to seem merely slow. Of course, Joseph Heller's book, which is a fragment of autobiography expanded into a black and satirical metaphor, could not have been easy to render down into a screenplay. This might be one of the reasons why no film version has emerged until now, although there were reports of various directors having their eyes on it ever since it was published in 1961. Over the years we have grown accustomed to black mirth, especially in respect of war and the official pressures that work against individual freedom. Even so, the Nichols putdown has an impact comparable at its fitful best to the 1963 onslaught of Kubrick's *Dr. Strangelove*. And one advantage of the time lapse is that Yossarian's defection at the end, when he finally evades the World War Two corruption and paddles a rubber dinghy towards Sweden, takes on an affinity to the ethos of latterday deserters who have eschewed the conflict in Vietnam.

Alan Arkin is good at the peaks of Yossarian's terror, when he can magnify realism, but I found him wanting in the [48] correct degree of straight-facing where it was needed. It is a performance, however, that brings out the main point strongly: the fear in a man who has been driven beyond reason. His traumatic experience, when a gunner died a horrible death which he was powerless to prevent, is recalled in bleached flashbacks, each a little bit longer and more detailed than the one before it, culminating in a swift but gruesome glimpse of the dying man's intestines and a masterly evocation by Arkin of the long and silent scream.

The case-history of Yossarian's breakdown is often represented against ironic visual charms. Dawn steals across the landscape of a US air base in the Mediterranean area (location shooting was done in Mexico, where the chosen site provides a reasonable substitute). Silence is disturbed by small

SOURCE: *Films and Filming*, November 1970, pp. 48–50. Reprinted by permission of the author.

noises, bird calls, a distant dog barking, a general ambiance of placidity to be disrupted by the roar of bombers. The ponderous old B-25s, dangerously massed in a haze of heat, rising awkwardly with their lethal burdens, are serving a deplorable purpose. The war against Italy has been virtually won: it is 1944. But Colonel Cathcart (Martin Balsam) keeps his men at it, sending them on pointless raids to form neat patterns of explosions that will photograph nicely from the air and get the colonel's name into the papers back home, where too many of his counterparts in other battle areas have been hogging publicity for their maximum efforts.

Impervious to destruction, the colonel lends a ready ear to a milk-fed and bright-brained lieutenant, Milo Minderbinder (Jon Voight), who enters to fill half the screen with a fresh egg, displayed with a showman's flair, introducing a profiteering scheme whereby commodities are filched and traded internationally. Flying the odd plane on lucrative missions from one needful country to another, Minderbinder builds up a syndicate for the benefit of the base, and especially for himself. In the film's best single take, he outlines his plan to the colonel as they walk by the site of an airstrip while a bomber comes streaking down in a cloud of black smoke: as it passes and crashes, the Minderbinder voice goes on, eager and articulate, and neither he nor the colonel pay the slightest attention to death, which is familiar, because a more interesting subject is blossoming freshly in their hard little heads.

This opportunist theme is ultimately the most successful part of the film's satire. It relates directly to Yossarian's plight, because Minderbinder strips the combat planes of their vendible silk parachutes and medical supplies, regardless of the added threat to sanity. Therefore Yossarian the bombardier has no possibility of escape from his bubble of space in a B-25, and no medication to help the dying gunner, whose funeral he will watch from a distance, high in a tree, naked and aloof (another link with latterday dropouts), until Minderbinder climbs up to offer him a chocolate-coated wad of cotton: there is a glut on the market and the businesslike lieutenant has accumulated an embarrassing quantity of the stuff. The cotton crisis leads on to an episode both hilarious and horrific, in which buildings around the airstrip are efficiently bombed and flames proliferate, under the cool control of Minderbinder who has made a complex deal with the Germans —a thing inadequately explained by the few lines that are shouted amid the confusion. There is a brilliantly black climax, however, when Minderbinder lords it over a crippled Italy, a dictator in the bud, while Yossarian walks through dark and dreadful streets after curfew, taking bewildered note of the few who are still outdoors—the mindless fornication on a sidewalk, the flogging of a fallen horse, the long line of servicemen waiting their turns at the Minderbinder brothel, the bloody corpse of a girl who has been raped by a formerly insipid soldier.

The all-purpose official regulation, the "Catch-22" that covers any enormity, is amusingly defined near the start of the film by a doctor, and sadly underlined towards the end by a hopeless woman in an empty house. But, apart from this short sequence, the film's excursions into solemnity are plodding. The worst, glum where it ought to be wry and astringent, is an aged Italian's dissertation to a young American on the benefits of national weakness as a guarantee of survival, as distinct from the power of the USA which invites destruction: this is a keynote, sounded inadequately.

A lesser blight spoils Yossarian's incidental love affair with an Italian girl. It begins well, after one of the movie's long takes (at which Nichols is good): on location in Rome, outside a café, conversation and detailed background movement have continued for a fascinatingly long time, observed from a fixed camera position; then Yossarian is left on his own and his glance falls upon the girl. With the cut to her approaching legs, and a camera glide to her breasts and face, the soundtrack bursts into *Also Sprach Zarathustra*: possibly a jaunty nod to Kubrick's *2001—A Space Odyssey* but valid in its satirical pointing up of the Persian philosopher's definition of man's choice between darkness and light. But things begin to congeal when they dance in a slow revolve-kick, *Vertigo*-style, to a mournfully orchestrated version of the "September Song" from *Knickerbocker Holiday* (bang-on for 1944 downbeat pop, admittedly), and their aftergloom is maudlin.

At the other extreme, General Dreedle (Orson Welles) brings in his wake a son-in-law and a WAC mistress who seem to have sprung half-alive from a comic strip. The balance of satire is unsteady. It would have been wiser, perhaps, to forget about delicate mood changes and stick to one sharp genre: the incident of the man who is cut in half (unintentionally) by a low-flying plane is precise in its fusion of true horror and sick relief-laughter (as well as being a neat little effort from the special effects department); and incidental performances that are pitched to perfection, in addition to Voight and Balsam [49] who have the best lines, are those of Anthony Perkins as a befuddled chaplain and Richard Benjamin as a major who delivers his briefings like an entertainment officer at a holiday camp. Altogether, when you make allowances for the difficulty of getting a quart into a pint pot and biting off more than most people would be able to chew, Mike Nichols has done pretty well, although his memorable filming of *Who's Afraid of Virginia Woolf?* (a serious satire more contained than this but far from easy) led me to expect better of him. [50]

Wayne Charles Miller
'Catch-22':

Joseph Heller's Portrait
of American Culture—
The Missing Portrait in
Mike Nichols' Movie

In some ways Mike Nichols' *Catch-22* was an enjoyable movie, but it is unfortunate, I think, that the film so little resembled Joseph Heller's book. In making the usual antiwar statement Nichols succeeded about as well as Robert Altman did in the less-pretentious, less-expensive *M*A*S*H*. If Altman erred by running the football sequence too long and by grossly sentimentalizing his heroes' trip to Japan, at least his mistakes were minor. Nichols' blunder involved a major misunderstanding. Put as simply as possible, he misread the book. Seeing it almost exclusively in terms of an antiwar framework, he precluded effective use of practically all of Heller's arsenal of barbs, arrows, lances, and blockbusters. In fact, while watching the movie, I had to conclude that Nichols did not even know who the enemies were or recognize at which targets the satirical thrusts were aimed. He may have handled Heller's frame with some cleverness and good film techniques, but he missed the substance of the portrait itself.

For *Catch-22* is not simply or even primarily an antiwar novel. It is not merely a part of that long antiwar tradition in American fiction that includes some of the best work of some of our major writers (See *An Armed America—Its Face in Fiction: A History of the American Military Novel* [New York: New York University Press, 1970]). Published in 1961, *Catch-22* is concerned primarily with the directions that life in the United States has taken in the years since World War II. In fact, it is a portrait of our culture since that war. Heller uses the military unit at Pianosa as a microcosm of American society at large and aims his satire more at our absurd values, life styles, and institutions than at the follies of men at war. Certainly, it is a disturbing fact that he can find in the totalitarian world of a military establishment most of the institutional ingredients of life in a "democratic" country, but that is, after all, the fundamental paradox upon which he bases his satire. Heller is telling us that the nation which began so idealistically less than two hundred years ago as an experiment in de-

---

SOURCE: This essay was written especially for this book.

mocracy is now a nation whose religion is capitalism, whose people are motivated by the pursuit of corporate power and affluence, and, most importantly, whose military establishment now typifies the corporate nation-state itself. The nation of Paine, Adams, Washington, and Jefferson now belongs to Cathcart, Korn, Peckem, Dreedle, Daneeka, Scheisskopf, and Minderbinder. It is a nation in which Washington Irving has become Irving Washington and one in which all too many of its citizens resemble characters out of Walt Disney—Donald Duck's nephews, complete with the same silly conformity, the same capacity to get in line and follow their leader, and the same compunction to play at the games of violence. Loveless, other-directed, and lost, most of Heller's characters are victims of fear and victims of the traditions and values that constitute the culture.

It is a disturbing portrait that Heller paints, but it ought not be a shocking one. In fact, it ought not even surprise us. Beginning with Harold D. Lasswell's pioneering study in 1951, *National Security and Individual Freedom*, people as diverse in their political philosophies as Walter Millis, C. Wright Mills, Fred J. Cook, Tristram Coffin, Kenneth Galbraith, and J. William Fulbright have warned that the United States has drifted toward government by elitist groups, toward international commitments based simply on the application of military power, toward reliance on military spending as the backbone of the economy, and, in general, toward a highly structured, rigid society of a corporate order. In retrospect, it seems culturally significant, I think, that one year before the publication of *Catch-22*, Dwight D. Eisenhower warned in his Farewell Address that the military-industrial complex had grown so large and so powerful that it could eventually threaten democracy in America. Since then, Pentagon spending has nearly doubled, and as early as 1957 Samuel Huntington, in *The Soldier and the State*, was already picturing a culture modeled on the "ordered serenity" of West Point, and suggesting that "modern man may well find his monastery in the Army."

It is this state of American society—a dangerous one, and in Heller's view, one based on absurd values and traditions—that *Catch-22* is all about. Yossarian is not merely trying to escape the war. He is trying to escape the culture that produced the war and the traditions that produced the culture. Heller's satire is aimed at those traditions, at the institutions that capitalize on them, and at the individuals who adjust to the system and thrive within it. To miss the social and cultural satire is to miss the most important dimension in the novel. Incredibly, Nichols managed to miss it in his film.

It would be unfair to fault him for the way in which he lopped off characters, conversations, and situations in transposing the book to the screen. Just in terms of sheer bulk, *Catch-22* would present any director with mammoth problems. But one can quarrel with Nichols' choices for exclusion—Scheisskopf, Peckem, Sanderson, Chief White Halfoat—since so many of them are essential to Heller's presentation of a national portrait; and one *must* quarrel with the manner in which Nichols dealt with the characters he did include. For the ways in which he brought them to the screen reveal his shallow and superficial interpretation of the book.

Consider, for example, his treatment of Major Danby, Colonel Cathcart, Doc Daneeka, and Milo Minderbinder. In the film, Danby is a smart-aleck operations officer who gets his biggest laugh by making an anachronistic announcement on the flight line in the saccharine and soporific tones of an airline hostess soothing her passengers with coffee, tea, or milk—a comic "bit" more reminiscent of a skit by Nichols and May than of Heller. The film's Colonel Cathcart, played by Martin Balsam, is a slovenly wheeler-dealer whose biggest laugh-getting moment involves a straight sight gag as he barks orders while seated on a toilet bowl—an impression of the colonel that is hard to justify when one considers the character in the book. In the film Doc Daneeka just seems to pop up here and there. He appears once to watch Hungry Joe cut in half. (It is Kid Sampson in the novel, but for no clear reason Hungry Joe in the film.) Another time he ushers in the Italian-American family whose members are willing to accept Yossarian as their dying son or brother—another short "bit," isolated in the novel, that Nichols could not resist. All of these interpretations of character are wrong—but Nichols is nowhere more wrong than in his heavy-handed treatment of Milo Minderbinder.

Near the end of the film Nichols' Milo, surrounded by goons and riding triumphantly at the head of a column of troops, looks more like one of the fascist perverts of Luchino Visconti's *The Damned* than the character Heller created. Heller's Milo is not an insidious and conniving power-hungry fascist. In fact, it is testament to Heller's genius that he could create a figure simultaneously so innocent and so destructive as is his representative of American business values and perhaps capitalism itself. Milo is frightening precisely because he is such a perfect product of the culture. Industrious, competent, pleasant, engaging, sexually moral or perhaps sexless, he is destined for success. In fact, Milo is the kind of son that most American parents wish their boys to be, and, of course, it is Heller's point that this controller of the Syndicate embodies exactly the kind of success story that Americans generally admire. He is a bright young man who would not intentionally hurt anybody but who just happens to be absolutely committed to a business ethic—that is to say, in an echo of Charles Wilson's statement about General Motors, what's good for M & M Enterprises is good for the country. Yossarian may doubt Milo's motives, but Heller makes it clear that Milo always operates with a clean conscience.

Yossarian turned slowly to gaze at Milo with probing distrust. He saw a simple, sincere face that was incapable of subtlety or guile, an honest, frank face with disunited large eyes, rusty hair, black eyebrows and an unfortunate reddish-brown mustache. Milo had a long, thin nose with sniffing, damp nostrils heading sharply off to the right, always pointing away from where the rest of him was looking. It was the face of a man with hardened integrity who could no more consciously violate the moral principles on which his virtue rested than he could transform himself into a despicable toad. One of these moral principles was that it was never a sin to charge as much as the traffic would bear. (pp. 65–66)*

Milo does not believe that he is morally wrong when he sells the men's parachutes or steals the morphine that the dying Snowden and others like him need so desperately. He knows that they may be inconvenienced a little, perhaps even die, but that over the long term he has everyone's best interest in mind. Furthermore, it is not immoral for Milo to bomb his own squadron. Since his morality is based on the business ethic, he can explain to the men who again might suffer a little, again perhaps even die, that in the final analysis what's good for M & M Enterprises is good for the country—and good for them. He can point out that most of the victims benefit from the bombing because they are members of the Syndicate. Like many lower-middle- and middle-middle-class families in America who pride themselves on small stock or mutual fund holdings, they may own only two or three shares but they are members in good standing and will ultimately profit from the destruction. Warfare, Milo might add, is an important part of the normal business cycles of the Western world. After all, wars come and go but the laws that Milo worships, the laws of supply and demand, are unalterable; besides, Milo knows that the only way one can measure a nation's greatness is by measuring its economic might, its gross national product. In a brief paragraph Heller describes the ways in which Milo operates.

Milo had been earning many distinctions for himself. He had flown fearlessly into danger and criticism by selling petroleum and ball bearings to Germany at good prices in order to make a good profit and help maintain a balance of power between the contending forces. His nerve under fire was graceful and infinite. With a devotion to purpose above and beyond the line of duty, he had then raised the price of food in his mess halls so high that all officers and enlisted men had to turn over all their pay to him in order to eat. Their alternative—there was an alternative, of course, since Milo detested coercion and was a vocal champion of freedom of choice—was to starve.

---

* Quotations from the novel are from the Dell edition (1962).

When he encountered a wave of enemy resistance to this attack, he stuck to his position without regard for his safety or reputation and gallantly invoked the law of supply and demand. And when someone somewhere said no, Milo gave ground grudgingly, valiantly defending, even in retreat, the historical right of free men to pay as much as they had to for the things they needed to survive. (p. 377)

Occasionally he must go to great lengths in order to keep the market bullish and so guarantee future prosperity and happiness for all. As he explains to Yossarian when he finds Heller's hero sitting naked in a tree, the masses may have to learn to like chocolate-covered cotton since M & M Enterprises is stuck with a load of Egyptian cotton that Milo cannot unload in any other way. True, they may suffer a bit, perhaps even die as a result of eating the stuff, but it would be good for them financially. My guess is that if Milo could find a clever enough advertising agency, he might be able to pull it off. After all, how long have we been watching the tobacco industry sell us cancer cloaked in coolness, springtime, orgiastic splendor, and supermasculine cowpunching. No, Milo is no immoral conniver who would seek to organize such "dirty physical stuff" as the prostitution industry; nor would he be interested in personally taking political power. Rather, he would be much more likely to disappear behind the scenes—say, to a Las Vegas hotel or an island in the Bahamas or to a Wall Street board room—and call the shots from there. In other words he could play Krupp to an American Hitler but he would never become a Hitler himself. In Heller's book Milo is the perfectly innocent embodiment of a business ethic whose primary principle is that money is more important than men—that profit is all. Operating on the basis of that value judgment, he enjoys immense success in the markets of the Western world.

While Minderbinder is an archetypal embodiment of the business ethic, Doc Daneeka exists in the book in order to show what happens when that ethic is applied within a profession. It is no accident that Heller chooses medicine. While Daneeka hardly emerges in the film, he is important in the book as a means of attacking one of the most notable American authority figures, the medical doctor. In this light, Daneeka embodies the worst instincts of the medical profession in America. Daneeka's attitudes are not entirely his own fault, however. As he tells Yossarian, he simply does not know what is expected of him. " 'All they ever told me was to uphold the ethics of my profession and never give testimony against another physician.' " (p. 179) He admits that his two most important medical instruments are his adding machine and his typewriter, and announces at one point: " 'I don't want to make sacrifices; I want to make dough.' " (p. 33) His response to the war is all too typical. He thinks it a godsend—

until *he* gets drafted. " 'I had it made, I tell you. Fifty grand a year I was knocking down, and almost all of it tax-free, since I made my customers pay me in cash. I had the strongest trade union in the world backing me up. And look what happened. Just when I was all set to really start stashing it away, they had to manufacture fascism and start a war horrible enough to affect even me!' " (p. 52) Clearly, to Doc Daneeka, medicine is a business. He does not treat patients; he charges customers. Once in the Army, where he makes the same amount of money regardless of how hard he works, he stops practicing altogether.

Representative of another profession, Heller's Danby hardly resembles the character Richard Benjamin portrayed in Nichols' movie. In the book Danby is a well-intentioned, liberal college professor who regards the war as a necessary evil in an imperfect world. Although he, like Yossarian, has difficulties with the morality of the war, he fears fascism enough to justify his participation in a system that he feels is somehow wrong. Like many liberals, he is, in some ways, weak, but his indecision results from moral compunctions, not from the superficiality that characterizes Benjamin's portrayal. Near the close of the book it is Danby and Chaplain Tappman, two liberal and idealistic men, with whom Yossarian talks before making his attempt at escape. They are the only two left in the squadron who can still understand Yossarian's desire to reject the sordid world that surrounds him. Out of the whole menagerie at Pianosa, they may be the only two who can understand Yossarian's statement that he would not want to live his life without misgivings—the only two left who are not first, members of the Syndicate, and second, human beings.

Certainly, the same cannot be said for Colonel Cathcart, Heller's representative of the millions of organization men in America. In the book, Cathcart is an other-directed, success-oriented corporation climber. He is a lonely and friendless man who evaluates himself solely on the basis of how his superiors react to him. Ecstasy, for Cathcart, is seeing his name high on the organization chart. He feels envy and despair when he discovers that men younger than he have risen a rank or two above him, and is filled with "foppish delight" when he thinks of all those older men who will never attain the rank he already holds. Unfortunately, Cathcart brings his ambition to the "business" of war. His promotion depends upon how much destruction his Group can deliver, how many towns and cities and lives his Group can destroy. Since he views all his actions in terms of his rise in rank, for him there is no moral question when he raises the number of missions or when he orders the bombing of a defenseless town of no strategic value. He is a miniature Milo willing and anxious to operate the machines that the Syndicate owns. In treating him as a gross and eccentric buffoon, Nichols misses the point that Cathcart's values are those of many clean-cut, well-dressed commuters who funnel in and out of our cities and manage America's industries.

In addition to satirizing particular types of Americans and American institutions, throughout *Catch-22* Heller explodes myths concerning the freedom of the individual in a moral Christian country. Captain Black's Glorious Loyalty Oath Crusade is a replica of McCarthyism. The C.I.D. agents, representative of the numerous "intelligence" agencies in the nation, are simultaneously sophomoric, silly voyeurs, and dangerous tools of a remote power establishment. Education at Pianosa, symbolically located in Captain Black's tent, is "open and free" until the students begin developing the wrong attitudes and asking questions that probe the values of the culture; then it becomes clear that only those who believe in the system are allowed to question it—and, naturally, they will not. Religion in America, represented finally by the atheist Corporal Whitcomb rather than the Anabaptist Chaplain Tappman, is a public-relations operation aimed at rationalizing whatever actions the Syndicate thinks necessary. Neither Whitcomb nor Captain Black appears in Nichols' movie.

General Dreedle does. But in order to understand his role as an aging and defunct warrior-leader slowly losing his power to a new kind of service elite, the military managers, one must compare him with the more public-relations minded General Peckem. Peckem does not appear. Neither does Scheisskopf. Beginning as a lowly lieutenant in charge of cadets, his emergence as General Scheisskopf near the end of the novel indicates the kind of person Heller feels finds success in the military establishment. A natural fascist, at the end he wants everybody in lock step; he wants everybody to march.

Because of the absence in the film of the important dimension of social satire, it is difficult for the viewer to understand the levels of Yossarian's disenchantment and rebellion. Given the problem, Alan Arkin succeeds admirably in his portrayal. How much easier it would have been for him if Nichols had included just one scene involving Yossarian's "treatment" in the hands of the staff psychiatrist, Major Sanderson, for, clearly, Heller sees psychiatry as just another morally bankrupt method of desensitizing the individual in the name of adjustment to the existing order—the order established by the Syndicate. And how much easier if Nichols had included one of the book's three trial scenes to show how much the men have to fear from their own superior officers, justifying Yossarian's claim that everyone from Hitler and Tojo to Cathcart and Korn was out to get him.

When the psychiatrist Major Sanderson accuses Yossarian of being crazy because of the young captain's inability to adjust to misery, ignorance, persecution, violence, slums, and warfare, it becomes most obvious that Heller's central contention in *Catch-22* is that Yossarian may be the only sane one left in a highly structured and insane society built upon systems and institutions that justify massive killing and destruction in the name of an economic system. While sitting on the limb of what he calls "the tree of life" during Snowden's funeral, Yossarian finally realizes the simple and essential truth that is the heart of Heller's book—that which promotes life is good, that which destroys life is evil. From the point of that realization it is inevitable that he must make his break with the existing order, and, like Huck Finn, light out for the territory—not for Huck's unformed American West but for the apparently sane and socialistic Sweden. Unlike those indoctrinated, brainwashed American innocents— Nately, Mudd, Kraft, Clevinger, Huple, McWatt, Wren, Kid Sampson, and Snowden—he is unwilling to give up the only life he has in the name of a system he abhors.

Because Nichols missed or ignored the dimension of social concern essential to Heller's book, his audiences cannot comprehend the significance of Yossarian's decision. As is so often the case with complex, multi-level novels of real significance, *Catch-22* lost a great deal when packaged to make a profit in movie theaters. Nichols reduced *Catch-22* to the level of just another antiwar film, and a slick one at that. My guess is that the thousands who saw the film without reading the book must now think that Heller's work is merely a series of obvious "bits," skits, and vaudevillian "turns." My advice to them is to read the book.

And, then, perhaps, reread it.

BIBLIOGRAPHICAL NOTE

Since the publication of *Catch-22* in late 1961, there has been an outpouring of commentary, much of it very serious, seldom equaled by that about other American novels. *Catch-22* itself enjoyed a steady, healthy sale in its first year, but never reached the best-seller lists in the United States, although it did so in Great Britain. Since then, of course, it has been one of the most popular books of our time, enjoying a new surge of interest in mid-1970, when the film appeared—in fact, it set a record for paperback sales during one six-week period. The stage version of *Catch-22*, written by Mr. Heller (Buck Henry wrote the screenplay), revived interest again in 1971 and 1972. When Mr. Heller's new novel *Something Happened* makes its debut, no doubt there will be even more.

The serious student will want to examine much more than the core material provided in this text. The following bibliography provides a good second step. The best single location for studies of *Catch-22* is the Special Collections Room at Brandeis University Library, where most of Mr. Heller's working materials and a large body of the early reactions to the novel are gathered. In addition to primary materials like working notecards, there are many letters about the book, reviews, articles, and several copies of translations into other languages. This collection also includes most of Mr. Heller's earlier writings, the bulk of which is a large group of short stories.*

The following is an informal list of materials that might have been included in this text but for necessary limitation of space.

---

* In order to avoid making an unreasonable imposition upon the Special Collections Librarian and his staff, one should make definite arrangements prior to visiting the collection and understand that someone must accompany a user at all times, and that no material may be taken from the room.

As a critical focus for *Catch-22*, Leslie Fiedler's essay "No! In Thunder," from *No! In Thunder* (Boston: Beacon Press, 1960), and often anthologized, has much to suggest.

Among the early book reviews that should be examined are these:

Whitney Balliett in *The New Yorker*, December 9, 1961, pp. 247–48.
William Barrett in *Atlantic*, January 1962, p. 98.
Ralph J. Gleason in *The San Francisco Chronicle*, August 27, 1962, p. 41.
"Good Soldier Yossarian" (anonymous review), in *Time*, October 27, 1961, pp. 97–98.
Granville Hicks in *Saturday Review*, October 14, 1961, p. 32.
William Hogan in *The San Francisco Chronicle*, May 3, 1962, p. 39.
Spencer Klaw in *New York Herald-Tribune Books*, October 15, 1961, p. 8.
Orville Prescott in *The New York Times*, October 23, 1961, p. 27.
Bernard Share in *Irish Times* (Dublin), June 30, 1962, p. 26.
Richard G. Stern in *The New York Times Book Review*, October 22, 1961, p. 50.
Robert Taubman in *New Statesman*, June 15, 1962, p. 871.
John H. Thompson in *The Chicago Sunday Tribune*, November 26, 1961, Pt. 4, p. 3.
Raymond Walters, Jr., in *The New York Times Book Review*, September 9, 1962, p. 8.

Significant criticism concentrating on form and genre include the following five pieces. The second, though marred by inaccuracies, has interesting suggestions about sources.

Cockburn, Alex, "*Catch-22*," *New Left Review*, Nos. 13 and 14 (January–April 1962), 87–92.
Lehan, Richard, and Jerry Patch, "*Catch-22*: The Making of a Novel," *Minnesota Review*, 7 (1967), 138–44.
Lewis, R. W. B., "Days of Wrath and Laughter," *Trials of the Word* (New Haven: Yale University Press, 1965), pp. 184–85, 226–27.
Ryan, Marjorie, "Four Contemporary Satires and the Problem of Norms," *Satire Newsletter*, Spring 1969, pp. 40–46.
Way, Brian, "Formal Experiment and Social Discontent: Joseph Heller's *Catch-22*," *Journal of American Studies*, 2 (October 1968), 253–70.

The following two articles concentrate on structure.

Chanan, Gabriel, "The Plight of the Novelist," *Cambridge Review*, 89A (April 26, 1968), 399–401.
Gordon, Caroline, and Jeanne Richardson, "Flies in Their Eyes? A Note on Joseph Heller's *Catch-22*," *Southern Review*, 3 (1967), 96–105.

The next four articles analyze theme. The second, though marred by factual errors and gobbledygook, ranges widely across the contemporary novel.

Blues, Thomas, "The Moral Structure of *Catch-22*," *Studies in the Novel*, 3 (Spring 1971), 64–79.

Greenberg, Alvin, "The Novel of Disintegration: Paradoxical Impossibility in Contemporary Fiction," *Contemporary Literature*, 7 (1966), 103–24.

Hassan, Ihab, "Laughter in the Dark: The New Voice in American Fiction," *The American Scholar*, 33 (Autumn 1964), 636–39.

Pinsker, Sanford, "Heller's *Catch-22*: The Protest of a *Puer Eternis*," *Critique*, 7 (Winter 1964–65), 150–62.

The following criticism centers about The Absurd and Black Humor.

"The Black Humorists" (anonymous review), *Time*, 85 (February 12, 1965), 94.

Byrd, Scott, "A Separate War: Camp and Black Humor in Recent American Fiction," *Language Quarterly*, 7, 1 and 2 (Fall–Winter 1968), 7–10.

Kostelanetz, Richard, "The Point Is That Life Doesn't Have Any Point," *The New York Times Book Review*, 70 (June 6, 1965), 3.

Littlejohn, David, "The Anti-Realists," *Daedalus*, 92 (Spring 1963), 250–64.

McNamara, Eugene, "The Absurd Style in Contemporary American Literature," *Bulletin de l'Association Canadienne des Humanities*, 19 (Winter 1968), 44–49.

Schulz, Max F., "Pop, Op, and Black Humor: The Aesthetics of Anxiety," *College English*, 30 (December 1968), 230–41.

Waldmeir, Joseph J., "Two Novelists of the Absurd: Heller and Kesey," *Wisconsin Studies in Contemporary Literature*, 5 (1964), 192–204.

These next five articles place Catch-22 among the body of war novels.

Bryant, Jerry H., "The War Novel: A Blood-Spattered Utopia," *The Open Decision* (New York: The Free Press, 1970), pp. 156–64.

Kazin, Alfred, "The War Novel from Mailer to Vonnegut," *Saturday Review*, February 6, 1971, pp. 14–15.

Miller, Wayne Charles, "Joseph Heller's *Catch-22*: Satire Sums up a Tradition," *An Armed America: Its Face in Fiction* (New York: New York University Press, 1970), chap. 7.

Muste, John M., "Better to Die Laughing: The War Novels of Joseph Heller and John Ashmead," *Critique*, 5 (Fall 1962), 16–27.

Stern, J. P., "War and the Comic Muse: *The Good Soldier Schweik* and *Catch-22*," *Comparative Literature*, 20 (Summer 1968), 193–216.

Criticism dealing more generally with Catch-22 and the nature of recent fiction follows.

Aldrich, John, "Contemporary Fiction and Mass Culture," *New Orleans Review*, 1 (Fall 1968), 4–9.

Amis, Kingsley, "What We Need Is Savage Laughter," *Opinions and Perspectives from The New York Times Book Review*, ed. Francis Brown (Boston: Houghton Mifflin, 1964), pp. 279–83.

Barnes, Hazel, "Literature and the Politics of the Future," *Denver Quarterly*, 5 (Spring 1970), 41–64.

Brewer, Joseph E., "The Anti-Hero in Contemporary Literature," *Iowa English Yearbook*, 12 (1967), 55–60.

Charyn, Jerome, Introduction to *The Single Voice* (New York: Collier Books, 1969), pp. ix–xi.

French, Michael R., "The American Novel in the Sixties," *Midwest Quarterly*, 9 (1968), 365–79.

Hassan, Ihab, "The Character of Post-War Fiction in America," *English Journal*, 51 (January 1962), 1–8.

Tanner, Tony, "The Great American Nightmare," *Spectator*, No. 7192 (April 29, 1966), 530–31.

Yates, Norris, "What Makes the American Novel Modern?" *Jahrbuch Fuer Amerikastudien*, 11 (1966), 59–68.

The following are additional interviews with Joseph Heller.

Janeway, Elizabeth, ed., "Fiction: The Personal Dimension," *The Writer's World* (New York: McGraw-Hill, 1969), pp. 137–40, 159–73.

Mandel, George, "Dialogue with Joseph Heller," *Penthouse*, May 1971, pp. 54–56, 59, 60, 98.

"So They Say" (anonymous interview), *Mademoiselle*, 57 (August 1963), 234–35.

Shenker, Israel, "Did Joe Heller Bomb on Broadway?" *The New York Times*, December 29, 1968, D3, D11.

Stories and articles by Joseph Heller that bear in one way or another upon *Catch-22* are these.

"Catch-18," *New World Writing* (New York: New American Library, 1955), pp. 204–14.

"Castle of Snow," *Atlantic*, March 1948, pp. 52–55.

"MacAdam's Log," *Gentleman's Quarterly*, December 1959, pp. 112, 166–76, 178.

"World Full of Great Cities," *Nelson Algren's Book of Lonesome Monsters* (New York: Bernard Geis, 1963), pp. 7–19.

"Irving Is Everywhere," *Show*, April 1963, pp. 104–5, 126–27.

"A Man Named Flute," *Atlantic*, August 1948, pp. 66–70.

"How I Found James Bond, [Etc.]," *Holiday*, June 1967, pp. 123–25.

Readers interested in Mr. Heller's second novel, *Something Happened*, unpublished at this time, should read the condensation of part of the manuscript in

Esquire, September 1966, pp. 136–41; and the interview by James Shapiro in *Intellectual Digest*, December 1971, pp. 6–11.

Additional reviews and background pieces on the film *Catch-22* follow.

Alpert, Hollis, "The Catch," *Saturday Review*, June 27, 1970, p. 24.

Bass, Milton R., "*Catch-22*," *The Berkshire Eagle*, October 6, 1970, p. 22.

Blazer, Sam, "World War II [Etc.], *Los Angeles Free Press*, July 2, 1970.

Blevins, Winfred, "*Catch-22*—No Cinematic Equivalent to the Novel," *Los Angeles Herald-Examiner*, June 21, 1970, pp. F1, F7.

Canby, Vincent, "Nichols Captures Panic of *Catch-22*," *The New York Times*, June 25, 1970, p. 54.

Cuskelly, Richard, "*Catch-22*—Brilliant, Contradictory," *Los Angeles Herald-Examiner*, June 21, 1970, pp. F1, F8.

Ephron, Nora, "Yossarian Is Alive and Well in the Mexican Desert," *The New York Times Magazine*, March 16, 1969, pp. 30 ff.

Flagler, J. M., "Mike Nichols Tries the Impossible—A Movie of *Catch-22*," *Look*, June 30, 1970, pp. 55–59.

Genauer, Emily, "There's No Catch to It," *The New York Post Magazine*, July 4, 1970, p. 10.

Gross, Beverly, "*Catch-22*," *The Nation*, July 20, 1970, pp. 60–61.

Henry, Buck, "A Diary of Planes, Pilots, and Pratfalls," *Life*, June 12, 1970, pp. 46, 48.

Holzschlag, Phyllis, "Is *Catch-22* Male Chauvinist?" *Commonweal*, October 6, 1970, pp. 69–70.

Kauffmann, Stanley, "*Catch-22*'s Broken Promises," *New Republic*, July 4, 1970, pp. 22, 32.

Miller, Edwin, "*Catch-22*," *Seventeen*, August 1970, p. 80.

Morgenstern, Joseph, "Into the Mad Blue Yonder," *Newsweek*, June 22, 1970, pp. 81–82.

Robin, Steve, "*Catch-22*," *After Dark*, July 1970, pp. 66–67.

Sarris, Andrew, "Catch-23," *Village Voice*, June 25, 1970, pp. 49, 54–55.

Schickel, Richard, "One of Our Novels Is Missing," *Life*, July 4, 1970, p. 12.

Schjeldahl, Peter, "Is *Catch* Really a Miss?" *The New York Times*, July 19, 1970, p. D9; and "The Pitch on *Catch-22*" (letters in reply to Mr. Schjeldahl), *The New York Times*, August 2, 1970, pp. 2, 10.

Schlesinger, Arthur Jr., "*Catch-22* 'disappointment,' " *Vogue*, August 1, 1970, p. 40.

Seligson, Marcia, "Hollywood's Hottest New Writer—Buck Henry," *The New York Times Magazine*, July 19, 1970, pp. 10–11, 49–50, 52.

Shaber, David, "The Magical Man Behind *Catch-22*," *True*, July 1970, pp. 39–40, 78–80.

Sokolov, Raymond A., "There's a Catch—*Catch-22*," *Newsweek*, March 3, 1969, pp. 52–56.

Zall, P. M., "*Catch-22* Uncaught," *Satire Newsletter*, Fall 1970, pp. 69–73.

Other sources of comment on *Catch-22* may be found in the reviews of Joseph Heller's play *We Bombed in New Haven* (appearing mostly from December 1967 to November 1968), and of his stage version of *Catch-22* (starting in the summer of 1971).

Finally, one should consult *Critical Essays on* Catch-22, ed. James Nagel (Encino, Calif.: Dickenson, 1973), which contains several useful essays not otherwise available.

DISCUSSION QUESTIONS

1. The Yossarian who "takes off" at the end of the novel is different from the Yossarian who leads his flight a second time over Ferrara. Discuss the key events that changed him.

2. Has Yossarian, because of this change, become a coward? Define cowardice, and indicate who the real cowards in the story are.

3. If you conclude that Yossarian is *not* a coward, what then has he become?

4. To what degree has Milo Minderbinder's enterprising caused Yossarian's change?

5. Is McWatt, who is "perfectily sane" and still does not mind the war, a hero? Is Aarfy, who "does not have brains enough to be afraid"? Is Colonel Cathcart, who "had courage and never hesitated to volunteer his men for any target available"? What is heroism?

6. "Everybody who knew" Appleby, Heller says, "liked him." Why, then, does Yossarian growl, "I hate that son of a bitch"? (Chapter 2)

7. Compare Yossarian to Plato's man of the caves, who returns to the darkness to tell others what sunlight is and is thought crazy. What exactly is Yossarian's insight, and what has given it to him?

8. "Ripeness is all," Shakespeare's Edgar concludes (*King Lear*, V, ii, 9–11). Yossarian reads life's secret differently (Chapter 41). Or does he? Discuss.

9. In J. D. Salinger's *Catcher in the Rye*, Holden Caulfield's word for hypocrisy is "phony." Does Yossarian's word "dedicated" describe a similar quality? Dunbar, for instance, is to Yossarian "a true prince, one of the finest, least dedicated men in the whole world." Who are the "dedicated" men in *Catch-22*? Can you group their motives? If dedication is wrong, what are the alternatives?

10. Yossarian loves or makes love to several women. What do the women who appeal to him have in common? What do women dislike about him?

11. Beginning with the discussions of God in Chapters 1 and 18 discuss God's place in such a Catch-22 world. For one opinion, see Victor Milne's article.

12. Who is "the enemy"? (See, for example, Chapter 12 and 29.) Is that a gratuitous charge, or does it have extensions of meaning beyond the humor?

13. Major —— de Coverley "was an ominous, incomprehensible presence." What does his presence in the book mean, or is he simply there for the humor's sake? Compare him to the major in Heller's play, *We Bombed in New Haven*.

14. Major Sanderson (Chapter 27) says to Yossarian, "The trouble with you is that you think you're too good for all the conventions of society." Does Yossarian reject his entire society? If you feel he doesn't, what specific aspects of it does he accept?

15. Yossarian may not speak completely (if at all) for Heller. What does the book as a whole seem to offer—that is, what *does* make life worth living? What values are worth preserving or defending? Compare your answer and Heller's story with William Faulkner's Nobel Prize acceptance speech, as well as with his novel, *The Sound and the Fury*.

16. Clevinger, the clever sophist (Chapter 8), "knew everything about literature except how to enjoy it." Is it possible to disagree with much of a novel that questions certain old values (as *Catch-22* does) and still enjoy it? How?

17. Heller treats sympathetically all of the characters who want to stay alive—Yossarian, Orr, Dunbar. But these might have been "messy" characters in Ernest Hemingway's stories and novels, in which men of courage face their equally inescapable fates. What posture in the face of death is "right," or does it matter? What similarities are there in Heller's and Hemingway's characters? For example, compare Dunbar's quest for a long life (Chapter 4) to Robert Jordan's satisfaction with a life three days long in *For Whom the Bell Tolls*.

18. In most novels, the protagonist struggles with an antagonist, a conflict that is resolved toward the end of the book. To what extent does *Catch-22* follow this tradition? Is Yossarian's escape, in other words, "a cop-out," or does it grow out of the struggle? *Is* it an escape?

19. Some readers squirm because Yossarian "takes off," claiming this is artistically, patriotically, or morally no way to end the book. Yet in what Hemingway called the source of modern American literature, Mark Twain's *Huckleberry Finn*, the puckish hero (after surviving a river's length of encounters with man's hideous inhumanity to man) also "lights out" for the Indian Territory. The similarity is even more striking when we realize that Yossarian left rather than be comfortably tamed and returned to the civilized States, and Huck leaves to avoid the comfortable (but to him confining and compromising), civilized family life. Therefore, can you think of other American fictional heroes (or legendary or factually famous ones) who "take off" in quest of individual rather than conventional fulfillment? Is there perhaps a more widespread tradition of radical individualism in American life and literature than some have realized in criticizing *Catch-22*, making Yossarian at the end of the story not a maverick or a cop-out (or if he is, at least not uniquely so), but one of many individualists in a land of such? In your study, consider the last half of "An Impolite Interview with Joseph Heller," reprinted in this casebook.

20. Reread the "tree of life" episode (Chapter 24). Yossarian has changed qualitatively; an experience (an insight, a revelation, what James Joyce called "an epiphany") has sent him up into the "tree of knowledge of good and evil," and he decides that he does not want to wear the uniform again. He has become in

a sense a conscientious objector in wartime—or a coward—or a casualty. Is his a moral choice? Does he have the "right" to "desert," to refuse to fight anymore? Does *anyone* have the "right" to refuse to fight, to support, or to serve his country? Does Yossarian in a sense make "a separate peace," as certain Hemingway heroes do (for example, Frederick Henry in A *Farewell to Arms*)? Compare Yossarian's desertion to Henry's. What leads to each one's decision to leave? Is either justified? If so, on what basis?

21. Yossarian's American prototype may be Henry David Thoreau. Consider Yossarian's dilemmas and final resolution in light of the conclusion of Thoreau's *Walden* and the opening pages of his essay "Civil Disobedience."

22. Consider the ending of *Catch-22* in light of the various articles that dispute over it (for example, "The Best Catch There Is," and the Henry, Stark, Castelli, Denniston, and Milne articles). In your judgment, which one seems closest to the best possible reading, in terms of the novel itself?

23. Is Yossarian insane, or the only sane character in the novel? Examine the discussions of sanity in the Protherough and Monk essays.

24. Heller has said *Catch-22* is organized around a metaphor. Assuming the metaphor is Catch-22, explain its meaning and how the novel is organized around it.

25. Given the appeal, the persuasiveness, the emotional power of fiction, does an author have a responsibility to create certain kinds of protagonists with whom readers will identify? Do readers necessarily adopt the attitudes of the fictional characters they like?

26. How does Heller make the reader like Yossarian? Find as many general devices as you can, then illustrate them with specific examples.

27. Discuss foreshadowing in *Catch-22*. Suspense. Flashbacks. Study the articles by Stark, McDonald, and Mellard on Heller's use of *déjà vu* as a structuring device.

28. The novel progresses hesitantly toward the moment of discovery (when Snowden spills the secret to Yossarian in Chapter 41), as if imitating Yossarian's reluctance, yet obsession, to approach that horrible moment again. The movie, though drastically different in some aspects, shows a similar bit-by-bit progression toward the awful scene. Does this technique work in the novel? In the movie? What does the technique do for the story? How important is Snowden's death to Yossarian? Is the final scene of Snowden adequately foreshadowed, psychologically prepared? If you feel that the technique, with its culminating scene, works, does it answer the charge of some critics that the novel is formless, without a plot?

29. In a larger sense, *Catch-22*'s structural pattern may be recurring phantasmogorical nightmares: "So many monstrous events were occurring that [Chaplain Tappman] was no longer positive which events *were* monstrous and which *were* really taking place." (Chapter 25) In this sense, does the book's form appropriately imitate the content of such a world of violence, greed, and nightmarish perception?

30. "That crazy bastard," says Dr. Stubbs of Yossarian, "may be the only sane one left" (Chapter 10). Discuss Heller's scheme of crazy versus sane. Does he succeed? Why or why not? Consider Dr. Stubbs' remark in light of the quotation in Question 29. Does Heller seem to have consciously integrated characterization, and the motif of crazy versus sane, with the rest of the book's madness? Is Tappman's puzzled vision (expressed in the quotation in Question 29) identical with Yossarian's?

31. For all of its comic madness, *Catch-22* is about dying. How can they kill me, Yossarian seems to chant, let me count the ways. "Everywhere [Yossarian] looked was a nut, and it was all a sensible young gentleman like himself could do to maintain his perspective amid so much madness. And it was urgent that he did, for he knew his life was in peril." (Chapter 2; see also the end of Chapter 27). Granting Yossarian's claim, what can you do with such fear, such dangers, in a world such as ours? What does the book say or imply?

32. "I don't want to wear a uniform anymore," Yossarian announces in Chapter 24. In a sense, this scene states the crux of Yossarian's change. Discuss its place in the novel, and explain how Heller stacks other details to make us side with Yossarian against what the uniform represents to him.

33. Milo Minderbinder ("What's good for M & M Enterprises is good for the country") is of course like Al Capp's cartoon character General Bullmoose. One critic has said that Milo's motto is based on "the notorious indiscretion of Charles E. Wilson, President Eisenhower's secretary of defense and former president of General Motors: 'What's good for General Motors is good for the country.'" Find other analogues for Milo in literature or in life.

34. The bureaucratic satire *The Peter Principle* (1969) by Lawrence J. Peter humorously proposes that the reason for widespread inefficiency within organizations is that people are steadily promoted to their "level of incompetence." In 1961, Heller had General P. P. Peckem say essentially the same thing. Describing an entirely unnecessary mission, Peckem says, " 'That's the way things go when you elevate mediocre people to positions of authority." (Chapter 29) Discover as many such promotions to incompetence in the novel as you can.

35. Compare *Catch-22* with other novels that use to some extent the motif of comic craziness—for example, Ken Kesey's *One Flew Over the Cuckoo's Nest*.

36. Perhaps the father of comic antiwar novels is Hasek's *The Good Soldier Schweik*. Read and compare it to *Catch-22*. (See J. P. Stern's article, listed in the Bibliographical Note in this book.)

37. Compare *Catch-22* with the following novels: Sy Bartlett and B. Lay's *Twelve O'Clock High*; Hugh Fosberg's *View from the Air*; Norman Mailer's *The Naked and the Dead*; Thomas Heggen's *Mister Roberts*; John Hersey's *The War Lover*; Gunther Grass' *The Tin Drum*; Evelyn Waugh's *Vile Bodies*; George Mandel's *The War Boom*; J.P. Donleavy's *The Ginger Man* (see "The Best Catch There Is"); Irwin Shaw's *The Young Lions*; and James Jones' *From Here to Eternity*.

38. Compare *Catch-22* to Heller's play *We Bombed in New Haven*.

39. Compare *Catch-22* to the movie *Dr. Strangelove*. What are the differences between Milo Minderbinder and Strangelove?

40. Compare Yossarian to the following characters: Holden Caulfield in J.D. Salinger's *Catcher in the Rye*; Robert Jordan in Ernest Hemingway's *For Whom the Bell Tolls* and Frederick Henry in his *A Farewell to Arms*; and Henry Fleming in Stephen Crane's *The Red Badge of Courage*.

41. Compare the novel to the film version of *Catch-22*. Compare the film with *M*A*S*H*.

42. In the interview "So They Say," Heller says that he had William Faulkner's

Absalom, Absalom in mind when structuring *Catch-22*'s time, its recurring scenes. Compare the techniques of the two novels.

43. John Wain claims that after a few pages of *Catch-22*, the circular, scrambled method of the narration becomes completely justified. Discuss.

44. Study Wayne Miller's *An Armed America—Its Face in Fiction: A History of the American Military Novel.* (Compare Miller's article in this casebook.) How does he fit *Catch-22* into the history of the American military novel? How would you? (See Eric Solomon's article.)

45. Critic Brian Way says, "It is impossible to establish an orderly time-sequence for the novel." Do you agree? Stark, Jan Solomon, and Gaukroger maintain that the time-sequence can be worked out and is in fact important. Which one comes nearest to your reading of the book?

46. Way goes on to claim that "it would be a falsification to suggest that there could be any orderly development of this situation, in time, towards a resolution." Consider the articles by McDonald, Gaukroger, Milne, and Monk. With whom do you agree?

47. Jan Solomon finds that past events in the novel "are not related through conventional flashbacks. At first, numerous brief references to an event are inserted into the current action; then somewhat fuller allusions; and finally, for each specific important episode, a fairly extended direct narration." Do you find this pattern? If so, does it seem merely repetitive, or does it strengthen the novel? How? Find as many events dramatized through this pattern as you can.

48. Constance Denniston finds two plots in the novel, "one concerning the aggressors in their struggle to gain power, the other concerning the hero, Yossarian, in his struggle to live." Can you find extensions of this second plot—subplots, perhaps—as other "victims" struggle to live? Consider, for example, Orr, Dunbar, Doc Daneeka.

49. Denniston finds that Yossarian can bring no order to his society because "it seems past redemption." Does it? Consider what happens to the heretofore spineless Major Danby and Chaplain Tappman when Yossarian refuses to sell his soul to the colonels. Are the major and the chaplain really converted disciples who will remain to make changes for good? Or will they knuckle under once Yossarian is gone? Or will their efforts simply be futile? What does Heller seem to intend?

50. Milne calls the attacks by Nately's Whore "puzzling." Also, there seems to be no explanation for her attacks in the movie, aside from the assumption that in her grief she lashes out at Yossarian, who brings the news of Nately's death. But see the end of Chapter 33 and the start of Chapter 34. Does this episode adequately predispose her to blame Yossarian? (See also the start of Chapter 38.) How obvious must a writer be in motivating his characters for later actions? Discuss the phenomenon apparent in your own class, or in this casebook, of the way readers react so differently to the same novel, even to the point of devaluating a book on the basis of charges that can clearly be disproved by textual evidence. How can we determine when a writer has clearly made his point?

51. Eric Solomon lists four categories of characters. Would you agree with his categories? Would you agree with those characters he puts in them? Why or why not?

52. How well did the movie fulfill Heller's 1962 expectations? (See "An Impolite Interview with Joseph Heller.")

53. Summarize and classify the derogatory criticism of Heller in this casebook. Are the derogatory judgments founded on the novel itself, in its own demonstrable terms, or do they spring from the critics' moral, political, or aesthetic presuppositions?

54. Is there anyone in *Catch-22* like Colonel Ross in James Gould Cozzens' *Guard of Honor*?

55. Are there characters in Mailer's *The Naked and the Dead* who seem to step right out of *Catch-22*?

56. Is Yossarian an existential hero? Compare him with Meursault, the hero of Camus' *The Stranger*, and Harry Haller in Hesse's *Steppenwolf*, and victims like Yossarian of forces larger than himself.

57. Read E.E. Cummings' poem "I Sing of Olaf." Is Olaf in any way like Yossarian?

58. Read Leslie Fiedler's essay "No! In Thunder," cited in the Bibliographic Note, which appeared just before *Catch-22* was published. Does Heller's novel answer the plea Fiedler makes?

59. Compare Chapter 39 of *Catch-22* with the Ulysses in Nighttown section of James Joyce's *Ulysses*. Could that have been Heller's source?

60. Read the Humpty-Dumpty section of Lewis Carroll's *Through the Looking-Glass*. Would Humpty-Dumpty have fit into *Catch-22*? Is he embodied there in any character?

61. Read Martin Esslin's *Theatre of The Absurd*. Is *Catch-22* an "absurd" novel?

62. Several reviewers of the book in 1961–1962 and of the film in 1970 call Yossarian's attempt to get to Sweden at the end of the work "a cop-out." Is it? Or are those reviewers missing Heller's point?

63. How would you describe Yossarian's religion?

64. Is *Catch-22* the product of applying the principles of the Theatre of The Absurd to the genre of the war novel?

65. Look at the *names* Heller has given his characters! Analyze his use of this old satiric convention. You may have to do some translating and use an unabridged dictionary. For example, what does Tappman mean in German? And Kraft? And of course Scheisskopf? Why do you suppose that in the first Scheisskopf chapter, Heller has another character refer to Scheisskopf by the English translation of that name and furthermore uses a capital S? What is the name of the dead man in Yossarian's tent? Why is it Major ———— de Coverley? How are several of the names ironic—for example, Clevinger, Kid Sampson, Nurse Duckett, Hungry Joe? What does Orr's name suggest? What is the dictionary definition of *towser*? Does the definition fit Sergeant Towser? Do the same for Dreedle. What does Nately suggest as a name? Wintergreen? Appleby? What general patterns do you find at work in the names of the characters? Is there even a mad dirty joke hinted at in the death of Hungry Joe? What reference is suggested by Snowden's name? Is there irony in Luciana's name? In Chief White Halfoat's?

66. The original title of the novel was *Catch-18*, but it was changed to avoid confusion with Leon Uris' novel *Mila 18*, published about the same time. The new name was to be *Catch-14*. Then *Catch-22* was selected as being somehow funnier. Would you have titled the novel differently? Why?

67. In the film, the pilot cut in half on the raft by McWatt is identified as Hungry Joe. Who is it in the novel? Why do you suppose such a change was made? McWatt flies a different kind of plane in this scene in the film. Why?

68. One of the funniest moments in the film is the first entrance of Luciana accompanied on the sound track by a massive orchestral rendering of the opening section of Richard Strauss' tone poem *Also Sprach Zarathustra*. This is the same music used in the opening scene of the film *2001: A Space Odyssey*. What is the point? Is it witty or just cute? Is it apparent or just "inside"? (See Heller's "On Translating *Catch-22* into a Movie.")

69. One technique Heller uses throughout the novel is the juxtaposition of jarring incongruities. Does this pattern carry over to the film?

70. It is always fun and sometimes revealing to play the old game of who-should-play-the-part-in-the-movie-version. Make up your cast of characters for the film. For example, Paul Newman, Steve McQueen, Peter O'Toole, Anthony Quinn, and others were said to be interested in the Yossarian part. How do you see them in the role? Would James Garner have made an ideal Yossarian? Or Henry Fonda, Major Major? Or Peter Fonda, if Henry Fonda looks too much like Henry Fonda?

71 Norman Mailer, in *Cannibals and Christians*, has said that *Catch-22* is a man's book "written on the face of solemn events and their cockeyed contradictions," relieving "the frustration men feel at the idiocy of their work," and that women are puzzled by it. Do you agree? Do the differing reactions Mailer suggests really depend upon sex, or something else—like exposure to the workaday world?

72. In an interview with the editors, Heller suggested as an epigraph for this casebook Dylan Thomas' poem "Do Not Go Gentle into That Good Night." How does the poem comment on the novel? What other poems might serve as epigraphs?